Tracing and drawing together the precursors of contemporary approaches to urban security, Jon Coaffee offers an authoritative account of how the city irrevocably changed as a result of the mundane and exceptional measures introduced as a result of the U.S.-led War on Terror. Building on Professor Coaffee's long-standing engagement with the field and marshalling and interrogating an unparalleled range of empirical studies and interdisciplinary insights from both before and since 11, this important book showcases how national governments, city administrations, technology companies, the military, policing and intelligence agencies, and citizens have become increasingly implicated into countering the enduring threat of urban terrorism. Informed by a range of critical social theory, this account further addresses important questions concerning the intensification of social control and surveillance and the reshaping of civic responsibility. At the same time, this unique analysis illuminates how ideas of militarism, preparedness, pre-emption and resilience have become institutionalised within systems of security governance and emerged as an integral part of normal everyday city life.

Pete Fussey, Professor of Criminology,
University of Essex, United Kingdom.

Jon Coaffee's most recent book is a timely and welcome addition to the *Interventions* book series. In this groundbreaking text, many of the conventions of IR and global politics are critically challenged as post-9/11 counter-terrorism interventions are interrogated and their implications for everyday life detailed. In this synthesis of critical theory and an understanding of security practices and behaviours across an ever-expanding range of security actors and civil society, a greater focus is placed on better understanding the role of security's many audiences than in traditional scholarship. The result is a detailed rendering of the rescaling and refocusing of security concerns to the metropolitan level and below as a result of anxieties about 'new terrorism' and the purported need to enhance resilience. Whether this is through concerns for the protection of vulnerable crowded locations, the 'lockdown' security that has become an accepted part of staging high-profile events, attempts to counter the radicalisation and violent extremism of individuals and certain communities, the impact of state-level threats assessments and public warning and informing campaigns or the overlap between counter-terrorism and pandemic response practices; this book provides a grounded account of the importance of understanding how 'spaces of security' have been steadily intensified over recent decades and the wider implications of this 'new normal' for the securitisation of everyday life.

Nick Vaughan-Williams, Professor of International
Security and *Interventions* book series editor,
University of Warwick, United Kingdom.

The War on Terror and the Normalisation of Urban Security

This book explores the processes by which, in the 20 years after 9/11, the practices of urban security and counter-terrorism have impacted the everyday experiences of the Western city. Highlighting the localised urban responses to new security challenges, it reflects critically on the historical trajectory of techniques of territorialisation and physical protection, urban surveillance and the increasing need for cities to enhance resilience and prepare for anticipated future attacks and unpacks the practices and impacts of the intensification of recent urban security practices in the name of countering terrorism.

Drawing on over 25 years of research and practical experience, the author utilises a range of international case studies, framed by conceptual ideas drawn from critical security, political and geographical theory.

The book will be of interest to students and scholars of politics, war studies, urban studies, geography, sociology, criminology, and the growing market of security and resilience professionals, as well as non-academic audiences seeking to understand responses to terrorist risk.

Jon Coaffee is a professor in Urban Geography in the Department of Politics and International Studies at the University of Warwick, United Kingdom and is an international expert in counter-terrorism, security and urban resilience. His work includes *Terrorism, Risk and the City* (2003); *The Everyday Resilience of the City: How Cities Respond to Terrorism and Disaster* (2008), *Terrorism, Risk and the Global City – Towards Urban Resilience* (2009), *Sustaining and Securing the Olympic City* (2011), *Urban Resilience: Planning for Risk Crisis and Uncertainty* (2016), *Futureproof* (2019) and *Resilience and Planning: Planning's Role in Countering Terrorism* (2020).

Interventions

The Series provides a forum for innovative and interdisciplinary work that engages with alternative critical, post-structural, feminist, postcolonial, psychoanalytic and cultural approaches to international relations and global politics. In our first 5 years we have published 60 volumes.

We aim to advance understanding of the key areas in which scholars working within broad critical post-structural traditions have chosen to make their interventions, and to present innovative analyses of important topics. Titles in the series engage with critical thinkers in philosophy, sociology, politics and other disciplines and provide situated historical, empirical and textual studies in international politics.

We are very happy to discuss your ideas at any stage of the project: just contact us for advice or proposal guidelines. Proposals should be submitted directly to the Series Editors:

- Jenny Edkins (jennyedkins@hotmail.com) and
- Nick Vaughan-Williams (N.Vaughan-Williams@Warwick.ac.uk).

'As Michel Foucault has famously stated, "knowledge is not made for understanding; it is made for cutting" In this spirit The Edkins – Vaughan-Williams Interventions series solicits cutting edge, critical works that challenge mainstream understandings in international relations. It is the best place to contribute post disciplinary works that think rather than merely recognize and affirm the world recycled in IR's traditional geopolitical imaginary.'

Michael J. Shapiro, University of Hawai'i at Manoa, United States.
Edited by Jenny Edkins, Aberystwyth University and Nick Vaughan-Williams, University of Warwick

Emotional practices and listening in peacebuilding partnerships
The invisibility cloak
Pernilla Johansson

Subversive pedagogies
Radical possibility in the academy
Claire Timperley and Kate Schick

For more information about this series, please visit: www.routledge.com/series/INT

The War on Terror and the Normalisation of Urban Security

Jon Coaffee

LONDON AND NEW YORK

First published 2022
by Routledge
2 Park Square, Milton Park, Abingdon, Oxon OX14 4RN

and by Routledge
605 Third Avenue, New York, NY 10158

Routledge is an imprint of the Taylor & Francis Group, an informa business

© 2022 Jon Coaffee

The right of Jon Coaffee to be identified as author of this work has been asserted by him in accordance with sections 77 and 78 of the Copyright, Designs and Patents Act 1988.

All rights reserved. No part of this book may be reprinted or reproduced or utilised in any form or by any electronic, mechanical, or other means, now known or hereafter invented, including photocopying and recording, or in any information storage or retrieval system, without permission in writing from the publishers.

Trademark notice: Product or corporate names may be trademarks or registered trademarks, and are used only for identification and explanation without intent to infringe.

British Library Cataloguing-in-Publication Data
A catalogue record for this book is available from the British Library

Library of Congress Cataloging-in-Publication Data
Names: Coaffee, Jon, author.
Title: The War on Terror and the normalisation of urban security / Jon Coaffee.
Other titles: War on Terror and the normalization of urban security
Description: Abingdon, Oxon; New York, NY: Routledge, 2022. | Series: Interventions | Includes bibliographical references and index.
Identifiers: LCCN 2021021228 | ISBN 9781138617551 (hardback) | ISBN 9781032120133 (paperback) | ISBN 9780429461620 (ebook)
Subjects: LCSH: Terrorism–Prevention–Case studies. | Public safety–Case studies. | Emergency management–Case studies. | Crime prevention and architectural design–Case studies. | Internal security–Case studies. | City planning–Case studies. | City and town life–Case studies. | War on Terrorism, 2001–2009–Influence. | September 11 Terrorist Attacks, 2001–Influence.
Classification: LCC HV6431 .C557 2022 | DDC 363.325–dc23
LC record available at https://lccn.loc.gov/2021021228

ISBN: 978-1-138-61755-1 (hbk)
ISBN: 978-1-032-12013-3 (pbk)
ISBN: 978-0-429-46162-0 (ebk)

DOI: 10.4324/9780429461620

Typeset in Times New Roman
by Newgen Publishing UK

Contents

List of figures	ix
List of tables	xi
Acknowledgements	xii

PART 1
The search for urban security   1

1 Introduction: Security and the urban imagination   3

2 The city as target   19

3 Detonation boulevards   36

PART 2
Conventional tactics and techniques of urban security   57

4 Padded bunkers   59

5 Territorial security and the panoptical gaze   76

6 The fearful shock of 9/11 and the rise of military and urban geopolitics   98

PART 3
The longer term implications of 9/11   117

7 Normal protective streetscapes   119

8 Preparation and anticipation in the global War on Terror	143
9 Everyday terror prevention	164

PART 4
The future of urban security — 187

10 Towards impenetrable and smart security	189
11 Pop-up security and the politics of exceptionality	217
12 Conclusions: Normalising urban security	244
References	273
Index	301

Figures

2.1	Haussmann as 'Artiste Démolisseur' Paris: capital of the nineteenth century	26
3.1	The maximum extent of the Belfast security segment (ring of steel) in 1976	45
3.2	The devastation caused by the U.S. Embassy bombing in West Beirut	51
4.1	A typical example of security put in place in New York after the 1993 bombing	69
5.1	The initial extent of the Experimental Traffic Zone or 'ring of steel'	88
5.2	Signs put up in 1996 warning drivers they were entering the Docklands security cordon	92
6.1	The ring of concrete established outside the Houses of Parliament	103
7.1	Security bollards placed on turntables to allow vehicle access. Bronze 'no-go' blockers were placed on either side	120
7.2	Granite benches sited in the newly pedestrianised Times Square	122
7.3	An indicative spectrum of visible security	134
7.4	Security balustrade along Whitehall, London	136
7.5	'ARSENAL' – Ornamental Security Façade for the Emirates Stadium	137
7.6	Crash-rated seating outside a federal building in Boston, Massachusetts	138
7.7	An example of a Tiger Trap in Battery Park, New York	139
10.1	The new U.S. Embassy in Baghdad	195
10.2	The new U.S. Embassy in London	197
10.3	New security cameras and signage installed in Manhattan in 2007	204
10.4	Multipurpose surveillance devices, 2013	206
11.1	Policing a protest in Manchester amidst 'island security'	225
11.2	Security fences and steel blockers sealing the conference site	226
11.3	Cordon blue around the Olympic Park, 2007	232

11.4	Electrified security fences, 2009	233
12.1	Barriers established in December 2016 to restrict vehicle access to the Christmas market in Birmingham	248
12.2	Retained steel blockers planted with flowers to 'soften' their appearance	249
12.3	Granite security outside the Christiansborg Palace, Copenhagen	251
12.4	#Bollart protests in Melbourne	251

Tables

11.1　Key features of the standardised Olympic security model　　227
11.2　The spatial imprint of London 2012 security　　231

Acknowledgements

Empirically this book draws from the author's extensive portfolio of research over the last 25 years focused on different, but interconnected, strands of urban security and counter-terrorism research and further reflects active engagement with a wide raft of urban security professionals in many countries. Data collection has included hundreds of research interviews with those active in urban counter-terrorism, the deployment of surveys to businesses about the impact of terrorism on everyday life, the development and assessment of training courses for security and built environment processionals, and advocacy work for city and policing leaders regarding contemporary developments in counter-terrorism. Much of this research has been supported by an array of grant funding from the United Kingdom research councils and from the European Union. I wish to acknowledge the following grants from the UK Research Councils (now UK Research and Innovation) and other national funding bodies: The Everyday resilience of the City – how provincial cities respond to threat, RES-228-25-0034; The Urban environment: Mirror and mediator of radicalisation, RES-181-25-0028; Resilient Design for counter-terrorism, EP/F008635/1; Science and Security: Research Impact and Co-Production of Knowledge, ES/K011359/1; Norway Research Council – Rights, institutions, procedures, participation, litigation: embedding security, ES637445; EU Framework 7 projects DESURBS, and HARMONISE and EU Horizon 2020 projects RESILENS, and MEDI@4SEC. These projects have been co-produced and/or co-funded by an array of national- and city-level security and counter-terrorism services, policing bodies, built environment associations and emergency planning and resilience organisation across the Western world.

The range of interconnected topics and examples covered in this book has meant that the work supporting it has been a collaborative effort. Special thanks must go to numerous research partners with whom I have worked over the last 25 years, and I would particularly like to thank John Gold, Steve Graham, Paul O'Hare, Lee Bosher, David Murakami Wood and Pete Fussey for their advice and support over many years.

Acknowledgements xiii

The vast majority of the images used in the book have been taken by the author during empirical fieldwork. The following images have been sourced using Creative Commons or are publically available for use: Figures 2.1, 3.2, 7.2, 10.1, 10.2 and 12.3. A note attached to each figure details its source.

Part 1
The search for urban security

1 Introduction

Security and the urban imagination

Cities have always been crucibles of civilisation and modernity: sites of visionary planning, democratic forums, rich agglomerations of cultures and economies and a place where hope for a better, more modern future, resided. They have also always been places where risks, threats and vulnerabilities have been concentrated and equally where populations have been controlled and trades protected through various techniques of fortification, surveillance and ordering. Such a paradoxical relationship between security and urbanisation has long been highlighted, perhaps most notably by Lewis Mumford in *The City in History* (1961) in his discussion of the origins of war and the city that questioned whether there is an inherent pathology within 'dreams' of security, which leads inevitably to violence. As he famously noted, 'no matter how many valuable functions the city has furthered, it has also served, throughout most of its history, as a container of organized violence and a transmitter of war' (p.58). More recently, in *Discipline and Punish*, Foucault (1977) also saw the design and management of towns and city as 'punitive' or 'carceral' where landscape markers continuously reinforced a code of control. As he noted,

> this, then, is how one must imagine the punitive city. At the crossroads, in the gardens, at the side of roads being repaired or bridges built, in workshops open to all, in the depths of mines that may be visited, will be hundreds of tiny theatres of punishment.
>
> (p.113)

Within this long-running historical context, this book concerns itself with the intersection of security and city life and, particularly, with the security interventions undertaken in the name of reducing the threat of late-twentieth- and early-twenty-first-century urban terrorism. In doing so, the forthcoming chapters take a novel view of urban security and articulate this through reconfigured and rescaled approaches to international relations (IR) and geopolitics that in many ways decentre the traditional Westernised way of viewing and practising security that focused on identifying the referents, selecting the threats and determining legitimate knowledge. Conventional approaches to security and IR have commonly been conceived on a national, trans-regional or global scale and largely in terms of traditional notions of state sovereignty and broad governance coalitions or macroeconomic institutions or 'interests' (Booth, 2004).

Since the 1990s, emerging ideas of 'human security' began to highlight the importance of sub-national and localised responses to new security challenges, which required analysis through a different frame of reference from the realist state-centric security studies orthodoxy, 'placing the needs of the individual, not states, at the centre of security discourses' (Chandler, 2012, p.214). However, whilst such work has tried to wrench security away from its institutional bias, to focus it on the needs of people and populations, such challenges have remained for the most part marginal within security studies until recently. Within this framing, this book will seek to rethink scale in urban security, highlighting the localised and everyday *urban* responses to new security challenges and grounding these in new forms of spatial practice and critical analysis. Particularly, since 9/11, security has been rescaled, as exemplified by the way in which major cities are dealing with terrorist threats to core business, financial and governmental functions and the protection of public spaces and events. Security as a concept and a practice has 'come home': in other words, the discourses, procedures and, in many cases, material examples of national and international security are influencing and/or are directly employed at subnational scales, placing the needs of the cities at the heart of emerging security practices (Coaffee and Murakami Wood, 2006).

Although the empirical focus of this book is predominantly upon the present and future, importance is also placed on providing the historical context for such developments, including the targeting preferences of intruders or terrorists, as well as critically reflecting upon the conceptual ideas that sought to understand and influence the spatial and material security practices that emerged. Contemporary debates about the role of security in urbanisation have only had a minor role for historians, often limited to the observation that there is a long history and a brief summary of the accepted wisdom. Other accounts focus solely on 'exceptional' events that are often viewed as one-off occurrences. Whilst this book intends to focus on emerging practices of urban security during the ongoing War on Terror, tracing the deeper development of both the discursive and the material aspects of the risks faced, and vulnerability felt, by city civilisations of the past is vital to understanding the roots of contemporary security dilemmas.

The initial chapters of this book (Part 1) are thus spent developing a historical perspective from the ancient world up to the end of the twentieth century – a *longue durée*[1] sweep. Rather than solely focusing on what French sociologist François Simiand (1906) called *histoire événementielle* (event-driven history), the foregoing chapters give priority to a synthesis of long-term historical processes that collectively symbolise the evolution of ideas and practices of security over time. Such a historically-driven analysis does not preclude the analysis of important 'events' that, in some cases, act as tipping points in the battle between the need for security and freedom in the everyday city. The focus on this long historical sweep is further undertaken in the broad spirit of the genealogical method advanced by Foucault (1980), where progress is not seen in terms of a linear evolution but rather as a form of counter-history where attention is placed upon the multiple and sometimes conflicting interpretations of the past that reveal the influence of power on social development and everyday life. As Arais (2011, p.373) has argued,

> genealogical approaches to the issue of security are necessary, if not urgent, since they expose the institutional and discursive apparatuses that condition our interpretation of reality with respect to risk, and allow us to adopt a critical position toward these dispositifs.

Such an approach, as Erlenbusch-Anderson (2018) has more recently noted in her genealogical study of terrorism, is a form of engaged critique in which norms can be excavated from the historically contingent conditions that shape their emergence and, 'from the practices of those who are fighting' (p.179).

Boulevards of broken dreams

As cities evolved, particular morphological features came to symbolise the open, democratic nature of urban spaces. Notably, central public places where citizens assembled – what the ancient Greek city-states called an agora – came to represent the centre of spiritual and political life. Agorae were also the symbolic locations where citizens would meet for military duty or to hear proclamations from rulers and, in time, commonly morphed into a central marketplace. These were classically open and democratic spaces but were changed in character when city walling trends began as a result of war, social segregation and the underlying need to separate the known and controllable city from the relative chaos and danger of the outside world (Chapter 2).

As modern cities began to emerge from the 1700s, the construction of boulevards came to form a key skeletal element of the urban fabric, signifying the antithesis of the city wall, that had historically provided security but were increasingly becoming obsolete as a defensive measure. However, the emergence of the boulevard was infused with security meanings and etymologically comes from the French meaning bastion or rampart. Here a boulevard referred to the flat structure of a rampart, projecting outwards from the wall of a fortification, most commonly angular in shape. This feature offered greater scope for defence in the age of gunpowder artillery, compared with the medieval fortifications they superseded.

Whilst these early boulevards often replaced old city walls in encircling a territory, in later times boulevards morphed into wide avenues that radiated from the central city. The classic city boulevard emerged in France (Paris) in the nineteenth century as a tree-lined promenade that ran alongside the former city wall. In many cities, as with the classical agora, the boulevard became the centre of cultural life; a thoroughfare bordered by shops, flower beds, fountains and footbridges that came to symbolise the vibrancy, publicness and social benefits of open and accessible public spaces. However, beneath the conventional image of these modern boulevards lurked an implicit security function that enabled the easy access and egress of military troops into and out of the city to repel attackers, or to quell internal disturbance, as best exemplified by Baron Haussmann's Paris master plan in the mid-1800s. Over time, the boulevard system also became a central element in Cold War military planning, providing an escape route from the city in the event of a nuclear strike (Chapter 2) as well as being exploited as a delivery corridor by car bombers in the late-twentieth century (Chapter 3).

Most recently, the accessible and straight-line design of the historical boulevard has become a relatively easy target of terrorism through vehicle-as-weapon attacks such as those on the Promenade des Anglais in Nice, France in 2016 and on La Rambla, Barcelona in 2017.[2] These high-profile attacks, and many others worldwide, led to the increased defence of boulevards and publically accessible locations, with the deployment of protective security infrastructure and security personnel (Chapter 12). In essence, the public and accessible nature of these places of public gathering had been upended by the ever-increasingly requirements for security, and that were in danger of becoming sterile spaces where hyper-security dominated the urban scene. These once public corridors have, in many cases, become boulevards of broken dreams.

The rise of everyday practices of security

As urban areas evolved so too did the risks faced as well as the sophistication of security interventions intended to protect civilians, create liveable places and maximise the orderly flow of commerce. Notably from the second half of the twentieth century onwards, plagued by high crime rates and civil unrest, large tracts of Western cities became synonymous with risk and labelled dangerous and indefensible. In reply, urban authorities commonly resorted to pseudo-military responses to keep the population under control and to reduce the threat from crime and, increasingly, urban terrorism. In such circumstances, ethological and anthropological ideas of human territoriality commonly informed the deployment of security interventions, where territory was viewed as both the definition of a space and the attempt to influence thinking and behaviour with regard to that space. Creating a sense of territoriality, especially through urban design or boundary reinforcement, became associated with the filling of space with power and worked on levels from the purely symbolic to the material (Newman, 1972; Sack, 1986). Combined with the active targeting of urban areas in a Cold War era of mutually assured destruction, the Western city in the latter decades of the twentieth century was a place where defensive design, 'bomb proof' living and panoptical surveillance provided by new technologies, became *de rigueur* and, for many, an increasing part of everyday urban life.

Here, what is meant by the everyday city and how this intersects with terrorist risk is important. In the context of this book, it refers to how the discourses and practices of urban terrorism and counter-terrorism impact individual and collective experience, leads to new forms of collaborative decision-making regarding security and is conceptually framed by Michel de Certeau's (1984) study of everyday spatial practices. These observation-based studies were inspired by views from the top of the newly completed (at the time) World Trade Center (WTC) in Manhattan, New York; a building that in time was to play a pivotal role in global security discourses as a result of terror attacks in 1993 and 2001. Gazing down from the newly completed WTC, de Certeau proposed his highly influential ideas about how individuals alter, re-appropriate or subvert the repetitive nature of everyday objects – from city streets to literary texts – to make them their own. In *The Practice of Everyday Life* (1984), he reflected on the WTC as an embodiment of structural polarity – of the commanding elevated, privileged optical point versus the space of the streets below – where the devices and tactics of everyday life were deployed, often invisibly, to subvert, resist and restructure the spaces of the city. From this vantage point, the geometric, planned and readable city was transformed from an 'operational' view to 'another spatiality' as the everyday nature of the city created additional complexity, blind spots and opaqueness through the deployment of everyday spatial practices (ibid., p.93).

Moreover, the way individuals experience the everyday city through such *spatial practices* drew an important distinction between the top-down Cartesian-inspired spatial strategies, and the tactics deployed from the ground up. *Strategies* were seen as 'the calculation (or manipulation) of power relationships that becomes possible as soon as a subject with will and power…can be isolated… and targets and threats…can be managed' (ibid., p.35–36). For example, urban life and urbanisation more broadly are historically framed through meta-scale socio-economic, political and planning/architectural strategies that regulate everyday life and leave little room, by design, for protest or resistance.[3] Such a strategic set of procedural rationalities served to catalyse advances in measuring, observing and controlling city spaces through making the urban terrain readable and legible and by suppressing alternative ways of viewing the urban terrain. In counter-distinction, *tactics* were seen by de Certeau as 'the space of the Other…a manoeuvre within the enemy's field of vision and within enemy territory' that seeks to vigilantly make use of the cracks that particular conjunctions open in the surveillance of the proprietary powers (ibid., p.37). Here, by their very essence, tactics were opportunistically deployed to disrupt both the physical and psychological spatiality produced and governed by more powerful strategies.

de Certeau explicitly connected his ideas to Foucauldian structures of power and control where tactical spatial practices, and conditions that determine 'lived space', were viewed as a consequence of the exertion of disciplinary power on the social body that was marked by the tension between 'the collective mode of administration and an individual mode of reappropriation' (ibid., p.96). In complementing Foucault's work, de Certeau sought to explore how everyday spatial practices are amalgamated into broader strategies that seek to control space, creating resistances and fissures that may in time reconfigure the totalising structure of strategic control through 'pedestrian rhetoric'. This work represented a more grounded and socially engaged analysis of the structuring of everyday urban life than Foucault, who focused his initial analysis of power on specific institutional sites of repression such as the prison or hospital, where carceral strategies were seen to be punitively deployed within the public realm and embedded within the design and management of urban safety and security. Marxist geographer David Harvey (1990, p.213) further argued that de Certeau provides an 'interesting corrective' to Foucault in that he 'treats social space as more open to human creatively and action' rather than as a metaphor for a site or container of power which usually constrains. Foucault's (2007, p.11) later work notably in *Security, Territory, Population* did, however, situate and problematise security within the general governance of populations[4] and processes by which 'spaces of security' can be constructed and naturalised as a result of social threats in the form of resistance or 'counter-conduct'.

In the late 1980s and into the 1990s, the study of the everyday and the inscription of political knowledge and power into material things, notably the built environment, were further reflected in wider 'material', 'aesthetic' and 'spatial' turns in the humanities and social sciences that sought to reassert the importance of space within critical social theory (Soja, 1989). These critical endeavours focused on the dialectical relations between materiality, space and the social in the organisation of power and in the production of everyday cultural practices and political landscapes (see, for example, Latour, 1992; Harvey, 1990; Jackson, 2000; Duineveld et al., 2017). More specifically, such 'turns' focused attention upon the spaces of the built environment as a means to understand how historical and social processes help shape urban landscapes and provided a context for social action (Soja, 2003). Such approaches were readily applied in analysing the wider societal implications of material security in the city and how the formation of defensive territories and landscapes could express political power (Coaffee, 1996b; Gold and Revill, 1999; Chapters 4 and 5).

The constant state of emergency and securitisation

The more grounded approach to the study of urban life advocated by de Certeau and others has gained greater traction in more recent years as various conceptual approaches to (urban) security have sought explanations for how the changing threat of terrorism has been responded to through new forms of 'securitisation' by which State rhetoric promotes defensive responses, material changes to the built environment, as well as reconfiguring security governance. For example, Vaughan-Williams and Stevens (2016) drew upon recent 'vernacular' and 'everyday' turns within security studies to analyse attempts to bring non-elite knowledge back into security politics and advocating how such viewpoints could be incorporated into state-level security strategies and public space design to make them more democratic (see also Huysmans, 2014). Such work also illuminated how security was received by citizens in particular ways that unsettle traditional security approaches and policing styles. For example, recent studies have consistently identified how 'vernacular' or 'popular' citizen terror threat perceptions differ according to identity, ethnicity, religion, class and gender and, importantly, how these perspectives were almost invisible to national-level policymakers, who typically enact one-size-fits-all policy guidance (Jarvis and Lister, 2013; Gillespie and O'Loughlin, 2009).

In parallel to the everyday turn in the humanities and social sciences, post-9/11 security studies further embraced insights about how citizen voice could disrupt local security approaches and sought to develop a political sociology and geography of community resilience that went beyond an elitist focus (Coaffee and Rogers, 2008; Noxolo and Huysmans, 2009; Guillaume and Huysmans, 2013).[5] Such work on everyday urban security further privileged an analysis of how and why security discourses, practices and embodiments become reproduced and normalised, and increasingly formed a backdrop to city life.[6]

Whilst such analysis of everyday life was significantly influenced by major terror events, notably 9/11, that for some, signalled a paradigm shift in security thinking, we should avoid uncritical assumptions about the influence of such events in changing the direction of travel of security and counter-terrorism policy and scholarship. Most notably, it became almost assumed knowledge that 9/11 'changed the world' and that nothing would ever be the same again, with the event forming and indelible watershed that would 'divide history' as before and after the attacks. Whilst, of course, these events were significant in catalysing enhanced attention being placed on the need for homeland security and in the necessity of geopolitical change through the War on Terror, they *were not* the *start* of a new and dramatic militarised urban counter-terror response (Coaffee et al., 2008b). Rather the events of 9/11 should be viewed as *accentuating* trends in security that, in many cases, have a long historical trajectory and that were already in train in September 2001. That said, the immediacy of response required after 9/11 did starkly illuminate the outdated nature of many security approaches and mechanisms and led to a constant stream of pronouncements about how the West should secure itself and make their homelands more resilient in what was referred to breathlessly as the age of terrorism. This notably had the effect of shifting the relationship between security and the future and, in particular, seeking to advance exceptional, unprecedented and 'pre-emptive' approaches in the present to account for anticipated future threats.

As with de Certeau's analysis, the WTC played a pivotal role before and after the devastating attacks on 9/11. From its iconic status as 'Ground Zero' to the site's rebirth as 'Freedom Tower', the ruins and emerging built form of the WTC site symbolised the start of the global crusade against international terrorism, as well as showcasing how the city can regenerate itself with security and resilience concerns at the forefront of development practices. More generally, the 9/11 attacks also led to an instant response that enlisted the securitised rhetoric of the War on Terror to enhance 'homeland security' and promote and legitimise the national and local security state. In parallel, this led to an alteration in thinking about the response to terrorist risk through urban counter-terrorism. As Gregory and Pred noted in their landmark book *Violent Geographies* (2007), intense security became the new normal with many advocating 'a purely technical and instrumental response to 9/11, drawing on political technologies to profile, predict and manage the threat of terrorism as an enduring mode of late-modern government' (p.1). A key part of such emergent strategies was centred on advanced risk assessment and the technical modelling of the spaces of the built environment that were seen to be particular vulnerable to devastating attack. In a short space of time, such approaches sort to anticipate future disruptions and to focus pre-emptively on the potential of unknown threats. This has been characterised by Louise Amoore (2013) as a shift from the politics of probabilities to the politics of possibility – or from risk to resilience management (Coaffee and Clarke, 2016) – where the future is colonised by the ever-present need for security, the rolling out of emergency powers allied to detention, heightened surveillance, the curtailing of civil liberties and linked to anything what the State deems dangerous and threatening.

Over time, the responses to 9/11 became emblematic of how Western society coped with emergencies in the new Millennium and reflected what Arias (2011) referred to as the most significant experience of our times – 'the urgent need for security and the impossibility of political contingency' (p.364). Here, urban security imagineering was increasingly driven by the possibility of surprise or 'black swan' events – low probability but high-impact 'shocks' – that had dramatic, far-reaching effects on both localities and global society and that perpetuated a permanent state of emergency. Most vividly, Giorgio Agamben's (2005) philosophical treatise on exceptionality focused on the near ubiquitous state of emergency, siege or martial law that was ushered in by the events of 9/11, but the seeds of which were sown long ago by medieval to Roman juridical conceptions of sovereign authority. Here, framed by the War of Terror, sovereignty could easily step outside of the normal rule of law to dramatically effect everyday urban life (see also Greene, 2018). In such an emergent state of security-obsessed urbanism, the notion of a constant emergency was perpetuated in evermore elaborate counter-terrorism practices and seen as the 'new normal'. Historically speaking, the resort to exceptionality is far from a novel explanation but has undoubtedly become more widespread post-9/11. As Bishop and Phillips (2002, p.94) argued in terms of what they termed 'manufactured emergencies', where military use has merged fully and completely with civil defence, protecting the populace from disasters...Emergency – being on alert, preparedness – has been our steady state for some half a century now; only now, we have more of it and the stakes get even higher.

In the years and decades proceeding 9/11, and in response to other major terror attacks, state-level responses dominated as government's around the world attempted to keep their populations safe by whatever means necessary, enveloped by a broader process of what many termed, 'securitisation'. Securitisation was a concept coined by Ole Wæver from the so-called Copenhagen School (of security studies) in 1993 and become commonplace in studies of IR and geopolitics after 9/11. Orthodox securitisation studies aimed to understand 'who securitizes (securitizing actor), on what issues (threats), for whom (referent object), why, with what results, and not least, under what conditions' (Buzan et al., 1998, p.32). Although a highly complicated theory associated with the power of 'speech acts', securitisation is, at its core, a process-based explanation that explores how state actors transform subjects into security issues and hence allow extraordinary means, the full power of the state and a disproportionate amount of state funding and attention to be deployed in the name of enhancing security.

Despite the statistical evidence highlighting that you are more likely to die as a result of falling off a ladder or slipping in a bathtub than from a terror strike, international terrorism after 9/11 performs the role of the *bête noire* of our age, inducing fear and dread and lowering the threshold to take action (Gardner, 2009; Moltoch, 2012). As a result, amidst doomsday warnings of existential terror threats, counter-terrorism and national security has, since 9/11, systematically siphoned up an increasingly large proportion of Western government's emergency budgets. Emerging security policies have further been critiqued as being deliberate attempts to heighten fear, based on the premise that a fearful population is easier to control and activate as part of a state-wide response. In other words, the rolling-out of new security discourses created heightened threat perceptions that were mobilised by government to generate shared national purpose, to frame policy responses militarily and in terms of war and conflict and to identify a known or unknown referential enemy abroad, all of which were solely 'designed to make visible the government's much advertised commitment to fighting the "war" on terror ...' (Massumi, 2005, p.33). Simultaneously, utilising military and war framings to promote counter-terrorism efforts undoubtedly spread what Ingram (2008) referred to as 'geopolitical anxiety' that provoked the need for national cohesion to combat emerging threats and promoted an ordered and peaceful homeland whilst portraying disorder abroad (see, for example, Gregory, 2010).

Such studies of securitisation, despite shining a light on governmental processes and discourse, can also be seen as particularly narrow when seeking explanations for securitising behaviours across an ever-expanding range of security actors and civil society. As McDonald (2008, p.10) highlighted, an exclusive focus on language is problematic in the sense that it can exclude forms of bureaucratic practices or physical action that do not merely follow from securitising speech acts but are part of the process through which meanings of security are communicated and security itself constructed.

This subsequently led to a greater focus upon seeking to better understand the role of the audience (citizens) and cultural context that do not form the basis of classic securitisation theory (Eriksson, 2001; Meyer, 2009).

This opening up of the actors analysed in security processes beyond the traditional emphasis on only the most elite actors (Bigo, 2002, 2008), alongside more sociological approaches (Balzacq, 2011), called for, a more 'pragmatic' approach that 'stresses the variety of symbolic technologies through which securitization can take place' (Williams, 2011, p.213). Similar to de Certeau's concerns to include the influence of civil society through an understanding of everyday practices and analysis undertaken in security studies on vernacular and everyday turns, reworked securitisation approaches have increasingly sought to ground security in local reality that has illuminated a key repercussion of 9/11, namely a rescaling and refocusing of security concerns to the metropolitan level and below.

In parallel to the evolution of securitisation ideas in the wake of 9/11, orthodox studies of state-centric terrorism were being challenged by the rise of the broad sub-discipline of critical security studies that drew on critical theory to revise and widen the conventionally narrow focus of mainstream approaches to security (Peoples and Vaughan-Williams, 2010). More specifically, within this wider discourse, critical terrorism studies emerged and similarly deployed critical theory to deconstruct traditional discourses, focus upon the multitude of actors involved in developing the language of terrorism and, notably, to 'interrogate the exercise of power' (Jackson, 2005, p.188). Although initially linked to the 1970s, such studies were mainstreamed by the publication of *Terror and Taboo: The Follies, Fables and Faces of Terrorism* (Zulaika and Douglas, 1996) that saw terrorism as socially constructed and context dependent. Critical terrorism studies, using increasingly interpretative and emancipatory methods, expanded rapidly after 9/11 as a lens through which to problematise the labels, language narratives and prominent assumptions about terrorism, counter-terrorism and the War on Terror (Michel and Richards, 2009; Smyth, 2007).[7] As Jackson (2007b, p.225) reflected, much of the terrorism-related research following 9/11 'lack[ed] rigorous theories and concepts, [wa]s based primarily on secondary information, lack[ed] historical context and [wa]s heavily biased towards Western and state-centric perspectives' (see also Silke, 2004). Gunning (2007) further argued that attention must be drawn towards 'fragmented voices' from outside the traditional terrorism studies field, alongside and policy actors and 'end users' (p.388) and in so doing facilitate the discovery of what terrorism and counter-terrorism mean for citizens in the everyday city spaces they inhabit.

Rescaling and redesigning security

In the last 20 years, the policy responses to the occurrence of crime, fear of crime and the evaluation of cities as strategic sites for a spectrum of large-scale increasingly destructive 'perturbations' in everyday urban life, such as riots, protest and particularly acts of terrorism have elicited ever-advanced security responses. These are detailed in a vast academic literature that has developed in recent decades around the concept of 'militarising' or 'securitising' cities and their public spaces. Whilst historically, terrorism concerns have generally been referenced to a national, trans-national or global scale more recently, localised responses to new security challenges, which require analysis through different frames of reference, have emerged as the key focus of study. Similarly, prior work on how contemporary society has become increasingly anxious and ordered according to a preoccupation with 'bad' risks (Beck, 2002) or, as previously noted, ideas of securitisation that sees democratic societies increasingly governed by and through security measures, have influenced the post 9/11 modus operandi of counter-terrorism that is increasingly penetrating the urban civic realm and everyday life. As has been argued, 'security is becoming more civic, urban, domestic and personal: security is coming home' having significant implications for the *local* management of terrorist risk (Coaffee and Murakami Wood, 2006).

Much of this city-scale commentary was framed by the emergence of a new body of work on critical urban geopolitics that focused upon interrogating the links between political violence and the built fabric of cities, particularly those in the Anglophone world. This work recognised that in the post–Cold War era, 'new' twenty-first-century conflicts would be largely urban in orientation, with the city becoming both the target and the crucible of political violence (Graham, 2006; Coward, 2006; Weizman, 2007). As Stephen Graham noted in his landmark collection *Cities, War and Terrorism: Towards an Urban Geopolitics* (2004), recent decades have seen a 'geopolitical and strategic reshaping of our world based heavily on a proliferation of organised, extremely violent acts against cities, those that live in them, and the support systems that make them work' (p.4). Notably, the threat of large-scale terrorist attack against Western urban areas led to an increased requirement for security considerations to be an integral part of the urban design and planning process (Coaffee, 2004a). This especially centred on the complex political ecologies involved in developing physical security for public spaces – that are seen as 'soft' targets – and emerging configurations of metropolitan governance – or 'hybrid' sovereignty – where state *and* non-state actors are increasingly involved in the management of contested cities (Fregonese, 2012). More recent elaborations in urban geopolitics have seen the operation of counter-terrorism increasingly going beyond the representational, state-centred and territorial framings of national security to focus upon the 'banal terrorism' (Katz, 2007) work of local security initiatives in ways that attempt to better understand the impact of materialities, aesthetics, bodily experiences and ambiances/atmospheres that compose the changing urban landscapes of everyday terror (Rancière, 2004b; Adey et al., 2013; Fregonese, 2017).

As will de detailed in this book, previous security and counter-terrorism techniques that focused on territorially 'designing out' threats have commonly led to the use of ever-advancing surveillance technologies and the construction of fixed borders, security cordons, enclosures and 'rings of steel' to protect locations deemed vulnerable (Coaffee, 2004a). Such techniques have often been supported by an array of legislative powers and regulatory guidance that targeted the design of space and the control and monitoring of particular activities deemed unacceptable, with some even suggesting that security design be recognised as a kind of regulation, or legal measure, given its exclusionary potential (Schindler, 2015). Here, local studies of 'lockdown' urban security have sought to show how such regimes of counter-terrorism perpetuate a range of uneven geographies, are maintained and made permanent and, become the 'normal' option for cities on the frontline in the War on Terror (Chapter 11).

In parallel to the spatial design implications of counter-terrorism, significant recent work has also been undertaken on new forms of security governance and the practical and social ramifications of the changing mode and operation of security discourses for those charged with delivering them in situ. Conceptually, as has already been noted, the broadening out of securitisation discourses has sought to make the everyday experiences of non-elite actors, notably citizens, a key object of study. This work shone a light on how different cities have responded to the complex challenges of urban terrorism by devising new forms of governance as a way of better mobilising collective action. Such a shift became increasingly important in the early-twenty-first century as a result of outdated, hierarchical and 'command and control' Cold War rationalities that continued to dominate 'emergency planning' procedures and the enactment of urban security and counter-terrorism (Coaffee, 2019).

Such state-level collective action, initiated during the ongoing War on Terror, increasingly emphasises both the drawing in, or co-opting, of different individuals, community groups, private sector firms and professional stakeholders beyond traditional elites (including urban planners, architects and engineers) into security decision-making at a city level. For example, this has focused attention upon the power that communities can exercise to either assist with broader security efforts or, conversely, to negotiate or resist the imposition of certain policies and practices (Chapters 8 and 10). Equally, there has been much critical discussion about the role of technology companies in national security agendas and, in particular, the synergistic relationship between the military and a selected band of innovators whose security devices seek to both control and profit in equal measure (Chapter 11). Where once it was common for military technology to be redeployed in the civic realm to counter the threat of terrorism, as with automatic number plate recognition technology (Coaffee, 2000), increasingly we are seeing laboratory-generated technologies that have undergone urban trials, being appropriated for the battlefield (such as biometric technology) in what has been referred to as the security-industrial complex or surveillance-industrial complex (Wood et al., 2003; Ball and Snider, 2013). Whilst approaches to contemporary security governance further emphasise the importance of safety advancing alongside new policy discourses about place quality and improving collaboration among stakeholders (Bevir, 2010; Cross, 2008), vital questions still remain about the impact of security interventions on everyday life, including their effect on human rights and civil liberties.

Towards security-driven urban resilience

Today, urban security threats emanating from conventional as well and new and emerging forms of terrorist *modus operandi* are seen an ever-present risk in many major cities. Large-scale attacks such as in Madrid (2004), London (2005), Mumbai (2008), Moscow (2010), Oslo (2011), Boston (2013), Sydney (2014) and most recently in Paris (2015 and 2016), Brussels, Istanbul, Berlin and Nice (all 2016) and London, Manchester and New York (all 2017) have highlighted the risk faced by cities in the seemingly never-ending War on Terror, and showcase how the urban condition is shaped by and through IR at a range of scales. Such attacks have also illuminated the wide-ranging tactics of terrorists who seek to exploit the vulnerability of cities as key geopolitical entities. Counter-responses on behalf of the state and urban authorities, in many cases, have arguably been (too) quick, aimed at reassuring a fearful public that everything is under control and have led to an almost uncritical acceptance of an increasingly militarised built environment, constant states of emergency and a rapid expansion of associated surveillance and security management practices.

In this drive for evermore security, new rhetorics have surfaced to frame urban security process, most notably, *resilience* (Chapter 8). In the immediate wake of 9/11, amidst fear of further terror attacks against global cities, 'resilience' was rapidly mobilised as the dominant rhetoric of Western governments in seeking 'stability' and enhancing the ability of social and economic systems to bounce back from shock events as quickly as possible (Coaffee, 2006; Flynn, 2007). Historically, the world before 9/11 was one with a greater confidence in the capacity of states and governments to secure and control events where solutions to problems could be learnt, generalised and applied elsewhere. After 9/11, in policy arenas connected with counter-terrorism, resilience discourse quickly metamorphosed out of a fixation with future security challenges required to reduce the exposure of places to terror risk through material interventions, as well as a focus upon pre-emption and new modes of risk scanning – in other words, a reappraisal of who, what and where is vulnerable to terrorism and how people, places and processes can be made more resilient.

As a result, security-driven urban resilience has continued to rise in prominence as a governing logic and spatial practice to meet the 'new' security challenges of twenty-first century (Coaffee et al., 2016). More critically, the rolling out of such security practices under the aegis of resilience has had significant impacts on the ability to generate effective, transparent and legitimate governance in the face of nationally derived counter-terrorism policy. Arguably, resilience framing has tended to refocus policy on absorbing and rebounding from shocks rather than strictly on the traditional security approaches of prevention and deterrence, despite the calls for new flexible and proactive strategies for managing terrorist risk. This has occurred in a number of ways that will be scrutinised in forthcoming chapters: the increased use of electronic and digital surveillance in public urban spaces; the imposition of boundaries and barriers to delimit territory and restrict access to public spaces, governmental buildings and financial districts; the enhanced sophistication and cost of anticipatory techniques and preparedness planning; and the linking of urban resilience and security strategies to competition for footloose global capital and the hosting of major events (Coaffee et al., 2008).

Emerging models of 'resilient' urban security represent a response to existential or material vulnerability, insecurity and, ultimately, change in the way terrorist risk is imagined and dealt with. This hybrid conceptualisation draws on, and complements, existing contributions within interdisciplinary security and terrorism studies, and urban geopolitics and, in so doing, seeks to ground the complex decision-making around the materialities and local management of terrorist risk. As such, and utilising the conceptual scaffolding laid out in this introductory chapter, this book will situate, contextualise and critically examine emerging theories and practices surrounding attempts to enhance city security and counter-terrorism. In doing so it will:

i Chart the surfacing and progression of different ways in which the need to secure the city from acts of terrorism has been enacted and driven by different threat environments, risk assessments, terrorist tactics and emergent technologies;
ii Examine the continual (re)emergence, and changing role and remit, of discourses and practices enacted in the name of securing the city and explore how everyone in society is increasingly being asked to contribute to this agenda;
iii Unpack some fundamental political questions of security for whom and by whom, highlighting the increased importance of embodied experience and of social and spatial justice considerations, within the implementation of urban security policy; and
iv Illuminate the processes by which exceptional notions of security become reproduced and normalised in the urban environment.

Using a range of international case examples, the book is structured into four main parts focused upon the underpinning principles and key discourses, practices and techniques of urban security in both the pre- and post-9/11 world, as well as reflections upon new and emerging counter-terrorism trends. Initially, the book historically locates the field of study, situating the city as the territorial device that served to control populations through a range of military and surveillance practices, but also as the key catalyst for the development of states and subsequent empires and civilisations. This highlights how security and urbanism have always been interlinked and, in the recent past, stresses the important developments in the second half of the twentieth century that saw strategies of urban defence enter a new phase, driven by Cold War threats, concerns over crime, disorder and violence and latterly terrorist targeting against commercial and government targets.

Moving into what has been defined as the era of 'postmodern' terrorism in the late twentieth and early-twenty-first century (Laqueur, 1996), the latter chapters showcase the increasing requirement to protect complex and evolving urban environments from multiple forms of terrorist attack and illuminate the effects of such securing strategies and techniques on citizens and the wider population (Neumann and Smith, 2008). Whilst avoiding grand narratives of hyper-security and focusing upon the local and contingent examples, this book further explores how the political rationalities underpinning neoliberal democracies have been reconfigured by and through the biopolitical *nomoi* of security, crisis, emergency and, more recently, resilience (Minca, 2006; Coaffee and Wood, 2006). As the book proceeds, it will further showcase how scale in security has been rethought, highlighting the importance of localised *urban* responses to new global security challenges that have become almost ubiquitous. This emphasises how security and counter-terrorism interventions are increasingly moving from the exceptional to the normal as they become socially accepted, are often uncritically mapped onto the design and management of the city and are increasingly permeating the everyday lives of citizens.

Notes

1 The *longue durée* (or the long term) is an expression used by the French Annales School of historical writing to designate their approach to the study of history.
2 In Nice, on July 2016, a 19-tonne cargo truck was deliberately driven into crowds of people celebrating Bastille Day on the Promenade des Anglais killing 86 people and the injuring around 500 others. In Barcelona, in August 2017, a van was driven into pedestrians, killing 13 people and injuring at least 130 others.
3 As was further noted, strategic thinking of this kind 'is an effort to delimit one's own place in the world bewitched by the invisible powers of the Other. It is also the typical attitude of modern science, politics and military strategy' (de Certeau, 1984, p.36).
4 Here, the relationship between space and security is often subsumed in governmentality techniques and wider discussions on biopolitics and biopower – the style of government that regulates populations.
5 Such vernacular and everyday accounts are, however, not identical. Most notably, whereas scholars associated with the vernacular turn have primarily focused upon

the linguistic constructions of citizens' accounts of threat and (in)security in their daily lives, those who take a more everyday perspective are interested in security practices negotiated in the context of citizenship more generally (see Vaughan-Williams and Stevens, 2016).
6 Here, approaches to analysing everyday urban security sought to avoid any unnecessary distinctions between macro and micro-levels in unpacking how everyday risks impacted upon individual and collective decision-making.
7 Perhaps one criticism of critical terrorism studies is that, until very recently, it has not really engaged in a discussion of space and spatiality.

2 The city as target

There is a deep historical lineage of urban security, and, in particular, strategies of fortification and walling, that altered urban mobility, modified spatial relationships and were invested with power (Brown, 2010). As Denman (2020) noted, in conditions of warfare, 'the design of the built environment and the organisation of space are intertwined' (p.231) with city walls serving 'as both a military devise and an agent of effective command and control over the urban population' (Mumford, 1961, p.82). As Mumford further noted, the physical form and institutional life of the city from the very beginning of the urban implosion were shaped in no small measure by the irrational and magical purposes of war (p.58).

Although requirements for urban security are central to contemporary polices that seek to defend the city from terrorist action through the hardening of city infrastructure and the mobilisation of civil defence, many of its characteristics are not new; they are adaptive versions of techniques and strategies that date back to the start of human civilisation. In this sense, security can be viewed as core to urbanism and urbanisation.

Defence has therefore always been a factor influencing the material and social structure of cities, becoming an ever-present preoccupation as the ruling powers sought to defend and secure their interests through creating increased feelings of safety (Forbes, 1965; Postgate, 1992). As early urbanisation proceeded, so the defensive systems deployed by city authorities became increasingly sophisticated to repel the improving strategies of intruders, in particular, through 'target hardening', with the construction of physical barriers such as gates, walls and ditches emerging as the most common features of urban defence and fortification (Morris, 1994). The earliest cities were synonymous with defensive features that have endued over the centuries. Uruk, in Mesopotamia, perhaps the first great city civilisation, had multiple walls, as recounted in an anonymously written poem, *The Epic of Gilgamesh:*

> Of ramparted Uruk the wall he built,
> Of Hallowed Eanna (temple) the pure sanctuary,
> Behold its outer wall, whose cornice is like cooper,
> Peer at the inner wall, which none can equal!

DOI: 10.4324/9780429461620-3

Pre-modern notions of defensive enclosure were not only formulated to protect cities from the 'dangerous' outside but also presented those in charge with an opportunity to control their internal citizenry (Keegan, 1993). Walls were seen to embody a 'seemingly physical, obdurate, premodern signature' (Brown, 2010, p.80), and as Mumford (1961) further described, 'the city with its buttressed walls, its ramparts and moats, stood as an outstanding display of ever-threatening aggression' (p.57).

Conceiving the relationship between urban space and security through a historical *longue durée* sweep, rather than the numerous ahistorical accounts that dominate the academic security studies literature – that according to military historian David Betz (2016, p.297), rarely 'pay more than lip service to how constant, widespread, and successful wall building has been as a strategic practice' – means returning to the central question Mumford raised in *The City in History* regarding the links between conflict and urban form and whether security is possible when urban societies are predisposed to war. The natural reaction to what Thomas Hobbes had famously referred to in *Leviathan* (1651) as a 'war of all against all', where the safety of people was seen as the supreme law, was an 'elaborate system of fortifications, with walls, ramparts, towers, canals, ditches that continued to characterise the chief historical cities down to the eighteenth century' (Mumford, 1961, p.57). Defensive needs shaped city spaces and became a perquisite if cities were to survive and thrive. Here though, the development of security features was not necessary a defensive strategy to prevent imminent attack, but rather to pre-emptively prepare for future attacks or warfare. In later work, notably, Clausewitz's famous treatise *On War* (1873 [1984]), defensive fortifications were seen as an integral part of the overall strategy of war, where accordingly, the organisation of war was inherently connected to the organisation of city spaces (Virilio and Lotringer, 2008, p.20).

Within this historical context, this chapter is divided into three main parts that foregrounds the development of more sophisticated modern approaches to managing collective security and territorially controlling populations, through military-inspired city planning. The first part will unpack the pre-modern and medieval notions of how best to cope with violent urban incursions and war, predominantly through walling and the generation of visible defensive landscapes. The second part focuses upon the surge in hybridising military strategy and urban planning during the seventeenth and eighteenth centuries that focused upon Baroque ideas, and notably the construction of boulevards as security corridors. The third part of the chapter draws on more recent history and deciphers Cold War notions of civil defence where the city emerged as a key locus of targeting as well as city-wide defence and set the scene for the holistic urban security strategies we see today.

Warfare and walling: The obduracy of urban security

Cities have always been characterised by feelings of insecurity, invasion by competing groups and the fear of crime and insurrection, with the need for defence against external attack being an ever-present preoccupation for urban authorities (Chermayeff and Alexander, 1966). Most accounts of the birth of cities stress how much fortification and warfare are bound up with its origins and development. In *The City* (1996 [1921]) Max Weber argued that 'the city in the past, in Antiquity and the Middle Ages, was also a special fortress or garrison', whilst the earliest settlements that are commonly recognised as cities are commonly known to have been walled. Archaeological records show that the early urban areas on the floodplains of great rivers such as the Nile, Tigris, Euphrates and Yangtze were often surrounded by walls, ditches and other defensive features to delimit the 'known' from the chaos and danger of the outside world. Such defensive features – typically a combination of a wall, tower and ditch – in time, became the universal blueprint for the fortified city. This was a design that was to change little between the building of the Wall of Jericho in approximately 8000 BC, and the introduction of gunpowder some centuries later (Keegan, 1993).

The relationship between walling and warfare is, however, a complicated one. Weber also acknowledged that walls as a property of cities 'was not universal even in the past' and that the 'city was not the sole nor the oldest fortress' (1966 [1921], p.75). In other words, warfare did not catalyse the rise of cities in a general sense, with many of the first cities showing few signs of either defensive or aggressive preparations. In many cases, war seems to have been subsequent to the founding of cities. Mumford's (1961) classic account of urbanisation additionally argued that war was an outcome of cities rather than cities as consequence of war. For Mumford, the origins of war were linked to the assertion of 'sovereign powers' by egotistical political rulers who were displacing earlier cooperative or religious institutions and ways of life, with the walling of cities, providing 'a permanent structure to the paranoid claims and delusions of kingship, augmenting suspicion, hostility, non-cooperation, and the division of labor and castes' (p.46). Many cities were also established as centres for storage and trade, with the wall representing the protection and enclosure of wealth as well as people. Put simply, the walled city was, at least potentially, a pathological entity where leaders felt compelled to defend the city from the dangerous 'other' outside the city wall whilst at the same time being cognisant of the value of walling for socio-economic purposes (Coaffee et al., 2008).

Inside the walled city was often found a 'citadel' – literally little city – representing the fortified core of the urban area. Initially as Mumford (1961) illuminated, the earliest citadels in the settlements in Mesopotamia were stores where the chieftain's grains and other produce were kept safe from resentful villagers but soon became the places where shrines were housed, making it a sacred and inviolable enclosure. As cities developed, so the citadel commonly took the physical form of a castle, stronghold or fortress that acted as the city's last line of defence, should the enemy breach the outer wall and other fortifications. Citadels subsequently became especially common in Greek and Roman towns and, as Betz (2019) noted, functioned as an element of 'strategic architecture' that 'were designed to command and control both literally and symbolically' (p.32) and provided the location for dispensing justice, organising policing and regulating commerce, becoming material symbols of power (Pepper, 2000). Hence, the citadels' primary function was not necessarily defence but control of the city and, by extension, wider territories where 'the strategic uses of fortification extend[ed] greatly beyond the mechanical necessities of battle' (Betz, 2019, p.33).

The relationship between war, defence and city design was not a universal blueprint and varied historically and geographically with fortification, and in particular, walling, becoming important in many entirely unconnected places and times (Owens, 1999; Hansen, 2000). Whilst knowledge is complicated by the reliance on archaeological evidence, with few written records, it is acknowledged that walls became more common in all the regions of what is now Italy from around the fifth century BC, although it was not until the period of the later Roman republic that 'a walled enceinte, complete with towers and formal gateways, [became] an essential symbol of city-status' (Cornell, 2000, p.218). The Roman *municipia* were partly defined by their possession of walls that were 'fully integrated urban defences with the city plan and the street system' (Owens, 1999, p.151). This continued in Imperial Rome, with evidence of extensive building of more sophisticated fortifications in many different shapes that reflected innovation in defensive thinking, and the particular, military threat (Campbell, 2002). Lanciani (1897) further indicated that Rome was fortified seven times by seven different lines of walls between the fifth century BC and the third century AD with outer walls being set beyond inner ones in a process termed 'multivallation'.

Such defensive designs, especially the city wall, also became associated with class distinction and the dual processes of inclusion and exclusion as the social élite lived within the defended citadel, whilst the poor often lived in relative danger outside the city wall (Sjoberg, 1960). More generally, we also know that where centralised modes of governance began to be established, construction of strategic defences around cities or regions became increasingly widespread. As Gold and Revill (1999, p.230) noted, these defences secured 'the *interests* of an imperial power, serving to establish a presence and create and image of power that might impress an indigenous population or rival colonialists'. The development of such urban assemblages inside city walls meant that the urbanisation process could therefore be read as an agent of social control where the threat of external attack meant that rulers could justify the dense concentration of population into an easily regulated and controlled space (Wittfogel, 1957).

As pre-modern cities developed, defensive systems became more complex to cope with new threats and the improving strategies of intruders. The castles and the walled towns of Medieval Europe exemplify this historic trend where designs for stone-clad castles were imported into Europe from Arabia, and which formed the centre of new settlements as urbanisation spread within the safe confines of the city-wall (Poyner, 1983). As such the wall, whilst serving a defensive purpose, also became 'a symbol of the sharp distinction between the city and the country, and stood as formidable reminders of class distinction' (Dillon, 1994, p.10; see also Fumagalli, 1994).

In time, the extent of city walling and fortifications waxed and waned in accordance to levels of threat, advances in military technology, new practices of warfare and the general growth of cities that made previous lines of 'barrier' defence superfluous. Walls, however, still remained as symbols of wealth, privilege and sovereign power (Brown, 2010). In essence, the technologies of fortification changed little in most places in the world beyond the initial burst of walling until the advent of modern techniques of warfare (Parker, 1996). Then, confronted by siege guns, and utilising advances in geometric methods, walls increasingly became more elaborate and sophisticated. This led to key developments in the fifteenth and sixteenth centuries such as the angle bastion which, when put together, created a star-shaped fortification that for many years served as a model for fortress building (De La Croix, 1963; Maier, 2016). As Pollak (2010, p.63) noted, 'the pentagonal citadel, like the head of a comet, drew behind it the whole discourse of military urbanism'.[1] Here, in the late sixteenth century we saw the ascent of specialist military architects to plan fortifications, replacing more 'universal' architects who engaged in both civilian and military domains (Denman, 2020, p.236).

The mobile and open city (or, the rise of the military engineer)

Over time, as urbanisation proceeded alongside industrialisation, the parallel assent of the modern state with its civil and military bureaucracies saw urban master planning become increasingly prevalent to catalogue and order the apparent chaos of urban life. This often had a particular focus upon opening up the unplanned urban fabric that had become dense and overcrowded, to ensure that people and goods could move around the city effectively and that the increasingly unknowable city could be observed through new techniques of urban surveillance. This saw the value of fortifications 'not only on the resilience of walls but also on lines of sight, the ability to survey the battlefield, and the possibility of strategic manoeuvre' (Denman, 2020, p.232).

New models of urban planning were advanced particularly from the start of the Renaissance (approximately 1300–1500) that provided the cultural bridge between the Middle Ages and the early modern era. Here, city builders sort to create utopian schemes that were open like the classical Greek agora and permitted easy intra-urban mobility. Initially there were a number of great cities in the mid-fifteenth century in Italy, notably Florence,[2] that took on a star-shaped layout adapted from the star fort, and were designed to resist cannon fire, with radial streets extending outward from a defined centre of military, communal or spiritual power (Giedion, 1962).[3]

As the Renaissance bleed into the Age of Enlightenment (approximately 1650–1800), the atmosphere of scientific advancement gave increasing room for progressive opinions to be voiced about how cities should be planned. Here new Baroque[4] styles of planning became popular as a means to transform the

24   *The search for urban security*

layout of the medieval city, with an emphasis on the creation of space and movement (Zucker, 1955).

During this period, rulers often embarked on ambitious attempts at redesigning their capital cities as a showpiece for the grandeur of the nation. Here though, military conflict or other forms of disaster were still a significant stimulus for redesigning cities. For example, in Brussels, following the 1695 bombardment by the French troops that destroyed a large part of the city centre, reconstruction efforts centred on transforming the medieval city that included a more geometric street layout, with straight avenues offering long, uninterrupted views. Ultimately such grandiose plans failed to garner enough political and public support to be constructed, although what did emerge were many wider streets to improve traffic flow, and by default, would serve to aid the movement of military troops into and out of the city.

As with warfare, disasters were often a major catalyst for planned reconstruction. In London after the Great Fire of 1666, radical rebuilding schemes that emphasised wide avenues spreading out from piazzas and a multitude of green spaces were promoted by architects such as Christopher Wren but were impossible to achieve due to the complexities of land ownership claims. In contrast, in the wake of the Lisbon earthquake of 1775 the King of Portugal launched efforts to rebuild the city that led to the construction of big squares, large avenues and widened streets in a grid system that replaced large sections of the old city.[5]

More generally, the town plans of late-seventeenth and early-eighteenth-century Europe also reflected increasingly powerful and centralised governments also had the resources necessary to impress themselves upon the design of the city. Whilst the morphology of the modern city was in drastic need of reordering as a result of burgeoning population which led to overcrowded living conditions, in many locations the need for defence and security also played a significant part in reconfiguring the cityscape into one that was more open and mobile, rather than one obsessed with walled defence. New architectural styles were particularly noticeable through the accelerated construction of new town halls, sculptured parkland and wide diagonal avenues that sought to advertise the grandeur of the city to the wider world.[6] Crucially, such broad avenues or boulevards also permitted military control of the approaches to the city.

In this process of rebuilding, demolishing the older parts of a city were often the result of plans drawn up by what Mumford (1961, p.442) described as 'military engineers' that had specialised knowledge in the mathematics of fortification techniques that separated them from earlier military architects (DeLanda, 1991). More specifically, as Denman (2020, p.236) highlighted, Euclidean/Cartesian geometry and the application of science to everyday life – a hallmark of the Renaissance era – meant 'the military engineer sought to emulate pure geometric form, equating mathematically defined order with effective defense. This was a matter of deriving the design for fortifications from regular polygons'. Essentially, this meant that 'fortification was easily transposed from the design of battlefields to the design of urban systems' (ibid., p.237). As a result, spatial control was rethought and as Elden (2013) noted into relation to the birth of territory, 'within Cartesian geometry', space was rendered 'measurable, mappable, strictly demarcated, and thereby controllable' (p.291).[7] Advances in urban defence thus shifted the focus from defined urban spaces to broader notions of territory with a particular emphasis on the circulation of goods and the mobility of people (and troops). In this era, defensive tactics were further utilised to stop the spread of disease through the construction of barriers or a *cordon sanitaire* (sanitary cordon) to restrict the movement of population into or out of a defined geographic area. In cities, the outer edge of a *cordon sanitaire* was usually a fence or wall with armed troops patrolling the perimeter.[8]

In practice, the term 'military engineer' had a two-fold meaning. First, it referred to the military tactics of clearing the ground of 'encumbrances' to allow the mathematical lines of new designs to be enacted (Mumford, 1961). Second, it signified how urban design 'regulated the movements of populations and defined the telos of war as the realisation of life in the ideal city' (Denman, 2020, p.237). Most notably, central places with radiating avenues gave an unparalleled vantage point where 'the artillery could command every approach' (Mumford, 1961, p.444). For example, in Moscow in 1774, Ekaterina II ordered the destruction of the rundown fortification walls of the White City that had protected the city for 200 years and created a boulevard ring instead. The first completed boulevard in Moscow – Tverskoy Boulevard – was opened in 1796 and was 872-metre long. Almost immediately the boulevard was used as an encampment by French troops, led by Napoleon, during the Patriotic War of 1812 given its strategic viewpoints.[9]

In this era, the French military were at the forefront of developments in urban warfare, and in 1847, after a long campaign in Algiers, produced a strategic manual that promoted the creation of large thoroughfares or 'military highways' through cities to circulate troops and enhance the surveillance of local populations. As Evans noted in *City without Joy* (2007), this 'street-fighting' manual, *La Guerre des rues* (The War of the Streets), 'outlined flexible street tactics of fire and movement designed to allow French columns to penetrate the maze of buildings and narrow alleyways that made up the Algiers Casbah' (p.4). Such operations essentially involved demolishing much of Arab Algiers, 'to facilitate the easy urban deployment of French troops in case of insurrection' (ibid.).

Such 'military operations as urban planning' (Misselwitz and Weizman, 2003) were to foreshadow Baron Haussmann's scheme to rebuild Paris that was commissioned by Napoleon a few years later. Here, building work took place between 1853 and 1870 and included the demolition of medieval neighbourhoods that were deemed overcrowded and unhealthy.[10] The old city was to be replaced by the building of wide avenues, or boulevards, that completely remodelled Central Paris and its surrounding areas, with building

26 *The search for urban security*

regulations imposed on façades, public parks, sewers and water works, city facilities and public monuments.

A less well publicised but essential element embedded within Haussmann's plan was to enable territorial control of populations and the crushing of popular uprisings by the army. Therefore, beyond aesthetic and sanitary considerations, the wide thoroughfares crucially facilitated troop movement, policing and social and military order. The nineteenth century in France, and especially Paris, was a revolutionary time and during periods of disorder, working-class Parisians had built make-shift barricades, which blocked off Paris' notoriously narrow streets and prevented government soldiers restoring order. Haussmann replanning of Paris essentially bulldozed wide new boulevards through the fabric of old Paris preventing the construction of effective barricades (see Figure 2.1). More strategically, the boulevard system

Figure 2.1 Haussmann as 'Artiste Démolisseur' Paris: capital of the nineteenth century.[11]

also allowed troops to enter and exit all corners of the city effectively to restore order (and collect taxes), essentially functioning as military corridors.

Haussmann's ideas further inspired a legacy of city rebuilding internationally. In the Austrian capital Vienna, the thirteenth century walled fortifications that had become popular bastions, and the surrounding *Glacis* – a wide, flat defensive belt that for military reasons was subject to a building ban – were demolished in 1858, with the broad circular 'Ringstraße' boulevard built in its place. This created a new urban landscape that was seen as easier to police and to restrict barricades, and heralded as an imperial show of power by Emperor Franz Joseph I. Further afield, in America, Daniel Burnham's 1909 plan for Chicago utilised Haussmann's ideas of large open public spaces and boulevards as part of what became known as the 'City Beautiful' movement, by which cities could reinvent themselves through their urban design and comprehensive urban planning. Similarly, to Haussmann, ideas of defence were never far from the surface, especially given Chicago recent history of civil unrest and rioting. As Krohe (1993) noted, 'the memory of mobs of strikers paralyzing the movement of troops through the city by rail must have caused more than one person to look favorably on the wide, straight boulevards laid out in the Plan'. As in Paris, the rationale for wide and easily accessible boulevards was to speed up the movement of goods, but in advancing the city defensible, they also sped up the movement of troops and made such routes more difficult to blockade.

The beginnings of everyday militarisation and urban decentring

Similar military corridors that emerged in Paris and elsewhere in the nineteenth century were also to remerge as a key part of new urban plans in the interwar era alongside an increasingly anxious form of urbanism that was fermented as a result of new visions of future war. Notably, from the late 1940s onwards the city was seen as being in the crosshairs of atomic targeting leading to Cold War anxieties, and what many historians have referred to as the beginnings of the militarisation of everyday urban life. As Mumford (1961) noted of the city in the early 1960s, 'the metropolitan regime now threatens to reach its climax in a meaningless war, one of total extermination, whose only purpose would be to relieve the anxieties and fears produced by the citadels' wholesale commitment to 'weapons of annihilation and extermination' (p.632). Here the city was perceived as a 'universal extermination camp' that had a 'death wish' (ibid., p.635). The city as target – an assumption that was underpinned by significant research effort and new forms of risk assessment – stimulated new waves of civil defence activity that passed responsibility for safety and security to all citizens, led to morphological and urban design responses that would aid civil evacuation and military access and egress, and perhaps more pervasively, the laminating of military-style thinking into managing all manner of urban problems. These Cold War trends were particularly stark in the United States where fears of atomic strike led to the military becoming embedded in a full range of metropolitan decision-making tasks. What is also striking about such trends, when viewed in the rear view mirror of history, is just how similar such ideas were to those that emerged to deal with the post-9/11 city (Chapter 6).

Whilst visions of conflict and war in the latter parts of the twentieth century were focused predominantly on the threat of 'total war' from nuclear strikes – framed by the appropriately named acronym M.A.D. (mutually assured destruction) – it was airplane-inspired future war that dominated military discussions in the 1920s and 1930s as the fear of devastating aerial bombardment increased through developments in aeronautical science. Particularly in America, as Corn and Horrigan (1984) noted, this led to the emergence of ideas for 'bomb-proof cities', and 'underground cities to protect against attack from above' (p.118). In the interwar years, many popular magazines depicted such cities in minute detail in response to the outlook that future wars were going to be wars that targeted urban centres. Such visions predicted that mass casualties would occur amongst citizens and not, as in previous wars, the military, given the imprecise targeting of aerial bombing. In such circumstances, civilians became 'legitimate targets' and in the 'total war' made possible by mechanisation, going underground seemed the only way to avert 'annihilation' (ibid., p.119). Whilst no underground cities were ever fully built, during World War II, the idea of digging down was a common strategy as underground shelters became widespread, with bunkers being built in house basements and with millions of people preparing to utilise underground train systems to protect themselves from aerial attack.

The dropping of the atom bomb in 1945 essentially put pay to the dream of underground cities that would not be able to survive the nuclear contamination from such strikes. The birth of the atomic battlefield of the future further led to the vast funding of scientific research and the development of an array of weaponry that once again painted cities as key targets for destruction by bombs given their concentration of buildings, infrastructure and population.[12] Such targeting, as Farish (2004, p.95) noted, led to a reconfigured geography of risk enveloping the city that was visualised through a series of 'concentric circles of destruction inscribed over various urban topographies' that got progressively riskier as you neared the central city. Such risk diagrams were reproduced in many popular periodicals of the day as well as being used strategically by the military as target analysis maps to plan a response.

Whilst the existence and circulation of such diagrams was to have impact on the built form of the city, and upon the way in which everyday life was structured, it was also to have an existential impact upon the anxiety of city living. This was visibly represented by Herbert Matter's 'Atomic Head' image that adorned the cover of the American Journal of *Arts and Architecture* in 1946 (Pavitt, 2008). This striking image of a head in profile with a mushroom cloud from an atomic strike rising to fill the brain cavity provided a powerful icon of the anxiety that swept across urban areas after the atomic bombing of Japanese cities after August 1945 (ibid., p.101). Whilst such anxiety was often hidden by the optimism that accompanied post-war technological advancement, it was never too far from the surface.

Such underlying fear of attack, and the explicit targeting of cities, not only prompted a resurgence of designs for bombproof living, but also led to new concepts of civil defence and citizenship being rolled out as part of the gradual process of distributing responsibility for security and defence to all citizens as part of a gradual militarisation of everyday life. As Farish (2004, p.94) noted of the situation in America at this time:

> Even before the development of frightening tensions with the Soviet Union, many Americans had reflexively mapped the devastation of Hiroshima and Nagasaki over their own metropolitan spaces, an exercise in *anxious urbanism* that...inspired an array of efforts to prepare both residents and landscapes for the arrival of the bomb (italics in original).

Programs of civil defence or civil protection – generally seen as the effort to protect citizens from military attacks and environmental hazards using the principles underpinning emergency management – were initially conceived in the West as early as the 1920s and 1930s as the threat of a Word War II, and in particular aerial bombardment developed, but only became widespread after the threat of atomic weapons became manifested after 1945 (Vale, 1987). Such domestic emergency management perquisites of national security meant preparing citizens for the arrival of the A-bomb through newly established civil defence initiatives that involved education, awareness raising and participation in mock exercises. Collier and Lakoff (2008) characterised this political logic as one of 'distributed preparedness' where, in accordance with the relationship to the target city, and plans made for managing the consequences of a nuclear strike, 'responsibility was delegated to different levels of government, and to both public and private agencies according to their competencies and capacities' (p.128).

Strategic war plans with civil defence as a core element were further advanced at this time, whilst a series of underground bunkers 'beneath the streets' that were for the exclusive use of the political and military elite and those who could afford them, were simultaneously developing (Laurie, 1979; Campbell, 1982). By contrast, and more surreptitiously, such war planning also ran in parallel with the rolling out domestic surveillance and psychological management programs in many advanced nations. As Oakes (1999, p.68) detailed, such programs of civil defence-inspired propaganda in the United States had three aims: first, emotion management plans designed to control fears of nuclear attack that would harness anxieties about nuclear war for civil defence activities, and the need to convincing citizens that nuclear annihilation fear were groundless; second, 'using managerial rationality – careful planning, organization and training' – to persuade the public 'that they could protect themselves by learning the requisite civil defence procedures and techniques', with the need for 'Duck and Cover' drills in schools being a widely used example; and third, the development of 'a Cold War ethic that interpreted civil defence as an *obligation of every household* and construed the practices required by family preparedness as *civic virtues* indispensable to the American way of life…and the *moral foundation* of national security' (emphasis added).

U.S. programmes exemplified the underlying aim of many Western civil defence programs as providing moral education about self-responsibility and the upholding of national values whilst, somewhat paradoxically, managing panic (which was arguably being instilled by such State propaganda) and militarising the nation; not just through traditional military means but also through the co-option of ordinary citizens into an array of traditional State security tasks. This was not a straightforward task. For example, in his analysis of U.K. civil defence during the Cold War period, Grant (2010) illuminated how the propaganda utilised to recruit civil defence volunteers in the 'atomic age' suffered from mixed messaging concerning citizenship and participation, and perpetuate tension about the conflict, patriotism and voluntarism. Initially, in the 1950s recruiting to the U.K. civil defence effort was through Government propaganda such as the poster 'What are YOU doing about Civil Defence' with a focus on obligated notions of duty and patriotism of everyone to defend the nation.[13] Despite strong early public engagement, over time, the changing (a)political culture in the U.K., and the growing amount of wealth and leisure time, made such messaging less effective (ibid.).

Overall though, the iconography and messaging of civil defence as displayed on billboard posters such as 'Protect and Survive', in popular magazines, and through transmissions over the radio and television, served to both nationalise and normalise militarism during the Cold War, with cities as its laboratory. Here citizens were enrolled in the experiment by default whether they liked it as not so they 'can learn what they can do to protect themselves and the freedoms they cherish' (U.S. Federal Civil Defense Administration (FCDA), cited in Farish, 2007, p.102).[14]

In more extreme cases, such notions of responsible citizenship that had been inculcated within a broader framework of civil defence morphed into a citizen's actively spying on fellow citizens at the State's request (Kackman, 2005). Notably in America, massive intelligence gathering efforts by U.S. agencies immediately after World War II involved operations where surveillance and intelligence were also gathered by citizens whose consciences compelled them to inform on other citizens. As Reeves (2017) noted in *Citizens Spies: The Long Rise of the Surveillance State*, how a range of habits and anxieties about political dissidents and ethnic minorities were inculcated through the Cold War 'red threat', and perpetual vigilance towards neighbours and citizens, was seen as a patriotic and moral duty. Here we saw a form of the civic regulation of morals in action within a climate where everybody was under suspicion, and everyone was seen to have a duty to be enrolled in civil defence. Over time, this has arguably led to the pervasive and taken for granted surveillance of public spaces and 'suspect communities' in the twenty-first century (Chapter 9).

Whilst preparing (urban) citizens for nuclear war was one key strand of national security efforts, a second strand of material landscape alternation – both real and imagined – was arguably more pronounced and advanced through ideas of deconcentrating urban cores and highway dispersal. A key linkage between these strands concerned how motor vehicles could be used for the key civil defence task of urban evacuations.[15] Here, the construction of the U.S. interstate highway network in the 1950s can also be seen in starkly military terms with the arterial routes in and out of most major cities being a strategic evacuation route or 'defensive highway' in the event of an atomic strike (Graham, 2010).

However, such urban visions predated the Cold War. The Eisenhower administration, having seen the efficiency of the German Autobahn system during World War II,[16] envisioned the emerging interstate system as having 'a duel military purpose of aiding evacuation and facilitating the movement of troops and equipment during war' (Fairish, 2007, p.104). As the Cold War got underway and the potential targeting of cities was most feared, impetus grew in the United States for major interstate expansion that resulted in the 1956 Federal-Aid Highway Act that was subsequently renamed the National System of Interstate and Defence Highways. From the outset of building work on the Interstate System, the U.S. Department of Defence fed military input to all phases of construction, ensuring it was designed to allow mass evacuation of cities in the event of a nuclear attack.

Whilst evacuation schemes as a key civil defence measure were widely heralded in the United States, built environment professionals, the military and politicians became increasingly concerned with what they saw as the over-concentration of urban areas that presented an inviting target to enemy bombardment. This led to a push for schemes that aided de-concentration and dispersal that would create small scale, and relatively uncongested, suburban communities. As Pavitt (2008, p.108) noted, the rationale for such dispersal was simple:

> a congested, large scale city was vulnerable to attack not only because of the concentration of industry, resources and people, but also because it would render the community unable to respond with retaliatory action in the chaos that followed. Smaller communities banded by empty green space (which could act as firebreak) were not only seen as more efficient, but disturbingly more expendable.

Planners and atomic scientists such as Tracy Augur and Ralph Lapp subsequently suggested visionary urban masterplans based on de-concentrated living. These often mirrored principles of the English Garden City movement of the early twentieth century that envisioned a series of self-contained urban communities, or, more contemporary visions of a Doughnut City where population is dispersed to perimeter rings. One proposed scheme that captured elements of both Garden City and Doughnut approaches was Cybernetics expert Norbert Wiener's 'lifebelt city' where green belts (seen as lifebelts) separated the central city from the suburbs. Entitled *A Civil Defence Plan for American Atomic Age Cities*, the plan was publicised in *Life Magazine* in 1950 (Leydenfrost, 1950). Drawn rather chillingly as a series of concentric circles that mirrored targeting and impact maps used by scientists of the time to measure the effect of atomic strikes on cities, the essence of the plan was to provide 'a place for bombed out refugees to go'. Spatially this consisted of a circular highway that was connected to a series of spoke roads (or contemporary boulevards) that radiated out from the centre and which, functioned as escape routes. Around the circular highway was 'a safety zone' where zoning regulation would prohibit building, thus enabling large tent cities to be constructed quickly in the event city evacuation was required.

Although in actuality such atomic city master plans were never constructed as envisioned, in part as a result of the development of Cold War weaponry that would make evacuation of cities futile, it did cement the idea of the active involvement of military-thinking into urban design and planning that bleed through into subsequent suburbanisation schemes, as well as the types of public spaces we see today. Here, as one commentator noted, as a result of the atomic threat 'the city...had become a bunker of sorts, a Survival City where the reproduction...of the environment was not viewed as an emergency measure but an everyday condition' (Vanderbilt, 2002, p.132). As Farish (2004, p.94) further summarises, 'from the pages of popular magazines...civil defence exercises, simulations of atomic attack turned the city into a "laboratory of conduct" subject to the spatialisation of risk and virtue' (see also Osbourne and Rose, 1999, p.740). Such a pervasive militarism in how cities were designed and expected to function in this period, arguably reinforced a constant state of emergency, or vigilance, that was to have repercussions beyond this era, and become expressed through the material configurations of the built environment.

Conclusion

In this chapter, a number of historical sweeps have illuminated urban security and the material configurations of defence and fortification as a system of territorial dynamics. Initially, the rulers of early cities sought to defend space as a display of sovereignty that utilised barrier methods that, over time, broadened out into a more rational and calculative technique that sought to organise space and wider territories for defence, based on geometric principles and practices of military engineering. These later approaches were a response to the changing nature of war and an appreciation that in the art of war, pre-emptive defence is strategically as important as offensive tactics. More recently, Cold War efforts to secure the city further exemplified the circular nature of history and illuminated how defensive efforts in the 1950s and 1960s were a reflection of the changing nature of threat but at their core drew significantly on previous episode of urban security. What history therefore tells us is that there is a repetitive pattern of political arguments that emphasise new dangers to justify more power for the rulers and usually more elaborate forms of security and defence.

As will be detailed in forthcoming chapter, the resurgence of fortification strategies that we have seen after the Cold War drew to a close, and in the post-9/11 era that are often articulated through ideas of urban resilience (Coaffee et al., 2008) or military urbanism (Graham, 2010), are not new, novel or unsurprising if we take a *longue durée* view. As Betz (2016, p.300) has argued 'there has been no point in history since the invention of the city in which armed forces have not been concerned about war in urban terrain'. One way in which urban historians have conceptualised this truism is through the idea of a palimpsest that sees the interpretation of multiple layers of security that emerged in different historical periods and which, superimposes over each other whilst still bearing visible traces of its earlier form. Ever-present in such layering has been a military mindset that has influenced decision-making over the nature and scale of urban defences to be employed.

Long sweeps of history have also served to illuminate how the past can be used to inform the present and how urban security trends recirculate over time. The nuances of such arguments were often lost in the wake of 9/11, with many proclaiming a paradigm shift in how were conceived threat and responded through physical and technical means (Huber and Mills, 2002; Marcuse, 2002; Warren, 2002). What this chapter has illuminated are the security approaches from prior eras of urbanism that have largely been reproduced and laminated into different spatial and geopolitical contexts where cities continue to be sites for both strategic and opportunistic violence that can no longer respond with external fortification or abandonment and retreat.

In this sense, urban security can no longer be viewed as strictly about enclosure and regulating movement between and through walls that separated the inside from the dangerous outside. In more recent times, this understanding has produced a number of dominant city narratives in the twenty-first century that have become central to counter-terrorist responses (Murakami Wood and Coaffee, 2007). These are narratives that view security as 'techniques of power working through a combination of modulated control by obstruction and heightened detection' (Denman, 2020, p.232) that involves how space is produced, organised, received, controlled and surveilled.

Three overriding accounts can be identified. First, a heightened focus upon emergency or contingency planning in the *prepared city*. Here, earlier civil defence structures and other process of regulatory management have been reinvigorated and reimagined for contemporary threats, and to decrease urban vulnerability and increase preparedness for 'inevitable' attack. As in prior era's, there is a proclaimed need for 'distributed preparedness' and for all citizens and stakeholders to be prepared and resilient, and play a part in national security. Moreover, if we examine the history of the citizen spy, we also see these same patterns embedded in contemporary policing trends and the actions of security services aligned to our current moment in surveillance culture that sees reporting suspicious activity as a moral imperative.

Second, we see a ratcheting up of territorial control through ideas of the *defensive city* where internal physical or symbolic notions of the boundary and territorial closure seek to regulate urban flows. Most starkly, this has resulted in an 'architecture of fear' emerging with aggressive forms of exclusionary urban designs, the continued 'citidelisation' of wealthy citizens into gated compounds and the widespread creation of 'exclusion zones' or 'cordon sanitaires' around particular 'at risk' sites. In extreme cases, we have seen ideas borrowed from strongholds, medieval castle architecture or from Cold War bunkering, remerging as design tropes in the construction of high-profile buildings and public spaces. The post-9/11 era further saw heated discussions, almost identical to those in 1950s America, about urban decentralisation.

Third, increasing and more sophisticated surveillance that has been rolled out in the *watchful city* through electronic surveillance within public and semi-public urban spaces, that since the late twentieth century, came to be seen as a remedy for many of the problems of criminality. Here the focus on surveying fixed bounded spaces has been extended to the entire population via the use of digital methods of categorising entry into certain city spaces, tracking circulating objects around the city and, pinpointing of suspect communities and behaviours. In subsequent chapters, we will see how these three main strategic urban security trends remerge in different configurations in both the latter decades of the twentieth century in response heightened levels of crime, civil unrest and car-bombing and in the post-9/11 era as key governmental responses to multiple forms of urban terrorism.

Notes

1 Cited in Denman (2020, p.236).
2 This 'ideal' planning model was widely transferred given the immense cultural power of Florence at this time.
3 The central areas of great cities were remodelled industrial suburbs characteristic of this era which remained disorderly and characterised by crowding and organic growth.
4 Historically, the Baroque period started in 1545 with the death of Michelangelo and continued until the mid-eighteenth century when neo-classic style becomes popular.
5 Here great philosophers of the day such as Rousseau and Kant had implied blame for the impact of the 'first modern disaster' should be associated with the unplanned and crowded urban patterns of modern cites.
6 Similar city building schemes were also taking place in the United States – Burnham's 1909 plan for Chicago being perhaps the most elaborate example.
7 Cited in Denman, p.237.
8 The term *cordon sanitaire* dates to 1821, when French troops were stationed on the border between Spain and France, to prevent the spreading of yellow fever (see Taylor, 1892).

9 The French referred to the war as the Russian Campaign. Here French soldiers dramatically altered the boulevard's appearance by cutting down all the lime trees on the boulevard for firewood. The boulevard was gradually restored after the war, with the planting of additional trees, and the siting of benches, bridges and fountains. In time it became the favourite place for promenading (Fedosuk, 2009).
10 The population of Paris had exploded from 759,000 in 1831 to more than a million in 1846 – despite regular outbreaks of cholera and typhoid that killed tens of thousands.
11 Brown Digital Repository. Brown University Library, https://repository.library.brown.edu/studio/item/bdr:80929/.
12 Notwithstanding the suburbanisation movement that was in full swing at this time.
13 This had a strong resonance with World War II messaging of self-sacrifice and public service.
14 One emblematic example Fairish gives in this 2007 work entitled 'panic in the street' concerns a U.S. FCDA roadshow developed in 1951. This was a convoy that travelled around the nation visiting a number of 'target cities' and offering citizens a dramatic view of what the atomic threat might look like in their location if an A-bomb detonated.
15 In the U.K., there was not a comparative scheme put in place, with a number of commentators highlighting that the focus was more upon invacuation to home-made shelters than the evacuation of cities via highways (see, for example, Preston et al., 2015).
16 The system has also been used to facilitate evacuations in the face of hurricanes and other environmental disasters.

3 Detonation boulevards

Introduction: Protecting territory through design determinism

As highlighted in the previous chapter, defensive strategies to deal with urban insecurity are not new and have a long genealogy that were periodically revisited as urban leaders sought solutions to deal with the impacts of late-twentieth-century terrorism. As this chapter will illuminate, in the 1970s and 1980s, danger was increasingly seen to originate from within, rather than outside, the urban area leading to defensive features such as new walled and gated spaces, and secure transport corridors, being developed *within* city boundaries to protect civilians from terrorism and political violence. At this time, security was especially enacted as protection against vehicle-borne improvised explosive devices (VBIEDs) or car bombs. As Thomas Freidman[1] noted in the *New York Times* in 1983, 'nothing terrifies…more than car bombs – not only because they are utterly indiscriminate, but because they transform a totally innocuous object from daily life into a deadly weapon'. At certain historical junctures, the frequencies of such vehicle attacks have led to issues of defence and security being inscribed into the everyday fabric of city life, both materially and socially, and often as a result of the actions of city planners who became key stakeholders in the construction of an increasingly normalised securityscape.

Car bombing tactics were no stranger to the twentieth century, being a weapon deployed since the 1920s as an act of radical protest and, increasingly, from the 1970s as a mode of political violence. In *Buda's Wagon* (2007), Mike Davis described how Mario Buda, an Italian anarchist, exploded his horse-drawn wagon near Wall Street, New York, in 1920, killing 40 and injuring over 200. The governmental response was swift, with the incident quickly being labelled a national emergency with the rapid rounding up local communist sympathisers. Labelling such improvised attacks as a 'poor man's air force', Davis further documented how, from the late 1940s to the 1960s, the car bomb was sporadically deployed as a weapon of urban warfare by guerrilla groups, and how the 'gates of hell' were opened as a result of American Vietnam protests and strategic Provisional IRA attacks against urban economic interests in Northern Ireland in the early 1970s. This showcased the

DOI: 10.4324/9780429461620-4

global diffusion of this simple, yet effective technology, that were cheap to manufacture from ammonium nitrate fertiliser, simple to deploy, challenging to prevent and impossible to overlook. As Davis noted,

> These new-generation bombs, requiring only industrial ingredients and synthetic fertilizer, were cheap to fabricate and astonishingly powerful: the elevated urban terrorism from the artisan to the industrial level and made possible sustained blitzes against entire city centers as well as causing the complete destruction of ferro-concrete skyscrapers and residential blocks.
>
> (ibid., p.5)

Such improvised weapons were delivered to targets by means of the road network where they were either left on a rudimentary timer switch to explode at a designated time or, more simply, driven at speed into the target as a suicide mission. Road and traffic management thus became essential to help secure the city from terrorism that involved reconfiguring the road layouts, blocking entrances to locations with makeshift barriers, and initiating innumerable armed checkpoints on strategic routes, all of which impacted urban mobility.

Human territoriality

Underpinning security responses to such changes in terrorist targeting techniques were conceptual ideas of territoriality that many felt could explain the impact of defence as a key feature shaping and separating urban space, both physically and socially. The concept of territoriality was originally developed at the beginning of the twentieth century to describe patterns of animal behaviour, in laying claim to, marking, and defending their territory against rivals (Gold, 1982). During the 1960s, a renewed interest in such ethological studies amongst urban planners argued that the concept of territoriality could be utilised to gain insights into human behaviour (Flaschsbart, 1969).

Politically, emerging ideas of territory at this time also began to question ideas of sovereignty as traditionally conceived in international relations through the dominant Westphalian model of state sovereignty, with questions emerging about the legitimisation of central state authority and territorial control of states, and the importance of different spaces (such as cities) and actors within organised politics and protest (Agnew, 1994, 2005). In this era, the expression of territoriality that saw defence in the city as emanating from sovereign power became complicated by the state increasingly acting with, or in parallel to, an array of non-state actors, militias or paramilitary groups to enhance security.

Prior conceptions had often used the idea of territory in a naturalistic way, assuming what is effectively a biological determinist conception of territory, deriving from Hobbes' (1651) 'war of all against all' as the natural state. Instead, the theory of territoriality that became widely utilised by the 1980s was derived from geographer Robert Sack's classic work, *Human Territoriality* (1986). For Sack, territoriality was both the definition of a space and the attempt to influence thinking and behaviour with regard to that space as a geopolitical strategy, as opposed to innate instinct. It was the filling of space with power and 'the results of strategies to affect, influence, and control people, phenomena, and relationships' (Sack, 1986, p.19).[2] This way of viewing territory and territorially, although theoretically underdeveloped at this time, does evoke Elden's (2010) more recent historical genealogy of the term that sees territory as a political technology that 'comprises techniques for measuring land and controlling terrain, [where] measure and control – the technical and the legal – must be thought alongside the economic and strategic' (p.799).

In the later part of the twentieth century, the territorial analogy was most frequently applied in urban research to describe segregation in terms of 'conflict interpretation', with social groupings reacting to a hostile environment by evoking territoriality or creating 'turfs' to preserve the character of a defended area and to instil a sense of cultural solidarity (Clay, 1973). In practical terms, city planners, as well as the police and military, became more aware that the built environment was a political infrastructure that could reveal and reproduce society's power structures and values. In this case, where there was a perceived necessity to control space and territory to reduce criminality or protest, political power produced the formal discourses, developed the plans and set strategies that reinforced existing spatial divisions and rules of conduct. In a more everyday sense, this often came down to unproven assumptions that the design of the built environment could significantly influence, or even determine, behaviour.

In this chapter, it will be highlighted how, from the late 1960s, initial ideas of territorial defensive design were increasingly utilised by a combination of policing, the military and a range of built environment professionals in attempts to increase urban safety and security. This will note the synergies made between urban designs and crime management when built environment professionals started to manipulate the built environment to curtail opportunities for crime and disorder – termed defensible space (Newman, 1972) and, in particular, how such notions were adopted by particularly military planners to counter civil disorder, terrorism and political violence.

Notably, from the early 1970s until the early 1990s, such militaristic urban security planning was perhaps most advanced in Northern Ireland, Israel and Lebanon as an active counter-terrorism and security strategy (Brown, 1985; Jarman, 1986; Soffer and Minghi, 1986; Monroe, 2016). This broader process of militarisation was made visible through 'the deployment of troops, the installation of checkpoints, watch towers and other surveillance apparatus' (Smyth, 2004, p.546) that came to transform everyday life. Moreover, such approaches to militarisation went beyond the visible apparatus of military security or policing regimes and could be seen as inverting politics and prioritising military goals, decisions and methods over those of civil society (Bulchotz, 1999).

Design, behaviour and security

Sixty years ago, Jane Jacobs in *The Death and Life of Great American Cities* highlighted how inappropriate urban design could contribute to diminishing community safety, and developed the concept of 'eyes on the street' to enhance informal urban surveillance (Jacobs, 1961). Such observations also elucidated the importance of urban design in producing or mitigating potential criminogenic environments, influencing human behaviour and affecting quality of life. For Jacobs, one of the main characteristics of a thriving place was that people felt safe and secure, despite being among complete strangers. Here the importance of safety and security sought to ensure that everyday experiences were represented in public spaces that she saw as central to the dynamics of city life. Essentially, if such locations are accessible, attractive, and safe, they can encourage a range of uses and activities. Conversely, when public spaces are neglected, they can create feeling of insecurity. The logic was simple: the more people on the streets, the safer they become with 'eyes on the street' providing informal surveillance of public locations. Urban security was therefore not simply a matter of policing space but was related to the physical design of the built environment and the quality, accessibility and conviviality of public spaces. This in itself was seen in relation to ideas of clear borders or demarcated territory using walls, fences and other built forms that could give a sense of ownership to communal areas and help animate or, conversely to segregate, urban space.[3]

Jacobs' pioneering work became inspirational in stimulating research and thinking on the relationship between certain types of environmental design and reduced levels of violence. This led, from the early 1970s, to urban design and planning tools commonly being used to address both the causes of crime, disorder and incivility, and its impacts. Notably, in America, defensive architecture and urban design were increasingly used as a direct response to the urban riots, which swept many U.S. cities in the late 1960s, as well as the perceived problems associated with the physical design of the modernist high-rise housing blocks, that were viewed by criminologists of the day as breeding grounds for crime. Here, urban renewal strategies were felt to be destroying the social framework needed for self-policing with such places were sometimes described as 'indefensible' space and where, for many, urban fear was becoming increasingly institutionalised.

There were further concerns that enhanced urban fortifications were socially and economically destructive and that the provision of security was becoming increasingly privatised as individuals, having lost faith with the public authorities to provide a safe environment, increasingly sought to defend themselves. As one commentator noted,

> The urban environment is being fortified today, not primarily by public decisions, but mainly through a multiplicity of private choices and decisions, individuals make in our decentred society. The private market

is responding to growing demand for an increasing range of crime control devices and other means of safety. In some cases, safety has become a commodity that is explicitly sold or rented with real estate.

(Gold, 1970, p.153)

Research suggesting a tangible link between crime and the built environment was, however, throwing up possible solutions. Initially, in the early 1970s, criminologist C. Ray Jeffery (1971) developed an approach called *Crime Prevention through Environmental Design* (CPTED) that suggested that the design and arrangement of buildings could create environments that would discourage normal patterns of social interaction and encourage criminal behaviours. The key idea was that opportunities for crime could be reduced by modifying the design of the built environment, leading to a decrease in crime and the fear of crime. As Jeffery stated, 'in order to change criminal behaviour we must change the environment (not rehabilitate the criminal)' (1971, p.178).

Jeffery's work was followed by a host of studies on architectural and design determinism that highlighted how certain material elements could affect behaviour. Notably, it was the publication of architect Oscar Newman's *Defensible Space – Crime Prevention through Urban Design,* in 1972, that stimulated the most intense debates on the relationship between crime and the built environment after a study of large public housing estates in St Louis and New York. For Newman, defensible space encompassed a 'range of mechanisms – real and symbolic barriers... [and] improved opportunities for surveillance – that combine to bring the environment under the control of its residents' (ibid., p.3). Defensible space was offered as an alternative to the target-hardening measures that were being introduced to American housing at this time. It became a means by which the residential environment could be redesigned 'so they can again become liveable and controlled not by the police, but by a community of people who share a common terrain' (ibid., p.2). Newman did not rule out the use of security fences or electronic surveillance technologies, but relying on these measures was seen as a last resort if subtler design solutions were unsuccessful. Echoing Jacobs, the notion of defensible space fundamentally incorporated ideas of civic responsibility:

> The designs catalyse the natural impulses of residents, rather than forcing them to surrender their shared social responsibilities to any formal authority, whether police, management security guards, or doormen.
>
> (ibid., p.11)

In practice, Newman proposed that outside spaces become more defensible if they are clearly demarcated and also proposed four interrelated design features that contributed to secure residential environments:

1 *Territoriality* – Creating a sense of ownership and of community of shared space amongst local residents by the zoning or demarcating of public space;

2 *Natural surveillance* – The use of environmental design to improve the ability of residents to observe their locality;
3 *Image* – Alteration of the structure of buildings to counteract the 'stigma' of public housing;
4 *Milieux* – Alteration of environmental surroundings of residential areas to merge with areas of the city considered safer and enhanced their security.

Newman's ideas, like those of CPTED, were inexorably linked to the early 1970s and as such reflected the growing interest of the planning and architectural professions in the relation between environment and behaviour. This type of research work was very much in vogue given the growth of behavioural approaches in human environments and, in particular, the growth of behavioural geography in response to the overly quantitative turn in spatial sciences that occurred from the 1950s (Eriksen, 1980). At this time, a great dealing of attention was further placed upon so-called 'design determinism' (Knox, 1989) – how the design of the built environment negatively effects human behaviour – and, more specifically, concern that the micro-arrangement of urban spaces might discourage normal patterns of social interaction and elicit deviancy and criminality. As a result, defensible space was considered attractive in this era as it emphasised the use of the environment to promote residential control and the potential to return to a more humane and less threatening environment.[4]

Defensive design for anti-terrorism

Since their incorporation into mainstream urban planning and design decision-making in the early 1970s, defensive design measures were further advanced as a result of an increase in attacks by terrorist groups against urban infrastructure and populations. This inevitably led to an increasingly sophisticated array of fortification, surveillance and security/traffic management techniques being deployed by urban authorities and the police, often guided by planners, to protect perceived urban vulnerabilities based on the principles of defensible Space/CPTED.[5]

Since the pioneering work of Jeffrey, Newman and others, defensive design schemes subsequently evolved to increasingly include measures such as access control, tactics such as 'target hardening', and advanced surveillance technologies such as CCTV. The underpinning assumptions of defensive design also came under scrutiny as many examined the behavioural expectations that underpinned defensible space; notably that the visibility of security features may not deter all potential offenders, and that those acting irrationally (because of drugs, mental illness or ideological fervour) may decode environmental cues differently. Such approaches were also seen have significant visual impacts, with many perceiving a very real risk that defensive design could produce a ' "fortress effect" whereby structures or sites are so festooned with bars, locks and barricades that at best their aesthetic value is degraded and at worst their appearance only serves to increase fear and unease among the pubic' (Conzens et al., 1989, p.342). Similarly, many pointed to the exclusionary potential of places that incorporated defensive design inappropriately and disproportionality, arguing that if applied without sufficient community participation, defensive design may become over-reliant upon target hardening and develop a 'fortress mentality' and create sterile public areas that 'effectively works against CPTED concepts, designed to support social interaction and "eyes on the street"' (ibid.).

Because of the 1970s and 1980s zeitgeist for design-out crime ideas, in many Western countries the police, often through associated ideas of *Secure by Design*,[6] and in some cases the military, became increasingly incorporated as an influential stakeholder in planning and place-making processes as crime rates soared and bombs exploded in divided cities. This subsequently saw ideas associated with defensible space – of territoriality, boundary enclosure, access/traffic management and target hardening – utilised in a number of contexts from the early 1970s to thwart urban terrorism. The particular concern here was to stop or mitigate the impacts of car bombs that emerged as the terrorist's weapon of choice. Such attacks, as part of 'long war' insurgent strategies, were depicted as 'an implacable virus' that once they have 'entered the DNA of a host society and its contradictions, their use tends to reproduce indefinitely' (Davis, 2007, p.6).

In counter-response to the rise of car bombing, the 1970s and 1980s saw ideas of defensible space merged with military and policing tactics, leading to approaches to security that privileged fortress design and access control at the expense of community-centred schemes. This saw the urban planning and design profession playing a more active role in decision-making than was the case in Haussmannian boulevard schemes or Cold War survival city master plans (Chapter 2). This era saw the birth of the military planner who acted as a guide to where defensive fortifications and secure corridors were strategically placed, increasing the scope and scale over which mitigation measures were deployed, and thereby extending the design and construction focus of earlier military architects and military engineers.

In the following sections, the material and social responses to car bombing as a specific technology of terrorism will be noted and the strategic elements of this territorial reaction depicted in relation to three cities; Belfast, Jerusalem and Beirut. This will be undertaken through a genealogical lens that showcase a number of asynchronous accounts that emphasise context and historical contingency in understanding the local webs of relations that determine what decisions regarding security are made, by whom and with what level of authority and effect. This demonstrates a truism, long accepted in the spatial sciences, that the design and organisation of space is a political and strategic activity (Lefebvre, 1991 [1974]), despite planning being seen as a depoliticised activity in the popular imagination. In reality, in these instances, planning functioned as an arm of the modern nation-state focused on security and social control as its chief priority (Yiftachel, 1998).

Belfast's ring of steel

In the late 1960s and early 1970s, Belfast, in Northern Ireland, experienced widespread defensive 'walling', with Boal's classic study of the Shankhill/Falls 'interface' in West Belfast illuminating one of the best-known examples of human territorial behaviour (Boal, 1969). This study depicted how Protestant and Catholic communities were kept apart by a range of symbolic landscape markers such as flags, bunting, graffiti, family names, bus routes, and media and political attachments, which were radically concretised in the built environment by a series of physical 'environmental' barriers. These barriers started as hastily erected barricades and then morphed into full-scale defensive walls, or 'peace lines' that acted as territorial ciphers in the urban landscape (Boal, 1971).

Consequently, as the 'Troubles' proceeded from the late 1960s, the residential geography of Belfast became fragmented into a series of religious enclaves based on 'safe' territories for particular communities, essentially hardwiring segregation into the physical and social landscape (Boal, 1995). This further led to many new residential communities being designed so that access to housing estates was restricted to a small number of roads, making them easier to monitor by the police and army.

Defensible space became the order of the day as ideological division, and a permanent sense of conflict, became a concrete part of the increasingly militarised built environment through not only the interface walls, but the widespread adoption of razor wire, metal gates and police and army checkpoints (Shirlow and Murtagh, 2006). Belfast in the 1970s quickly became a laboratory for radical experiments on the fortification of urban space with ideological divisions becoming 'a concrete part of the physical environment, creating an ever more militarized landscape' (Jarman, 1993, p.107). Notably, in relation to the specific need for anti-terrorist security in Northern Ireland, it was argued that the ultimate level of security provision in a city was defensible space (with its emphasis on territoriality) existing alongside physical barriers (the target hardening mechanisms that Newman saw as a last resort) (Boal, 1975; Coaffee, 2003).

From the early 1970s onwards, attempts to militarise defensible space therefore became part of the everyday city, being particularly stark in and around the central shopping area. During the first years of the 'Troubles' (1968–1970), the commercial core of Belfast was seen as a relatively neutral space within the segregated sectarian landscape and was relatively unaffected by terrorism. All this changed in July 1970 when a large vehicle bomb was detonated in the city centre, without warning, outside the premises of the Northern Bank, injuring 30 people, 3 seriously.[7] More attacks were to follow. Between late 1971 and mid-1972, the Provisional IRA went on 'car bomb blitz' in an around the centre of Belfast, fuelled by knowledge of the destructive power of new home-made ammonium nitrate fertiliser bombs (Davis, 2007, p.56).[8]

The bombing campaign of the Provisional IRA against the city centre was centred on economic terrorism and aimed to cripple the city's commercial life. In little over a decade, it led to the destruction of over 300 retail outlets and the loss of a quarter of all retail space (Brown, 1985). In response, on the July 18, 1972, new traffic restrictions were imposed, without warning, as barbed wire fences were thrown across the main streets in central Belfast creating a number of 'defensive segments' with access controlled by the British Army. The city centre in effect became a 'besieged citadel' initially leading to fears that these security measures would destroy the city centre in a way the Provisional IRA never could, by keeping the customers out (Jarman, 1993, p.115).[9] These drastic security measures, implemented by the authorities to tackle the security problem through restriction of access and mobility, can be seen as a radical example of territoriality as encompassed in notions of defensible space.

The bombing campaign against Belfast city centre peaked in intensity on July 21, 1972, 3 days after the construction of the makeshift security cordon, when the Provisional IRA detonated 22 car bombs in and around the central area within the space of 75 minutes. Seven people were killed and over 130 injured, with the centre of Belfast, according to one commentator, resembling 'a city under artillery fire' (Moloney, 2002, p.116). All of the explosions, however, occurred *outside* of the new restricted traffic zones. By 1974, the barbed wire fences encircling the central area of Belfast had been replaced by a series of tall steel gates, with civilian search units established. The initial placement of this reconfigured security cordon around Belfast city centre was made up of a series of different zones, the entry into which was dependent upon a body search undertaken at an armed checkpoint. Further changes were made in March 1976 when the four main security segments were amalgamated to form a single security zone ringed by seventeen steel gates (see Figure 3.1), that become locally known as the 'ring of steel' (Brown, 1985; Coaffee, 2000).[10]

Subsequently, as the relative threat of terrorism against Belfast city centre decreased during the 1980s and early 1990s,[11] city officials sought to re-image the city in an attempt to attract businesses back. Reduced levels of security, decreases in the number of terrorist attacks and significant redevelopment and pedestrianisation, subsequently, helped to re-patronise central Belfast as part of the city's attempts to market itself within the global economy as a post-conflict city (Coaffee, 2003). Further landscape 'softening' also occurred as attempts were made to remove visible territorial barriers and boundaries, including the 'ring of steel', to increase access between previously contested territories and promote a less threatening environment, given the reduced risk from terrorism.

However, this re-imaging of Belfast was only perceived as partially successful and often as superficial. Here, the outside world was largely viewing the city through media images of bomb-damaged buildings and colourful paramilitary murals that significantly ignored the radical planning transformations that were taken place. As such Neill (1992, p.9) concluded that Belfast city centre, at this

Detonation boulevards 45

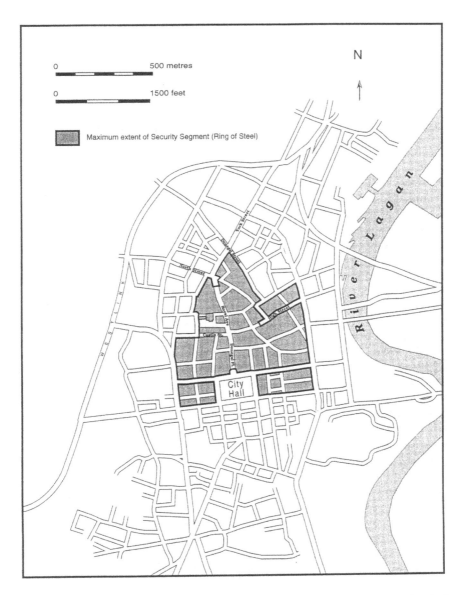

Figure 3.1 The maximum extent of the Belfast security segment (ring of steel) in 1976.

time, exhibited 'a condition of visual schizophrenia' where 'a post-modernist consumerist kaleidoscope of images floats uncomfortably on top of the squat brutalism of terrorist-proof buildings and the symbolism of the past'.

Overall, through the 1970s and 1980s, and into the early 1990s, Belfast provided an example of a city with a 'hardened' urban landscape, where the spatial configurations within a defined area, especially borders and boundaries, became more pronounced in an attempt to create territoriality by delimiting buildings and territories from their surroundings through defensive architecture, access restrictions and demarcated boundaries. Importantly, in such restructuring of the urban landscape the security forces – the police and army – became key agents in the city planning process.

Israeli securityscapes

Turning to another notable example, Israel during the 1980s and early 1990s became synonymous with militaristic security planning that significantly impacted land use and the day-to-day experience of places. As in Northern Ireland, the link between the military and city planning in Israel must be viewed as a long-term historical mission with plans to embed security thinking into the design of settlements dating back to the 1930s and 1940s. As architect Eyal Weizman (2006) noted, a 1948 military document *Security Principles in the Planning of Agricultural Settlements and Workers' Villages'* by the Israeli Defense Force (IDF) stressed the importance of 'strategic and tactical considerations' in regional planning and the internal design of settlements. *Security Principles* effectively hardwired different strategies of defensive intervention at national, regional and local scales creating a preoccupation with 'impending threats, defence strategies and precautionary measures' (Soffer and Minghi, 1986, p.28). Over time, defensive responses created what Azaryahu (2000) referred to as a 'securityscape' that encompassed not only physical interventions but also public alertness to risks and threats that became part of the everyday experience (p.103). This focus of security, away from military action and warfare, and towards counter-terrorism as a key aspect of public safety associated with policing, served to enhance the notion that security increasingly concerned the 'home front' (p.104).

Compact, dense and heavily fortified dwellings and perimeters – protected spaces – were to be the planners' design of choice as cities and settlements were targeted, by not only car bombs and mortar shells, but also a variety of small-scale explosive devices left in the urban environment and retail outlets, as well as suicide attacks against transport infrastructure. As Weizman Israeli highlighted 'planners working in private offices or within in the map rooms of the military centers of operation, further imagined homes ... as physical fortifications and adopted their layout according to the trajectories of vision, fire and supply' (2006, p.160).

In occupied areas, such as the Gaza strip, where large Palestinian refugee camps had been set up in the early 1970s, the military adopted the principles of Baron Haussmann and broke up the dense and complex maze of alleyways with mass building clearances and the construction of military corridors and perimeter security zones that enabled troops to access the camps to maintain security and collect taxes. Under the leadership of IDF commander Ariel

Sharon – who would eventually become Israeli Prime Minister between 2001 and 2006 – planning was deployed as a tactical military tool to gain territorial control and to destroy the areas from where possible terrorists would emerge (Weizman, 2007). These were security principles *and* planning tactics that would be constantly redeployed in forthcoming decades, sometimes by Sharon, to literally destroy the city to remove potential terrorist threats with tanks literally bulldozing population from strategic sites. As Graham (2002a) argued, Sharon's long-term strategy had always been one of 'urbicide'; 'the deliberate denial or killing of the city, the systematic destruction of the modern urban home'[12] that was centered on security and counterterrorist philosophes 'linked to a broader strategy of destroying the landscape in the creation of settlements and mobility spaces that are supposedly less vulnerable to Palestinian attack' (ibid.).

If the concerns for secure territorial design prior to the 1980s were predominantly focused on threats from the 'outside' of settlements, the rapid urbanisation of Palestinian communities in the 1980s and 1990s led to the threat of civil disruption, terrorism and political violence being conceived as something that was internal to cities, and which required a modified territorial design strategy. These overcrowded and deprived urban areas were commonly viewed by the Israeli state as the 'habitat of terror' with Palestinian inhabitants seeking to destabilise territorial control and which, in response, required a 'jihad of building' to reshape facts on the ground (Weizman, 2010).

This increased requirement to embed the design of protected spaces into everyday life stemmed from master planning documents prepared by the World Zionist Organisation in 1980 that proposed bisecting Palestinian areas with Jewish settlements to disrupt 'territorial contiguity' and enforce migration (Weizman, 2006, p.162). As in Belfast, areas such as the West Bank and East Jerusalem saw military planning fragmenting the cityscape through a series of strategically positioned settlements, roads, checkpoints and the separation of the urban areas into what were perceived as safe and unsafe zones.

In particular, the development of transport corridors provided a graphic example of how security was made in concrete form. Pullan et al. (2007) illustrated the case of how a major boulevard – Road 1 – in and around Jerusalem – became an axis of exclusion and dispossession. Spatially, this six-land carriageway, since the 1970s, had dissected Jerusalem north-south, separating Israeli and Palestinian sectors and 'bringing the frontier into the centre of Jerusalem while at the same time contributing to Israeli spatial continuity' (p.176).

This deeply political highway was a vital ingredient in the post-1967 war ideas for Israeli planning that sought to connect to settlement construction on occupied land.[13] The road, as it evolved, was constructed largely on the de facto border of Palestinian East Jerusalem and Israeli West Jerusalem and was severed by military checkpoints as it neared Ramallah and Bethlehem. Used predominantly by Israelis, the road functioned to enhanced mobility for some whilst curtailing it for others. As Pullan (2007) argued, the road was emblematic of urbanism underwritten by conflict, where unequal mobility reinforced segregation and was seen to enhance security. Specifically, with regard to Road 1,

> the way the thoroughfare has been conceived and constructed in the post-1967 period has shifted from a naive and one-sided dream of unity via an inner city boulevard, to a hard frontier that has brought to this critical area of Jerusalem new levels of restriction and manipulation.
>
> (ibid., p.192)

The development of this road served a national (security) agenda of division and occupation of Jerusalem. This was reflected in planning culture in the 1970s and 1980s (Nitzan-Shiftan, 2005), where road building was linked to territorialisation and where master plans, once conceived, had a tendency to remain in place, unaltered for some time. For example, Nasrallah (2014) highlighted how the last comprehensive plan for Jerusalem developed under the British Mandate, and published in 1949, remained as the principle development brief for the city for well over 50 years.[14] Such outdated plans were a powerful statutory instrument in the 1980s that restricted Palestinian development at local level and especially the linking of Palestinian-administered towns through the development of transport infrastructure. This is especially the case with Jerusalem, where, as Chiodelli (2012, p.6) noted:

> Planning is one of the privileged tools of a "low intensity war," which combines the "dramatic violence of some events (bombs, killings, missiles and bulldozers) … with slower and more consequential events (the construction of buildings, streets, tunnels) no less violent or destructive. The Israeli-Palestinian conflict becomes, within the Holy City, "a war of cement and stone".

Such long-standing practices were discussed at a UN General Assembly in December 2006 where it was explicitly argued that 'urban planning was being used by Israel as a tool of ethnic segregation and control, and as a weapon of physical and psychosocial fragmentation'.

Other studies further pointed to a combustible mixture of ethnonational and religious conflict, combined with urban planning, that marginalised Palestinian communities in Jerusalem (Bollens, 2011). Subtle planning and building regulations, unequal service provision and housing allocation policies *combined with* electrified fences and defensive walls that snake through neighbourhoods, created a landscape of security and separation. As architect Omar Youseff (2011) recounted of the built form in Jerusalem, it 'tells stories about laws, politics and visions of power that shape them; through daily encounters, they influence behaviours and whisper, or sometimes cry, with cultural and political meanings, as people use the space'.

The 'Beirutization' of space

The long war in Lebanon (1975–1990), although often described as a civil war, was a multinational conflict fought by members of Lebanese, Palestinian, Syrian, Israeli, the United States and other foreign militia groups and state armies, notably from France and Italy.[15] Such complexity made territorial congruity impossible to maintain and led to notions of hybrid sovereignty (Fregonese, 2012) being put forward to explain Lebanese sovereignty and territorial claims, as a result of complex fusion between state and non-state actors. In the 1980s, this amalgamation of competing interests was summed up by a U.S. Marine quoted in Freidman's 1989 opus, *From Beirut to Jerusalem*:

> To me it was a civil war, only it wasn't just the North against the South. It was North against South, East against West, Northeast against Southwest, Southeast against Northwest, and we were in the middle of it all. There were just too many different sides. If we picked one, we had four others against us.
> (first cited in Friedman, 1984, p.32)

On the ground, such a situation destabilised understandings of sovereignty as the exclusive control by a state over a bounded or fixed territory (see, for example, Agnew, 2005), instead postulating that 'both state actors and non-state militias perform sovereignty practices increasingly resembling each other, and co-constituting each other through Beirut's physical environment' (Fregonese, 2012, p.655). As in Belfast and Jerusalem, during the late 1970s and throughout the 1980s, Beirut became spatially divided along sectarian lines with militias enforcing the boundaries of different city territories, and where defensive architecture and an extensive apparatus of security and surveillance measures contributed to the normalisation of segregated geography.

This was a long war that was 'waged against the background of an ever-present fear of car bombs' (Khalidi, 1986, p.88) that fragmented and territorialised space into warring parts in a process that became known as 'Beirutization' (see Monroe, 2016). Such terroristic and security practices led to citizen immobility as free movement was entangled in a complex geography of closely guarded territorial boundaries that demarcated 'friendly' and 'enemy' enclaves that were themselves palimpsests of complex histories of political violence and emergent terrorist threats (ibid.). As Freidman (1983, p.12) further noted of Beirut, 'the city lives in that half-light between security and insecurity, war and truce, in which there is usually enough security to go about one's day but never enough to feel confident that it won't be your last'.

In Beirut, the nadir of this tactical car-bombing-inspired violence came in the early 1980s as warring factions sought to out-bomb each other, whilst simultaneously trying to devise countermeasures to thwart deadly vehicles packed with explosives reaching their intended targets. Whilst car bombing as a strategic tactic of the Lebanese war had been used sporadically through the

1970s, and in Beirut in particular, these were small scale attacks compared to 'Hell's kitchen' (Friedman, 1989) that was to follow in the early 1980s. Such terrorisation tactics were used by both 'sides': on the one hand, the Christian fraction backed by Israel that sought to remove the Palestinian Liberation Organisation (PLO) from Muslim West Beirut, and Lebanon more generally, and on the other hand, the Muslim faction backed by pro-Iranian militia Hezbollah, who sought the removal of international 'colonists' from Lebanon.

As Davis (2007, p.68) recounted, attempts to remove the PLO from the Israeli-Phalangist campaign meant that 'for 18 months [between late 1981 and early 1983] a hellish chess game was played out with TNT-packed taxies and trucks in a vain attempt to intimidate…'. By the beginning of September 1981, American troops had supervised a major withdrawal of the PLO from Beirut and then had withdrawn themselves, but the bombs still continued. Notably, on September 17, 1981 a large vehicle bomb exploded outside a Palestinian political office killing 29 people and injuring over 100. Over the following days, many other car bombs were either diffused or wrought havoc in West Beirut as crowded locations were targeted. In counter-response, extra layers of security were added outside of PLO offices, including sniffer dogs. This was to no avail as a massive explosion ripped through West Beirut on October 1 killing over 50 people and causing widespread devastation. Dozens of further attacks in the next 6 months brought the estimated death toll from such attacks to around 2000 (Davis, 2007, p.70).[16]

Illuminating the complex geopolitical landscape of Lebanon, in May 1982, the seemingly impregnatable French embassy compound in Muslim West Beirut suffered a car bomb attack killing 12 and injuring many more.[17] This attack was largely seen to have been ordered from Syria and precipitated the invasion of Lebanon by the IDF in June 1982, alongside the cluster bombing of Syrian military positions and West Beirut more generally. This military operation was also in reprisal for repeated attacks and counter-attacks between the PLO operating in southern Lebanon, and the IDF, that had caused civilian casualties on both sides of the border, and the attempted assassination of the Israeli ambassador to the United Kingdom which was blamed on the PLO. The response from the repressed Islamic population in West Beirut was the formation of Hezbollah as part of an Iranian-inspired effort to aggregate a variety of militant Lebanese Shia groups into a unified organisation, the main goal of which was the expulsion of 'colonialists', such as the Americans, French and Israelis, from Lebanon. Further conflict followed. In September 1982, a multinational peacekeeping force that included the United States, French, Italian and British personnel entered Lebanon intending to negotiate a ceasefire between Lebanon and Israel, who had invaded the country 2 months before[18] and after Israel's Lebanese allies slaughtered nearly 1,000 unarmed Palestinian civilian refugees.[19]

In time, Hezbollah was to rise to become perhaps the most influential militia group on the planet and took car bombing to new depths. As Davis (2007, p.79) noted, Hezbollah added a new element to car bombing – 'a decisive ingredient from Beirut cuisine: the grimily determined *kamikaze* ready to crash through security barriers and past startled security guards in order to bring his deadly payload into the very lobby of an embassy or barracks' (emphasis in original). From early 1983 until late 1984, the relative calm of Beirut life was shattered by a series of devastating Hezbollah car bombings against the United States and overseas targets. Notably, in April 1983, the U.S. embassy in West Beirut was targeted by a suicide car bombing when a pickup truck packed with over 2000 pounds of explosives was driven through the embassy gates and hit the building. The resultant explosion killed 67 people, including dozens of Lebanese workers and eight members of the Central Intelligence Agency (CIA) (Figure 3.2).

At the time, whilst devastating, this attack was very much seen as a one-off event with the city under a de facto ceasefire, with hopes high for Syrian reconciliation talks. This resulted in perimeter fences around U.S. compounds remaining relatively unfortified despite occasional grenade or sniper attacks. But this was the calm before the storm. In October 1983, a yellow Mercedes[20] truck laden with explosives rammed through the guard post at the entrance to the U.S. Marine Battalion Headquarters Building in Beirut.[21] The resultant blast decimated the four-story, concrete, steel-reinforced structure with 2-foot-thick walls – considered one of the most robust buildings in Lebanon at the time.[22] Two minutes later, a nearly identical attack targeted the French Multinational Force building less than 4 miles away.

Figure 3.2 The devastation caused by the U.S. Embassy bombing in West Beirut.

The attacks collectively killed over 240 U.S. Marines and 58 French paratroopers. These attacks focused attention on U.S. foreign policy, and in February 1984, U.S. officials announced the withdrawal of the U.S. troops from Lebanon, which was followed shortly after, by the pull-out of Italian, British and French soldiers. This did not immediately stop the attacks, and in September 1984, Hezbollah carried out another suicide car bombing targeting the U.S. embassy annex in East Beirut, killing 16 people. This time, however, the suicide attacker had to expertly swerve his vehicle around the concrete dragon's teeth defences that had now been placed outside U.S.-controlled compounds. As Davis (2007, p.89) highlighted, recovered intelligence documents show that Hezbollah had photographs showing the exact position of the defence features and that the car bomber had been practising his approach in advance denoting that Hezbollah was literally 'running professional car-bombing school'.

The impact of these 1984 attacks on security and defensive architecture was pronounced. First, it reinforced the need to have secure diplomatic or military compounds that in time led to bunker-style designs being developed for Lebanon, and which have since become a regular feature of overseas embassies and military barracks (see Chapter 4). Second, the constant car bombing in Beirut led to material changes in the everyday built environment linked to ideas of defensible space and territoriality. This occurred through the barricadisation of the city with a series of barriers, checkpoints and blockades constraining mobility and demonstrating in concrete form, a blurring of the action of state and non-state actors. Such security installations became ever-more widespread as car bombing became an accepted part of everyday life and, as Freidman (1983, p.13) noted, 'nothing terrifies more than car bombs – not only because they are utterly indiscriminate, but because they transform a totally innocuous object from daily life into a deadly weapon'. In response he further noted how checkpoints across the city had become endemic, shatter-resistant window coatings hugely popular, and where 'shopkeepers and embassies all over town...placed barrels, box springs or huge boulders on the street outside their doors to keep potential car bombers at a distance'.

Conclusion

This chapter has highlighted the first phase in the evolution of how city builders came to consider counter-terrorism as a core consideration within planning processes. From the late 1960s until the early 1990s, ideas underpinning defensible design and the manipulation of the built environment, first used for crime prevention, were incorporated into anti-terrorism interventions that sought to reduce the impact of urban terrorism. These approaches tended to be reactive and defensive-minded, focusing on the target hardening of individual buildings, destruction of swaths of the urban fabric, or defending public places alongside traffic management/control interventions that restricted access to mobility corridors or boulevards.[23]

Here the intervention of the security services and the military led to stark forms of anti-terrorist protection embedded within the built environment, at times so widespread to effectively normalise heightened security and make effectively permanent, 'temporary' security tactics. In addition to the fortification and bounding of public and shared spaces, segregation was formalised and partially institutionalised as a method of managing and containing civil conflict, and was mainstreamed within national security and counter-terrorism strategies. Such planning-led interventions, although crude, were generally acknowledged to be, superficially effective, in that they prohibit the penetration of targets and the permeability of spaces by potential perpetrators of attacks, notably car bombers. Urban planners in this sense were an initial guide to the siting of defensive features, with the planning system and processes facilitating the adoption of territorial defences but had little influence over construction or design of anti-terrorism features (Coaffee, 2020).

The examples from Northern Ireland, Israel and Lebanon in the 1970s and 1980s illuminate how security became spatialised in the urban environment through a patchwork of enclaves, an array of walls and fences, 'apartheid highways' and no-go areas and street blockades, and foreground more recent post-9/11 explorations that focus on spatial intervention as a key tool of urban security strategies. In the 1970s, the anti-car bomb security set up around Belfast city centre, and in other Northern Irish towns, became a 'prototype for other fortified enclaves' (Davis, 2007, p.58) as 'rings of steel' have been adopted in other targeted cities to protect against vehicle attacks (Coaffee, 2000). In Jerusalem and Beirut, the techniques of large-scale urban destruction to quell insurgency foregrounded more widespread 'urbicide' incidents in the late 1980s and early 1990s most notably related to conflict in the former Yugoslavia. Here, the term came to define the violence against the city fabric. For example, work by Marshall Berman (1987) on the destruction of Sarajevo, and the 'Mostar '92' group of Bosnian architects (Šego, 1992), saw the phrase increasingly used by architects and urban planners to understand how cities can no longer be considered safe havens from war, but rather as part of the battlefield. More sociocultural interpretations have further argued that the aim of urbicide is annihilating not only critical infrastructure but destroying symbolic architecture to erase social differences and cultural histories (Coward, 2008).[24]

Furthermore, in Israel and Lebanon, the territorial and segregation approaches have been extended and enhanced over time as security planning has infiltrated all aspects of everyday life in ways that left a marked legacy in terms of design techniques used for micro-scale defences such as security barriers and concrete slab dividing walls that seal off roads, the continual upgrading of 'apartheid' road networks,[25] and in terms of the robust engineering of individual buildings to withstand a large explosive blast. In the next chapter, we will see how, in the 1990s, such territorial approaches and target hardening measures were applied in a number of cities, aided by planning and engineering processes, as terrorists targeted government buildings with large vehicle bombs, and which led to the use of bunker architecture as a core defensive technique.

Notes

1 Freidman worked as the *New York Times* reporter in Beirut at the start of the 1982 Israeli invasion of Lebanon. His coverage of the war, won him the Pulitzer Prize for International Reporting.
2 In time, both biological ideas associated with ethology and Sack's notion of spatial 'containers' have come to be seen as limited, in new reworkings of historical ideas of territory and territorially.
3 As Jacobs noted, 'a border – the perimeter of a single massive or stretched-out use of territory – exerts an active influence' (1961, p.257).
4 Newman's ideas subsequently became popular, in the U.S. and further afield as a concept underlying the design of new residential communities (see, for example, Newman, 1996). This early work on defensive design was not unproblematic and was criticised for its poor statistical analysis and normative statements about causal links between physical design and crime.
5 Closely aligned to both defensible space and CPTED approaches was situational crime prevention that emerged from the late 1970s. This technique focused generally on methods for reducing opportunities to commit crime, as opportunity is a consistent causal factor in crime. The behavioural logic underpinning situation crime prevention was based on the concept of rational choice – that every criminal will assess the situation of a potential crime, consider how much they may gain, could potentially lose, and the probability of failing or being caught, and then act accordingly (see, for example, Clarke, 1982).
6 For example, in the late 1980s, the U.K. Home Office pioneered a new approach to reduce crime – *Secured by Design* – (SBD), which sought to embed CPTED, situational crime prevention and defensible space ideas into new residential developments because of rapidly rising burglary rates. Its growing popularity has led to trained police officers working closely with architects, designers, developers and municipal planners at the early design stage to incorporate crime prevention measures into the physical security of buildings and the layout and landscaping of the adjacent environment. Most notably in the United Kingdom, police forces begun to employ Architectural Liaison Officers (ALOs) to introduce crime prevention issues into the planning system and to advise upon, rather than to prescribe, reduction measures on crime and in time, terrorism.
7 In the following years, the defensive landscape transformation in Belfast, and in particular its central area, became the model that other towns in Northern Ireland adapted to their own local circumstances. For example, in July 1972 concrete barriers were placed around the shopping district of (London)Derry by the British Army to seal off direct access to the centre from the Bogside, the western area of the city from which the majority of Provisional IRA attacks were believed to have originated. The central area was not completely sealed off, but rather the number of entrances were limited, making the control and the searching of vehicles easier.
8 Before the early 1970s, most car bombs were comprised of the conventional explosive, TNT.

9 In the mid-1980s researchers also highlighted that the usual forces of city centre decline, such as population dispersal, the impact of out of town shopping centres and increased car ownership, in part, contributed to the decline of central Belfast's retail core.
10 This made shopping in the centre easier as only one search was required, although many shops employed their own searching teams to supplement zonal security. This arrangement also meant that the personal needed to run the scheme was minimised. There were only two vehicle entry points with the others being exit-only.
11 In large part because the target of attack had shifted to the British mainland in general and London specifically – see Chapter 4.
12 Urbicide is a term that literally translates (Latin: *urbs*: city + Latin: *caedere* to cut, kill) as 'violence against the city' and was periodically used by critics of 1960s urban restructuring (and destruction).
13 As Pullen et al. (2007) noted, this route dates from at least as early as the caravan routes of the Roman Empire, was in use during the British mandate (1920–1948) as national road 60 and became a two-land highway that went through Jerusalem to link Palestinian areas on Ramallah in the north and Bethlehem in the south under Jordanian control of the West bank (1950–1967).
14 The British Mandate aimed, but failed, to update the regional plans every 5 years. The Regional Outline Plans expressed a philosophy of planning that focused upon restricting development, whereas in the 1980s and 1990s planning was increasingly seen as a means of enabling development. The last outline plan for the city in fact dated back to 1959 (Local Plan No. 62) and it wasn't until 2004 that a new master plan for Jerusalem was forged and even this has yet to be agreed.
15 Lebanon was, and remains still, a strategic battleground for internal and regional power plays.
16 In addition to car bombings, cluster bombs and white phosphorus shells fell regularly in West Beirut at this time.
17 This explosion was the latest in a series of attacks against French personnel and institutions in West Beirut. It came less than a year after a former French Ambassador, Louis Delamare, was shot and killed by unidentified gunmen as he was driving near his residence.
18 Some U.S., French and Italian peacekeeping forces had arrived in Lebanon in 1981.
19 Known as the Sabra and Shatila massacre that occurred between September 16 and 18, 1982.
20 The Mercedes vehicle was very much the vehicle of choice for Hezbollah car bombings.
21 The building was formerly an old Army barracks near the airport.
22 Eyewitnesses recalled that the force of the blast caused the entire building to float up above the ground for a moment with FBI investigators noting that it was the most powerful car bomb ever detonated.
23 As opposed to counter-terrorism which tends to be more proactive and offensive, and within the context of planning can be seen as more deliberative and collaborative attempts to blend security concerns with other planning functions.
24 After 9/11 the use of the term became more popular (see, for example, Campbell et al., 2007; Shaw, 2004).
25 See, for example, www.haaretz.com/israel-news/.premium.MAGAZINE-new-apartheid-road-opens-separating-palestinians-and-west-bank-settlers-1.6827201.

Part 2
Conventional tactics and techniques of urban security

4 Padded bunkers

Introduction: Boom and bust terrorism

Whilst the previous chapter focused attention on how military gaze, juxtaposed with planning ideas and political complexities, sought to actively destroy the city (urbicide) or reduce the risk of insurgent attack (anti-terrorism), this chapter focuses upon the growth of militarily hardened structures in the 1990s and attempts to 'design-out' terrorism in and around valuable, targeted buildings. The responses of urban authorities and the agencies of security at this time were both related to local circumstances of place and the evolving tactics of terrorist groups. As Hoffman (1998, p.205) noted, at the end of the twentieth century 'terrorism [was] among the most fluid and dynamic of political phenomena ... constantly evolving into new and ever more dangerous forms in order to evade security procedures and surmount defence barriers placed in its path'. Here, he continued, by noting that effective counter-terrorism must also move with the times which, 'will inevitably depend on its ability to understand the fundamental changes that distinguish today's terrorists from their predecessors. Only in this way can the array of required counter-measures be first identified and then brought to bear with genuinely positive results' (ibid., p.206).

More specifically, at the beginning of the 1990s there was a growing realisation by terrorists that by targeting high-profile buildings, they could not only cause severe damage and significantly disrupt trade and economic transactions, but also cause reputational damage to the city and nation where the attack took place. Notwithstanding the highly destructive vehicle bombings in Beirut in the 1980s that had used vehicle bombs to damage buildings (Chapter 3), the 1990s, saw a shift from an array of relatively small-scale terror attacks using car bombs and other weapons to much larger and destructive modes of attack capable of killing hundreds of people and destroying large areas of the material built environment. Indeed, through the 1990s, whilst the number of terrorist incidents worldwide declined, the percentage of large-scale 'spectacular' attacks that resulted in mass fatalities grew significantly as terrorist groups engaged in highly selective acts of lethal violence against symbolic targets to capture the attention of politicians, the

DOI: 10.4324/9780429461620-6

media and public alike (Lesser et al., 1999). Concomitantly, this led to urgent discussions amongst engineers and security professionals, about how to best protect 'at risk' buildings; first with a dedicated focus on overseas embassies, and then increasingly upon valuable commercial infrastructures.

Whilst a novel kind of better organised terrorism was evolving from the late 1980s, that led to new anti-terrorism efforts, widespread adaptation to this new reality didn't really take effect until after the 1993 World Trade Center (WTC) bombing in New York. This event catalysed a noticeable shift from 'the old terrorism to the new' where the primary motivation for engaging in acts of terror became the oppression of identify and culture overseas (of largely Muslim's), where in perpetuating the attack 'rage and malice had no limit', and where the organisation of the attacks spanned many actors operating on many continents (U.S. Government, 2004, p.71). The WTC attack was quickly labelled 'a virus of which these individuals [who committed the WTC atrocity] were just the first symptoms' (ibid.). In the United States, although this bombing heightened awareness of a new terrorist danger, there was still a widespread underestimation of the threat that, in part, was linked to cuts in national security expenditures as a result of the ending of the Cold War. The WTC attack in 1993, alongside the 1995 Tokyo poison gas attack on the city's subway by the doomsday cult, Aum Shinrikyo, saw U.S. intelligence agencies classify urban terrorism as a major threat both at home and abroad, with an emphasis placed on thwarting such acts through better intelligence operations. Notably, at the time of the Tokyo attack, Aum Shinrikyo had an office in New York but neither the FBI nor the CIA had ever heard of it. Following this assault, the subsequent 1995 bombing in Oklahoma City had been blamed initially on Middle Eastern terrorists, which turned out to be incorrect. As a result, in June 1995, Presidential Decision Directive 39 noted that the U.S. should 'deter, defeat and respond vigorously to all terrorist attacks on our territory and against our citizens' with counter-terrorism given the highest priority. This Directive particularly focused attention, resources and effort upon not just intelligence gathering but the material protection of valuable structures.

Event response, material protection and the critical turn in analysis

Whilst in the previous chapters the change in urban security and defence were looked at over longer periods of time – a *longue durée* – this chapter, and those that follow instead focus upon the production, detection and reaction to specific terrorist incidents – an event-driven analysis – whilst taking into account historical precedent. Here an event is seen in broad terms as representing what Lowenthal (1992) referred to as a 'rupture of continuity', or as Žižek (2014) saw it, an occurrence that shatters ordinary life, transforms reality and leads to new thinking and practices emerging to counter the impacts of such happenings. Prime examples of such terror events in the 1990s included large-scale vehicle bombs that exploded in the financial core of London in 1992 and 1993 (see Chapter 5), the WTC bombing in New York in 1993 where a van bomb positioned in an underground car park exploded killing six, injuring thousands and causing extensive damage; the bombing of Central Bombay in 1993 when a series of 13 bombs were detonated in India's financial centre killing over 250 people; the Tokyo subway attack in March 1995 when the Tokyo subway system was attacked with improvised chemical weapons containing the nerve agent Sarin, killing 12 people and injuring more than thousands; the 1995 bombing of the federal building in Oklahoma killing 168 people; and, a massive vehicle bomb left outside a light-railway station in the London Docklands in 1996 that killed 2 people and devastated a large area (Chapter 5).

One common reaction in the West towards this upsurge in targeted 'spectacular' urban terror attacks was the increased attention that was paid to the material protection of buildings through 'bunker' architecture, as a result of a great deal of introspection about the 'mortality' of buildings, and the wider impact of defensive structures on the cityscape. Conceptually, this growing interest reflected a reassertion of the importance of space as the contextual setting for social interaction in cities (Soja, 2003) and, relatedly, a 'material turn' in the humanities and social sciences (or new materialism), at this time (Latour, 1992; Law and Mol, 1995). The material turn specifically focused attention on the relations between materiality and the social in exploring new understandings of the role of material infrastructures in the organisation of state power, everyday cultural practices and political landscapes. Such a 'turn' was broadly seen as a reaction against a wave of discursive cultural theory that for many removed the material configuration of things as a primary focus of research, and in particular that material entities are 'partially formed by the aspects of other events from their environments' (Whitehead, 1985, p.133). As Barry (2013) has more recently argued, materials play a significant role in political life and questions of governing materiality: 'no longer can we think of material artefacts...as the passive and stable foundation on which politics takes place; rather...the unpredictable and lively behaviour of such objects and environments should be understood as integral to the conduct of politics' (p.1–2). In parallel, the 1990s also saw emerging work in urban cultural geography that was also focusing on the materiality of individual buildings (Domosh, 1989; Lees, 1997), the everyday impact of such vernaculars, and upon the links between buildings and place-making that involved a hybrid analysis of both material and immaterial (see also Chapter 5).

From a security perspective, the 1990s also saw the growth of the broad field of critical security studies that sought to utilise critical theory to politicise conventionally static approaches to studying international security (Krasue and Williams, 1997; Booth, 1997). More specifically, within this wider field of scholarship, 'critical terrorism studies' emerged to interrogate the orthodoxy of traditional terrorism studies that had focused almost exclusively upon a realist state-centric prospective. The publication of Zulaika and Douglas's (1996) *Terror and Taboo: The Follies, Fables and Faces of Terrorism* is often held up as a crucial moment in the emergence of critical terrorism studies, viewing terrorism as a social construct and methodologically focused on the discourse of (counter)terrorism – 'the assumptions, narratives and labels about its primary subjects – as well as an accepted array of knowledge generating practices' (Jackson, 2009, p.67; see also Jackson, 2007). The approach taken in *Terror and Taboo* contrasted with conventional studies where 'the discourse of the terrorism expert is buttressed by the scientific idea that true knowledge must afford the objectivity that allows one to talk about society in terms of universal criteria' (p.181). By contrast, terrorism, for Zulaika and Douglas, was viewed as contingent upon the socio-cultural and political context in which it occurs, and, 'as a shifting representation that commands diverse perceptions from different actors and audiences in separate situations'. Here, in the context of securitisation ideas, they critiqued the idea that 'once something that is called "terrorism" – no matter how loosely defined – becomes established in the public mind, "counter-terrorism" is seemingly the only prudent course of action' (p.ix).

Within this conceptual and threat-driven context, analysis in this chapter looks at the significance of particular buildings before, during and after spectacular terrorist events in the 1990s. This will draw out how processes of production, protection and rebirth that framed such events were also deeply reflective of the political-economy, and, in many cases, military-style decision-making.

Falling buildings and enhanced bunkering

During the 1990s, the counter-responses to terrorism were also seen to embody how architectural forms produced highly uneven power relations often through explicit exclusionary security devices that impacted urban mobility (Davis, 1990; Cresswell, 2006). Here, buildings were viewed not as static objects in the urban landscape but seen as continuously in flux, incorporating new layers of material, and making incremental shifts to adapt and align with the imperatives of the day to remain suitable to its users and valuable to its owners. Moreover, whilst buildings as material objects had a lifespan, they could also be seen to live 'multiple lives' (Kraftl, 2010), reflecting the number of professionals involved in their design, construction and maintenance, as well as the numerous publics that interact with it in space. Put another way, building were not seen as

> empty static vessels, shells brought to life only by the people who inhabit them, but… are themselves animate systems [and] a product of complex interconnections of materials designed to constantly shift and transfer the forces of gravity, wind and water out of themselves and harmlessly into the ground or air. *They are built to bend without breaking*.
> (Baer et al., 2005, p.108, emphasis added)

Building also die, out of old age, functional obsolesce or in extreme cases collapse as a result of natural hazards, or man-made explosives. Buildings were can be viewed as not ever-present, but mortal structures that fall down or become redundant for a range complex reasons that architects and structural engineers constantly had to grapple with. Here, the focus of construction experts at the time, when faced with particular risks and threats, was to extend building lifespans though ever-resistance and robust structures to expected force loading. As engineers Levy and Salvandori (1992, p.13–14) noted in *Why Buildings Fall Down*:

> A building is conceived when designed, born when built, alive while standing, dead from old age or an unexpected accident. It breathes through the mouth of its windows and the lungs air conditioning systems. It circulates fluids through the arteries of its pipes and sends message to all parts of its body through the nervous system of its electronic wires. It reacts to changes in its outer or inner conditions through its brain of feedback systems, is protected by the skin or its facade support by its skeleton of columns, beams, and slabs, and rests on the feet of its foundations. Like most human bodies, buildings have full lives, then they die.

In taking forward the ideas of 'resisting' the felling of buildings, this chapter focuses specifically upon the emergent of militarily hardened structures in the civic realm during the 1990s, and the increased attention being paid to the physical protection of buildings and commercial districts through 'designing-out' terrorism techniques. Practically, from a built environment perspective, this necessitated adopting refined approaches to the structural integrity of buildings to blast, and to territorial security, that meant urban planners and architects needed to innovate their existing practices and engage with blast-resistant specialists and the tools they used to understand explosions, as well as the police and security services to restrict access to 'at-risk' target locations.

The proactive protection of buildings and built structures from explosions *per se* at this time was not, however, a new advance: blast resistant design specialists were, in actuality, a recent legacy of the Cold War fixation with creating bomb shelters and weapons silos. Now, however, in response to the threat of terrorist attack against key city buildings, such expertise was deployed in the civil realm but was required to balance security needs with other considerations of cost and visual appearance. Most notably, in the United States, the need for such defensive architecture was framed by a general narrative of the 'fortress city', where anti-crime measures were taken to the maximum, and where the destructive car bombs were considered a threat to take evermore seriously. This was especially the case in Los Angeles (LA) that became appropriated as the symbolic heart of 'fortress America', with such rhetoric reaching a crescendo after the terrorist bombings against the

64 *Conventional techniques of urban security*

World Trade Centre in New York, in 1993, and the Federal Exchange Building in Oklahoma, in 1995.

New city defences

In the early 1990s, new defensible space approaches and the operationalisation of security discourses are once again serving to influence the design and management of the urban landscape as 'form followed fear' (Ellin, 1997). This further represented a broader social shift towards a purported 'culture of fear', with fear being socially constructed and 'moulded by popular culture and institutionalised in the organisation of everyday life' (Furedi, 2006, p.3). Examples, especially from the U.S., indicated that 'fortress urbanism' with its walls, security guards, pedestrian partitions, traffic barricades, gates, cameras and other physical measures, was now *de rigueur* for creating well-defined pockets of urban civility, community and mutual support within an urban landscape that was often perceived as dangerous or unsafe. The response of urban authorities and populations was most dramatic in LA where it was argued that the implementation of crime displacement measures had been taken to an extreme in what, at the time, was commonly termed 'postmodern urbanism' (Soja, 2000; Dear, 1999).

During the 1990s, LA assumed a theoretical primacy within urban studies with an overemphasis on its militarisation that portrayed the city as a testing ground for anti-crime measures (Christopherson, 1995). Fortress urbanism showcased an obsession with security becoming manifest in the urban landscape with 'the physical form of the city... divided into fortified cells of affluence and places of terror where police battle the criminalized poor' (Dear and Flusty, 1998, p.57). The emergence of the fortress city in the popular urban imaginary also reflected the transformation of the city in the mirror of middle-class paranoia combined with the necessity of economic vibrancy. For example, it was reported that in 1991, 16% of Los Angelians were living in some form of 'secured access environment' that was viewed as an ultimate lifestyle choice and a dominant feature of contemporary urban life (Blakely and Snyder, 1995, p.1). As Haywood (2004, p.115, emphasis added) further noted, whilst employing historical security references to refer to the renaissance of downtown LA and its apparent blanket security and the privatisation of public space: 'this was the corporate Los Angeles *manning the ramparts in a bid to protect* its economic interests by excluding those individuals and groups no longer necessary for (or dangerous to) the perpetuation of profit in the city's new globalised economy'.

Mike Davis was the most cited author on 'Fortress LA', depicting how LA responded to the increased fear of crime by 'militarising' the urban landscape. His dystopian portrayal of LA in *City of Quartz* (1990; see also *Ecologies of Fear*, 1998) provided an alarming indictment of radical territorial defensive measures, with the LA Police Department (LAPD) becoming a key player in the development process (see also, Herbert, 1997). As Davis starkly highlighted: 'in cities like Los Angeles on the hard edge of postmodernty, one observes an unprecedented tendency to merger urban design, architecture and the police apparatus into a single comprehensive security effort' (1990, p.203). Here, the militarisation of commercial buildings and their borders became 'strongpoints of sale' (Flusty, 1994) with defensible space approaches reapplied to protect an ever-increasing number of city properties and residences through target hardening and advanced forms of surveillance. This everyday militarisation of the city, noted Davis, led to 'a proliferation of new repressions in space and movement', and security becoming 'a zeitgeist' or 'master narrative' in the emerging built environment of the 1990s (1990, p.223) reflecting the fragmentary and fortified urban spaces, or what were termed 'carceral cities' (Dear and Flusty, 1998).

The 1970s planning and design ideas of luminaries like Oscar Newman's, therefore, became a cornerstone of new urban security policies in 1990s America to reconfigure existing neighbourhoods, and to design new urban spaces so as to reduce the risk of both crime and, increasingly, urban terrorism. This was implemented hand-in-glove with advanced engineering approaches that used increasingly robust materials and protective designs to ensure the structural integrity of buildings, and to reduce the risk of the progressive collapse as a result of explosive shock waves emanating from explosions in a desire to 'pad the bunker' (Davis, 1990, p.223).

Resisting blast

In the 1990s, unprecedented terrorist attacks in the United States and in U.S. territory aboard from vehicle-borne explosive devices penetrating target buildings led to widespread calls to bombproof vulnerable sites. Notably, attacks against the WTC in New York in February 1993, the destruction of the Alfred P. Murrah Federal Building in Oklahoma City by a truck bomb in April 1995 led to increased attention being paid to the protection of buildings that were no longer seen as immortal. Although such attacks were neither entirely unprecedented nor unanticipated, attacks on the streets and against public buildings in continental America were significant in the mainstreaming of engineering-based anti-terrorism features into construction of the built environment, as well as displaying the destructive force of a new wave of terrorist *modus operandi* (Coaffee and O'Hare, 2008).

On February 26, 1993, just after midday a truck bomb detonated below the 381-metre-high North Tower of the WTC in Lower Manhattan, New York City, in what was the first ever international terrorist attack on American soil. The device comprised over 600 kilograms of a high explosive nitrate-based fertiliser. Three compressed gas cylinders were also placed in a circular configuration around the main charge to enhance the blast, mirroring the 1983 Beirut barracks bombing (see Chapter 3).[1] The terror operation, carried out by Islamic terrorists in apparent revenge for U.S. support for Israel against Palestinian insurgency, was intended to propel the falling North Tower into the South Tower, and in so doing, destroy the entire WTC structure and kill perhaps 30,000 people.[2] It failed to do so but killed 6 people and injured over 1000, mainly as a result of respiratory problems from breathing in fumes during evacuation attempts.

The blast, the most powerful and damaging improvised explosive device ever at the time, was centred in the underground parking garage and created a 100-foot crater several stories deep and several more high (FBI, 2008). The bomb severed the WTC's main electrical power line, knocking out the sprinklers, generators, elevators, public address systems, the emergency command centre, more than half of the high-voltage lines that fed electricity to the complex, and sent smoke rising to the 93rd floor (of 110) of both towers. Subsequently, an FBI investigation revealed that the WTC blast was intended as the first in a series of bomb attacks against New York landmarks, with a verified plot uncovered, to simultaneously attack the U.N. building, the Holland and Lincoln Tunnels and the FBI New York Headquarters.

A decade earlier, the WTC 'Twin Towers' was the backdrop to de Certeau's theorising on the practices of everyday life (1984), but now, in the wake of the 1993 attack, another philosopher – Paul Virilio – took centre stage in depicting the wider social and symbolic significance of the WTC atrocity. Virilio, who was appointed as an expert consultant in the wake of the attack, saw the episode as the start of a new post-Cold War age of imbalance, where a new form of terrorism had emerged and where arguments were not settled with guns, but with attempts to destroy the symbolic marketplaces of major cities:

> In the manner of a massive aerial bombardment, this single bomb, made of several hundred kilos of explosives placed at the building's very foundations, could have caused the collapse of a tower four hundred metres high. So it is not a simple remake of the film Towering Inferno, as the age-conscious media like to keep saying, but much more of a strategic event confirming for us all The Change in The Military Order of This Fin-De-Siecle. As the bombs of Hiroshima and Nagasaki, in their day, signalled a new era for war, *the explosive van in New York illustrates the mutation of terrorism.*
>
> (Virilio, 2000, p.18)

In further commentary on the significance of the attack, he noted that they were a type of 'pure war': a term he had first coined in 1983 to refer to the invisible war that technology is waging against humanity and, in which, distinctions between war and peace did not apply, with a military-industrial complex becoming highly visible. In a reworking of this famous essay in 1997, he further argued that terrorism had entered a new phase in its destructive evolution, as symbolised by the WTC attack, and that

> we have entered an age of large-scale terrorism... Small-scale terrorism happens in Northern Ireland, where bombs blow up a car and can kill

one hundred people. The large-scale version is a totally different matter... terrorist deaths used to be counted in their hundreds, now suddenly it could jump to 20,000 dead... the equivalent of a strategic cruise missile strike.

(p.190–191)

In further illuminating, the deeply asymmetrical nature of contemporary terrorism, he added that such attacks could have been perpetuated by 'a mere five men and a van... [and] If the van had managed to park at the base of the tower, instead of the access ramp, the whole Trade Center would have gone up' (ibid.). Focusing upon the emerging tread of terrorists targeting the economic hubs of global cities, Virilio also noted the symbolic and communication tactics of terrorism:

Terrorism uses the speed of mass communication...terrorism needs the media. If you manage to blow up the WTC without anyone knowing about it, that's pointless...They scheduled their bomb blast on time to catch the evening news. The explosion only exists because it is simultaneously coupled to a multimedia explosion.

(p.194–195)

In the wake of the WTC bombing, security was immediately tightened across New York (and nationwide), including at all three city airports and prominent landmarks. In the days that followed the attack there were anonymous, unfounded bomb threats at a number of locations, including the Empire State Building and Pennsylvania Station. More generally, the WTC attack horrified the U.S. public that had considered itself relatively immune from acts of terrorism and solicited a swift defensive response with both individual buildings and commercial districts increasingly attempting to design-out terrorism. The particular concern here was to be able to monitor and control the movement of large vehicles that might be carrying significant amounts of explosive material that could topple buildings if detonated. In New York's financial core, the militarisation of commercial buildings and their borders – to 'pad the bunker' – become a key element within the emerging cityscape as clean-up and reconstruction efforts begun. More specifically, in the aftermath of the bombing, and in particular, the chaotic evacuation which followed, many of the firms inside the WTC revamped emergency and evacuation procedures. The New York Port Authority, who governed security for the WTC buildings, spent in excess of $100 million to improve structural, physical and technological security upgrades. The buildings' owners further repaired the damage, upgraded elevators and electrical systems, put battery-operated emergency lights and luminous paint in the stairwells and set up a state-of-the-art emergency command centre.

In a post-incident report, written by the U.S. Fire Administration, a key question was posed of what constitutes acceptable protective security measures, and how a balance could be struck between 'easy entry and egress, free circulation of pedestrians and vehicles, and an attractive and open environment [which] are important for doing business' (Hinman and Levy, 1993, p.109). For many commentators, advanced security measures seemed 'antithetical to these requirements and [brought] to mind a bunker or prison without windows surrounded by guards and walls' (ibid.). To advance a 'balanced security design', it was argued that engineering analysis of the target, its vulnerable areas and the threat scenario (in this case a large vehicle borne explosive device) should be undertaken. The layering of security – the militarily-inspired 'onion-skin approach' (ibid., p.110) – was also encouraged to make the targeting of a building less attractive. From an engineering perspective, key to such a security approach was to either maximise the stand-off distance between the places a bomb could be concealed, and the building, and/or to construct a blast-resistant building structure. Additionally, given that many injuries in a bomb blast were known to be caused by flying glass from windows, reducing window size, applying specialist film to the inside or putting in toughened glass were also encouraged to mitigate the impact of a blast.

Structural counter-measures were complemented by an array of security devices built into the fabric of buildings, or embedded into the wider urban landscape, that required the integrated effort of several types of professionals – security experts, planners, architects, urban designers and structural engineers. In the first instance, temporary protective security was instigated, with giant concrete planters filled with earth being put around the WTC sidewalks to prevent vehicle access, that in time evolved into permanent barrier structures. In adjoining parts of Manhattan, perimeter fences or walls, automated barricades, steel barriers and bollards, the most advanced security cameras available at this time and metal detectors were further added outside federal buildings (see Figure 4.1).

To boost security, public mobility was also restricted with a number of roads and access routes closed off, or redesigned, and screening to enter federal buildings was established with police stationed in bulletproof booths until permanent security gates were installed. Commentary in the *New York Times* illuminated how defensive landscapes, based on Oscar Newman's defensible space principles (see Chapter 3), quickly became a key determinant of urban morphology noting that 'barricades and bollards have become the newest accessory on this country's psychic frontier…You might call it the architecture of paranoia. They call it "defensible space"' (Brown, 1995). More specifically,

> After the World Trade Center was bombed in 1993, the principles of defensible space design were put into place there. In addition to concrete planters, parking is no longer open to anyone. Tenant parking is controlled and includes a hydraulic barrier – a latter day drawbridge – lowered by a guard, only after the proper credentials are shown, and capable of stopping a truck at 50 miles an hour.
>
> (ibid.)

Figure 4.1 A typical example of security put in place in New York after the 1993 bombing.

The overall impact of the WTC bombing was significant for both the material urban landscape and a broader acceptance of evolving techniques of counter-terrorism. The attack functioned as a symbolic tipping-point in the understanding of evolving terrorist methodologies and required defensive responses that saw Lower Manhattan increasingly pad the bunker. In the mid-late 1990s, as international terrorism intensified, and the U.S. homeland was hit again by a major truck bombing in Oklahoma (see next section) security in Lower Manhattan was further tightened, with much of it paid for with funding from Anti-terrorism Bills passed by Congress. New York's securityscape would escalate further after the events of 9/11, with an ever-expanding number of security guard's, barriers, security gates and electronic surveillance devices being deployed.

Domestic terror in the homeland

On April 19, 1995 just after 9 am, a large truck bomb exploded outside of the Alfred P. Murrah Federal Building in Oklahoma City that was home to 15 federal agencies and several Department of Defense services. The attack was initially thought to be the work of Middle Eastern terrorists but rapidly it was realised that the explosion took place on the second anniversary of the end of the Waco siege,[3] on Patriots day,[4] with it quickly becoming clear that the bombing was revenge attack perpetrated by domestic terrorists.

The bombing killed at least 168 people and injured around 700 more. The explosive mixture of ammonium nitrate fertiliser, nitromethane and diesel fuel detonated in front of the north side of the nine-story structure, destroying more than one-third of the building that then collapsed in under 7 seconds. This left a huge crater as well as shattering the entire glass facade of the building with the overall structure eventually having to be demolished 3 months later. The blast wave produced by the bomb destroyed, or damaged, over 300 further structures in the vicinity and shattered glass in all nearby buildings.[5] At the time, this was the deadliest terrorist attack in U.S. history and was estimated to have caused at least $652 million worth of damage (Hewitt, 2003). The effects of the blast were equivalent to over 5000 pounds (2300 kilograms) of TNT and could be heard up to 55 miles away (Mlaker et al., 1998).

The bombing was perhaps of more significance from an engineering viewpoint than the WTC attack 2 years earlier and signalled a further wave of concern about the need to 'harden' the built environment for protection from terrorism. In response, the U.S. Government quickly passed legislation for increased security for non-military federal buildings, and for the potential for 'bombproofing' through greater structural robustness and blast resistance. Notably, a great deal of attention was paid to the design of the Murrah building that had been so devastated by the explosion and collapsed like a pack of cards, significantly contributing to the death and injury count. As the truck exploded, it first destroyed the building column next to it, with the explosive shockwave forcing the lower floors upwards, before the fourth and fifth floors collapsed onto the third floor, whose supporting pillar could not hold the added weight, eventually causing the total collapse of the building.

In the wake of the bombing, the U.S. Government ordered all federal buildings in major cities to instigate temporary security measures in the form of concrete Jersey barriers to prevent similar attacks, and to convey an appearance of protection, whilst more permanent and structural measures were planned. No longer would protective design be optional with the total cost of improving security in federal buildings across the country in response to the bombing eventually exceeding $600 million (Linenthal, 2003). At most of the 8300 federal buildings, this security upgrade saw many of the temporarily deployed security measures replaced with permanent perimeter security, state-of-the-art CCTV and lighting systems, access control, truck-resistant barriers, the incorporation of deep set backs or standoff zones from surrounding streets to minimise a buildings vulnerability to explosion, the hardening of building exteriors and glazing and, structural engineering design implemented where possible to prevent progressive collapse (Nadel, 2007).

At the time, the extensive analysis of federal buildings that followed the Oklahoma attack utilised planning approaches to crime prevention alongside military engineering principles to assess how buildings could be protected in the future. A review of the impact of the bombing detailed how buildings could be 'hardened' and highlighted that, unlike military facilities, few standards for civilian facilities were available (Hinman and Hammond, 1997).[6] In the longer term, a plan for U.S. federal building security was initiated, including new regulations, agreed through the U.S. General Services Administration (GSA), to ensure that all federal facilities had some level of protection to blast and progressive collapse. The Department of Justice (DoJ) were further directed to set up an interagency working group, comprising security professionals from nine federal departments and agencies, to assess the vulnerability of all federal building to acts of terrorism. This working group reported in June 1995, recommending specific minimum security standards for federal buildings alongside criteria, guidance and timetables for evaluating security needs based on 5-level classification system (DoJ, 1995). Such guidelines were particularly relevant to newly planned buildings. This included the replacement New Oklahoma City Federal Building planned for Downtown Oklahoma City that was allocated a $40-million grant in July 1995 and was seen as vital for the revitalisation of the central city. The design process begun in 1997 when the U.S. GSA begun a design competition for a replacement complex a short distance away from the original site and worked with the city's planning department to promote a design that would both promote *both* safety *and* economic development. In essence, the design logic was to protect tenants with a hardened exterior and access restrictions to the site by way of security bollards and other devices whilst remaining open to the public and the wider city.

Advancing such secure design principles was not easy. At this time, knowledge about proactive defence of buildings and structures from explosions blast was restricted to a small cabal of structural engineers and were very much 'Cold War legacies' (Baer et al., 2005, p.109) where blast resistant specialists had been deployed, with unlimited resources, to defend not civilian buildings, but military facilities such as missile silos or command bunkers, from nuclear blasts. Now, in response to the threat of terrorist attack against civic buildings, they were tasked with bombproofing buildings from modern terrorist attacks that targeted specifically progressive collapse, but with the added challenge of 'budgetary and aesthetic considerations that were never meant to accommodate blast hardening' (ibid., p.117). Balancing out protective need, with cost and aesthetically appealing design that didn't give the appearance of a bunker, was a tricky task. This was especially the case in the commercial sector where developers and building owners were reluctant to pay for additional protection, viewing it as a sunk cost. In seeking to encourage security design principles, in 1998, the U.S. DoJ published enhanced security directives in their *Vulnerability Assessment of Federal Facilities* which argued that designing-in security at the early stages of the planning process could significantly reduce the cost of added security requirements.[7]

It was not just against the continent U.S. that domestic attacks were staged. The mid-1990s also saw series of devastating attacks against U.S. embassy compounds overseas. As Davis (2007, p.147), recounted, 'these demonstrations of Heartland DIY ingenuity, were scarcely the last word in destructive power; indeed, it was probably inevitable that the dark Olympics of urban carnage would be won by a home team from the Middle East'. A few months after the Oklahoma attack, in November 1995, a truck bomb exploded outside the Saudi National Guard Communications Center in Central Riyadh, Saudi Arabia, killing five American servicemen and two Indian police. This was followed, less than a year later, by another truck bomb attack on the Khobar Towers apartment complex,[8] near Dhahran, killing 19 U.S. airmen and injuring over 350 more.

The emerging Al Qaida network claimed responsibility for both these Saudi attacks. Whist in the mid-1995 Saudi Arabia was considered a relatively safe place to house U.S. service personnel, these attacks saw the urgent upgrading of security for such overseas compounds. Further embassy bombings in Dar es Salaam, Tanzania, and Nairobi, Kenya in 1998, led to the passing of the specific legislation in 1999 that replaced broad standard written in 1995 following the 1983 Beirut barrack attack (Chapter 3). For example, the Kenya embassy had been seen as an easy target by Al Qaida insurgents as it was possible to park up very close to it without attracting attention (U.S. Government, 2004, p.68). This begun a process of formalising official standards for security and protective design of federal buildings at home or overseas that was to expand considerably in the new millennium (Chapter 10). Such attacks further heightened concerns about terrorist targeting of U.S. military assets abroad and demonstrated that urban terrorism was a major threat to international security as the twenty-first century came into view (Lesser et al., 1999).

As the 1990s drew to a close and the threat level was increasing both from domestic (left and right wing and animal and environmental protestors) and international terrorism from the Middle East, particularly that linked to Al Qaida (FBI, 1999),[9] the physical security enhancement of federal buildings had continued apace. Notably, Government guidance was published by the GSA[10] which expanded the scope to consider not just individual structures, but entire urban 'security zones', and more broadly to enhance national dialogue on balancing security and access in public buildings and spaces (Hollander and Whitfield, 2005).

Conclusions

In the wake of 1990s incidents on American soil and against American interests abroad, the public became increasingly aware of the threat of terrorism and the inherent vulnerability and mortality of the built environment. The practical response by statutory agencies can be seen as reactionary, adopting crude but robust approaches to building and territorial security, and once again, pursuing the ideas of defensible space and target hardening as their key modus operandi. By extension, the potential role that a wider range of urban built environment professionals, including planers, architects and engineers, could play in 'terror-proofing' cities became more apparent as enhanced security requirements became an essential part of Government requirements. Moreover, social considerations were also beginning to be seen as critical as material and non-material considerations becoming increasingly blended in decision-making processes about the acceptance and design of anti-terrorism features.

Examples from the United States at this time illuminated how utilising specialist knowledge from structural engineers was increasingly applied to deal with blast resistance whilst simultaneously embracing principles of territorial control to limit the access of vehicles into vulnerable spaces to create full building security. During the 1990s, there was a growing emphasis on advancing 'safe' designs and retrofitting existing buildings for security, aligned with a structural engineering view of how to effectively protect structures. This led to many potential target buildings becoming little more than padded 'bunkers' – in effect turning buildings into steel and concrete shelters, with limited windows or glazing of any kind, little public or vehicular access, and with large 'stand-off' distances between the 'compound' and the public realm, becoming commonplace.

Similar concerns were also apparent in London at this time as a result of a series of large explosions in the financial core. Here, crude defensive cordons were established in an attempt to prevent attacks, with research commissioned into the siting and impact of such protective security infrastructures (Coaffee, 2000). Such bunker-esque building design was seen by one critical commentator as an apocalyptic vision of *Terminal Architecture* (Pawley, 1998) that would foreground the end of architecture and the city as we know it, with extreme target-hardening increasingly initiated because of an upsurge in urban terrorism. Such attacks were targeting 'the highly serviced and vulnerable built environment of the modern world', where it was argued that the new-wave of signature buildings of global finance could be replaced by an 'architecture of terror', because of security needs (p.148). This, it was further argued, could well have the function of making buildings 'anonymous' and bunkered, and thus, it was concluded, a less unattractive terrorist target. Perhaps more importantly, Pawley, using examples from Israel, Sri Lanka, North America, Spain and the United Kingdom, argued that this 'architecture of terror' could be self-reproducing as planning guidelines, once drawn up, would be difficult to withdraw. This vision implied that such defensive architecture would become 'impossible to resist' once the threat was, in effect, realised through a successful terror strike (ibid., p.180–181).

Whilst such security upgrades were commonplace in locations that had suffered large-scale terror attacks and in some ways made certain buildings less attractive targets and in so doing improved the security perception of occupants, they had also increased the intrusiveness of security measures and made access to the building more difficult. This raised a fundamental challenge of providing an effective design that does not interfere with the essential functioning of the building. One strategic security approach that further advanced in the 1990s, from initial approaches in the 1970s, was the idea of securing a geographical area through territorial means and restricting and monitoring access and egress with updated surveillance technology. Such urban fortification, tactically resembling Belfast's ring of steel in the 1970s (Chapter 3), subsequently evolved in the financial zones of London in the early-mid-1990s as a supplementary 'area-based' approach to padding the bunker. It is to these advanced territorial and panoptical approaches that the next chapter turns.

Notes

1 There was also a widespread belief at the time that there was cyanide in the bomb, given cyanide gas was as later found in a locker rented by one of the bombers, but no forensic evidence at the blast scene was found to substantiated this (see, for example, Lance, 2004).
2 The FBI and the New York Joint Terrorism Task Force had been tracking Islamic fundamentalists in the city for months and were close to thwarting the planning of this attack. In addition, security teams at the WTC had identified the underground parking lots as a place where car bombs could be detonated – analysis that was not acted upon at the time and subsequently formed the basis of a series of trials in the twenty-first century over liability for the attacks.
3 The Waco siege was the police and military siege of the compound that belonged to the religious sect Branch Davidians between February 28 and April 19, 1993 in the community of Axtell, Texas, 13 miles from Waco. The siege ended when the FBI launched an assault and in an attempt to force the Branch Davidians out of the ranch and a large fire started resulting in the deaths of 76 Branch Davidians. April 19, therefore, became a highly symbolic dates for right-wingers, who perceived the mass murder of the Branch Davidians movement by the Federal government.
4 Patriots' Day, April 19, is an annual event commemorating the first battles of the American Revolutionary War on 1775.
5 The broken glass alone accounted for 5% of the death total and nearly 70% of the injuries outside the Murrah Federal Building.
6 This led to a wave of studies into the effect of explosive blast on building structures that today still forms part of training for many policing professionals involved in counter-terrorist security.
7 To prevent access to security design consideration by potential terrorists, the federal government set up a list of preferred engineers to whom they released design standards after they had signed an agreement guaranteeing that they would not reveal the details of the proposed design.
8 At that time, Khobar Towers was being used as living quarters for coalition forces who were assigned to police Iraqi no-fly zones. The important lesson from this incident is that the towers didn't collapse and were seen by structural engineers as more 'ductile' than other buildings that were destroyed by bomb blasts. This led to many studies looking at how earthquake resistant construction techniques could be applied to buildings.

9 In particular, there was concern about the potential of major attacks on crowded spaces where Millennium celebrations were planned.
10 Notably, the GSA issued a number of reports: *Physical Security Criteria and Standards* (GSA, 1997), *Balancing Security and Openness: A Thematic Summary of a Symposium on Security and the Design of Public Buildings* (GSA, 1999a) and *Urban Design Guidelines for Physical Perimeter Entrance Security* (GSA, 1999b).

5 Territorial security and the panoptical gaze

Introduction: Old wine, new bottles

During the 1990s, the changing nature of global terrorism catalysed a change in thinking by policy makers, security professionals and scholars, with new working definitions and different ways of thinking, seeing and countering terrorism being developed as a response to the catastrophic potential of 'postmodern' terrorist attack (Laqueur, 1996). As detailed in previous chapters, historical responses from urban authorities to the risk of terrorism were, in large part, extrapolations of ongoing trends that are already employed to reduce violent crime or blast-harden building structures.

Security infrastructures that emerged during the 1970s and 1980s (Chapter 3) to protect 'at risk' sites subsequently evolved in the 1990s to territorially control space through the deployment of (de)militarisation design logics and the adoption of new technologies. For example, in Jerusalem, overt *militarisation* and fragmentation of Palestinian territories into bordered enclaves was intensified by the first permanent Israeli checkpoints being introduced in East Jerusalem in 1993 in an attempt or stop suicide bombers striking in Central Jerusalem.[1] This set the scene for prolonged 'national security' inspired incursion and a major expansion of Jewish-only settlements in the traditional Palestinian side of the city that created ever-more brutal and visible territorial defences. This led, in 2002, to the Israeli Defence Force commencing the construction of a 'separation' wall around substantial sections of the Palestinian West Bank and Gaza strip, linking earlier fences and walls in a formidable barrier in the name of protection of Israeli areas and Jewish settlements.[2] Here in stark terms, we saw the materiality of the built environment as an explicit tool of control and of territoriality where 'the mundane elements of planning and architecture [became] tactical tools of dispossession' (Weizman, 2007, p.5) and, which, made a significant contribution to conflict's endurance and intensification.

In contrast, in the 1990s Northern Ireland, a very different process of *demilitarisation* occurred, signified by a reduction of military and security deployment, operations and installations, and with vehicle control zones rescinded, barriers removed and checkpoints relaxed (Smyth, 2004). In Belfast, a more

DOI: 10.4324/9780429461620-7

symbolic approach to defending the area subsequently emerged as attempts were made to portray the city centre as a neutral space and to encourage inward investment. At this time, such demilitarisation of the built environment was an attempt to project 'an air of normality, accessibility and prosperity central to attempts to attract both British and foreign investment' through the removal of visible security infrastructure (Jarman, 1993, p.116). More specifically, the main security gates in the main shopping streets were slowly removed and replaced with much smaller swing gates in 1995[3] with any decrease in security offset by a centralised CCTV scheme, which became operational in December 1995.[4] Similarly, in Beirut, the end of the civil war in 1990 ushered in a decade of relative peace as the city sought to remodel its material built environment and undertake economic growth in the image of neoliberalism, until a return to violence in 2004, saw militarised security intensify to protect political figures and public buildings from car bombings (Monroe, 2016) and, in so doing, overlap with lines of demarcation, security zones and secure residencies that emerged during the civil war (Brand and Fregonese, 2013).

Economic targeting

From the early 1990s, such territorial and security imperatives had been particularly evident within global cities as a result of a growing targeting by the world's terrorists of financial centres; not only to cause severe physical damage, produce great uncertainty about future insurance coverage, but also to dent the reputation of the area through negative media exposure. In what Davis (2007, p.117) referred to as the 'globalisation of car bombing', important economic, political and cultural centres were targeted with increasingly lethal attacks – from Buenos Aires, Lima and London in 1992; New York, Bombay, London, Florence in 1993; Johannesburg and Buenos Aires in 1994; Algiers, Oklahoma and Riyadh in 1995; and Colombo, London and Manchester in 1996. In response, global financial districts sought extra protection against possible attack. As Timothy Hillier from the City of London Police noted in 1994:

> Massive Explosions in London, New York and other major cities worldwide clearly demonstrates that important financial districts have become prestigious targets for terrorist organisations, regardless of their motives. In addition to causing significant loss of life, these bombs severely disrupt trade and economic transactions.
>
> (p.1)

Entering the 1990s, the increased target of economic zones by terrorists meant that the physically, regulatory and technological control of the urban landscape was ratcheted up to minimise the disruption to commercial flows with the latest cutting-edge technology deployed. As the use of surveillance technologies continued to first 'creep' and then 'surge' in vulnerable urban areas (Graham and Wood, 2003), many proclaimed that cities were becoming a technologically managed system based on automated access and boundary control (Lianos and Douglass, 2000).[5] Here increased danger and risk was leading to what Beck (1999, p.153) termed a 'protectionist reflex' where a 'withdrawal into the safe haven of territoriality becomes of intense temptation'.

Within this evolving historical context, this chapter charts the changes to the urban landscape in the U.K. capital, London, during the 1990s, as its leaders and security agencies sought to defend its financial heartlands from terrorism through the construction of territorially bounded security cordons. First, it will illuminate how a combination of regulatory management, fortification and digital surveillance strategies was utilised to explicitly categorise, divide and control urban space, and which resulted in new ways of examining security landscapes. Second, this chapter will detail the attempts made by local state actors and security professionals, most notably the Police, to control and regulate space within the U.K.'s financial heart, the City of London (also referred to as the Square Mile, or the City) as the threat of attack from the Provisional IRA intensified. It will also be highlighted how such a security cordon was established in another part of London, based on the same territorial and security principles.

Modern-day cordon sanitaires

In the 1990s, terrorists were increasingly targeting key economic areas, creating security threats to which municipal and national governments were forced to respond to alleviate the fears of their citizens and business community (Wilkinson, 1996).[6] As a direct result, individual buildings, as well as financial districts in a number of global cities, attempted to 'design-out terrorism' through the introduction of physical barriers to restrict access, advanced surveillance techniques in the form of security cameras, insurance regulations and blast protection, as well as innumerable indirect measures that operated through activating individual and community responses. Space and populations were thus increasingly seen as under siege, controlled and territorially bounded by a modern-day *cordon sanitaire* – with the restriction and monitoring of the movement of people and vehicles into or out of a demarcated area, in what were seen as highly political acts.[7]

Here, political power deployed in the city could be viewed as the 'perpetual use of silent war' (Foucault, 1976/2003, p.12) that shaped the social dynamics of daily urban life through inculcating and institutionalising the logics, forces and architectures of war. Such ideas that emphasised the ubiquity of coercive techniques further influenced the 1990s scholarship in urban security, linking to ideas of enclosure and techniques of ordering that become normalised through the imposition of evermore elaborate security assemblages. At this time, the writings of Foucault's (notably those in *Discipline and Punish*, 1977) came to the fore to analyse how landscape markers continuously reinforced a code of control and were exercised through a range of discourses such as media, policies, behaviours and architecture that were strategically assembled and, 'rendered functional as well as institutionalised into coherent bodies of power/knowledge' (Reid, 2003, p.4).

Driven by the ongoing and escalating threat of terrorism, modern-day *cordon sanitaires* were rapidly constructed with counter-terrorist polices focused upon police-driven, territorially bounded security cordons, monitored by cameras; a trinity of regulatory management, fortification and surveillance which explicitly attempted to secure urban space whilst not damaging economic growth (Coaffee, 2000).

As illuminated in Chapter 4, the 1990s saw an intensification of such territorial enclaves through the privatisation and militarisation of contemporary urban life, where 'form follows fear' (Ellin, 1996). Here, gated and heavily guarded residential and commercial areas became common, where control was increasingly asserted through an array of evermore sophisticated physical and technological measures (Jones and Lowrey, 1995). This new enclaving of the city often led to certain areas of economic development and consumption excluding themselves from the rest of the city through their 'hardened' territorial boundedness.

Such an approach to urban security – and by implication counter-terrorism – relied on an intertwining for approaches that sought to regulate, defend and watch the city. At this time, regulatory management put in place in an attempt to restrict the opportunities for criminality and terrorism, predominantly involved the forces of law and order. In the 1990s, regard to how the police strategically utilised the notion of territoriality was first promoted in *Policing Space*, Steve Herbert's ethnography of the Los Angeles Police Department (LAPD) (Herbert, 1997). This work illuminated how police strategies involved creating boundaries and restricting access as they attempted to regulate space and became increasingly active in the planning process, allowing the 'power of the police is inserted within the fabric of the city' (ibid., p. 6/7).

Concomitantly, approaches to fortification took the form of turning office blocks, shopping centres and residential communities into territorial enclaves through methods of restricted access and the introduction of defensive measures such as walls, barriers and gates that furthered the 'replacement of public access with private spaces that can be controlled by security guards and the ability to pay' (Wekerle and Whitzman, 1995, p.6). Such fortressing was often based on principles of defensible space, but as critical research at the time pointed out, it could have a dual impact. Marcuse (1993, p.101), for example, argued that city walls can be seen as both 'walls of fear' and 'walls of support', whilst Ellin (1996) additionally noted that, 'the gates, policing and other surveillance systems, (and) defensive architecture…do contribute to giving people a greater sense of security. But…also contribute to accentuating fear by increasing paranoia and distrust among people' (p.153).

These regulatory and fortification approaches were further complemented by watchful city approaches and an explicit use of state-of-the-art and increasingly automated surveillance cameras, particularly at the entry into a territory. For Deleuze (1992), writing on 'societies of control', this showcased how new technology served to facilitate the increased automation of everyday life, further illuminating the relationship between surveillance and subjectivity observed by Foucault in the Modern period, and expressed through the idea of the panopticon.[8] The conceptual usage of the *dispositif panoptique* continued to evolve in the 1990s, being extended beyond the confines of individual buildings and into the public realm through the use of public space CCTV systems as a key part of the selective ordering of the contemporary city.[9]

In the United Kingdom, where such surveillance practices for urban spatial control were initially pioneered, the first centralised CCTV scheme was established in the southern seaside town of Bournemouth in 1985. The year before had seen the Provisional IRA mount a devastating bomb attack on the ruling Conservative Party conference in nearby Brighton, almost killing the Prime Minister, Margaret Thatcher; Bournemouth was to be venue for the next conference.[10] Crucial to this process was the role of the state in providing funding and limiting regulation. Thus, whilst CCTV was expanding, it was also able to be normalised as an expected feature of public space, or even a 'fifth utility' (Graham, 1999).

In the 1990s, CCTV was seen to have 'more of an impact on the evolution of law enforcement policy than just about any technological initiative in the last two decades' (Davies, 1996b, p.328).[11] Driven by the fear of terrorism, CCTV systems advanced – from simple analogue systems to more sophisticated digital systems – that were 'waved aloft by police and politicians as if it were a technological Holy Grail ... for urban dysfunction' (Davies, 1996a, p.328). However, many critical commentators illuminated how CCTV seamlessly reordered and controlled urban life (Sorkin, 1995) creating little more than 'a carceral city', a collection of surveillance nodes designed to impose a particular model of conduct and disciplinary adherence on its 'inhabitants' (Soja, 1995, p.25).[12]

Materiality, spatiality and security

As well as the analysis of emergent security infrastructures in the 1990s through the lens of regulation, fortressing and surveillance trends, more conceptually, architecture – and the material landscape more generally – was seen to have the capacity to transmit a range of dominant ideologies, illustrating how a particular society was inscribed into space (Harvey, 1990; Ellin, 1997). This stream of theorisation saw the built environment of the city as a key site for encounter within the 'material turn' in the social sciences and humanities, where spaces and landscapes evolved through entanglements of human and non-human elements that co-constituted each other.[13] In particular, this led to a focus upon what built spaces get spatially constituted through everyday activities, and their relationships with organisations and organising (Miller,

1998). Here an understanding of 'governing materials' became crucial, especially 'the contention that material objects should not be thought of as the stable ground on which the instabilities generated by disputes between human actors are played out; rather, they should be understood as forming an integral element of evolving controversies' (Barry, 2013, p.12).

Architecture and urban design were increasingly being seen as having the power to order society through environmental determinism, with such embodied experiences often serving to in/exclude particular groups from certain spaces of the city (Sennett, 1994). Drawing upon such assertions, and from a security perspective, the built landscape was seen to possess the power to condition new forms of subjectivity, with spatial performances of identity and (in)security becoming linked to how subjects internalised fear.

More specifically, in the early 1990s, work, particularly in urban and cultural geography and architectural studies, portraying landscapes as texts that could be 'read', revealed a range of interpretations of conflict, war and terrorism in a more culturally sensitive way. Drawing on postmodern and post-structural ideas, landscape was seen as 'a medium in which social relations and processes are formed and reproduced' (Daniels, 1993, p.1026) and which 'reveals' the symbolic importance of their constituent elements (Cosgrove and Daniels, 1988; Barnes and Duncan, 1991; Duncan, 1995). Whilst such work drew on the long tradition of seeing landscapes as materially reflecting human culture (Sauer, 1963), the new focus was on the politics of representation of material culture (Jackson, 2000).

These and similar such 'textual' modes of analysis were quickly employed to analyse the upsurge in urban fear in the 1990s, recognising how the latter's visual aesthetic came to symbolise conflict, violence and terror. Studies at the time highlighted how symbolic markers of territorial conflict – counter-terrorism features – produced highly symbolic (and often contested) landscapes (Jarman, 1993). These so-called landscapes of defence (Coaffee, 1996b) with a focus upon territorial security were conceived as

> a landscape shaped or otherwise materially affected by formal or informal defensive strategies to achieve recognisable social, political or cultural goals…[which] may be seen in terms of rich diversity which extends from the loci of violently contested conflict to places heavily invested with symbolic meaning that helps provide a reliable background to everyday life.
> (Gold and Revill, 1999, p.235; see also Coaffee, 2000)

Within this context, the following section of this chapter showcases the spatial and material imprint and impact of attempts to counter the terrorist threat in the City of London in the 1990s,[14] and which, provided a clear example of the convergence of regulatory, fortification and surveillance practices in tackling terrorism.

Hard and soft boundaries: Rings of concrete and rings of surveillance

During the 1970s, Provisional IRA attacks in Northern Ireland aimed at disrupting the economy took a variety of forms with incursions made against central business districts, energy and raw material resources, communication facilities and transport infrastructure (Murray, 1982), and that led to security measures being built into the physical landscape of Belfast, and other towns (Chapter 2). Such attacks, specifically directed against economic targets, were the precursor to the 1980s and 1990s Provisional IRA bombings in Central London with the experience of Belfast, in particular, providing a historical context for the defensive landscape changes introduced in London.[15]

This switch of operational theatre occurred for two key reasons. First, there was a change in Provisional IRA tactics, which increasingly saw England as the key target as it became clear that the 1970s protracted bombing campaign in Northern Ireland would not put sufficient pressure on the British Government to withdraw from Ulster. Second, there was the belief by some that the success of the security cordon around Belfast city centre forced a change in Provisional IRA targeting priorities towards 'softer' targets in England. The Provisional IRA thus extended their campaign to England in the hope of thrusting the 'Irish question' back into the centre of the political agenda. This also had the additional effect of restricting bombings in Northern Ireland and would 'take the heat off Belfast and Derry' (Bishop and Mallie, 1987, p.250). More specifically, a Provisional IRA Army Council meeting in June 1972 decided that an English bombing campaign should be restricted to targets in Central London with minimum civilian casualties (Dillion, 1994).

In the proceeding decades, a number of Provisional IRA bombing campaigns in England were carried out, striking at the economic, military, political and judicial targets, including major hotels[16] and banks in Central London, army career centres and the assassination of prominent Members of Parliament (Clutterbuck, 1990). In the late 1980s, there was a shift in specific Provisional IRA tactics towards attacking non-civilian 'economic' targets; a shift that was aided by a new form of explosive. As highlighted in previous chapters, there had been an evolution in explosives used for military attack, or terrorism, over centuries – from gunpowder, to TNT and then to ammonium nitrate-based substances that were extensively used in the 1970s and 1980s. In the latest evolution of explosive power, the mid-1980s saw the Provisional IRA receive Libyan shipments of a 'new' type of plastic explosive called Semtex – an odourless explosive, invisible to X-ray, and many times more powerful than ammonium nitrate fertiliser (O'Brien, 1995).[17] This 'explosive of choice' was subsequently used in virtually every Provisional IRA bombing attack in England to great effect.

London calling

The British Security Services cite the bombing of the Mill Hill Army barracks, in North London in August 1988, as the moment when the Provisionals began to move away from previous strategies (Coaffee, 1996b). By the early 1990s, the majority of bomb attacks were against industrial, commercial or transport infrastructure – in short, economic targets. As Rogers (1996, p.15) commented, 'in the early 1990s PIRA continued with a range of paramilitary actions... but there was a progressive move away from the deliberate targeting of civilians and towards economic targeting'. Dillon (1996, p.265) further noted that whilst 'political assassination was always favoured by the IRA, ... their main aim for the 1990s was to bring terror to the heart of London with a ferocity never before experienced in the capital'.

The first major Central London attack of the decade – a mortar bomb attack on Downing Street on February 7, 1991 – symbolically carried the Provisional IRA's message to the heart of the British establishment, in an attempt to force the British Government into further political dialogue.[18] The Security Services had previously installed tall steel gates at the entrance of Downing Street in 1989, in response to the threat of car bombing. After this attack, the Provisional IRA began to extend their campaign to cause maximum civilian disruption, for instance attacks against transport facilities. Such attacks included a litterbin bomb at Victoria Station, which injured 43 and killed 1 person during the morning rush hour. This led to the bins on the London Underground being removed to prevent similar incidents.[19] Aware of the state of the developing recession in Britain, and the pressure on government finances, the Provisional IRA at this time also began to appreciate the value of inflicting massive economic damage on Britain, in terms of actual damage caused, insurance and compensation claims, as well as negatively affecting London identity as a global financial hub.

This targeting of London's economic infrastructure through the early to mid-1990s, using much larger and more powerful bombs from those previously deployed, centred predominantly on the historic City of London – the Square Mile of global financial institutions. Nevertheless, the Provisional IRA had long regarded London's docklands development, dominated by the Canary Wharf tower – Europe's tallest building and seen by many as a monument to the neo-liberal economic policies of Margaret Thatcher – as a prime target in its U.K. bombing campaign. This tower was specifically targeted in November 1992, by a 1-tonne van bomb that failed due to a faulty detonator. Following this attack, security managers at Canary Wharf initiated their own 'mini-*ring of steel*' essentially shutting down access to 'their' private estate within the Docklands complex (Coaffee, 1997). Such an approach combined attempts to 'design out terrorism' with changing approaches adopted by the police and private security industry. Security barriers were thrown across the road into and out of the complex, no parking zones implemented, a plethora of private CCTV cameras were installed and identity card schemes initiated.

Overall, in through the 1990s, the Provisional IRA, in its 'economic disruption' bombing campaign, successfully attacked a number of key economic targets in London with large bombs exploding in the City of London (the Square Mile) in April 1992 and April 1993, and the London Docklands in 1992 (unexploded) and February 1996. These bombings and the subsequent reaction of urban authorities and the police served to highlight the use made of both territorial and technological approaches to counter-terrorist security, creating a series of interlocking hard and soft boundaries to counter the terrorist threat. This resulted in material changes to the urban landscape that evolved during the 1990s, as a result of the strategies of a number of key stakeholders – the police, local government, planners and private businesses – to defend themselves from terrorism (Coaffee, 1996a). Such security-driven alterations ultimately brought distinct changes to the cityscape that saw these financial areas increasingly separating itself from the rest of London in both physical and technological terms.

Defending the city

The first attack in the City of London occurred in the centre of the Square Mile, at the Stock Exchange on July 20, 1990. This bomb blew a 10-foot hole inside the main tower causing large-scale damage to the public gallery. No one was injured due to a telephone warning being received 40 minutes prior to the explosion that allowed the building and surrounding area to be evacuated. During the early months of 1992, a number of bombs were planted in and around London to coincide with the forthcoming General Election, which aimed to keep the Northern Ireland issue at the top of the political agenda. Election arrangements thus determined the timing of the Provisional IRA's strikes, whilst economics dictated the targets of attack.

In early 1992, over 15 bomb hoaxes were received directly relating to the area covered by the City of London, and in February a small terrorist bomb exploded in the northeast of the Square Mile (Coaffee, 1996a). However, the Provisional IRA's main economic bombing campaign in the 1990s was perhaps being underestimated by the security forces with the perceived threat level not considered high enough for the police to establish any special proactive security measures around potential targets. A more overt police presence coupled with a general security planning process was seen as a proportionate response to the threat faced. All this changed with the devastating bombing of the Baltic Exchange at St. Mary Axe in the heart of the City in April 1992, which led to attempts to contain the evergrowing threat.

On April 10, 1992 at 9:20 pm, the day after the General Election, a huge bomb was detonated in front of the Baltic Exchange Building on St Mary Axe. The 1-tonne truck bomb was assembled from a mix of nitrate fertiliser and 100 pounds of Semtex, and at this time was the biggest detonated on mainland Britain since World War II.[20] The bombing killed 3 people, injured 91 others and severely damaged surrounding buildings. The financial cost of the attack was initially put at over £800 million that was significantly more than the total cost of damage caused by the 10,000 explosions that had occurred during the ongoing troubles in Northern Ireland, up to that point.[21]

Territorial and panoptical security 85

This was the first major bomb in the City of London, and it was felt that an increased police presence, with officers carrying out spot checks on vehicles, was a suitable response. Strategically, the police, stretching the Police and Criminal Evidence Act (PACE) to its limit, instigated a number of short-term roving armed police checkpoints on the major entrances into the City. However, in May 1992, a month after bombing, an evaluation report argued that the Local Plan and draft Unitary Development Plan (UDP) for improving the City's environmental and movement policies called *Key to the Future* should be implemented. Under these proposals (drawn up *before* the bomb), it was planned to pedestrianise a central part of the City around the Bank of England, to improve traffic flow and reduce pollution. These policies became central to the City's construction of territorially based counter-terrorist security measures in the preceding months and years.

Subsequently, traffic management measures were introduced on an experimental basis on three City roads.[22] The police at this time wanted to set up permanent vehicle checkpoints on all entrances to the City, which they felt could be undertaken in line with the City's *Key to the Future* policies. However, a combination of legal issues (related to PACE), financial restrictions (primarily that City businesses would not want to pay for such measures) and public opinion (the fear of a disproportionate response) made this impossible to do. There was a feeling that a permanent security cordon would be an overreaction given that this was the first major bomb in the City and could have made the City 'look like Belfast', giving a propaganda coup to the terrorists (Kelly, 1994a,b). However, minor changes to the everyday urban landscape did occur at this time, including the removal of over 1000 litter bins that could not be made bombproof, and reducing the time black refuse sacks were left on the street, in an attempt to reduce the number of places a bomb could be concealed. In addition to random road-checks and vehicle access restrictions, the coverage of traffic management CCTV was extended and adapted to focus on incoming traffic, whilst businesses were encouraged by the police to install additional private CCTV cameras. Two months later, in June 1992, another minor bombing further increased calls for improved security measures. This bomb, although only a small device, showed that existing security in the Square Mile could easily be breached.

Calls for a Belfast-style solution

Overall, the period of containment after the St. Mary Axe bomb sought to enhance the control of space, limiting the ease with which terrorists could move around the City, and ensuring that vehicles parked suspiciously could be easily identified. In hindsight, the police were well aware of the limitations of their powers which prohibited permanent checks on vehicles coming into the City. By using mobile communications and a scout sent ahead to tell them whether or not there was a police check operating, terrorists could still easily plant a bomb in the City. During the early months of 1993, with the delicate state of political dialogue aimed at brokering a Provisional IRA ceasefire, the risk of further attack to the City significantly increased, as the mainland bombing campaign, aimed at making the cost of the staying in Northern Ireland unacceptably high for the British government, was in full swing.

The worst fears of the City police were realised in April 1993 when a Provisional IRA bomb exploded in Bishopsgate in the east of the Square Mile. This device, which was similar to the one used at St Mary Axe a year earlier, killed 1 person, injured 94, caused extensive damage to buildings in a 500-yard radius and shattered over 500 tonnes of glass from windows. Damage was initially estimated at £1 billion (subsequently reduced to around £550–600 million). The edition of *An Phoblacht*[23] on April 29, 1993 gave the Provisional IRA's version of events and highlighted how 'having spotted a breach in the usually tight security around the City' they planted their bomb and issued several warnings. They further noted how their 'surveillance operatives' exploited a loophole in security, which allowed builders' vehicles to park on the double yellow lines on Saturday mornings without being searched or asked to move by the City Police.

It was well known that close to this bomb site, and at the time of explosion, the European Bank of Reconstruction and Development had been meeting to decide on the location of the soon-to-be-established European Central Bank.[24] As such the Provisional IRA could not have picked a better day to attack the Square Mile. Through the precise placement and timing of this bomb, the Provisional IRA succeeded in making sure that the impact of the bomb was felt politically as well as economically. As the Provisional IRA further noted: 'as well as the huge cost of structural damage, the loss of buildings and the knock on effects of insurance costs, the City of London is assessing the damage to its prestige as a world financial centre' (ibid.).

In the wake of this bombing, the media and sections of the business community also began to suggest that drastic changes should be made to City security. An editorial in the *Sunday People,* the day after the bomb, captured the popular view that security must be enhanced:

> If we are to wage effective war against the IRA, there must now be an urgent review of security at their most likely target. Since the IRA mortar-bombed Number 10 from a waiting van, nothing is allowed to park in Whitehall. IF IT CAN BE DONE FOR DOWNING STREET IT CAN BE DONE IN THE CITY.
>
> (April 25, p.2, emphasis added)

Leading City figures cited in *The Times* further indicated that 'The City should be turned into a medieval-style walled enclave to prevent terrorist attacks... (p.3). In private there is talk about a "walled city" approach to security with access through a number of small "gates" and controlled by security discs ...' (April 27, p.27).[25]

In a similar vein, *The Sun* newspaper published a six-point plan 'which would keep the IRA bombers out', but only at a great cost. They proposed a 'ring of steel' directly based on the Belfast model, which they thought would cost £100 million to initiate plus £25 million a year to run. Under this proposal they suggested that access be restricted to 8–10 entrances, which were fitted with security barriers manned by armed guards.[26] By extension, the article also suggested that a national identity card scheme, a new National Anti-Terrorist Squad and the bombproofing of vulnerable buildings could also help prevent attacks.

Other views differed, with some highlighting the pitfalls of high levels of overt security. For example, the City Engineer, who also evoking medieval metaphors, stated that 'we wouldn't want the City turned into a castle with a moat around the outside'.[27] At this time such 'draconian security was dismissed as a propaganda gift to the Provisional IRA as well as being difficult to implement legally'.[28] In May 1993, given the heightened risk of further attack, and severe pressure from the business community (especially foreign institutions) to improve security, the police confirmed that they were considering radical plans, in the form of a security cordon, to deter terrorists from the City. The construction of the proposed scheme was essentially the same strategy as *Key to the Future* that was being suggested on movement and environmental grounds prior to the Bishopsgate bomb (see Corporation of London, 1993a). The emphasis of the rationale behind the scheme had, however, taken on a very different persona, being seen as a direct response to the Bishopsgate blast rather than the move towards environmental improvements.[29]

Given the perceived risk of further attacks, construction of the security cordon began in June 1993, with the introduction of security checkpoints to bar all non-essential traffic. Such modifications were criticised by those who felt that it would cause traffic chaos at the boundaries of the City and could geographically displace the risk of terrorist attack to other areas. Kenneth Clarke, the Home Secretary at that time, summed up the situation the City faced: 'There is a balance to be struck between having roadblocks which will frustrate what the terrorists can do, and creating enormous traffic jams which would disrupt the life out of the City'.[30]

Eventually, on the weekend of July 3–4, 1993, a full security cordon was activated in the City. The majority of routes into the City were closed or made exit only, leaving seven routes (plus one bus route) through which the City could be entered (see Figure 5.1). On these routes into the City, road-checks guarded by armed police were set up. Locally, the cordon was often referred to not as the ring of steel but as the 'ring of plastic' as the access restrictions were based primarily on the funnelling of traffic through rows of plastic traffic cones, as the scheme was still officially 'temporary'. The cordon provided a highly visible demonstration that the City was taking the terrorist threat seriously, even if many entering the City did not realise its counter-terrorist use.

88 *Conventional techniques of urban security*

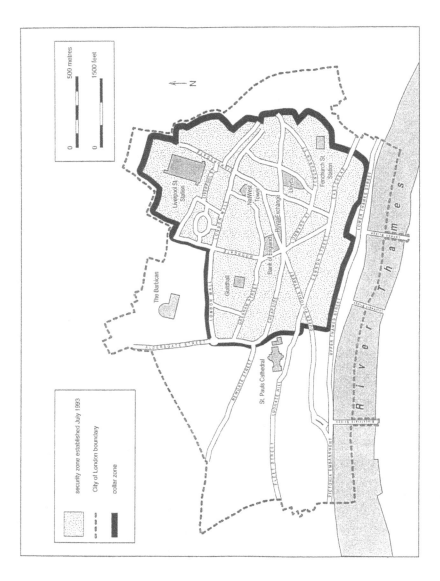

Figure 5.1 The initial extent of the Experimental Traffic Zone or 'ring of steel'.

This 'Experimental Traffic Scheme' as it was officially called, was put in place for an initial period of six months.[31]

As one commentator noted at the time, 'motorists attempting to cross the City are getting used to closed access routes and diversions ... and few would be surprised if they were stopped at a roadblock by a policeman toting a sub-machine gun: welcome to Fortress London, 1993' (Pratt, 1993, p.5).

In parallel to initiating access restrictions, surveillance capabilities were enhanced with camera technology emerging as perhaps the single most important factor in the City Police's counter-terrorist campaign. Heightened surveillance of the Square Mile was enacted as the traffic camera network was extended by the addition of 11 colour cameras to provide coverage on minor roads. Additionally, new police-operated security cameras were erected to monitor the entrances into the Square Mile, 24 hours a day, so that every vehicle entering the security cordon was recorded. From November 1993, there were two (or more) cameras filming at each entry point into the security cordon – one that recorded the number plate, and another that scanned the front profile of the driver and passenger. These provided high-resolution pictures, which could be compared against intelligence reports and an image database. The Commissioner of Police indicated that almost nine months after this camera technology was first used; it had been exceptionally successful and was attracting a good deal of attention from elsewhere.[32] By the end of 1993, there were more than 70 police-controlled cameras covering the City (traffic management and entry point), aimed at creating a highly surveilled environment where would-be terrorists could not hide.

However, there was still inadequate coverage of many public areas due to the lack of private cameras in situ. In September 1993, the police therefore launched an innovative scheme called CameraWatch, to coordinate camera surveillance and create an effective, and highly visible, private camera network (Corporation of London, 1993b), and by early 1996, over 1000 private security cameras, in over 375 camera systems, were operational in the City. The panopticon of surveillance that started construction after the Bishopsgate bomb served to reinforce the access restrictions that were imposed. Through these territorial strategies, space within the Square Mile was increasingly organised in such a way that almost complete surveillance coverage became possible, reducing the perceived opportunity for terrorist attack.

As well as developing territorial security and surveillance strategies, the police, in liaison with the private security sector, set about creating an extra layer of security around individual buildings through the addition of landscape features, and the implementation of security strategies as the private security industry was co-opted to help the counter-terrorism effort. Typical security plans adopted, at this time, aimed to deter an attack and deny the terrorist access to premises through a fortified and 'hardened' urban landscape, by altering the spatial configuration of areas immediately outside buildings to stop parking and to create 'stand-off' areas, by increasing surveillance through vigilant security guards and CCTV and to control access to buildings through limiting the number of entrances and the screening of visitors by security personnel. There were other precautions that were also taken by many businesses to reduce the effects of a bomb blast such as application of anti-shatter window film, safety glass (a legal requirement under building regulations at certain critical locations), the installation of blast curtains and the construction of internal shelter areas.[33] Risk communication campaigns also improved emergency readiness and contingency planning practices amongst public and private-sector institutions, enhancing their organisational resilience.

In time, many aspects of this overt security-driven territorialisation moved away from the popular 'conflict' approach, which witnessed the urban landscape fragmenting and dividing into mutually hostile units. Instead, more symbolic and subtle notions of territoriality were displayed that expressed a shared concern with defence, but which attempted to balance the need for protection with the continual functioning of the City as a business centre. For example, immediately after a Provisional IRA ceasefire was called in August 1994, the security cordon was scaled down with armed guards taken off most of the checkpoints.[34] Moreover, permanent bollards, paving, and in some cases, flower beds began replacing temporary traffic cones, creating a less visible form of landscape alteration. Here, the Commissioner of the City Police indicated that over the next few years, the street environment of the City around the security points would be 'landscaped to give the scheme an aesthetic permanence in keeping with City street architecture' (Kelly, 1994a). This demonstrated a noticeable 'softening' of the landscape as a result of reduced threat levels and led to a campaign from some City businesses, around Christmas 1995, to disband the security cordon. However, at the same time plans to further extend the security cordon westwards were developed by local government, representing a continuation of the *Key to the Future* philosophy in relation to reduced pollution, traffic and crime (and terrorism).

The police camera network had also been continually upgraded to meet the terrorist threat in the wake of the Bishopsgate bombing. In the early months of 1995, new high-resolution cameras for the traffic system were installed and 13 further cameras were added to monitor cars *exiting* the City. Exit cameras were particularly important, as police could now monitor traffic into the City and, if needed, track suspect vehicles across the City.

Reactivating and extending the security cordon

By early 1996 it was becoming clear that the Provisional IRA's 17-month ceasefire was in trouble as the understanding that their Political wing, Sinn Fein, would be allowed to take part in peace talks was not being met, with the British government demanding full disarmament before such talks could proceed.[35] This cessation of terrorist violence lasted until early February 1996, when a new mainland bombing campaign against symbolic and economic targets commenced with a large lorry bomb that exploded at South Quay in the London Docklands, seen as a symbolic extension of the Square Mile.[36] The 1400-kilogram bomb consisted of ammonium nitrate fertiliser and sugar packed into sacks and surrounded with tubes stuffed with Semtex to boost the power of the blast. The Provisional IRA had sent warnings 90 minutes beforehand, but the area was not fully evacuated. As well as the 2 people who were killed, more than 100 were injured with the blast devastating the surrounding office blocks and showering the area with broken glass.

Following this bombing, a 'fortress mentality' returned to the City with the full pre-cease-fire ring of steel being reactivated and made operational within a number of hours due to fears that the City would be attacked. Initially, there was a large increase in high-visibility policing both at the entry points and on the City streets in general. There was also an increased frequency of roving checkpoints as the City 're-steeled' itself. Furthermore, the plans developed during the ceasefire to extend the ring of steel westwards were enacted in early 1997. Coinciding with the opening of this extension to security cordon, the police's surveillance capability was once again enhanced when in February 1997, new cameras were installed at police checkpoints and were linked, first to the Police National Computer, and then to the vehicle database and 'Hot List' of vehicles at the Force Intelligence Bureau. These cameras were capable of zooming in and out and swivelling through 360 degrees and were fitted with lights, which enabled round the clock monitoring. The digital automatic number plate recording (ANPR) technology used – developed from technological advances made during the first Gulf War in 1991 – was able process the information and give a warning to the operator within 4 seconds, considerably increasing the speed and capability of the City of London Police to run vehicle checks.

In the aftermath of the Dockland attack, territorial security was also quickly established across the London Docklands as a result of the business community successfully lobbying the Metropolitan Police to set up an anti-terrorist security cordon to cover the whole of the Docklands – the so-called *Iron Collar* specifically modelled on the City of London's approach[37] – amidst fears that high-profile businesses might relocate away from the area. Subsequently, a security cordon was initiated for entire Dockland peninsula comprising four entry points, which at times of high-risk assessment, would have armed guards. High-resolution ANPR CCTV cameras were also installed. The most noticeable difference between the scheme initiated in the Docklands and that in the City was the overt advertising of the Docklands security cordon on the large signs at entry points into the cordon instead of downplaying the zones anti-terrorism purpose (Figure 5.2).

Whereas the City of London and the London Docklands were able to initiate a counter-terrorist scheme relatively easily given the perceived risk of attack and their powerful business communities, other urban areas in the United Kingdom did not find it so easy. This was especially true in Manchester in North West England where, on June 15, 1996, a bomb exploded outside the Arndale shopping centre in the central city.

Figure 5.2 Signs put up in 1996 warning drivers they were entering the Docklands security cordon.

In this attack, the Provisional IRA detonated a 1500-kilogram lorry bomb – the usual mixture of Semtex and ammonium nitrate fertiliser – that became the biggest bomb detonated in Britain since the World War II. Telephoned warnings about 90 minutes before the attack saved lives, allowing

75,000 people to be evacuated from the area. More than 200 people were injured and a large area around the bomb blast was devastated. This led to the Manchester business community calling for enhanced City of London-style counter-terrorist measures to secure the city's commercial heart against further bomb attacks. As the Chief Executive of the Chamber of Commerce noted on the day after the blast:

> No economy can stand this sort of disruption and the cost of putting it right. I think the business community will be calling for the sort of secure ring of steel that was put in place after the City of London bombing.[38]

However, upon closer inspection, it was not considered financially viable to implement such a cordon in Manchester. Subsequently, the city undertook an unprecedented level of urban regeneration activity as Central Manchester was physically remodelled, creating a series of innovative urban spaces and commercial environments where security features were subtly designed into the landscape from the outset.[39] Higher levels of security were eventually retrofitted in the mid-2000s when vehicle access to the central shopping zone was restricted by retractable bollards. In addition, secure 'standoff' areas were developed for high-profile buildings, with bombproof litter bins installed as part of the street furniture (Coaffee and Rogers, 2008).

Conclusion: Lessons from London

Since the early 1990s, London has provided some concrete scenarios of the relationship between terrorist risk and future urbanism, and in particular the mindset of the police, planners, architects and security personnel in designing cities in relation to risk-management criteria. Such accounts placed great emphasis upon 'target hardening', although increasingly more covert approaches, especially digitalised surveillance, took over as the counter-terrorist planner's favourite tool. During the 1990s, London Police sought to control and regulate the space within the financial zones, attempting to create a particular image based on a balance between a flourishing business environment, and safety and security concerns – a balance seen as vital if the area was to remain competitive within the global economy.

Such territorially focused security was constructed to thwart particular terrorist modus operandi that sought to bring economic life in London to a halt by causing unprecedented financial losses and sowing fear of possible future attacks. Such security cordons highlighted a number of trends at the time linked to the increased securitisation of urban space where the relationship between fear and form determined the extent of fortification measures. Here, the defensive landscapes that were constructed attempted to control space through physical and technological measures, reflected 1990s postmodern urbanism that saw the city fragmenting into disparate enclaves, driven by a 'master narrative' of embedding security into everyday life through 'street barriers', 'electronic guardian angels' and policing tactics (Davis, 1990, p.193).

The spatial imprinting of these trends was evident through the construction of London's landscapes of defence that became a concrete and technologically embedded part of the 1990s urban scene, and where individuals could expect to be filmed by, on average, around 300 cameras a day (Norris and Armstrong, 1999). The City of London, in particular, was transformed into the most surveilled space in the United Kingdom and perhaps the world, with over 1500 surveillance cameras operating, many using ANPR technologies (City of London Police, 2002). This highly advanced networked infrastructure was a forerunner of the surveillance 'surge' in the post-9/11 era where automation, miniaturisation and pervasiveness of electronic surveillance became key trends in urban counter-terrorism (see, for example, Lyon, 2003). Similarly, in proceeding chapters, we will see how hardened territorial boundaries and the creation of rings of steel, or *cordon sanitaires,* were expanded in London, as well as becoming part of the everyday urban experience in other locations around the world.

London's response to terrorist bombings in the 1990s saw it occupy a pivotal place within 'War on Terror' in the new Millennium and showcased two possible scenarios for how counter-terrorism measures can be aligned with urban management and landscape changes. First, a security arrangement that combines territorial control and advanced surveillance through the lens of traffic and environmental improvements as shown in the City of London. Second, as illuminated by the London Docklands, a security cordon overtly advertises its function as a counter-terrorist deterrent to maintain the areas image of 'safety and security' and retains its business functioning. However, more critically, these examples from London also revealed that security cordons promoted a disconnection of these protected zones, both physically and technologically, from the rest of the city through the development of their 'rings of confidence' (Coaffee, 1996b, 2004), creating a condition of 'splintered urbanism' (Graham and Marvin, 2001). Importantly though, from a public and social policy viewpoint, these rings of confidence were also seen as a panacea for heightened levels of terrorism and quickly became normalised by business coalitions, motoring organisation, commuters and governing authorities as part of London's everyday life.

Notes

1 This was the antithesis of the ongoing 'peace process' that was apparently in full swing at the time.
2 'The wall', which was estimated to cost US$1.5 billion, consists of 8-metre-high concrete slabs, with sections of electronic fencing topped with barbed wire, and is surveilled by radar, security cameras and observation posts. Access is only through armed checkpoints containing X-ray scanners and its entire length is patrolled by thousands of security guards.

Territorial and panoptical security 95

3 If shut, these gates could still create a security cordon if the threat level was increased. These new gates themselves were removed in the mid-2000s, limiting the ability of the police to seal off the area if required.
4 Security cameras were seldom used at the height of The Troubles due to expense and technological deficiency (Coaffee, 2003).
5 Lianos and Douglas's (2000) arguments regarding the surveillance and control are concerned with ordering around indices of risk rather than more comprehensive (Foucauldian) notions of 'soul-training' (Fussey, 2007, p.176).
6 This type of targeting was most prevalent in the early-mid 1990s with such attacks becoming less widespread in recent years given the fluid *modus operandi* of international terrorist groups or networks.
7 The term *cordon sanitaire* dates to 1821, when French troops were deployed to the border between France and Spain to prevent the spread of yellow fever into France (see Taylor, 1882).
8 For Foucault, the ideal type of controlling environment was envisioned as the panopticon where the few see the many and where the centralised surveillant gaze constitutes 'visible and unverifiable' power (1977, p.200).
9 This type of networked surveillance as part of a modern 'disciplinary society' further differs from Foucault's panopticism that implied an all-encompassing gaze, in that it only monitors selective spaces (Williams and Johnstone, 2000).
10 That CCTV soon penetrated British towns and cities so thoroughly was not entirely due to the fear of terrorism. The neo-liberal relaxation of planning laws and expansion of out-of-town shopping had seen traditional space of consumption in town centres decline. Other fears were also used to justify the installation of CCTV systems: particularly football hooliganism, and high-profile crimes against children, in particular the kidnapping and murder of a small child – James Bulger – in 1993.
11 In the mid-1990s, Fyfe and Bannister (1996) noted that over 100 towns in the United Kingdom had centralised CCTV systems, manly instituted in high-rent commercial areas.
12 More broadly, the plethora of surveillance technologies within the city were seen to evoke fears of an Orwellian society based on 'Big Brother', or rather a variety of 'Little brothers' (Lyon, 1994, p.53). Notably, the amplified use of surveillance technologies after a spate of spectacular terrorist bombings led to initial fears that the mushrooming of increasingly automated and hi-tech systems would further erode civil liberties as democratic and ethical accountability are given a back seat to the introduction of new digital surveillance devices.
13 As noted in Chapter 4, the material turn was part of a much wider spatial turn in thought which saw to the spaces of built environment as a means to understand both historical and social sciences.
14 This section draws on the prior and ongoing work of the author in researching this targeted space, and in particular, Coaffee (2000, 2003, 2020).
15 Economic targeting in England, and especially London, by the Provisional IRA was not a new phenomenon. The Provisional IRA has periodically targeted London since the 1930s, although the City itself was not specifically targeted until the 1980s.
16 Notably, Grand Hotel in Brighton in 1984 during the Conservative party political conference.

96 *Conventional techniques of urban security*

17 Semtex was initially developed and manufactured in the former Czechoslovakia, as B1 – a military explosive. It has been referred to as Semtex since 1964.
18 During this attack, three bombs were launched from an improvised mortar launcher attached to a van, which was parked approximately 200 metres from Downing Street. One of these bombs landed in the garden of 10 Downing Street during a meeting of the Gulf War Cabinet. The other two shells failed to explode.
19 This had been preceded by an earlier explosion at Paddington Station, and a threat that bombs were planted at all of London's main line railway stations. Police had been searching Victoria Station (and others) when the bomb went off and evacuated all the main line terminals in London immediately afterwards for the first time in London's history.
20 The attack was planned for months and marked an advance to the Provisional IRA's explosive manufacture.
21 A few hours later, another similarly large bomb went off in Staples Corner, a large road junction in North London, also causing major damage.
22 At this time, no official reference was made in such discussions to the counter-terrorist security implications of these changes, as the Corporation was keen to downplay the impact of the bomb.
23 The newspaper of the Republican Movement in Ireland.
24 This demonstration of the City's vulnerability could well have damaged the chances of London being chosen as the location for the European Central Bank. This was eventually established in Frankfurt in 1998.
25 Walled City mooted to thwart the terrorists. *The Times*, April 27, p.23.
26 *The Sun*, April 26, p.4. These barriers, they proposed, would only operate during the evening between 7 pm and 7 am and at weekends, as they would be impractical to operate during working hours. During office hours, only valid business traffic would be permitted entry. Other security methods this article suggested were an additional 250 police officers on the streets of the City, and a lorry ban, which, it was estimated, would cost £5 million a year.
27 Running the Mile. *Independent on Sunday*, May 2, p.10.
28 Police resist demands for City ring of steel. *The Times*, April 27, p.3.
29 The latter would re-emerge, in time, as the City's main justification for the security cordon.
30 Cited in City security boosted in war on terrorism. *Evening Standard*, April 29, p.5.
31 Also established was a so-called collar-zone around the restricted area, which saw increased police patrols and roving checkpoints to alleviate the fears of those businesses within this area.
32 Cited in the 1993 Annual Report of the Commissioner of the City of London Police (1994).
33 The security precautions taken were implemented alongside advice from the police, and security services and in conjunction with Home Office Guidance for *Bombs: Protecting People and Property*, first published in 1994. This guide highlighted how preparation was increasingly playing a part in counter-terrorism thinking within organisations as well as strongly encouraging building occupants to 'participate in the counter-terrorist security planning in your community: communities defeat terrorism' (p.4).
34 This slight downgrading of security did, however, have a noticeable influence on recorded crime levels.
35 A demand that was dropped after the bombing campaign started again in 1996.

36 As previously noted, the Docklands was seen as a 'high-prestige' target for the Provisional IRA and had been previously attacked in 1992. The area was made up of many high-rise buildings, including Canary Wharf Tower, then the tallest building in Europe, where the offices of major banks, corporations, newspapers and television stations were located.
37 This was designed by the same security specialists that had put in place the City of London's cordon.
38 Cited in Traders call for 'a ring of steel'. *The Guardian*, June 16, p.6.
39 The cost of such ongoing regeneration has been well in excess of £1 billion (Williams, 2003).

6 The fearful shock of 9/11 and the rise of military and urban geopolitics

Introduction: The shock of 9/11

The 1998 U.S. Embassy bombings in Kenya and Tanzania that killed over 220 people (Chapter 4) took place eight years to the day after U.S. troops were ordered to Saudi Arabia in the aftermath of Iraq's invasion of Kuwait – an action that catalysed the growth of Osama Bin Laden Al Qaeda network that claimed responsibility for the embassy attacks as the first 'spectaculars' in a worldwide campaign against the United States. Prior to these bombings, in February 1998, Bin Laden had issued a fatwa, or Islamic religious proclamation, justifying large-scale attacks against the non-Muslim world based on new motivations linked to both theological and political ideas. Whilst traditional secular terrorist groups were often small in size, it was estimated that Al Qaeda could call on between 4 and 5000 trained fighters, making them a formidable adversary, with a significant capability of lethal violence and mass casualty attacks anywhere in the world (Hoffman, 1999). Such threats intensified as the twenty-first century approached with fears of a millennium eve spectacular in the United States leading to the deployment of extra security around prominent locations, such as Times Square and LAX airport. Moreover, in August 2001, a presidential daily briefing entitled 'Bin Ladin determined to strike in US' explicitly highlighted the rising threat level for attacks on the American homeland that came to fruition 36 days later.

As a result of these initial threat assessments, discussions were begun at the federal level regarding how best to embed security into the cityscape, as at this time, only U.S. Federal buildings were required to adopt robust protective security. For example, in October 2000, House and Senate Committees requested the National Capital Planning Commission (NCPC) provide professional planning advice to the Congress, the Administration and other federal agencies on the impact of security measures on the historic urban design of Washington's Monumental Core. This work was in progress, when the planes struck the Twin Towers.[1]

The Al Qaeda-inspired attacks of 9/11 were unique, both in terms of the combination of tactics employed – the simultaneous hijacking of four planes and the targeting of iconic buildings – the World Trade Center and

DOI: 10.4324/9780429461620-8

Pentagon – by aircrafts that were used as missiles – and the magnitude of the damage caused. At the time, it was the single deadliest attack in human history. Nearly 3000 people died and 2500 were injured with many suffering longer term health consequences.

More broadly, 9/11 was seen by philosopher Paul Virilio (2002a) as an example of his theory of the 'accident of accidents' – a generalised accident occurring everywhere at the same time through the power and reach of global media – where 'the Manhattan Skyline became the front of the new war' (p.82). At the time of the 1993 World Trade Center attack, Virilio had foreseen the trend by which small groups of well-organised terrorists would be 'determined not merely to settle the argument with guns' but would 'try to devastate the major cities of the world marketplace' using new forms of warfare (Virillio, 2000). Now, eight year later, these ideas for the future of humanity were to be put into practice exactly as predicted a *'total act of war*, remarkably conceived and executed' (Virilio, 2002a, p.82). Specifically, as Redhead (2006, p.14) noted,

> a generalized accident or total accident seemingly came tragically true as a small, tightly knit group of men, armed only with Stanley knives, were seen to have taken over the cockpits of the hijacked planes and flew jet airliners with masses of fuel into the highly populated buildings of the World Trade Center.

Prior to 9/11, Laqueur (1999) had argued that terrorism was moving away from the calculated use of violence for political gain towards the pursuit of catastrophic destruction. 9/11 brought to the fore wider concerns about different types of 'postmodern' or 'catastrophic', 'mega' or 'hyper-terrorism' (Laqueur, 1996; Carter et al., 1998) which further disrupted the status quo in the field of counter-terrorism, by confirming that the nature of the terrorist threat was evolving. Whilst 'old terrorism' was largely discriminate, selecting victims and targets carefully, increasingly such 'new terrorism' was viewed as indiscriminate, destructive, irrational and non-political in nature, often incorporating religious ideology and fanaticism as a core motive (Laqueur, 2004). Neumann (2009, p.3) additionally highlighted how old realties were giving way to new threats at the turn of the millennium that had enhanced lethality but reduced predictability. However, the 9/11 Commission report further identified that prior to 9/11 there was a 'failure of imagination' and 'a mind-set that dismissed possibilities' amongst the counter-terrorism community, that needed to be transformed (U.S. Government, 2004, p.336).

In the post-9/11 era, it became clear that the nature of potential terrorist threats had irrevocably changed, requiring alteration in counter-responses from governments and agencies of security at all scales; from defence of localities to the developments of international coalitions to fight the global War on Terror. Discussions in the wake of 9/11 also served to highlight the links between new forms of defensive urbanism, strategically targeted terrorism (using chemical, biological or nuclear products), military threat-response technology and more pre-emptive modes of emergency governance.

Immediate calls for action often focused on *de*territorialised responses and the necessity for coordinated international action, attempts to generate a consensus for tackling the global terrorist threat through the master narrative of the War on Terror, and for Western governments to maintain control of global security (Rogers, 2002). This included calls for less statist approaches to international relations and terrorism research amidst a stark realisation that traditional counter-terrorism mechanisms, often premised on state-on-state attacks, were insufficient to deal with the new terrorist threats. For example, Bauman (2002, p.81) highlighted the impact of 9/11 as the 'symbolic end to an era of space' where traditional territorial borders collapsed where 'no one can any longer cut themselves off from the rest of the world' and where security became 'essentially extraterritorial issues that evade territorial solutions' (p.82). Sociologist Ulrich Beck (2002) further articulated the 9/11 events in terms of newly emerging aspects of his world risk society thesis, noting that 'it is not a matter of the increase, but rather of the debounding of uncontrollable risk' (p.41) where 'national security is no longer national security as borders...have been overthrown' (p.46). For others, risk and its calculative management and measurement practices became central to governing the emerging War on Terror.

Whilst *de*territorialised responses played out in global governance responses to 9/11, a *re*territorialisation also occurred as states looked inward at 'homeland security' and the defence of the city, evoking protectionist reflexes based on securing particular territories. Security was coming home (Coaffee and Murakami Wood, 2006). This was especially the case in important urban areas where a combination of iconic structures and high levels of media exposure would generate spectacular devastation, and loss of reputation, if large-scale terror attacks were successful.

In response, new defensive approaches and strategic deployment of security infrastructure in the city encapsulated 'new ideas of geometry applied to warfare' (Denman, p.242). Here older territorial defences based on Cartesian ideas by which space was rendered 'measurable, mappable, strictly demarcated, and thereby controllable' (Elden, 2013, p.291) were supplemented by new defence technologies and network-centric approaches (Weber, 2004) and non-linear tactics that begun to redesign military doctrine to anticipate and account for unknown and incalculable threats. As Denman (2020, p.243) noted, 'if the design of early modern fortification found its highest expression in simple polygons, the fortifications of everywhere war have gravitated toward principles of non-Euclidean geometry'.

Within this context of altering territorial security fixes, the remainder of this chapter focuses upon the initial urban-scale reactions to 9/11. It first spotlights the reactive and makeshift security put in place to provide protective security to buildings and public locations that further politically demonstrated that the state was seeking to protect the public. Second, evolving types of urban security research approaches at this time are unpacked. In the post 9/11 world, reconceptualised terrorist realities led, in some cases, to new and dramatic urban counter-responses based on Belfast and LA-style target hardening as well as increasing use being made of sophisticated technology. At the urban scale, a number of accounts will highlight how the events of 9/11 served to influence the technological and physical infrastructure of targeted cities so 'urban flows can be scrutinized through military perspectives so that the inevitable fragilities and vulnerabilities they produce can be significantly reduced' (Graham, 2002, p.589). This wave of *new military urbanism* or *critical urban geopolitics* framed new ways of conducting security and terrorism research that challenged orthodox positions and concepts, as post-Cold War military doctrine was remodelled. Third, this chapter then reflects upon the immediate reactions of commentators regarding the shape and function of the future city. It does this through the reintroduction of ideas of defensible space and the utility of advanced technology, which were viewed as solutions to the immediate terrorist threat, after 9/11. The predicted social and political impacts of urban defences in the wake of 9/11 are also discussed, alongside the growing political rhetoric that emerged where we should all prepare for life in a constant state of emergency with its authoritarian-style politics and changing legal context (Wood et al., 2003). This chapter ends with a discussion about one key outcome of new militarised counter-terrorism; a normalisation of fear and the need to secure, as a leitmotif of everyday life. Here as Barkun (2011) has argued, in *Chasing Phantoms,* non-rational, emotion-driven policy making played an unrecognised role in sustaining the climate of fear that propels and perpetuates – normalises – the War on Terror.

Reactive and makeshift security

In a number of countries immediately after the 9/11 attacks there was substantial pressure for key structures, including iconic or landmark public and commercial buildings, to be protected from terrorist attack. This led to many robust yet unrefined and obtrusive features being almost literally thrown around key sites. Initially, such measures were referred to as *anti-terrorist*, implying a reactive measure to thwart attack, and in time morphed into being seen as *counter-terrorist* measures that projected a more thought-through approach. For instance, it was charged that the U.S.-wide effort to secure 'key' buildings after 9/11 had, in its rather haphazard and makeshift manifestation, prioritised safety of building occupants over regard for social, economic, aesthetic or transportation considerations (Hollander and Whitfield, 2005). Others described how the 'guns, guards, gates' posture adopted in the immediate wake of 9/11 was inappropriate, due to the way such measures 'actually intensify and reinforce public perceptions of siege or vulnerability, and thus heighten the sense of imminent danger and anticipation of attack' (Grosskopf, 2006, p.2). For example, the statutory planning body responsible for Washington, DC immediately expressed concern about 'the hodge podge of solutions that have no aesthetic continuity or urbanistic integrity' and that 'the hastily erected jersey barriers, concrete planters, and guard huts that ring our buildings...communicate fear and retrenchment and undermine the basic premise that underlies a democratic civil society' (NCPC, 2001, p.4). Others further asserted that the defences resembled a construction site – 'the nation's capital has become a fortress city peppered with bollards, bunkers, and barriers' – due both to a lack of funding for 'anything nicer' and a lack of strategic coordination between 'planners and other policy makers' (Benton Short, 2007, p.426).

This pattern of reactive and retrofitted fortification was repeated in many Western cities as reconceptualised terrorist realities led, in some cases, to new and dramatic urban counter-responses. In reality, though many security responses amounted to little more than extrapolations of ongoing crime prevention techniques employed, evoking metaphors of territoriality, to highlight the control of space through urban design modifications and target hardening.

Whilst the impact and counter-response to 9/11 within urban areas was spatially contingent, reflecting both the history and geography of different cities, it was perhaps in London that protective anti-terrorism measures were advanced most thoroughly in practice given the extensive security operations already in situ (Chapter 5). As in the United States, prominent landmark buildings were crudely fortified against vehicle-borne bombs. For example, the U.S. Embassy in central London became a virtual citadel, separated from the rest of London by fencing, waist-high 'concrete blockers', armed guards and mandatory ID cards. Furthermore, in May 2003, in response to a heightened state of alert regarding possible terrorist attack given recent suicide bomb attacks in Saudi Arabia and Morocco,[2] a vast number of waist-high concrete slabs were placed outside the Houses of Parliament to stop car bombers. This so-called 'ring of concrete', which was later painted black to make it more 'aesthetically pleasing' (Figure 6.1), was one of a number of planned fortifications set up in central London to protect prominent buildings (Coaffee, 2004a).

In the City of London, just as in the immediate aftermath of the Docklands bomb in 1996, the ring of steel swung back into full-scale operation, in the wake of 9/11. This was part of a coordinated London-wide operation that saw over 1500 extra police patrolling the streets of the capital in an attempt to reassure the public. In the Square Mile specifically, the police immediately undertook special liaison with U.S. firms to improve their security through extra patrols, as well as instigating a far greater number of stop and search checkpoints.[3] The initial approach adopted in the City, drawing on the previous experiences of terrorist attack, was very much 'vigilant but calm' to avoid a 'siege mentality'. As a Corporation of London Press release stated a day after 9/11:

> The City is carrying on with business as usual. The City of London has had robust security measures in place for many years to deal with any terrorist threat and these are in operation now, as they are 365 days a

Figure 6.1 The ring of concrete established outside the Houses of Parliament.

year. We have been in contact with many businesses across the City and our message to them has been to remain calm, be vigilant and ensure that their own contingency plans are in place.

9/11 refocused the Police's minds on counter-terrorism and added a new dimension to defending the City. As the Commissioner of Police noted, some terrorists, in contrast to previous threats from the Provisional IRA, are *unlikely* 'to be deterred by the high levels of technical surveillance we have successfully used against domestic terrorists who seek to avoid identification, arrest and prosecution as part of their operating methods' (City of London Police, 2002a). Here, the City was preparing for the possibility of a suicide attack, person-borne or vehicle-borne, with the realisation that high levels of technical surveillance, might be ineffective against such terrorist methodologies. As a result, material change in the built environment was increasingly promoted as a key security response to deter terrorism. As a result, from November 2002, specially trained Counter-Terrorist Security Advisors (CTSAs)[4] started working within the City of London Police to provide advice on protective measures that businesses could take to mitigate the impact of terrorism, as well as in assisting with the updating and rehearsal of contingency plans. In the early months of 2003, it was also announced that the Corporation had committed itself to raise the business rate premium for City businesses, to improve security through the further expansion of the 'ring of steel' security cordon.[5]

The war between security and urbanism

Such visible, reactive and often brutal, fortification of cities in the wake of 9/11 illuminated how 'military and geopolitical security now penetrate[d] utterly into practices surrounding governance, design and planning of cities and region' (Graham, 2002b, p.589) and became embedded into everyday urban life. Here, there was a pronounced shift from a Cold War focus on security attained through spatial containment 'to an emphasis on security won through effective spatial administration... that served to blur former binaries such as internal/external and policing and war' (Mitchell, 2010, p.289). The end of the Cold War that also provided the foundation for a surge in the procurement of military technology for civil governance functioning as relatively simple imaginaries of terrorism based on East versus West, gave way to far more complex security environments that characterised the birth of 'new terrorism' (Coaffee et al., 2008).

Such a process whereby the military and civilian spheres begun to hybridise had, however, been in train for decades, with a vast literature developing around the idea of a 'Revolution in Military Affairs' (RMA). The term was initially developed by Soviet academics in the 1970s to depict periods of history – 'military-technical revolutions' – where advances in technology could precipitate new forms of weaponry and military tactics, but, in the post 9/11 world, was increasingly seen to refer to work undertaken on new doctrines of military organisation.[6] Such a doctrine developed in parallel with advances in weapons technology, changing conceptions of the nation state and altered geo-political, social and economic features of globalisation, which, it was argued, would require new forms of future military intervention to cope with new forms of war and terrorist attack (Builder, 1996; Ek, 2000).[7]

Whilst in the 1990s, such RMA advances were predominantly used *offensively* – for example, in the network-centric warfare of the first Gulf War (1991) and its precision-guided munitions, which used advanced military technology to pinpoint precise targets from a distance (hence reducing vulnerability) and in the immediate post-9/11 War on Terror, through ideas of 'full spectrum dominance' – after 9/11, advances were sought to *defensively* to scan the 'homeland', particularly at territorial borders and within urban areas, for potential targets and threats (Dillon and Reid, 2001). Notably, military-style technology was appropriated and used overwhelmingly in cities, resulting in military practices and technologies being more fully merged into civil defence, anti-crime initiatives and counter-terrorism (Coaffee, 2006).[8]

Whilst such a blending of military and civilian are nothing new, in the wake of 9/11 the pervasiveness of military discourse and tactics to secure physical and social space was unprecedented, with the prevalence of ingrained militarised altitudes and activities making any binary between the military and the civilian meaningless (Woodward, 2004). As such, this was not a new type of policy response but rather catastrophic events such as 9/11 making the introduction of military approaches and technologies easier to adopt (politically) in the civic realm. In such a context, the ability of policy makers to analyse the city through a 'military gaze' gave new insights into the risks faced from new security challenges and the possibilities of response. As Crelinsen (2009, p.13) highlighted, counter-terrorism philosophies evolved between September 10 and 12 to become seen in primarily military terms with a war model rather than a criminal justice model dominating. Here, terrorism was viewed as a new form of warfare rather than a criminal act and, deterrence and containment, as the preferred counter-terrorism strategy, gave way to logics of pre-emption and the privileging of the use of force.

Critical urban geopolitics

Defending cities became central to emerging global geopolitics in the wake of 9/11, with a realisation that 'the world's geopolitical struggles increasingly articulate around violent conflicts over very local, urban, strategic sites' (Graham, 2004, p.6) and where 'old defensive responses... seem almost comically irrelevant in this new age of threat' (ibid., p.411). As a result, there was a rapid, emergence of a new body of work on critical urban geopolitics focused on the links between political violence and the built fabric of cities, with the city becoming both the target and the crucible of terrorist action (Graham, 2001; Coaffee, 2003). A number of key features of critical urban geopolitics quickly became central to emerging discourses of counter-terrorism, and the broader War on Terror, and grew out of a critical engagement with existing security work that was being conducted largely in the United Kingdom, United States and Israel/Palestine (Warren, 2004; Coaffee, 2004b; Weizman, 2004). The publication of an edited collection on *Cities, War and Terrorism: Towards an Urban Geopolitics* (Graham, 2004)[9] set the scene for the emergence of this sub-field of study that problematised existing orthodox scholarship in terrorism studies, urban geography and international relations that predominately focused on national, rather than sub-national, spaces and territories. Here attention was upon the 'systematic and planned targeting of cities and urban places' in the post-Cold War and post-9/11 era, the counter-responses in which 'cultures of fear are constructed to impact on debates about urban planning, governance and social policy', and 'how urban areas and organized, military conflict, shape each other' (ibid., p.24).

Whilst reaffirming the inherent historical linkages between war and the city, critical urban geopolitics sought to bring this relationship into the twenty-first century to expose the increased urbanisation of warfare, and in particular, the rise of a *new military urbanism*[10] (Graham, 2010) as a discourse that sought to control urban space in novel ways. Here, as Denman (2020) noted, that whilst traditional territorial defence involved lines of linear defence in depth that slowed attackers and gave more time to defenders, the new military urbanism was based on 'a more expansive sense of anticipatory action'[11] that sought to 'determine distributions of risk contained in possible futures and apply calculative logics to contain, ameliorate, or cancel said risk' (p.243). Security or counter-terrorism measures, in this sense, had a definitive pre-emptive and precautionary logic where perpetual vigilance normalised suspicion and non-calculable risks were central (Ericson, 2008), and where 'risk based calculative models and practices emerg[ed] as a key means of identify vulnerable spaces and suspicious populations in the war on terror' (Amoore and de Geode, 2008, p.6).

9/11 clearly signalled a surge towards an increasingly militarised city although, as Warren (2002) noted, 'it is misleading to assume that these military and paramilitary operations in urban centres began on September 11', rather, the 'War on Terrorism' has served as a prism being used to conflate and further legitimise dynamics *that already were militarising urban space* (p.614, emphasis added). This he continued included:

> ... the revision of long standing military doctrine to accept and rationalize multiple threats within the urban terrain; turning vast areas of cities into zones of video and electronic surveillance; and the repression and control of mass citizen political mobilization in cities. These phenomena have expanded and deepened in the aftermath of September 11.
>
> (ibid.)

As the need for security became rescaled away from the traditional territories of nation states and Cold War blocs, and towards the homeland and the spaces of the city, security destabilised existing conventions and led to an 'implosion of global and national politics into the urban world' (Graham, 2004, p.6). In the immediacy of the 9/11 attack, the rhetoric was very much that of 'cities under siege' (Catterall, 2001) or of 'cities as target' (Bishop and Clancey, 2004). Security, in this sense, became heavily *re*territorialised to focus on the 'homeland' and its critical national infrastructure that would usher in dramatic changes for everyday life. As argued at the time, the concept of security was 'coming home' with the discourses, procedures and material examples of national and international security were seen to be influencing, or were directly employed, at smaller scales alongside a wider ecology of fear (Coaffee and Murakami Wood, 2006, p.514).

The resulting intensified militarisation of the city had significant effects beyond the visible security hardware that was deployed, and served to influence the wider narrative in the domestic front in the War on Terror, where militarised discourses of 'homeland security' begun to permeate and reshape the civic realm and public policy debates (Graham, 2004, p.11). Here, security became an umbrella policy of nations and cities and permeated a range of everyday practices, ranging from urban planning, migration, social care and schooling and, in many ways, ratcheted up urban fear and insecurity that already plagued many cities (Davis, 1998).[12] Signs of terrorism were to be found, the public was told, in the most banal settings such as in parked cars, trash bins or a carried backpack (Katz, 2004).

Everyday urban security

As a result of the overwhelming centrality of security to urban life, accounts of post-9/11 cities tended to present bleak portrayals and worst-case scenario options that depicted hyper-intensification of security and anti-terrorist defences, which, if constructed, could mean the virtual death of the urban areas as functioning entities. Such accounts were articulated in three main ways, linked to prior trends of utilising principles of defensive design, increasing the use of technological surveillance and advancing exceptional legal and social measures where civil liberties took a back seat to security enhancement.

Defensible space revisited

Immediately after 9/11, some commentators argued that it was time that planners, developers and architects began to consider safety and damage limitation against terrorism when designing cities, particularly in relation to individual structures that were seen, in many cases, as ill-prepared to withstand a bomb blast (Hall, 2001). There were also concerns raised that counter-terrorist defences, if constructed, could result in the virtual death of the urban areas as functioning entities. More broadly, 9/11 heralded many discussions regarding how major cities might look and function in the future if the threat of terrorism persisted. In particular, there was an immediate reassessment of the viability of building iconic skyscrapers, with some even predicting their demise altogether due to the fears of building occupiers, with one commenter noting:

> The construction of glamorous ever-higher trophy skyscrapers will stop; the towers in Kuala Lumpur and Frankfurt have already felt the threat, closing and evaluating the day after the World Trade Center collapse; workers in the Empire State building in New York and the Sears Tower in Chicago are already reported to be afraid to go up to their offices.
> (Marcuse, 2001, p.395)

Kunstler and Salingaros (2001) in *The End of Tall Buildings* went further, predicting that 'no new megatowers will be built' and existing ones disassembled in a 'radical transformation of city centers...' In this vein, it was argued, after 9/11, that we might see 'the massive growth of relatively anonymous, low level fortressed business spaces' (Graham, 2001, p.414). Very quickly, this tendency to sound the death knell of 'building tall' was proved incorrect as skyscraper construction continued apace (Coaffee, 2003).

Others suggested that dispersal of key functions away from city centres could be a further spatial impact of 9/11. This was equated to 'defensive dispersal' in reaction to the Cold War fear of nuclear attack on American cities (Bishop and Clancey, 2004). For example, Vidler (2001a) writing in the *New York Times* on 'A City Transformed: Designing Defensible Space', alluding to Oscar Newman's classic work, hypothesised about the nature of experiencing future city life, noting that:

> The terrorist attack on the World Trade Center is propelling a civic debate over whether to change the way Americans experience and ultimately build upon urban public spaces. Are a city's assets – density, concentration, monumental structures – still alluring? Will a desire for 'defensible space' radically transform the city as Americans know it?

Vidler (2001b) further argued that urban fear might overwhelm the attraction of density leading to an 'understandable impulse to flee', for cities to disperse to suburbia in search of 'space and security', and questioned whether 'dispersal rather than concentration will be the pattern of life and work and where monumental forms of building will give way to camouflaged sheds, or dispersed all together into home offices?'

Other observers addressed the potential urban impacts of 9/11, highlighting both the potential desire to flee the city and the continual need for business clustering. Peter Marcuse (2002b), for example, hypothesised about a number of potential consequences for urban economies and the real estate industry, which he argued could further increase the partitioning of urban space. The net result he argued 'might be described as a decentralization of key business activities and their attendant services, but to very concentrated off-center locations in close proximity to the major centres' (ibid., p.596). This he referred to as 'concentrated decentralisation'. He further anticipated that in both these new areas of activity, and the older areas of concern (such as crime), increased 'barricading' and control of activities in public places would occur, as well as a 'citadelisation' of businesses and exclusive residences. In short, he noted, 'security becomes the justification for measures that threaten the core of urban social and political life, from the physical barricading of space to the social barricading of democratic activity' (Marcuse, 2002a, p.276).

In essence, this was 1990s fortress urbanism rewritten in response to terrorist threats and led to initially to reactive and temporary security measures to be put in place to protect key buildings and spaces. As previously noted, there were also concerns regarding the impact that such anti-terrorist features may have upon the urban fabric and for the permeability and liveability of places. In Washington, DC, guidance was issued in the month proceeding 9/11 with a view to creating a comprehensive security plan that promoted accessibility alongside defence (NCPC, 2001). In this plan, a number of key goals were highlighted in an active attempt to avoid such 'fortress' style security, including providing an appropriate balance security for sensitive buildings and the vitality of the public realm; delivering security in the context of streetscape enhancement; avoiding the monotony of endless lines of Jersey barriers or bollards, which only evoke defensiveness; and providing security in a manner that does not impede the city's commerce and vitality, or pedestrian and vehicular mobility (p.2). The subsequent National Capital Urban Design and Security Plan (2002) *Designing and Testing of Perimeter Security Elements* further detailed an inherent tension between 'escalating threat assessments and potentially extreme security responses' that undermine the 'objectives for a vibrant capital city that showcases democratic ideals of openness and accessibility' (p.A-8).

However, in the immediate aftermath of 9/11, and in proceeding years, obtrusive 'target hardening' became the defensive strategy of choice in many U.S. cities. This pattern of reactive and retrofitted fortification was also repeated in many countries where 'defences' were constructed at key government and business sites in a drive to induce confidence in employees and investors (Coaffee, 2004a). Such interventions, though often crude, were seen as effective in that they prohibited the penetration of targets and limited the permeability of spaces by potential perpetrators of attacks.

The promise of technological fixes in the watchful city

The relationship between surveillance and subjectivity, observed by Foucault in the modern period, continued to evolve rapidly in the wake of 9/11, as surveillance mechanisms became increasingly central to the monitoring of everyday life in many Western cities with an increasing convergence of surveillance strategies aimed at tackling both crime and terrorism. As Fussey (2007, p.121) noted in relation to the U.K., this trend continued with 'surveillance technologies increasingly introduced and legitimized in terms of counter-terrorism, and this association is routinely projected onto the public consciousness through such occurrences as the posthumous CCTV footage of the London suicide bombers following July 7, 2005'.

In a short space of time after 9/11, there was widespread evidence that the 'creep' of surveillance and other methods of social control were beginning to 'surge' in response to the new terrorist threat (Wood et al., 2003). David Lyon (2003), in *Surveillance after September 11,* presented a meticulous account of how different aspects of surveillance were advanced and integrated in the city after 9/11. First, that the reaction to 9/11 brought to the surface and clarified a number of pre-existing trends that had been developing relatively unnoticed. Second, that 9/11 provided an opportunity to give 'some already existing ideas, policies and technologies their chance' (ibid., p.4), and which became legitimised through public acceptance and new legislative powers. Ominously, Lyon noted that the result is that the response to 9/11, 'speed up and spread out such surveillance in ways that bode ill for democracy, personal liberties, social trust and mutual care' (ibid., p.5–6). In the post-9/11 city there were particular fears that the burgeoning of increasingly automated and hi-tech surveillance systems would evolve and further erode civil liberties, as democratic and ethical accountability was given a back seat in the commodification of surveillance.

Here, the technological drive to develop digital, automated and biometric systems, sometimes covering entire urban terrains, was often implanted with high-grade military technologies (Lyon, 2002; Introna and Wood, 2004). The Automated Number Plate Recognition system used by the City of London Police since 1997 in their 'ring of steel' (Chapter 5) provided a perfect example of such a system, that according to some (Rosen, 2001) would be reinforced by biometric (facial recognition) cameras as a result of 9/11.[13] This was a system that had the most advanced (at the time) military technologies developed during the 1991 Gulf War embedded within it, and which was extended across central London for use in traffic 'congestion charging' post 9/11 (Coaffee, 2004a). This system became operational in February 2003, using 450 cameras in 230 different positions.[14] In essence, central London became encircled by digital cameras, creating a dedicated 'surveillance ring' affording London's police forces vast surveillance gathering capabilities for tracking the movement of traffic and people, and by inference highlighting potential terrorist threats. It was further alleged that MI5, Special Branch and the Metropolitan Police began secretly developing the system in the wake of the September 11 attacks', creating 'one of the most daunting defence systems protecting a major world city' (Townsend and Harris, 2003). Not surprisingly, civil libertarians felt misled over this hidden use for London's scheme, which was solely promoted as an attempt to beat traffic congestion. Additionally in London, new types of high-tech camera algorithms were also developed, aimed at pre-event disruption through the identification of suspicious behaviour.[15] Notably, in response to the Madrid train bombings in 2004, parts of the London Underground trialled a 'smart' CCTV surveillance software system that aimed to automatically alert operators to 'suspicious' behaviour, unattended packages and potential suicide bombing attempts on the tube system.[16]

Across the Atlantic, it was reported, in July 2003, that the Pentagon was developing a digitalised surveillance network capable of tracking the movements of all vehicles in a city by identifying them by physical characteristics, colour, or the biometric features of the driver. This expansive 'tracking system' was also mainstreaming military technology for non-combat use (Sniffen, 2003) and, as Lyon (2003) noted of this comprehensive 'Total Information Awareness' scheme:

> ...the data-mining technologies had been available for some time in commercial settings, but until 9/11 no plausible reason existed for deploying them – and the customer data that they analyse – within a national security apparatus. The drive towards large-scale, integrated systems for identifying and checking persons in places such as airports and at borders, urged for years by technology companies, received its rationale as the twin towers tumbled.
>
> (p.4–5)

Further accounts of the potential role of advanced surveillance networks took such systems to extremes in adaptations of 'pervasive', 'ubiquitous' or 'ambient' computing (Cuff, 2003). Right-wing commentators in the United States went as far as to demand a war between 'our silicon' and 'their sons' and argued that a pervasive automated surveillance apparatus of micro-sensors would allow cities like New York 'to watch and track everything that moves [and] just about anything that may interest us – the passage of vehicles, the odor of explosives, the conversations of pedestrians, the look, sound, weight, temperature, even the smell, of almost anything' (Huber and Mills, 2002). More critical commentators further illuminated the potential for such systems to enable the 'automatic production of space' (Thrift and French, 2002) that could 'start to inscribe normative ecologies of acceptable people and behaviour' within the everyday city (Graham, 2002b, p.241). Ultimately, the development of such systems were dogged by inaccurate test results and it wasn't until 2006/2007 in New York that the Lower Manhattan Security Initiative sought to create a 'surveillance veil' to 'detect, track and deter terrorists' (Buckley, 2007) using hundreds of wireless police cameras, supplemented by thousands of private CCTV (see Chapter 12).

Social impacts and authoritarian politics

In the post-9/11 city, the enactment and changing governance of intensified security measures eroded civil liberties in the new era of 'anxious urbanism' (Farish, 2002), both in terms of the restriction of public access that many protective security measures necessitated and, concerns over privacy, monitoring and accountability of newly deployed technologies. The United States undoubtedly took the global lead in the legislative reform around counter-terrorism, throwing the agenda of balancing civil liberties and state security centre stage with the swift passing of the Uniting and Strengthening America by Providing Appropriate Tools Required to Intercept and Obstruct Terrorism (Patriot) Act 2001, supported with the establishment of the Department of Homeland Security (DHS) in 2002. The DHS, in particular, also acted as a focus for a critical appraisal by the civil rights movement in the United States, which questioned how democracies could fight terrorism, and still remain democratic? (Chang, 2002)

Whilst much commentary on the consequences of 9/11 for urban life focused heavily on the physical changes that might occur, or the technology that might be installed as a result of the increased militarisation of the city, equally important, but less emphasised, were the potential social impacts that were foreseen. Marcuse (2001), for example, argued that social polarisation on the basis of income and race would be exacerbated by the reaction to 9/11 'with the focus of upper income disproportionately white households concentrated in more tightly controlled citadels, and others more and more excluded and segregated, with sharper dividing lines between and among groups' (p.395). The same argument, he argued, applied to public space that will become increasingly privatised and 'tightly controlled', through CCTV and regulated in terms of access restrictions. In short, 'democratic conduct' by all would be an essential ingredient of a counter-terrorist response to maintain the quality of city life. A year later, Marcuse (2002b) illustrated ways this increased power of the state in urban development and formal planning process would come to represent the concerns of an increasingly elite group of participants (in this case the security services and police) at the expense of wider community concerns. Wood et al. (2003, p.144) further described this as part of the ever-growing 'cross-fertilization' between the military and the managerial where, in the governance of urban areas, new languages, logics and practices of security emerged to spatially administer, rather than necessary contain, the emergent terrorist threat.

For others, security measures put in place based on ideas of managing exceptionality, actually intensified and reinforced public perceptions of vulnerability, and heightened 'the sense of imminent danger and anticipation of attack' (Grosskopf, 2006, p.1). 9/11 thus provoked an immediate, yet somewhat incongruous, response in an attempt to protect buildings, despite the fact that the events of that day were virtually impossible to defend against. Perhaps understandably, responses were, for the most part, driven by a sense of urgency and a heightened degree of threat. In particular, politicians felt it important for the public to feel reassured that the state was responding to the threat in a robust way. This was notably manifest through overt physical security in public places – a politically easy 'quick-win'. That said, it was quite apparent that such a balance – between reassurance and 'scaring' the public – was difficult to strike, with it later being suggested that any measures taken by authorities, or those responsible for leading counter-terrorism efforts, must accept a certain degree of risk and prepare the public for the possibility that an attack might happen.

There were similar concerns raised with regard to the impact that counter-terrorism features have upon public accessibility and the permeability of city space. For instance, Benton-Short (2007), reflecting on the reaction in the United States to 9/11, concluded that issues of terrorism and national security have 'trumped' concerns regarding public access. Referring specifically to the Washington Mall as a national commemorative space and a stage for political protest, she questioned how the need for improved security can be 'translated into acceptable levels of fortification and the potential loss of public space' (p.424). This global trend of highly visible security and fortress architecture, she further argued, has a deeply symbolic impact and is often 'elevated to represent a national discourse of war, fear, and entrenchment' (p.431) that dominates national political discourse.

Other writers interrogated this post-9/11 tension between security and liberty through a more philosophical lens. Paul Virilio (2002b) argued at the time that and society, under the influence of the 24-hour media and an increasingly military logic, has created a local and global politics that precludes the possibility of negotiation and diplomacy, as responses must be immediate. In short, this equalled the 'end of reflection', where speed of response to terror threat was prioritised over deliberative decision-making as those with responsibility for security felt compelled to act swiftly (Coaffee, 2005). This, Virilio noted, necessitated an authoritarian politics:

> The place of politics in ancient societies was the public space ... Today the public image prevails over public space ... We are heading towards a cathode democracy, but without rules ... No politics is possible at the scale of the speed of light. Politics depends on having time for reflection. Today, we no longer have time to reflect, the things that we see have already happened. And it is necessary to react immediately. Is real-time democracy possible? An authoritarian politics. Yes....
>
> (2002b, 42–43)

Conclusions: Normalising fear in the wake of 9/11

The post-9/11 reaction to international terrorism exposed global security fears and drew a distinction between terrorist *attacks* and the terrorist *threat*, the latter becoming 'universal as a result of it' (Beck, 2002, p.46–47). Subsequently, the urban response was to intensify and legitimatise the ongoing securitisation of everyday life as a result of the pervasive fear of imminent attack and, in so doing, embed anxiety into artefacts of everyday life. This new military urbanism logic, as Graham (2010) noted, was based on 'the idea that new military ideologies of permanent and boundless war are radically intensify the militarisation of urban life…[and] *also involve the normalisation of military paradigms of thought, action and policy*' (p.60, emphasis added).

In the wake of 9/11 a 'culture of fear' in security decision-making pervaded that became increasingly focused on a 'security first' response taken by increasingly reactive decision-makers (Briggs, 2005). Initially, this was supported by the public. For example, in the direct aftermath of 9/11, 80% of Americans questioned in a *New York Times/CBS* poll indicated they were prepared to have less personal freedom if it meant the country as a whole could be made more secure from further terrorist attack (cited in Rosen, 2001). However, the potential impact, broadening scale, and unquantifiable nature of global terrorism, combined with political leader's claims of 'unique' and 'classified' knowledge of potential threats, increasingly justified the implementation of a raft of security policies that excluded civic consultation. Relatedly, the role of the private sector in homeland security and the effective 'marketisation of fear' were also further exposed by 9/11 as military and security firms rushed 'to exploit the nation's nervous breakdown' (Davis, 2001b).[17]

The use of a sense of impending risk and danger and the deployment of popular political and cultural narratives to gain public consent for enacting new civic policy is not a new political strategy. Earlier work by Massumi (1993, p.viii) argued that a low-level 'ambient' fear had infiltrated everyday life, highlighting how the materiality of the body and associated emotions are ultimately objects of 'technologies of fear' or of policy responses to perceived threats. Likewise, Deleuze (1992) highlighted that since the end of World War II, a new society – the society of control – had replaced the pre-war disciplinary society in which 'enclosures' maintained order through the management of wages and discipline, or, other regulatory networks. In a society of control, everyday control was seen as more pervasive, but hidden, and was, according to Hardt and Negri (2002, p.23), 'characterized by an intensification and generalization of the normalizing apparatuses of disciplinarity that internally animate our common and daily practices'. During the War on Terror, we have subsequently seen concepts of governing through technologies of risk supplement disciplinary control and, ideas of governmentality and biopolitics replace sovereignty and geo-politics, as governments sought to control risky populations and secure at risk places and, more broadly, ensure 'the appearance of securability and manageability is sustained' (Amoore and de Goede, 2008, p.9).

Overall, 9/11 forced urban leaders and security professionals to think more carefully when balancing security with mobility and risk with recklessness as they sought to incorporate both democracy and risk management responses in the new age of terrorism that cast a fearful shadow over urban life. Such a delicate balancing act posed serious consequences for urbanity and the civic realm, and in particular for social control and freedom of movement. Ultimately, it appeared that 'fear and urbanism were at war' (Swanstrom, 2002). Here, being prepared for the worst in terms of future, often unspecified, threat became a key driver of state security policy (Coaffee, 2006). As Elmer and Opel (2006, p.477) highlighted in the post-9/11 world 'what if' scenarios, relating to the likelihood of Western States being attacked, were replaced by 'when, then' scenarios where the inevitability of further attack was assumed, and pre-planned for. Such anticipatory logic further provided the justification for affirmative and pre-emptive action to remove unwanted or dangerous 'elements' and secure the homeland.

In some cases, State responses, in the ongoing War on Terror were critiqued as being deliberate attempts to heighten fear. For example, Massumi's (2005) work on the U.S. 5 colour-code public threat assessment system argued that the 'aim' of the alert system was to 'calibrate the public's anxiety', 'modulate' the fear of imminent attack and 'trigger' the public into action:

> The alert system was introduced to calibrate the public's anxiety. In the aftermath of 9/11, the public's fearfulness had tended to swing out of control in response to dramatic, but maddeningly vague, government warnings of an impending follow-up attack. The alert system was designed to modulate that fear. It could raise it a pitch, then lower it before it became too intense, or even worse, before habituation dampened response. Timing was everything. Less fear itself than fear fatigue became an issue of public concern. Affective modulation of the

populace was now an official, central function of an increasingly time-sensitive government.

(p.31)

This system, noted Massumi, was solely 'designed to make visible the government's much advertised commitment to fighting the "war" on terror ...' (p.33).

Since 2001, and against the context of the subsequent interventionist Western foreign and security policy, scholars and policy makers have discussed, in often rather reactionary terms, the counter-response to fear of further terrorist attacks. Here attention was seen to be increasingly being turned away from the Cold War orthodoxy and universal concerns with national security, military intervention and territorial integrity, and towards more nuanced ideas about global and local risk and interventions to ensure homeland security. In this situation, a universalising of fear of terrorist attack and a new politics of fear became crucial in developing responses to what is seen as an *inevitable* attack. Davis (2001, p.389), in an article on *The Future of Fear*, argued that fear and a reduction in civil liberties will ensue, especially in American cities, where 'deep anxieties about their personal safety may led millions of otherwise humane Americans to invest in the blind trust of the revamped National Security State'. Similarly, Jackson (2005) argued that the normalisation and institutionalisation of War on Terror counter-terrorism approaches has, and will continue to, damage democratic participation and undermine ethical values. As will be illuminated in subsequent chapters, the often exceptional ideas and practices underpinning urban security interventions have been embraced, and increasingly normalised, as a result of the scale and magnitude of counter-terrorism interventions that became embedded in the built form of cities, used to monitor and track everything that moves, communicated through an array of policy guidance and regulatory measures, and, made a permanent technology of government in a War on Terror without end.

Notes

1 The subsequent report – *Designing for Security in the Nation's Capital* – was hastily put out for consultation in October 2001, with a revised version issued in October 2002.
2 On May 16, 2003, Islamic terrorists, reportedly linked to Al Qaeda, rampaged through the streets of Casablanca, Morocco slitting the throats of security guards before detonating suicide bombs at five targets including bars and restaurants. At least 41 were killed and over 100 more injured. This attack had clear parallels with similar attacks in the Saudi capital, Riyadh, a few days beforehand which killed 34 people.
3 The Corporation of London also re-examined its own emergency procedures through collaboration with key private sector institutions and security professionals, as well as recommending to all businesses that they reassess their contingency plans with the help of the City Police (Coaffee, 2003).

4 CTSAs have been used to varying degrees in all Police Forces in the United Kingdom since 2002. The nationwide network of CTSAs is coordinated through the National Counter-Terrorism Security Office (NaCTSO). In advance of 2002, the City of London and Metropolitan Police had a series of Counter-Terrorism Crime Prevention Officers.
5 Corporation of London News Release – 'Committee recommends new business rate premium for City policing and a bigger "ring of steel' 18 February 2003'.
6 Notably by the RAND Corporation in the United States.
7 In particular, in the post-Cold War period, a reappraisal of new threats in the new world order were carried out by the American military and identified a large spectrum of potential threats (especially those from 'catastrophic terrorism') which came from non-traditional sources and, which required new and counter-responses.
8 Bernazzoli and Flint (2009) further highlighted a broad range of work on militarisation and militarism that was seen both as a continuation of traditional security apparatus, as well as a distinct form of security management.
9 This collection came out of a conference on *Cities as Strategic Sites: Militarization, Anti-Globalisation and Warfare* – Salford University, United Kingdom, held between November 6 and 9, 2002.
10 Many have argued that there is nothing new about military urbanism, pointing to the long history of relationships between military operations and the city (Betz, 2016).
11 Including pre-emption, precaution and preparedness (Anderson, 2010).
12 The need to defend the homeland, led to many anti-cosmopolitan polices and legal restrictions being adopted domestically to restrict the activities of certain urban diasporas and to identify hidden domestic enemies (Howell and Shryock, 2003).
13 This predication failed to materialise until the late 2010s (see Chapter 12).
14 All number plate images were captured when entering the zone and automatically matched against a database of those who are registered to pay or have exemption. Other cameras monitored the general flow of traffic throughout the area, with further mobile camera patrols operating throughout the zone.
15 This is potentially an important development given the clear indication that traditional surveillance is no deterrent against the new breed of urban ('suicide') terrorist.
16 The implementation of this system followed extensive trials, which initially had little to do with terrorism and pre-dated 9/11. The original intention was to develop a crowd flow monitoring system that morphed into something more as its potential to spot those waiting on station platforms to commit suicide, was realised.
17 Cited in Savitch (2008, p.149).

Part 3
The longer term implications of 9/11

7 Normal protective streetscapes

Introduction: Towards security-driven streetscapes

Defending vulnerable urban spaces of Western cities against the ever-changing nature of international terrorism has long occupied state security services but, until 9/11, the selective nature of targets under threat meant that this has seldom had major impacts on everyday life in the city, or, on the practice of built environment professionals, such as planners, civil engineers and architects. The events of 9/11 ushered in a new era in protective counterterrorist planning with crowded public spaces such as sports stadia, shopping malls, prominent streets, hotels and public squares, becoming a key priority. This reflected the changing modus operandi of terrorists that, since the millennium, had encompassed not only vehicle bombs targeting major financial or political centres, but also person-borne improvised explosive devices – especially suicide attacks – and subsequently, Fedayeen-style mass shooting attacks. These operations typically focused on mass casualty strikes or multiple coordinated attacks, aimed at 'soft targets' and, more generally, congested locations where terrorists attacked the 'urban body of the crowd' (Aradau, 2015, p.155).

Consequently, traditional territorial anti-terrorism approaches were rethought. As noted in Chapter 6, the initial implementations of security measures to counter such threats, and to manage post-9/11 anxieties, were reactive and focused upon the physical robustness and resistance of engineered security systems and were manifested through highly visible fortress-like security at high-risk sites. At this time, such security processes involved limited engagement with the built environment professions such as urban planners and architects who could have advised about design options and spatial layout (Coaffee, 2003).

Materially, the erection of steel barriers or crash-rated bollards around key sites exemplified this highly territorial response to security through attempts to *design out* terrorism and restrict vehicular traffic access to such locations. While the need to protect 'assets' within urban areas was necessarily reactive and obtrusive, it also served an economic and political purpose in terms of visibly demonstrating that the state or private security was acting to protect

DOI: 10.4324/9780429461620-10

valuable parts of nation from terrorism (Briggs, 2005). For many, however, this approach was seen as disproportionate to the uncertain security threats facing cities (Coaffee, 2010) and, in time, new counter-terrorist urban designs emerged that were increasingly camouflaged and subtlety embedded within the cityscape. These new approaches, focused upon *designing-in* security, have subsequently been embedded within many national and citywide security and counter-terrorism strategies.[1]

These more subtle protective measures tried to balance the effectiveness and robustness of security interventions with their acceptability to the general public and the impact on the everyday experience of the city. For example, in the year following 9/11, iconic locations in Manhattan, New York, were subject to security redesign due to fears of attack. Initially, this was most noticeable around the Stock Exchange/Wall Street district where an area-based security scheme to keep vehicles out was carefully planned. Here temporary bollards and concrete Jersey barriers were replaced with bronze 'no-go' barriers, and where vehicular access was required, crash-rated bollards[2] were placed atop turntables (see Figure 7.1). The project designed by Rogers Architects received praise for its comprehensive security-driven streetscape design response in urban dense conditions that combined cultural, historical and financial landmarks into a security plan.

Figure 7.1 Security bollards placed on turntables to allow vehicle access. Bronze 'no-go' blockers were placed on either side.

Normal protective streetscapes 121

The integration of security into overall streetscape design can be further exemplified by more recent mitigation measures put in place in Times Square, New York – one of the densest and most visited public areas in the United States – that has more recently been transformed from a congested vehicular space to a largely pedestrianised location in the name of enhancing security. The Times Square area has, from 2013, seen security embedded in its redesign of the public realm, replacing the large blocks of concrete that were used to restrict access to this space. This design scheme was premised on security advice received in 2012 and 2013 that noted vulnerabilities from vehicles used either accidentally or intentionally to cause harm. Specifically, the threat was seen to come from a number of sources: drunken drivers, drivers who lost control of their vehicles as well as terrorists who planned to leave car bombs in the Square (as they did in 2010) or to drive into crowds.

Through the use of strategically placed street furniture and pedestrianised landscaping the area has, as far as possible, limited the opportunity for vehicle access whilst not detracting from the vibrancy of the space. Two main elements combined to make Times Square more secure from vehicle attacks – bollards and granite seating – that were agreed in a new security plan in January 2013. As noted in the media, Times Square was to get 'Belts of Steel and Granite'.[3] Importantly for designers Snøhetta, security requirements in the plaza were integrated into the overall design:

> Our method has been to protect the plaza areas while also using design elements that don't overwhelm the public experience. We wanted to be sure safety measures did not define the public space while also creating highly effective protective features in the most populated areas. Bollards, in connection with other integrated security features, form the basis of the security design for the plaza.[4]

The 200+ bollards installed were also designed to blend in with other stainless steel elements in the wider landscaping plan. In addition to the fixed, but removable, security bollards, 10-15-metre long granite benches that act as 'hostile vehicle mitigation' barriers were fitted to define and frame the area's public plazas, 'act as a magnet for visitors, create an infrastructural spine for events, and provide a clear orientation device for tourists and locals alike' (see Figure 7.2).[5]

The Times Square Alliance, which runs the local business improvement district and commissioned the plan, noted in 2013, at the start of the security master plan construction phase, that the proposals sort to balance reasonable protection with keeping the city's most symbolic and visible public space both open and appealing. Here, they tried to move beyond the imposition of over numerous 'ugly' concrete blockers and embed security in more innovative ways within the streetscape as part of wider landscaping plans.[6]

The integrated security design of Times Square design builds on and showcases a number of key features of counter-terrorism philosophy as applied

122 *The longer term implications of 9/11*

Figure 7.2 Granite benches sited in the newly pedestrianised Times Square.[7]

to the protection of crowded areas that emerged in the early part of the new millennium: the need to integrate effective protective security into the design of at-risk sites; the increased importance of built environment professionals such as planners, architects and urban designers in security planning; and the need to consider the visible impact of security measures and, where appropriate, make these as unobtrusive as possible. These questions of *proportionality*, *collective responsibility* and, in particular, *visibility* of protective counter-terrorism security, will be addressed as the chapter progresses and their impacts on the everyday streetscape highlighted.[8]

Within this emerging context, the remainder of the chapter will be undertaken in four main sections. The first section will highlight the changing terrorist philosophies deployed against Western cities that were laid bare by 9/11 and subsequent attacks. Here the focus on 'soft targets' by dynamic no-warning attacks was seen to present a significantly new security challenge. Second, the chapter interrogates, what at the time was, an emerging aspect of critical terrorism studies – namely the relationship between space, politics and aesthetics, emphasised in a so-called literary and aesthetic turn in security studies and international relations – as well as critical work in human geography on the politics of aesthetics. Here, particular concern was placed on the role of the cityscape in mirroring state security policy, but also how such visual symbolism is perceived/received by different audiences. Third, these ideas are related to an analysis of state security policy in the United Kingdom and the United States emerging from the reaction to 9/11.[9] The implications of this are explored through a 'continuum of visible security' that showcases a mixed rhetoric related to how counter-terrorism security features at some sites are expected to be obtrusive, whilst at other sites conspicuous security is required for such measures to be publically acceptable. Using examples drawn from attempts in the early-mid 2000s to embed counter-terrorism features into contemporary streetscapes, this section unpacks the appearance and symbolic impact of both visible and more 'invisible' forms of security interventions.[10] The fourth section reasserts the importance of understanding the variety of ways in which security features are 'read' by different stakeholders, the implications for everyday urban experience, as well as how protective security and counter-terrorism policy has evolved in a more sensitive way at the urban scale.

Changing terrorist philosophies and the strategic protection of soft targets

In the new millennium, the modus operandi of international terrorists became increasingly fluid and transcended national borders. Ever advancing communications also meant that tactics and targeting options could be exchanged more readily. This situation inevitably meant that Western security services paid increased attention to the techniques of non-Western terrorism, given the fear of the migration of terror tactics to the Western city. Media reports in the early years of the millennium highlighted a plethora of vehicle- or person-borne (suicide) attacks in Iraq, Afghanistan and elsewhere, targeting crowded public places such as markets, schools, hotels and hospitals, as well as sites of symbolic and iconic value such as religious and tourist locations. These types of 'spectacular' attack (often seen by many as synonymous with Al Qaeda) aimed to maximise causalities and garner media exposure, and, utilised multiple coordinated attacks that often relied on hostage-taking.

Subsequent high profile and lethal attacks involving suicide bombers and/or vehicle bombs served to reinforce this view. Such terrorist events, notably attacks by Islamic terrorists associated with Al Qaeda included assaults against nightclubs frequented by Westerners in Bali, Indonesia, in 2002, killing 202 people[11]; simultaneous, coordinated bombings against the commuter train network in Madrid, Spain, in 2004 (11-M), killing 198 people[12]; coordinated suicide attacks on the transport system in London in 2005 (7/7), killing 56 people[13]; and the marauding gun and grenade attacks in Mumbai, India, in 2008 (India's 9/11) that killed 170 people.[14] Such attacks increasingly saw national security policy being rearticulated in terms of the need to respond proactively and to develop pre-emptive security solutions focused upon both the physical design of streetscape elements and the associated management systems associated with popular urban locations (Coaffee et al., 2008b).

Traditional emergency planning and counter-terrorist strategies were rethought given the increased appreciation of the multiple and fluid threats faced from international terrorism (Silke, 2004). Although this was initially framed in terms of the fear from chemical, biological, radiological or nuclear (CBRN) attack, the threat posed by no-warning, and often person-borne explosive devices in a multitude of crowded public places also began to set significant new challenges for security agencies, signifying a shift in targeting emphasis from 'hard' to 'soft' targets. Whilst at this time debate continued about the relationship between new and traditional threats, the methods and tactics adopted by terror groups were seen as novel, innovative and increasingly focused on mass casualty strikes or multiple coordinated attacks (Coaffee et al., 2008b) that necessitated novel counter-responses.

The targets of choice – crowded areas – had features in common most notably their easy accessibility that couldn't be altered without radically changing citizen experience of such largely public places. In the U.K., such crowded places were defined by the Home Office (2009, p.11) as

> sites [which] are regarded as locations or environments to which members of the public have access that, on the basis of intelligence, credible threat or terrorist methodology, may be considered potentially liable to terrorist attack by virtue of their crowd density.[15]

Protective policies for enhancing streetscape security

Following the initial reaction to post-9/11 security threats, many nations advanced detailed national security and counter-terrorism strategies that attempted to interface with broader urban planning and design agendas. This developed quickest in the United Kingdom and the United States. In the U.S., as has been noted in previous chapters, significant terrorist attacks on American soil and internationally in the 1990s had led to planning and building regulations for implementation protective security being introduced for federal buildings. This requirement was reaffirmed in the wake of 9/11 with an imperative to install security bollards and barriers to limit street access and to fit a wide variety of additional security devices into the cityscape. This did, however, pose a question on how to secure non-federal buildings and spaces in ways that did not make the built environment sterile, devoid of public activities and fortress-like in appearance. For example, one planning study in central New York argued that the anti-terror concerns of the owners and building managers 'have closed streets and fitted the surrounding space with concrete barriers, bollards and moat-like structures to prevent potential terror attacks' with such ubiquity that they can be considered a new type of land use. In this instance, it was argued that over 25% of public space in and around other buildings had, over recent years, been developed into a 'security zone' representing a rapid shrinking on public space (Nemeth and Hollander, 2010). Moreover, federal buildings 'must obey' design instructions that were initiated in the 1990s – and included setting the building back from the street; limiting the number of entrances; removing first floor windows;

having no underground car parks; and barrier protection around the site – conflicted with urban planning and design approaches of the early 2000s based on principles of new urbanism that encouraged compact development, accessibility, convivial public spaces and mixed-use developments.

Quickly after 9/11, overt security measures had become an everyday part of the landscape in nearly all American cities, and applied on an ad hoc basis, without regard for their wider impacts. As previously noted, in the short term, such measures could be justified in the interests of homeland security, but in the medium and longer term, adverse effects on economic and social life became apparent. Here, urban planners, specifically, were asked to confront and replace piecemeal approaches to security with ones that were more strategic and design sensitive. Such a planning approach, although nonmandatory, began to emerge in the early 2000s and was crystallised in the American Planning Association (APA) *Policy Guide on Security*, published in 2005. In this guidance, responding to the threat of terrorism was seen as a collective responsibility, and that it was

> imperative for planners, working in concert with first responders and other allied professionals, to facilitate the participation of all stakeholders and agencies to minimize security-related risks' and maintain a balance between security and personal freedom that enhances the quality of life.
> (APA, 2005)

These security efforts were explicitly set within the context of past planning efforts such as Jacob's eyes on the street, Newman's defensible space, Jeffery's Crime Prevention Through Environmental Design (CPTED) and more recent work connected to ideas of new urbanism called 'safe growth' (Zelinka and Brennanm, 2001; Coaffee and Bosher, 2008). The overall approach advocated by the APA further sought to promote effective collaboration in security planning among planners, architects and other design professionals working closely with emergency managers and first responders, so that security needs and concerns are integrated into the overall planning process and undertaken in a comprehensive fashion rather than stand-alone security interventions on a building-by-building basis.

This approach was exemplified by overarching security plans produced for the monumental core of Washington, DC, where planning guidance was issued by the National Capital Planning Commission (NCPC, 2001, 2002, 2004), in an attempt to create security that complemented, or even promoted, vistas, open spaces, accessibility and the iconographic significance of the city (NCPC, 2002, p.1). In 2007, the Federal Emergency Management Authority (part of the Department of Homeland Security) further outlined several core aspirations of better perimeter security design that focused upon 'streetscape enhancement and public realm beautification, rather than as a separate or redundant system of components whose only purpose is security' (FEMA, 2007, p.s4-1/4-2).

Protection and balance

In the United Kingdom, post-9/11 reviews of protective security followed similar principles to those in the U.S., increasingly perceiving attacks against 'soft targets' as a key priority. From 2003, the United Kingdom developed a long-term strategy for counter-terrorism (known as CONTEST), the central aim of which was to reduce the risk of terrorism, so that people can go about their daily lives freely and with confidence (HMSO, 2006). CONTEST was divided into four strands: *Prevent, Pursue, Protect*, and *Prepare*. Through the *Protect* strand, protecting crowded public places against attack became a national priority. Similar to the U.S. experience, the initial spatial expression of the *Protect* strategy on the cityscape was dominated by a combination of robust physical approaches and technology that utilised barrier methods to delimited access to public spaces. Most visibly this included the 'sealing off' of government sites and other potential 'target risks' through the use of concrete or steel barriers and reinforced security bollards (Coaffee, 2004).[16]

Whilst the initial focus on protecting key urban areas was necessarily reactionary, visibly demonstrating that the state was acting to protect the United Kingdom from terrorist outrage, over time such approaches became increasingly important to the way towns and cities were designed and managed, and how planners and other built environment professionals collaborated to enhance levels of safety and security.[17] Such initiatives posed significant challenges for planners charged with balancing the public interest and ongoing urban renewal projects with security considerations, not least new engagements with police and security services officials in pursuit of this objective (Coaffee et al., 2008b). These new relationships began to develop in the mid-2000s as a response to further terrorist attacks on U.K. soil.

On July 25, 2007, shortly after failed car bomb attacks against a London nightclub and Glasgow Airport, and two years after suicide bombers killed 52 and injured 770 people on London's transport network, the then Prime Minister, Gordon Brown, provided a *Statement on Security* in which he noted, 'the protection and resilience of our major infrastructure and crowded places requires continuous vigilance' (Brown, 2007a). Subsequently, in November 2007, Parliamentary Under-Secretary of State for Security and Counter-Terrorism (Lord West) presented a review to Government calling for counter-terrorism measures to be embedded within the design, planning and construction of public places to best protect crowded places, from terrorist attack.[18] More specifically, the review recommended that the national security state should now work with planners to encourage them to 'design-in' protective security measures to new buildings, including safe areas, traffic control measures and the use of blast-resistant materials. Additionally, the Prime Minister noted that there should be 'improvements to the planning process' to ensure 'more is done to protect buildings from terrorism from the design stage onwards' and that announcements would prepare 'the public for the possibility that they may start to see some changes the physical layout of buildings where people gather' (Brown, 2007b).[19]

In the United Kingdom, such a requirement for enhanced protection of the public realm emerged slowly up until 2010, taking time to be translated into broader legislative and planning policy. In March 2010, the U.K. government released a set of guidance documents for built environment and security professionals concerned with urban counter-terrorism. These documents reinforced the message that the threat from terrorist attack against crowded places was real, and that, in response, the government had developed a strategic framework – *Working together to protect crowded places* – within which a range of key partners, including local government, the police, businesses and built environment professionals, could reduce the vulnerability of crowded places to terrorist attack (Home Office, 2010a). This argued, 'crowded places remain an attractive target for international terrorists. Putting in place better counter-terrorism protective security reduces both the likelihood and the impact of a terrorist attack' (ibid.).

More specifically, for those involved in protective security, a series of technical and procedural guides were unveiled that showcased how counter-terrorism might be appropriately and proportionately designed into the built fabric of cities. Notably, *The Planning System and Counter-Terrorism* (Home Office, 2010b) aimed to promote counter-terrorism design principles that sort to 'create safer places and buildings so that people are better protected from terrorist attack' as well as 'sustainable, affordable, attractive, and also deliver social goals, for instance, by designing out crime' (p.9).[20] Similarly, in *Protecting Crowded Places: Design and Technical Issues* (Home Office, 2010c), practical advice was given on how best to blend protective security measures into proposed new development schemes that are 'appropriate, proportionate and balanced with other relevant material considerations' (p.11) whilst ensuring that high design quality.

Other professional guidance followed in a similar vein. In 2010, the Royal Institute of British Architects released a guide to its membership so they could 'develop their own measured response to the issue [and] incorporate counter-terrorism measures into their buildings and public spaces whilst maintaining quality of place' (RIBA, 2010).[21] This was followed a year later by a specialist design guide from the Centre for the Protection of National Infrastructure: *Integrated Security – A Public Realm Design Guide for Hostile Vehicle Mitigation* that provided information *and inspiration* to those responsible for integrating protective security measures into the public realm that are 'proportionate to the assessed threat and...to ensure that the correct level of protection is provided without compromising the ability to create aesthetic and functional public spaces' (CPNI, 2011, p.2).[22]

Key design principles

In the years proceeding 9/11, the need to reduce the vulnerability of crowded places led to a number of key principles emerging with regard to the embedding of protective security into the built fabric of cities, which were common across U.S. and U.K. experiences: proportionality; collective responsibility; and notably, visibility.

First, in the initial policy responses, it was argued that protective security measures deployed should be *proportionate* to the risk faced to minimise disruption to everyday activities and for the 'the ability of individuals and businesses to carry out their normal social, economic and democratic activities' (Home Office, 2009, p.5). In time, this desire to achieve proportionality was further prioritised, with risk assessment matrices being devised to allow the 'prioritisation of work to reduce the vulnerability of crowded places to terrorist attack' (ibid.), as well as to ensure a suitable balancing of security effectiveness with the social and aesthetical appropriateness of proposed interventions.

Second, the emerging U.S. and U.K. experiences highlighted that cooperation amongst a host of associated stakeholders, most notably private businesses and built environment professionals, was required to make crowded places safer. The need to protect buildings and spaces from terrorism – from an early design stage – became evident, as was the need for this to be conducted with the support of relevant professional bodies to raise the awareness and skills of architects, planners and police in relation to counter-terrorism protective security (Coaffee and O'Hare, 2008). Here, delivering a noticeable reduction in vulnerability was seen not just in terms of the delivery of guidance to city authorities and business by security specialists, but in the actually implementation of measures to increase the safety of those crowded spaces deemed to be at the highest risk of attack. Such an approach can, more critically, be seen to shift onus and responsibility for protecting against terrorism to other actors, such as a range of built environment professions, the private sector and, more widely, communities and individuals. Such 'co-option' of non-statutory actors for assistance in state security agendas challenged conventional approaches to delivering state security.

Third, it was noted that the imposition of additional security features should not, where possible, negatively impact everyday economic and democratic activities. This realisation of the importance of the social acceptability led to a wider appreciation that security interventions should be as unobtrusive as possible, and where finding the right balance between 'subtlety' and 'safety' was seen as vital (Coaffee and Bosher, 2008, p.75). In response to this challenge, in the early-mid 2000s, we began to see security features being increasingly embedded within the streetscape so that to the general public they do not obviously serve a counter-terrorism purpose (Coaffee et al., 2009). This produced an aesthetic paradox with regard to traditional counter-terrorisms interventions that ran in parallel to an aesthetic 'turn' in the social and political sciences.

Towards a theory of (in)visible security

In the post-9/11 era, scholars began to argue for the increased consideration of aesthetics in relation to terrorism and security studies. Reflecting a move towards more critical security and terrorism studies, there was a realisation that 'whilst security threats are becoming increasingly complex and transnational, our means of understanding and responding to them have remained largely unchanged' (Bleiker, 2006, p.77). Such approaches drew from ideas that evolved in the 1990s that illuminated how emotional insights, including the fear of attack, may arise from policy responses to (in)security concerns. This 'turn' towards such interpretative approaches could be seen as an attempt to understand how texts, art, architecture and other visual phenomena might reflect dominant political ideologies, and the role of particular agencies (not just the state, but professions such as urban planning) in the conduct of war and in pursuing national security (Campbell, 2003). Similarly, theories of aesthetics revealed how art and other forms of culture, such as architecture, can act as 'sites' of complex identity construction, potentially applicable to the visual realm of security and violence (Moore, 2006; Bleiker, 2000, 2006).

Such everyday emotions, as part of a broader biopolitics,[23] had been largely ignored in traditional (pre-9/11) scholarship in the international relations field.[24] In the immediate post-9/11 era, a number of authors articulated how policy discourses of security and crisis had been written in ways that privilege the worldviews of political leaders at the expense of the experiences of ordinary citizens (Jackson, 2005; Croft, 2006). Others, further, questioned whether an understanding of new fears associated with the 9/11 attacks can be adequately conceptualised unless the role of emotions is theorised in political policy (Saurette, 2006). Concomitantly, other scholars began to highlight how the 'aesthetic domains' of literature, visual art, music and, critically for the present chapter, architecture and design, might offer further insights into the symbolic and emotional impact of terrorism and the relationship between aesthetics and politics (Bleiker, 2006, p.82). In the early 2000s, such interpretive approaches were increasingly embraced within the boarder humanities and social sciences, leading Bleiker and Hutchinson (2008, p.115) to argue that those studying security should 'consider alternative forms of insight most notably those stemming from aesthetics sources, which…are particularly suited to capturing emotions'.

Similarly, Möller (2007) noted that despite a limited discursive and linguistic turn in critical terrorism studies, the focus remained predominantly on speech and language, with little attention, until the mid-2000s, being paid to visual images. One exception was work on how visual culture intersects with ideas of militarisation and securitisation in the post-9/11 world where it was argued that 'visual culture is implicated in new military strategies, at the same time as it enables critical practices contesting those military strategies' especially through visual artefacts and practices (Campbell and Shapiro, 2007, p.133). Emerging from this rang of research work was a much deeper appreciation that architecture, and the built form more generally, has the capacity to transmit a range of dominant ideologies, potentially illustrating how a particular society is materially inscribed into space. Here the built environment was seen to function as a 'technology of security' that disciplined and controlled the population and that works on and through existing spaces to create what Foucault (2007, p.11) referred to as 'spaces of security'. Drawing upon such assertions, the built form potentially possesses the power to condition new forms of subjectivity, with spatial performances of identity and (in) security becoming linked to how subjects internalise fear through participation in the surveillance and disciplining of individual and collective conduct (Coaffee et al., 2009).

In a not dissimilar way to the aesthetic turn in politics and international relations, human geographers at this time commonly deployed the work of French philosopher Jacques Rancière to examine the complex links between space and power and, in particular, the role of aesthetics. Here, aesthetics was seen as 'a system of a priori forms determining what presents itself to sense experience' (Rancière, 2004, p.13), both visible and invisible, and was seen as central to political discourse around emancipatory and suppressive control (Hawkins and Straughan, 2016; Duncan and Duncan, 2004). Rancière's work focused on the relationships between politics and aesthetics – where 'politics has an inherently aesthetic dimension and aesthetics an inherently political one' – and was linked to the ideas that 'the disruption that they effect is not simply a reordering of the relations of power between existing groups...It is an activity that cuts across forms of cultural and identity belonging and hierarchies' (2010, p.2).

These and similar modes of analysis were not unlike those employed to analyse the upsurge in urban fear in the 1990s that recognising how visual aesthetics came to symbolise conflict, violence and terror. These traditional conceptions regarding conflict and terrorism evolved so as to take account of an increasingly complex, interdependent and potentially more threatening security environment (Coaffee, 2004). At the city scale, such trends were perhaps most apparent when the 'meaning' of security landscapes was contested by citizens, illustrating the complexities of aesthetic politics in emerging insecure urban setting (Raposo, 2006). In the first decade of the new Millennium, the visible (and increasingly invisible) moulding of the built environment was progressively conducted as a result of social and political priorities associated with security and insecurity, illustrating 'the inseparability of war, terror and modern urbanism' (Graham, 2004, p.171).

As exemplified by U.S. and U.K. policy pronouncements at this time, there was increased interest in how the transmission and reception of such impressions were projected through the insertion of overt and covert security features into the everyday cityscape as a method of countering emerging and anticipated terrorist threat. The message from governments in many Western states was clear and disseminated widely: the defence of the city – of the places where people work, relax and live – is central to wider national security strategies. City builders – including architects, urban planners and designers – were increasingly expected to consume and, through practice, to rearticulate the risk-and-threat discourse in, often literally, 'concrete' forms. In essence, protective security became viewed as emblematic – a visual symbol of the War on Terror. Here, the power of aesthetics was seen to operate through an 'aesthetic gaze' (Marvin et al., 2020) where populations could be 'trained' to see material objects in a certain way, and that conditioned behaviour and emotions.

The aesthetic paradox of countering terrorism

Foucault (1977) argued in *Discipline and Punish* that as mechanisms of everyday control (of people's movement or behaviour) are viewed as unimportant by citizens and normalised, the role of such instrumentation is forgotten or masked. Such a 'cloaking' process played out in the contemporary city from the early years of the twenty-first century, where security features were sometimes designed to be obtrusive or alternatively camouflaged. Security features, particularly those that proclaimed to prevent, deflect or mitigate a terrorist attack, are 'transacted': they form part of a two-way process, being at once projected or transmitted (both intentionally and unintentionally) by the state and the security services, but critically also being consumed or received by the general public and other observers. Such transactions – between the transmission and reception of messages – are marked by a series of paradoxes. 'Messages' inherent within security features may also be somewhat contradictory or confusing, particularly when analysed through the prism of their 'visibility' – or, alternatively, 'invisibility' – to their intended audiences (Coaffee et al., 2009).[25]

These contradictions underlined the subjective nature of interpretations and perceptions of security interventions and have a long history in terms of design determinism going back to 1970s work on defensible space (see Chapter 3) where obtrusive features 'advertised' the message that a place or building is secure. In this instance, two messages are commonly 'sent'. The public is 'told' that a place can be used in safety, while would-be perpetrators are encouraged to think that their malign intent is likely to be in vain or at least will require a significant degree of effort. However, these assumptions contained a potential contradiction that became very evident in the post-9/11 era. While security regimes may attempt to 'transmit' feelings of safety and security through the built environment and to reassure the public, the 'reception' of these very same messages may be 'lost in translation' (ibid.). Ironically, for example, security features can arouse feelings of fear and anxiety by drawing attention to the fact that safety and security is threatened.

132   *The longer term implications of 9/11*

For instance, Boddy (2007, p.279) highlighted the difference between what he referred to as an 'architecture of reassurance' and the 'fear-theming' of an 'architecture of dis-assurance', as exemplified by the plethora of new counter-terror security features deployed in U.S. cities in the wake of 9/11.

This dis-assurance, on the one hand, may be intentional. Some protective counter-terror designs act as a form of regulation of access and movement and a method of control over the use of physical spaces and buildings. Security measures such as barricading, surveillance, the imposition of stringent and overtly signposted rules, security announcements and access restricting security checkpoints, clearly aim to intimidate the public. They may also promote other emotions – feelings of isolation, of being repressed or under constant watch or threat. For example, a 2006 report published by the U.K. Information Commissioner highlighted how surveillance, as a particular aspect of security, exacerbates and institutionalises class, race, gender, geography and citizenship (Murakami Wood et al., 2006, p.3). As a result, people might feel they are only able to use urban space in a particular way due to symbolic and psychological cues embedded in street design. On the other hand, unintentional filtering of activities might occur where some groups do not feel comfortable or welcome. This is precisely the aim of much contemporary terrorism that aims to make crowded places 'empty' of 'sterile'. As such, because of people's real or perceived fears, there can be a reticence to use public spaces. In extreme circumstances, this dis-assurance has been likened to a form of spatialised agoraphobia: an anxiety or mania of place (Janz, 2008, p.193), particularly crowded places, such as shopping centres and busy streets (Predmore et al., 2007; Coaffee, 2017a).

In the years following 9/11, others also highlighted how general security infrastructure, now common in urban space to combat crime and antisocial behaviour, had wider implications. Illustrating this, Németh and Schmidt (2007, p.285) identified developments in counter-terror spatial management techniques according to hard (or active) control and soft (passive) control features. Hard control features included electronic surveillance, private security guards and the laws and rules of conduct that can restrict actions, influence behaviours or impede interaction. Such 'hardened' features were often both pervasive and unsubtle, and with the intention to affect the behaviour even of those who do not aim to cause harm. Under such circumstances, while the general populace appeared defended, it is under siege both from the terrorist threat and, perhaps more accurately, from the governmental response to this threat that in many cases made urban landscapes look 'barren, sterile, and fortress-like' (Hollander and Whitfield, 2005, p.245). In contrast, 'soft' strategies are rather subtler and include aesthetic and 'streetscape' features discussed later.

To add another twist to the issue of visibility, it has also long been suggested that visible protective security might in fact increase vulnerability to attack (Coaffee, 2000). Conspicuous security may identify some organisations as targets by highlighting their presence (and perceived vulnerabilities) to would-be terrorists. By extension, the need for the state to illustrate that it is taking the terrorist threat seriously further contributes to this paradox. For instance, the swamping of potential targets by armed police and in some cases military hardware (such as the deployment of tanks at Heathrow Airport, London, in February 2003), or the 'temporary' manipulation of spaces adjacent to sites through the placement of concrete security barriers to create an exclusion area for potentially hostile vehicles, can be used to proclaim to the public that a verifiable threat is being heeded. This paradox is based on the presumption that the state wants to transmit feelings of security. The state is, in many regards, symbolically weakened by terrorist attacks, and therefore counter-terrorism responses are attempts to be seen to be in control and to demonstrate the state's ability to afford protection to its citizens. Elsewhere, though, and as noted in Chapter 6, security policies have been critiqued as being deliberate attempts to heighten fear, based on the premise that a fearful population is easier to control (Mythen and Walklate, 2006).

Elsewhere, questions have been raised about the rise of 'invisible security' that became an important point of concern in the mid-late 2000s when there was a concerted effort by many Western states to establish ever more unobtrusive security features in the built environment. A range of pressures converged to create such initiatives, many of which were propagated by the state itself. First, as mentioned earlier, governments believe that the terrorist threat and the War on Terror now have a degree of permanency, as well as a pervasiveness. Therefore, security interventions are increasingly required to consider concerns regarding public acceptability, increasing pressure to adopt design features that are both more aesthetically pleasing and less obtrusive (Coaffee and O'Hare, 2008). Further, there have been technological and aesthetic innovations regarding the development of robust security features and an associated implication that professional expertise may be co-opted to secure the built environment. By consequence, security features are being increasingly 'camouflaged' – or covertly embedded within the urban landscape. These counter-terrorism features may be 'invisible' to the unaccustomed eye and do not obviously serve a counter-terrorism purpose (Coaffee et al., 2009). They include, for example aesthetically landscaped barriers or street furniture, and collapsible pavements. Such interventions can serve to combat assertions that visible security features are in fact dis-assuring. However, in many respects, 'invisible' security features invert the contradictions that have been outlined earlier in this chapter. They potentially present areas as being insecure, therefore, statutory institutions charged with protecting the public are rendered prone to allegations that threats are not being taken seriously enough. That said, it is important to reiterate that such 'invisible' security features are often 'legible' to those who wish to do harm to, or attack, an area.[26]

Drawing upon these differing views, Coaffee et al. (2009) constructed a continuum that identified the visibility of security as being 'overt', 'stealthy' and 'invisible' (Figure 7.3), and which posed a number of questions regarding the everyday impact, and legitimation, of the protective streetscape security.

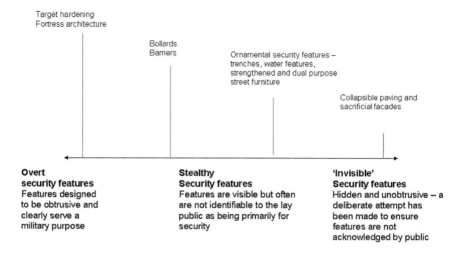

Figure 7.3 An indicative spectrum of visible security (after Coaffee et al., 2009).

Visible security in the wake of 9/11

During the War on Terror, and especially in the wake of attacks, or in the face of a perceived imminent threat, security services, and even private institutions, implemented initiatives and deployed security features with the principle goal of safeguarding particular spaces of 'critical importance' (Sternberg and Lee, 2006), including administrative buildings and places with iconographic or symbolic significance, as well as commercial or industrial centres.

Initially, these interventions typically took the form of concrete barriers and, later, steel bollards, as well as the implementation of regular security checks of building users. Such architectures of 'dis-assurance' were seen at the time to 'exploit the fears rather than the hopes' of citizens (Boddy, 2007, p.181). Such interventions, though crude and spatially specific, are (at least superficially) effective, in that they prohibit the penetration of targets through the limitation of the permeability of spaces by would-be perpetrators of attacks. In certain locations, such interventions were so widespread at times that heightened security was, in effect, normalised (Coaffee et al., 2009). It was also recognised that such features were implemented precisely because of their visibility to the public, which could potentially be 'calculated to manipulate awareness of the threat of terrorism' (Marcuse, 2006, p.921). With time, such interventions in many cities have been made de facto permanent. This has led to further critiques surrounding the aesthetics of counter-terrorism design. As noted in one newspaper article, in the light of national security pronouncements in the U.K. regarding the permanency of counter-terror

Normal protective streetscapes 135

features around key government buildings: 'we might live in dangerous times, but they don't have to be ugly ones too'.[27]

Over time, as the threats from terrorism became more acute and pervasive, and as responses become all the more widely adopted, significant effort has been invested to ensure that security features are installed on a more enduring basis with an increasing reluctance to deploy highly visible security features. For example, many people object to the intrusive character of many of the manipulated security responses, and some planners and architects have devoted themselves to the search for forms that conceal the anti-terror aspects of such interventions: making concrete barriers with flower planters on top, making bollards inconspicuous and finding social uses for extreme setbacks.

Western Government's protective counter-terrorism polices now commonly promote transparent security, 'invisible' to the public gaze through ever subtler, softer design features. Such policies are reflected by the fact that, in the U.K. and elsewhere, the state, through its security apparatus, is 'recruiting' built environment professionals to help combat terrorism amidst pressure to make security features more aesthetically pleasing (Coaffee and O'Hare, 2008). For example, public-realm 'streetscape' improvements in the Government Security Zone in central London had inconspicuous security features 'designed-in', in the form of balustrades (Figure 7.4). In the mid-2000s, the new Emirates Stadium in North London also actively promoted its ornamental counter-terrorism features that were held up as a model of best practice for designing-in counter-terrorism features to new buildings and spaces. Here, large fortified concrete letters spelling out 'Arsenal' were deliberately situated to prevent vehicle access (see Figure 7.5). Similar subtler streetscape security enhancement took place in Boston, Massachusetts where public seating that doubled as security barriers was added in front of a federal building (Figure 7.6).

Other counter-terror features may be even less obvious. For instance, expendable surfaces and building facades have been designed to dissipate when subjected to the pressure waves of a blast and strengthened or toughened glass that can withstand even significant attacks are increasingly designed into developments. In this respect, new design technology has become available to built environment professionals to help integrate perimeter and building security less visibly, and with more subtlety into the public realm. Another such feature, highly marketed in the early-mid 2000s as securing public areas in an almost invisible way, was a collapsible pedestrian pavement (promoted under the trademark 'Tiger Traps')[28] that gave way under the weight of a vehicle, trapping it in a pit some distance from potential targets (Figure 7.7).[29] As one newspaper reported:

> Outside the New York Mercantile Exchange, where oil and gold are traded just west of Ground Zero, a long row of bollards will be replaced this fall by a sidewalk punctuated with benches that will conceal a security device called a Tiger Trap: Just below a layer of paving stones is a trench filled with low-density, compressible concrete that will collapse under a heavy weight.[30]

Figure 7.4 Security balustrade along Whitehall, London.

These less overt forms of protecting urban spaces is indicative of the increased importance of visual aesthetics in the War on Terror and, as Boddy (2007, p.291) noted, potentially 'represents the future of the hardening of public buildings and public space – soft on the outside, hard within, the iron hand

Figure 7.5 'ARSENAL' – Ornamental Security Façade for the Emirates Stadium.

inside the civic velvet glove'. Importantly, this particular approach also further illuminated the rise of security as a marketable issue.[31] It is also raises a concern that 'invisible' forms of security may risk becoming an uncontested element of political and public policy.

Conclusions: The limits of visible protective counter-terrorism

This chapter has illuminated how public policy and political imperatives can be viewed in our streetscapes and city spaces and how, during the 2000s, the aesthetic turn in critical security and terrorism studies drew attention to the visual interpretation of counter-terrorism policies and their impact on the use of everyday urban spaces. In short, protective counter-terrorism policy can be seen as more than words and ideas as often studied by those focusing upon orthodox securitisation. It has become manifested within the built environment and can transmit powerful messages, both intentionally and unintentionally, eliciting a range of subjective emotional responses. In this way, security policy has had a tangible impact on the spaces in which we live, work and socialise (and how we do so), and has the potential to have an immense impact on how citizens interact with each other in locations deemed at risk.

138 *The longer term implications of 9/11*

Figure 7.6 Crash-rated seating outside a federal building in Boston, Massachusetts.

Such spaces of security illicit a range of conflicting transactions and messages that are projected. Urban defences can be formidable but are also foreboding – and on occasion are designed to be so. But, what is the overarching message that the state wishes to send in such circumstances? And, who receives it and in what fashion? Whilst, such policies are 'authored', predominantly by the state's security services under the premise that they are proportionate to the risk faced or anticipated threats, clearly, their 'readers' may assume different meanings from those intended – or at least from those projected by the state. The expansion of protective security in cities of recent years continues to raise critical questions over how different spatial and aesthetic arrangements of security features condition a 'range' of responses, and the possibility for the (re)production of different forms of subjectivity. As illustrated, despite pronouncements that the main task of the state is to protect its population, devices and designs for safety can achieve quite the opposite effect – fearfulness, suspicion, paranoia, exclusion and ultimately insecurity. In such instances, it is critical to note that in the face of likely attacks, the state's response may in itself serve to terrorise the very people supposedly protected. By extension, when the acceptability and effectiveness of security features are considered, it must be recognised that there is a degree

Figure 7.7 An example of a Tiger Trap in Battery Park, New York.

of fluidity. The source and target of threats can change over time, and so too can people's tolerance of invasive security or, alternatively, their desire to feel more secure (Coaffee et al., 2009).

Invisible form of security, though potentially more aesthetically pleasing, and offering a redress to the many drawbacks of obtrusive security interventions, must continue to be treated with a healthy degree of scepticism. Given the potential future omnipresence of 'stealthy' security, we must remain vigilant of the risk that citizens will provide passive consent to the rise to dominance of pre-emptive planning for 'inevitable' worst-case terrorist scenarios. Whilst it can easily be argued that (in)visible security measures are both about control of the public through a manipulation of threat perceptions, as well as physical protection, researching such perceptions of fear and insecurity has proved inconclusive. The argument that visible security measures increase insecurity and induce fear has found some empirical support from a University of Florida study in 2006 that argued that visible security features – both armed personnel and temporary concrete planters and bollards – increased fear (Grosskopf, 2006), whilst a 2010 Australian study of security measures introduced at airports, were mixed (Aly and Green, 2010). A more recent Danish study in 2016 also highlighted mixed results suggesting that the public is actually capable of being very nuanced and reflective about how to ensure public safety and security against security threats [and that] a democratic public will actually positively demand a broad and balanced range of counter-terrorism measures and even place special emphasis on "softer" measures.

(Dalgaard-Nielsen et al., 2016, p.709)

Undoubtedly, a more proactive and integrated approach to protective counter-terrorist security emerged throughout the 2000s where instead of reacting at pace, a more reflexive response became possible which accounted for issues such as proportionality and aesthetics of design, as well as developing a strategic framework whereby many more stakeholders are given responsibility for delivering the counter-terrorism agenda. Protective counter-terrorism and streetscape security has increasingly become a collective responsibility amongst not only the police and security services but also many professional and practice communities, who have been enrolled in the fight against terrorism, and in the development of a more resilient and robust urban landscape. Moreover, the everyday implications of these securityscapes for population control, subjectivities and broader techniques of governmentality have come under greater scrutiny where aesthetic norms were seen as part of the dominant framing of social order and control through what Ghertner (2010, p.2015) referred to as 'aesthetic governmentality'. In Chapter 12, illustrations of security aesthetics from the 2010s – both visible and invisible – will further illuminate how protective streetscapes and crowded locations have been remained a key element in a wider normalisation of urban security, amidst the constant evolution and migration of the tactics of terror and new integrated urban designs.

Notes

1 Such strategies often have a dedicated 'protect' strand to refer to interventions that can physically mitigate the impact of a terrorist attack. Examples include the United Kingdom, EU and UN counter-terrorism strategies.
2 In the United States, so-called K-rated standards were originally developed by the Department of State (DoS) in the 1980s and subsequently updated in 2003. Bollards are rated based on the vehicle speeds they can stop.
3 See *New York Times* blog at https://cityroom.blogs.nytimes.com/2013/01/13/times-square-bow-tie-is-to-get-a-beltof-steel-and-granite/.
4 See Architect's Newspaper, May 19, 2017 at https://archpaper.com/2017/05/snohetta-timessquare-car/.
5 Snøhetta Press Release, April 19, 2017 at https://snohetta.com/news/362-snohettacelebrates-opening-of-times-square-redesign.
6 This has served to assure businesses and those frequenting the Square that safety and security are being taken seriously.
7 Image supplied by © Snøhetta, Michael Grimm.
8 In January 2021, a similar large public realm improvement project was unveiled for Union Square in New York in which security was central. Here the Union Square

Normal protective streetscapes 141

and 14th Street District Vision plan, managed by the Union Square Partnership, was focused on integrating security features into the square in ways that did not detract from its vibrancy – see www.unionsquarenyc.org/vision.

9 As a counterpoint to this, it is clear that the type of counter-terrorist intervention varies according to context.

10 This section extends the prior published work of the author, see, for example, Coaffee et al. (2009) and Coaffee (2010).

11 The 2002 Bali bombings occurred on October 12, 2002 in the tourist district of Kuta. The attack killed 202 people and over 200 more were seriously injured. Three bombs were detonated – a device carried by a suicide bomber in a backpack and a large car bomb that was exploded in or near popular nightclubs. A third smaller device was set off outside the U.S. consulate nearby and caused only minor damage. The attacks were seen as a retaliation for the U.S. and Australian roles in the global War on Terror.

12 The 2004 Madrid train bombings of March 11, 2004 occurred three days before Spain's general elections. The attacks were directed by an Al-Qaeda terrorist cell and was seen as a consequence Spain participation in the Iraq War, and the wider War on Terror. In total ten explosions from improvised devices, detonated by mobile phones, occurred aboard four commuter trains.

13 The July 7, 2005 a series of three coordinated bombing attacks on the London underground during rush hour and a fourth on a bus left 56 people dead. The attacks were a response to the U.K.'s participation in the War on Terror.

14 The attacks in Mumbai between November 26 and 29, 2008, saw 10 members from Lashkar-e-Taiba, an extremist Islamist terrorist organisation based in Pakistan attack a number of pre-selected targets including the Taj Mahal Palace hotel with grenades and automatic weapons and use strategies such as mass hostage-taking to kill 170 people in attacks lasting four days. This attack was a relatively novel mode of operation and did not necessarily fit the 'pattern' of prior Al-Qaeda attacks of previous years.

15 This definition included the following sectors: 'bars, pubs and night clubs; restaurants and hotels; shopping centres; sports and entertainment stadia; cinemas and theatres; visitor attractions; major events; commercial centres; the health sector; the education sector; and religious sites/places of worship' (Home Office, 2009, p.11).

16 These security devices had been specifically designed to provide maximum protection and are intended to be used by designers, planners, architects, security managers and facilities managers within the public and private sectors.

17 This policy priority was backed up by streams of work being conducted by the National Counter-Terrorism Security Office (NaCTSO) on disseminating protective security advice to places deemed vulnerable to targeting such as shopping centres, bars pubs and clubs, and sports stadia

18 See House of Commons Debate. November 14, Col 45WS. Although, for reasons of national security, the review was unpublished, numerous statements were made in Parliament and to the press that provided an insight into proposed policy initiatives and their implications for the planning profession.

19 This would, he continued, be conducted with the support of relevant professional bodies (such as the Royal Town Planning Institute and Royal Institute of British Architects) to raise the awareness and skills of planners, architects and police Architectural Liaison Officers in relation to counter-terrorism protective security.

142 *The longer term implications of 9/11*

20 It was also emphasised that 'as with any design considerations, it is most effective if counter-terrorism protective security measures are considered as early as possible in the planning and development process'.
21 The author's research provided key inputs into the production of this guide.
22 The guide also identified security barriers and bollards that have Publically Available Specifications awarded by the British Standards Institute (PAS 69:2006, PAS 68:2007). These security devices had been specifically designed to provide maximum protection (generally to stop a 7.5-tonne truck travelling at 50 miles per hour) and are intended to be used by designers, planners, architects, security managers and facilities managers within the public and private sectors.
23 Biopolitics' is a term derived from Foucault's work analysing a type of political control. It concerns the regulation and control of populations through, for example, apparatuses of security like police forces and the exercise of power through micro-mechanisms of exclusion and surveillance
24 Coward (2006b, p.60) noted how, particularly among British international relations scholars, there existed a 'tendency towards qualitative, hermeneutic inquiry (as opposed to the quantitative methods that dominate American political science's analysis of global order) [that] seems well placed to investigate the conceptual contours of the discipline'.
25 These contradictions underlined the subjective nature of interpretations and perceptions of security interventions and have a long history in terms of design determinism going back to the seminal work of Oscar Newman in the 1970s on Defensible space (see Chapter 3) where obtrusive features 'advertised' in order to convey the message that a place or building is secure.
26 Research and post-attack analysis indicate that most attacks are conducted after a period of often quite intensive 'hostile reconnaissance', when would-be attackers survey, study and analyse (reconnoitre) potential targets.
27 From car bombs to carbuncles. *The Observer*, November 18, 2007.
28 See www.rogersmarvel.com/BatteryParkCityStreetscapes.html.
29 However, such interventions were widely reported in the media, somewhat undermining their rather invisible premise.
30 Defensive Devices Designed to Blend in with New York. *USA Today*, July 31, 2006.
31 As Light (2002, p.612) noted not long after 9/11, the fear of terrorism and the expansion of militarized urban space 'reminds us that many powerful economic and political interests are well served by the unbridled expansion of urban fear'.

8 Preparation and anticipation in the global War on Terror

Introduction: Redesigning security

In March 2008, the U.K.'s first National Security Strategy – *Security in an Interdependent World* (Cabinet Office, 2008) – was released and painted a bleak picture of an unprecedented array of threats faced across significant areas of the country. The overarching objective of the strategy was 'protecting the United Kingdom and its interests, enabling its people to go about their daily lives freely and with confidence, in a more secure, stable, just and prosperous world' (p.6). The old certainties of security during the Cold War had been replaced by increasingly complex and unpredictable security challenges, and loosely affiliated global terror networks, which presented threats that were 'qualitatively and quantitatively more serious than the terrorist threats we have faced in the past' (ibid.).

These new threats demanded new security responses that would complement recently enacted reforms of civil contingences and counter-terrorism, and that were collectively required to deal with an increasingly complex 'security landscape', link national authorities with those at a local level, as well as assessing Britain's place in an ever-more interdependent global world.[1] Notably, ideas of *resilience* were especially prominent in the strategy, as a government spokesperson noted on the BBC:

> Our new approach to security also means *improved local resilience* against emergencies, building and *strengthening local capacity* to respond effectively in a range of circumstances from floods to possible terrorist incidents...not the old cold war idea of civil defence but a *new form of civil protection* that combines expert *preparedness* for potential emergencies with greater *local engagement* of individuals and families themselves (emphasis added).[2]

In the wake of 9/11, the U.K. was not alone amongst Western nations in issuing state-level security strategies to reflect changed concerns over international terrorism and wider global threats. As Omand (2010, p.16) noted,

DOI: 10.4324/9780429461620-11

it is no coincidence that national security strategies were published in the years after 9/11 in Washington, Paris, Berlin, London, The Hague, Canberra, Singapore and elsewhere, where 'governments have recognised their responsibility for providing a sense of security to their publics... [but] are grasping for what it means to be secure in an independent world without a single dominant state adversary...and facing the serious threat of mass casualty terrorism'.

The consensus was that a new kind of security, designed for the twenty-first century, was required; one with different practices, governance and modes of operation that moved away from reactive response, to wards a greater focus on preparedness. In charting this endeavour, this chapter focuses on the complex political ecologies involved in developing security governance to prepare for, and anticipate, acts of terrorism at national and metropolitan scales. This represented the practical and social ramifications of the changing mode and operation of security discourses for those charged with delivering them in situ. Such a transformation in security governance, and the language that framed discussions of counter-terrorism (notably resilience), required a shift away from technical, functional, bureaucratic and incremental ways of working that had conventionally dominated the enactment of emergency planning and urban security (Coaffee, 2019). Countering complex terrorist threats was seen as a collective action problem where traditional security actors looked to draw in a range of additional emergency professionals and urban stakeholders to address new security challenges, whilst providing effective protection to the population and ensuring everyday life could continue in relative normality. In many countries, the obsolescence of traditional methods of counter-terrorism in the context of new terrorist threats led to a new lexicon being used to characterise the emerging approaches being adopted by urban security managers, based upon ideas of *resilience.*

The concept of resilience

Resilience is both a conceptual and policy metaphor that has been discussed at length in the academic literature, with various disciplines laying claim to its etymological evolution and applying it within different experimental and theoretical contexts. Work by ecologists, psychologists, disaster managers, geographers, political scientists, economists and the military have all contributed to academic discussion, with resilience ideas subsequently creeping into a range of policy debates in the new millennium in an attempt to capture the 'messy' realities of such change (Walker and Cooper, 2011; Chandler and Coaffee, 2016). Resilience has come to frame action in an increasingly interconnected and unpredictable world and recalibrated 'around a will to design, a drive or desire to synthesize drive forms of knowledge and develop collaborate cross boundary solutions to complex problems' (Grove, 2018, frontispiece).[3]

Historically, unpredictability and associated notions of crisis have commonly been presented objectively as events that governments must react to speedily. However, in the last twenty years, critical studies of security and neoliberal governmentality have begun to focus on how response to crisis has been used proactively, and seen as an opportunity by governments to instrumentally transform social reality and achieve desired policy goals. This has primarily been instigated through the promotion of preferred forms of subjectivity, framed in terms of resilience, and premised on enhancing responsibility, flexibility and resilience of individuals, communities and organisations to enhance capacities and capability to cope with an array of crises (Chandler, 2012; Aradau and Van Munster, 2007).

What most of the extant literature highlights is that the growth in scope of resilience policy means it must be treated as a 'translation term', 'boundary object' or 'floating metaphor' (Coaffee, 2006; Brand and Jax, 2007) as it has emerged in many Western nations as the central organising metaphor within the expanding institutional framework of national security and emergency preparedness in the post-9/11 era. Over time, the use of resilience rhetoric has helped reframe crises and the 'inevitable' terrorist attack as an opportunity to proactively confront uncertain and unknown threats within positive a language of assurance and comfort. In practice, the drive for such security-driven resilience (Coaffee, 2016) has drawn of an ever-increasing number of local citizens and government agencies into new frameworks operating under the guise of national security. For many, this changing governance of security, particularly the interactions between citizen and state, has progressively 'responsibilised' and put the onus for preventing and preparing for urban security challenges onto institutions, professions, communities and individuals rather than the state, the traditional provider of citizens' security needs. More practically, while the notion of resilience may have originally evolved in academia across a range of disciplines, its utility in the realm security became most evident through its ability to mobilise collective action through an explicit political rhetoric of national identity and solidarity.

This chapter focuses upon how ideas of preparedness and anticipation, as part of broader resilience approaches, were increasingly adopted by urban security professionals as they sought to operationalise integrated security, and counter-terrorism planning at the city scale. First, drawing on established ideas of securitisation that sees democratic societies increasingly governed by and through security, the chapter highlights how new security rhetorics and discourses emerged and were institutionalised at national and local scales. Second, the policy and practice implications of this 'resilience turn' in counter-terrorism are unpacked, drawing particular attention towards the governance of preparatory and anticipatory measures. How resilience ideas fed into counter-terrorism policy is further examined through examples from the United Kingdom, United States, Australia and mainland Europe. Third, the civic impacts of such measures are underscored, with a particular emphasis placed on problematising the balance between enhanced security measures and civil liberties.

Securitisation, resilience and the War on Terror

The politicisation of issues surrounding terrorism, counter-terrorism and especially the post-9/11 War on Terror, provided fertile ground for securitisation theorists from the Copenhagen School (Buzan, 2006; Roe, 2008; Aradau and van Munster, 2009). The War on Terror was presented as a key example of macro-securitisation (Buzan, 2006, 2008; Buzan and Waever, 2009) where securitisation processes took place at the international, as opposed to state scale. Not dissimilar ideas of 'collective securitization' were further developed by Sperling and Webber (2018) to describe the advancement of a shared concern and response to terrorism in the European Union (EU), noting that before 9/11 there was a 'lack of a shared perception of the terrorist threat and the virtual absence of counter-terrorism cooperation amongst European states' (Kaunert and Leonard, 2019, p.262). Importantly, within an overarching macro or collective securitisation process, it was argued that state actors are still able to 'link their own local problems' (Buzan, 2006, p.1104).[4]

As the War of Terror progressed, the need for enhanced security formed a regular part of public debates and emerging policy decisions, with new terror threats being portrayed, and commonly accepted, as posing an existential threat requiring emergency actions to ensure security and survival. This public imaginary of the War on Terror was further dominated by state-sanctioned risk assessments that determined what was and what wasn't a threat (Bigo, 2002). Such emergency, and increasingly militarised, actions were seen as key securitisation moves by the state to enforce new policy dynamics aimed at defending the homeland from grave and uncertain threat that, if not quelled, would impact upon 'normal' life. With hindsight we can now see how, over time, such 'active securitization' (Roe, 2008, p.633) became mainstreamed throughout a range of social, political and legal policy, affecting all aspects of life.

Here, every possible reaction to countering terrorist threat constituted securitisation, and where 'the necessary action required serious compromising of liberal values' (Buzan, 2006, p.1116). Such changes in policy and political rhetoric that sought to gain maximum acceptance from civil society would have been unimaginable without the spectre of impending and exceptional threat (Aradau and van Munster, 2009; Balzacq, 2011). Summarising the immediate post-9/11 security discourse, Jackson (2007a) noted that terrorism perpetrated by Al Qaeda posed 'a clear, unprecedented and existential threat to modern societies' and a challenge to 'democracy, civilisation and the international system itself' (p.236). This was a discourse of securitisation, shared across most Western states.

The commencement of the global War on Terror showcased a number of classic securitisation moves that further framed discussions about the rise of resilience as both an accepted language, and practice, of security. *First*, the declaration of 9/11 as an 'act of war' by the U.S. administration was significant, in that at times of war everything else a government does is secondary to defeating the enemy. Practically and administratively, this also meant that military logic predominated in seeking counter-responses. As Freedman (2008, p.386–387) noted, 'this securitising move was exceptional in character – the language of war helped justify a military (not simply a civilian) response, ...an elevated sense of patriotism and a demonization of al-Qaeda and its presumed accomplices'. *Second*, the need to 'prepare for the worst' amidst 'inevitable attack' that would destroy liberty and the everyday life became central to government rhetoric in ramping-up threat perceptions and, paradoxically, in attempts to assure the public that all was safe (Massumi, 2005). Concomitantly, this led to new forms of risk-based governance that allowed the uncertain future – the aleatory – to become statistically manageable zones of risk (Foucault, 2007, p.63) with the assertion of the necessity for 'pre-emptive strikes' against the 'enemy' ushering in new logics of warfare where anticipation of attack meant striking first.

Resilience becomes the new security

Preparing for such existential threats emanating from an identifiable, if amorphous, enemy and initiating counter-responses, required a more assuring and palatable language than that of disaster management, vulnerably or counter-terrorism. It was here that resilience came to the fore in many Western states to represent this rhetorical shift, with a focus on building capacity and capability in the face of terrorist threats (Coaffee, 2006). During the twentieth century, resilience was a term seldom heard within security circles, but the events of 9/11 destabilised the whole notion of security, who does it, how it is carried out and, in particular, how it is framed.[5] 9/11 brought to the fore wider concerns about new forms of terrorism and requiring a rethinking of existing security practices. Defending the homeland and making it more 'resilient' became the dominant rhetoric used by politicians in the Western world for how they should prepare for the next attack.

Such a twenty-first-century requirement focused on the need to better anticipate, and be adaptable to, known and unknown threats. In the contemporary period, the response to terrorist risk usually poses the question 'Are we prepared?' rather than 'Can we prevent it?' (Coaffee, 2003). As a result, national security policy became increasingly focused on how to restrict further 'inevitable' attack and embed resilience into physical defensive measures and local populations, foretelling the need to adapt to a changing landscape of terrorist risk. From this viewpoint, risks from terrorism can only be managed and prepared for but never completely eradicated.[6]

Communicating new terrorist threats through the vocabulary of resilience became ever-more central to the discussion of national security and attempts to convey a response that was proactive and had in-built adaptability to deal with the fluid nature of security challenges faced by many nations. In the context of security threats, resilience was more often than not seen as the ability of a society to absorb shocks and reorganise while retaining its essential structure and identity. At first glance, this type of approach appears to favour a 'business-as-usual' approach to handling disruption. But looking more deeply, the resilience-centred approach to counter-terrorism that began to emerge was radically different from pre-9/11 approaches and the reactive types of interventions seen in the immediate wake of terror attacks. The assumptions underpinning this new resilience philosophy saw terrorist attacks as impossible to predict and prevent, given the limitless array of targets, and the ease by which a handful of people can plan a strike. As a result, the emphasis shifted from the immediate post-9/11 rhetoric of 'defeating' and 'defending' ourselves from terrorism, to preparing for, mitigating and learning to bounce forward from an attack and, more generally, acquiring the capacity to adapt to persistent risk and danger.

Moreover, what emerged, most notably in the United Kingdom and the United States, was a move away from dealing with security risks through ideas of civil defence and civil protection as an outdated overhang of Cold War systems of emergency management. Even before 9/11, the collapse of the USSR, and a series of high profile domestic disasters, had stimulated calls to develop more contemporary ways of planning for civil emergencies that were less focused on wartime approaches and the involvement of the military. After 9/11, the concern that key sites would be targeted by terrorists, accelerated this process and made reform of emergency preparedness a key political priority on both sides of the Atlantic Ocean. This 'upping the ante' in disaster management, catalysed by 9/11, saw the concepts and practices of resilience, increasingly utilised towards this aim (Coaffee et al., 2008).

The resilience turn in counter-terrorism

At different scales, responses to 9/11 and subsequent attacks highlighted the importance of subnational and localised responses to new security challenges that required analysis through a different frame of reference from the realist state-centric security studies orthodoxy, 'placing the needs of the individual, not states, at the centre of security discourses' (Chandler, 2012, p.214). Just as the concepts and practices of security can be said to have 'come home' (Coaffee and Murakami Wood, 2006, p.504), so the ideas underpinning the political rhetoric of resilience also became more civic-centred and reapplied across a spectrum of largely local urban systems (Coaffee and Rogers, 2008). Here as Omand (2010, p.13) highlighted that governmental approaches to enhancing security-driven resilience meant a twin-track process of adapting government structures to 'strengthen strategic direction at the centre of government and breaking down departmental stovepipes' together with the 'decentralization of the detailed polices and tactics to deliver the strategy… to those closest to the frontline'.

Resilience quickly became a key organising principle of government action, providing a framework by which to respond to security threats involving the integration of two main 'threads' of work: the need for far-sightedness and the integrated governance of all-hazard response – alongside appropriate testing and exercising to boost responsiveness. First, a greater requirement for foresight, anticipation, and preparedness was required, where being proactive, rather than reactive, was the order of the day. Resilience practices therefore sought to foreground risk prevalence, where risk must be extensively planned for. As Lentzos and Rose (2009, p.235) highlighted, 'strategies of intervention are no longer focused on compensation after the event, but are those of anticipation, precaution and pre-emption'.

This simultaneously led to the rise of precautionary governance and created new models for anticipating an uncertain future, especially in relation to unpredictable and high-consequence 'what if' events. In practice, pre-emptive risk management activities were primarily undertaken to map urban vulnerabilities (often with an emphasis on worst-case scenarios), plan and test for high-impact 'shock' events, and to develop and enhance practical and technical expertise to aid both mitigation and recovery from disruptive challenges (Boyle and Haggerty, 2009; de Goede and Randalls, 2009).[7] Here, in conditions where the statistical calculability of terrorist risk is unknowable, logics of precaution dominated with a focus upon techniques such as stress testing, scenario planning and the rehearsal of disaster response planning (O'Malley, 2004).

Second, there was an assumption that society should organise the planning for multiple risks and hazards in a holistic fashion to bolster national resilience. Whilst terrorism, through its central role in national security discussions, was seen as both the key driver of the emergence of resilience policy, enhancing national resilience was not just a counter-terrorism plan, but a broader strategy to tackle a complex array of risks capable of causing insecurity. This new governance approach to enhancing resilience emphasised joined-up approaches to decision-making and devolving responsibility of a greater array of individuals and organisations within strategic resilience efforts. This move towards resilience focused on coordination of government efforts across scales and organisational units through an integration and adapting of existing structures, as well as the promotion of new nimbler governance configurations. Whereas traditional approaches to risk and security relied upon a narrow range of governmental stakeholders, post-9/11 schemas looked to draw a full range of individuals, professionals and community groups into decision-making at a range of spatial scales; from active citizens and locally coordinated systems to centralised and subnational organisations (Coaffee, 2013b).

The successful operation of security-driven resilience further relied upon testing governance procedures and arrangements; either during table-top training or simulated exercises resembling war games, to provide lessons for improvement, and to allow the emergency services, governments and other agencies to practice and plan for a variety of terrorist incidents. Here, as Anderson and Adey (2011, p.1092) asserted, such exercises are staged procedures that allowed emergency services to tackle particular scenarios – the what ifs – 'by rehearsing planned responses and as such become…part of the relational dynamics through which apparatuses emerge, endure, change, and function strategically'. They further noted in later work that it is through such exercising of scenarios that 'events are made actionable and thus governable' (Adey and Anderson, 2012, p.99). For example, resilience planners in London carried out a range of exercises to test terrorism-response scenarios, including *Exercise Capital Response,* in 2002; a table-top test that exercised the 'command, control, communication and consequence management issues following a catastrophic incident' to ascertain if current structures and provision could cope with an event on the scale of 9/11 (London Prepared, 2006).[8] Additionally, *Exercise Osiris II,* in 2003, aimed to test specific elements of the operational response to a chemical attack on the London Underground. This exercise focused on Bank Junction in the heart of the City of London and followed a desktop exercise, Osiris I. For this day-long test, the City of London was 'locked down' and London's emergency services were tested for their state of preparedness and their ability to work in a coordinated fashion, giving emergency services the opportunity to test the effectiveness of new specialist equipment, including chemical suits (Coaffee et al., 2008b).[9]

At a wider scale, in the early 2000s, London resilience teams further organised transatlantic counter-terrorism exercises, notably *Atlantic Blue,* in April 2005, involving the United Kingdom, the United States and Canada (known as Top Off 3 in the United States and Triple Play in Canada), that simulated internationally linked terrorist incidents. The United Kingdom used London's transport system as its simulation test bed to assess the vulnerability of passengers when bombs were left on buses and the underground (the events of July 7, 2005 followed this pattern). The U.K. command scenario involved 2000 personnel from the city's police services, the Ministry of Defence and numerous government departments and agencies, two London Borough councils, the fire and ambulance and health services, and provided the opportunity to test the existing procedures for domestic and international incident management and public information dissemination. The evaluation of this test also raised serious concerns over 'soft' targets in London.[10]

Rethinking civil protection: Towards resilience in practice

In the early 2000s, resilience emerged across many Western states as a key 'buzzword' in response to terrorist risk in major cities (Coaffee, 2003), but also the vulnerability of cities to natural hazards (Pelling, 2003), the susceptibly of critical infrastructure to attack (Perelman, 2007) and the recovery of cities and states from emergencies and disaster events (Vale and Campanella, 2005). Through the lens of resilience policy, it became possible to chart new forms of emergency governance in different territories and the drawing of a range of stakeholders to the resilience agenda, alongside the corresponding adoption of new roles and responsibilities in enacting policy priorities.

Whilst being sympathetic to critical accounts of resilience in practice, and especially their powerful expose of who wins and who doesn't in neoliberal governance (Coaffee and Clarke, 2016), the focus of the forthcoming analysis takes a more performative approach that views resilience as a multiplicity of related, and often experimental practices. Following Brassett and Vaughan-Williams (2015, p.34) resilience should be viewed 'as an ongoing interaction between various (and often conflicting) actors and logics, one which can be viewed as far more contingent, incomplete and contestable in both its characteristics and effects than is usually acknowledged in the existing literature'.

U.K. defence, protection and contingency planning

In the U.K. in the early 2000s, the increased complexity of disasters and their impact necessitated a rethink in the priorities of civil defence and protection, and emergency planning, based on ideas of resilience (Alexander, 2002). A series of high profile regional and international crises in 2000 and 2001[11] triggered a review of the performance and management of emergency planning, swiftly leading to a new review of what was commonly referred to as 'civil contingencies'.[12] However, as this review progressed, the 9/11 terror attacks, dramatically, changed the landscape of U.K. emergency planning giving new and significant impetus to the agenda of improvement and reorganisation. In particular, U.K. cities were deemed not sufficient prepared for major terror strikes (Coaffee et al., 2008).

Subsequently, a whole new governance architecture around ideas of enhancing resilience through the connected realms of civil contingencies and counter-terrorism legislation and guidance emerged, and a new set of powers, bodies and multi-agency connections were established to manage these issues. Such collaboration, it was argued, should be undertaken by government at all levels, service sectors and other emergency managers. Developing multi-scalar resilience was not just about coordinated thinking and multi-agency working *per se* but rather about such 'joined-up thinking' occurring at the appropriate scale. In the U.K., this was an exercise, led from the centre of government, with a focus on achieving a consistent level of 'resilience' across the country, that was able to respond effectively to all forms of emergency, but especially from terrorist attack.

Such activity encompassed wider reform of emergency planning and a reimagining of responses to new types of terrorism. These two major streams of work produced key pieces of national policy, notably the Civil Contingencies Act (CCA, 2004) and the Countering International Terrorism Strategy (CONTEST, 2006),[13] and whilst is difficult to quantify the extent to which the threat of terrorism drove this overall reform process, it certainly gave it significant impetus. Concerns about the lack of initial city-level preparation after the Manchester city centre bombing in 1996, and similar worries after the 9/11 attacks, clearly focused the government's mind on developing a response system that could cope with significant acts of terrorism (Coaffee et al., 2008). As the Home Secretary declared in November 2001, just after 9/11, our 'objective is to do everything that can be done to enhance our resilience'.[14]

In the reform of emergency planning, the vocabulary of resilience was adopted to describe this new and evolving process as it purveyed a holistic, positive and proactive approach. Resilience according to the Cabinet Office (2003) was seen as 'the ability to handle disruptive challenges that can lead to or result in crisis' (Paragraph 1.1) and was built around several key activities based on anticipation and *'scanning the horizon* for external threats' as well as 'to *prepare* to deal with a disruptive challenge' (ibid., emphasis added). To develop a relatively uniform approach, national resilience management evolved largely as a strategic, rather than directive tier – in a Foucauldian sense 'of governing at a distance' – with a requirement to coordinate central government action at different tiers in emergency response.[15]

The CCA regulations came into force in November 2005, setting out a simple framework that highlighted what resiliency tasks should be performed and by whom, and how cooperation towards this goal should be achieved. This Act was, however, primarily focused on insuring conformance at the local level[16] and aimed to establish 'a modern framework for civil protection capable of meeting the challenges of the 21st century' (Security Services, 2006). At city level, local resilience forums (LRFs) were mandated to improve responses to a range of emergencies and to break out of conventional and remote 'emergency planning' practices and develop a multi-agency environment across a defined geographical area, where preparing for emergencies was done in a more coordinated and effective way. The LRFs were tasked with developing strategic emergency plans detailing how public authorities, emergency services, utility providers and business and civic communities and others, would cope with, and respond to, disruptive incidents. The focus here was on both developing a generic plan based on capabilities required to cope with all types of disruption, as well as detailed plans for particular risks faced (notably terrorism). This new resilience governance system also sought to broaden the scope of the risks to be focused on, with priorities emerging from more detailed risk assessment and horizon scanning activities. So-called capability reviews were also central in identifying gaps in organisational ability, informing the planning process regarding the scale of response required and organising operational exercises to routinely test procedures and to learn from the experience.

Whilst the CCA 2004 focused on enhancing civil protection, predominantly at the local level, the other main strand of developing resilience in the United Kingdom came through the *Countering International Terrorism: The United Kingdom's Strategy* (CONTEST), first published in July 2006 (HM Government, 2006). The aim of CONTEST was to 'develop and implement plans and programmes to strengthen counter-terrorism capabilities at all levels of Government, the emergency services, businesses and the wider community' (p.3). Towards this resiliency objective, as with emergency planning reform, significant extra resources were utilised – approximately double the pre-9/11 level. Equally the partnership rhetoric in counter-terrorism was strengthened with envisaged cooperation between all government departments, links across all governance tiers, and with the emergency services. New government bodies were further established in the early 2000s linked to counter-terrorism – notably JTAC (Joint Terrorism Analysis Centre) and NaCTSO (the National Counter-Terrorism Security Office) – to further securitise the ongoing terrorist threat, and which, deployed the rhetoric of resilience.

The strand of work within the CONTEST strategy most closely connected with the previous discussions of civil contingences reform was 'Prepare' that sought to 'ensure that the UK is as ready as it can be for the consequences of a terrorist attack' (HM Government, 2006, p.25). This strand assumed the *inevitability* of attack and, hence, the need to prepare. As noted, achieving this 'involves developing the *resilience* of the UK to withstand such attacks. This means improving the ability of the United Kingdom to respond effectively, to recover quickly and to absorb and minimise wider indirect disruption' (ibid., emphasis added).

The Prepare strand placed great focus upon multi-agency and multi-tier working across the entire 'resilience community' to ensure an effective response to terrorism, as well as establishing 'processes which join-up work at the *local, regional and national levels* of government, and between the public, private and voluntary sectors' (ibid.). In this sense, the objectives of this strand were to identify risks from terrorism, assess the impact of potential risks, build the capacity and capabilities to respond and evaluate and test response through simulation, which were cross-cutting with the broader work on civil contingencies. As the 2006 CONTEST strategy noted, 'planning seeks to build generic capabilities and plans, able to be drawn on flexibly in the response to a wide range of terrorist (and other) events' (ibid.).

Securitising resilience for the U.S. homeland

This enhancement in disaster management and countering terrorism was felt around the globe but operationalised in different ways, often with a 'single response framework' being developed to deal with the ongoing threat from terrorism (Gregory, 2007, p.333). This was exemplified in the United States through the establishment of the Department of Homeland Security (DHS) in 2002, in response to heated debates about the ability of the American state, and its population, to cope with subsequent acts of large-scale terrorism. The DHS bundled up a range of domestic counter-terrorism operations that sprang from 9/11, and institutionalised and securitised the War on Terrorism.

More broadly, the U.S. undoubtedly took the global lead in the legislative reform around counter-terrorism, throwing the agenda of civil liberties and state security centre stage with the swift passing of the 2001 Patriot Act. The Patriot Act packed together a range of measures such as internal surveillance, border controls and intelligence gathering that restricted civil liberties, as well as enabling the detention of terror suspects – renamed enemy combatants – at the U.S. military's Guantanamo Bay camp in Cuba.[17]

154 *The longer term implications of 9/11*

As a result, the DHS and its terrorism remit was heavily criticised. The accusation from civil liberties lobbies maintained that the federal government had, through the establishment of extraordinary bodies for management of these issues, and the creation of emergency powers for dealing with terror suspects, contravened the principles of open government; eroded the right to privacy; unjustly targeted immigrants, refugees and minorities for differential policing; and jeopardised the fair and equitable treatment of security detainees (Chang, 2004; Doherty et al., 2005; Wolfendale, 2007). Whilst such approaches did not explicit use the term resilience, the actions they undertook were, effectively, anticipatory and preparatory resilience in action.

However, a few years after 9/11 it was questionable whether the required level of 'resilience' had been obtained. Stephen Flynn in *Edge of Disaster* (2007) painted a picture of an American nation still unprepared for dealing with a major catastrophe, arguing that terrorism cannot always be predicted and that more effort and resources must be put into preparedness training, infrastructure protection and the building of community and economic resilience. In short, argued Flynn, resilience should become the 'national motto' as the U.S. seeks to embed protective security and disaster management measures into nation organisations and the collective psyche. As such, 'a resilient society is one that won't fall apart in the face of adversity. Making infrastructures resilient makes them less attractive for terrorists. And preparing for the worst makes the worst less likely to happen' (ibid., p.154).

The emphasis here was both on the need to be prepared in the increasingly risky world of the unknown and versatile aggressor, and to build bridges and collaborative relationship, through this initial impetus of security towards other areas of disaster management. One key difference between the American and U.K. model is that 'U.K. Resilience' was a wide net cast to encompass a range of civil, natural and anthropogenic risks, hazards and threats from the beginning, whereas, in the U.S., widespread criticism was levied at the Office of Homeland Security for its focus on foreign threats at the risk of indigenous natural hazards (Committee on Homeland Security and Governmental Affairs, 2006; U.S. House of Representatives, 2006).

In this context, it took a while for the language of resilience to be officially designated at the DHS and in national security policy, although its programmes of action since its formation undoubtedly were focused on preparation and anticipation as policy goal priorities. Resilience as a process and program of activity became widespread in the 2010s amongst the homeland security community as 'it appears more "pro-active" – than the alternatives, vulnerability and protection. Vulnerability might be seen as implying weakness, while protection implies a purely defensive stance. Resilience, on the other hand, enables patriotic appeals to American values' (Sims, 2017, p.7). Notably, the first Quadrennial Homeland Security Review in 2010 offered recommendations on long-term strategy and priorities for both *security* – to protect the United States and its people, vital interests and way of life – and *resilience* – to foster individual, community and system robustness, adaptability and capacity for rapid recovery as key concepts 'that are essential to, and form the foundation for, a comprehensive approach to homeland security'.[18] The reinforcement of resilience ideas in U.S. security doctrine came in the 2017 National Security Strategy[19] where the enhancement of resilience included reference to the 'ability to withstand and recover rapidly from deliberate attacks, accidents, natural disasters, as well as unconventional stresses, shocks and threats to our economy and democratic system'. Here, a whole section was devoted to 'Promoting American Resilience' and, in particular, multi-scale collaborative working and information sharing amongst local, state and federal levels; building a culture of preparedness; and improving planning and the conducting of realistic exercises.

Europe and Australia

In other Western states, the development of resilience and the emphasis it gave to counter-terrorism emerged differently. Across the EU, 9/11 catalysed the advancement of a collective EU-wide counter-terrorism policy (EU, 2001; European Council, 2003, 2004) that was subsequently institutionalised through a number of mechanisms, such as an EU Counter-Terrorism Coordinator and the European Counter-Terrorism Centre within Europol (Kaunert and Léonard, 2019). Most notably, in 2005 the European Council adopted the EU counter-terrorism strategy to fight terrorism globally and make Europe safer. The strategy was established whilst the United Kingdom held the EU presidency and, as a result, mirrored the U.K. four-strand approach to (prevent, protect, pursue and respond [replacing prepare in the U.K. version]). As in the United States, it took a number of years for the language of resilience to be officially adopted as a core EU priority. As Joseph and Juncos (2019) noted, the resilience turn has more recently been 'promoted as the answer to a number of concerns regarding long-term development and short-term emergency intervention, disaster risk reduction and political and regional instabilities' (p.995). In practice, many cities and regions across Europe that have been afflicted by terrorism are increasingly adopting relatively similar approaches through coordinated and strategic preparations to allow themselves to be able to respond and recover from attack as quickly as possible. Whether this be the development of Swedish resilience regions, the U.K. city resilience partnerships or Dutch safety regions, the changing nature of terrorism means holistic and resilience-based approaches to counter-terrorism are becoming routinised in many locations in accordance with local and regional political realities (CTPN, 2019b).

Another example of the differential focus of security policy amongst Western states occurred in Australia, where the focal point of security in the wake of 9/11 was initially on immigration, border control and foreign relations and was strongly contested (McDonald, 2005). More recently, national-level plans for counter-terrorism, security and the protection of crowded places have adopted the language of resilience to refer to the advancement of policies for responding to know and unknown risks as effectively as possible. In the inaugural National Statement of Security in 2008, a focus was placed on 'resilience' as the need to respond more holistically and flexibly to a broadening of national security responsibility (not just terrorism) that were more complex and interconnected. Similar to the U.K. model, this can be viewed as a maturing of prior approaches to national security, with a shift from simply responding to an identifiable threat towards building a resilient community and enhancing the capabilities to resist, respond to and bounce back from any disaster. Furthermore, the Australian Government's 2010 Counter-Terrorism White Paper – *Securing Australia, Protecting Our Community* – listed resilience as one of the four key elements of the counter-terrorism strategy, and as a way of 'building a strong and resilient Australian community to resist the development of any form of violent extremism and terrorism on the home front'.[20]

Most recently, guidance about the protection of crowded places from terrorism released by the Australian Government in 2017[21] also sought to mitigate the impacts of terrorism and to 'protect the lives of people working in, using, and visiting crowded places by making these places more resilient to terrorism'. It also noted that this was 'a responsibility shared by all Australian governments, the community, and the private sector'. This strategy utilised the language of resilience to symbolise a protective, proactive and necessary approach that modifies the nature of terrorist targets by lessening their physical vulnerability in a proportionate fashion, commensurate with the level of risk faced.

Whilst the international idiosyncrasies define the structure, means and method of policy directions for enhancing resilience, consistency was apparent less in the specific policy of the nation-state or government body than in the rhetoric underpinning emerging policies. It was in this context that the elasticity of the term resilience came to the fore and driven by new slogans such as 'the War on Terror', but also through emphasis on the potential for a positive return to a new normality, giving a highly emotive rhetoric on which to attach a host of wider issues. In the 2000s, many commentators had expressed concern over the prioritisation of terrorist-related threats as the subject of resilience enhancement. As O'Brien and Read (2004, p.359) noted in relation to the U.K., 'resilience in the face of international terrorism is an obvious current priority ... but wider considerations should not be consumed by this current single course of threat'. From an American perspective, Flynn (2007) further argued that the overlooking of higher probability and higher consequence risk from natural hazards at the expense of terrorism has wide-ranging implications for society at large, and that 'the folly of a myopic focus on terrorism became abundantly clear when Hurricane Katrina struck New Orleans' (p.xviii).

The everyday impacts of security-driven resiliency

Governance architectures for civil contingencies and security that evolved in the early twenty-first century were driven by the ongoing terrorist threat and primarily developed to build up a consistent degree of resilience across a nation, to anticipate and prepare for a variety of threats faced. Whilst this enabled emergency planning, national security and counter-terrorism to enjoy unprecedented funding and profile at all scales, it was to have significant implications for everyday urban life; from the governance of control to institutional and personal responsibilisation in anticipation of inevitable attack. This means returning to the question urban historian Lewis Mumford raised in his discussion of the origins of war and the city, as to whether there is an inherent pathology within 'dreams' of security which leads inevitably to violence (see Chapter 1).

The impact of resilience politics

Many countries adopted increasingly introspective approaches to their own security in the post-9/11 era, reimagining traditional, and outdated, polices. As a result, a new protective and regulatory state emerged, often articulated through the rhetoric of resilience, replacing Cold War era conceptions of civil defence and protection, and leading to the dispersion of security responsibilities through all levels of government and beyond. This reterritorialisation of security can be seen as part of a process of social fragmentation that had occurred since the late 1960s and early 1970s, and which, has accelerated since the end of the Cold War. Neoliberalism has also helped spread regimes of privatisation that has increasingly transformed security into a commodity which is the responsibility of all levels of global society, rather than coterminous with national borders, or existing in the context of a consensual international order (Coaffee and Murakami Wood, 2006, p.514).

The concept of security – through the discourse of resilience – was subsequently rescaled and became increasingly ubiquitous in the 2000s and beyond; a trend that was especially pronounced in major cities that were tasked with dealing with terrorist threats. Security as a concept 'came home' whilst, at the same time, the terror threat was positioned as global, and 'terrorism' – rather like the market or democracy with which it is juxtaposed – was both everywhere and nowhere (ibid., p.504). However, the advancing 'security for all, and by all' rhetoric of national resilience programmes often provoked considerable criticism within civil society, not least with regard to issues of freedom of movement, the pervasive monitoring of everyday activities, and the impact on community cohesion and multiculturalism, creating a situation that was termed 'creeping authoritarianism' (Jenkins, 2006).

State surveillance and civil liberties

A key point in understanding the broader implications of resilience as a generative metaphor for security and counter-terrorism is that the scope of influence of the concept now transcends emergency planning and civil contingencies and extends through other related policy initiatives, underpinned by the rhetoric that we are living in a changing, uncertain and dangerous world. Through the exploitation of fear, security became part of an increasing number of policy domain and normalised notions of security – through resilience – began to pervade everyday life (Coaffee and Wood, 2006). In this sense, we are told we must be prepared – through enhanced resiliency – for life in a constant state of emergency (Wood et al., 2003), or what Agamben (2005) termed a 'state of exception', and where a 'politics of fear' permeates daily living.

The rhetorical links between the narratives of fear of crime and threat of terrorism, social order and quality of life, have increasingly and obliquely underpinned wider legislative reform. Wekerle and Jackson (2004), for example, argued with regard to North American cities that numerous policies have 'hitchhiked' on the anti-terrorism agenda and been implicitly embedded within numerous social and planning policy discourses, as 'a hegemonic project that insinuates itself into the interstices of everyday life, reframing policies relating to urban form, transportation and public space' (p.36). Commenting upon not dissimilar Australian experiences of the War on Terror, McDonald (2005) also discussed how the public discourses surrounding counter-terrorism were carefully constructed to resonate with concerns of domestic population and to justify an ever-advancing security state. Here 'political responses that potentially undermine individual security' and that are only 'marginally related' to counter-terrorism were evoked as the government sought to develop a broad discourse of the need for 'militarized vigilance in protecting Australia's security in an insecure world' (ibid., p.298).

Resilience as a policy metaphor and governance assemblage seemed to be a more nuanced approach to embedding security than the target-hardening and 'zero-tolerance' approaches seen in broad policy shift towards, for example, crime reduction in New York, following the Giuliani era, or in the mass policing of high profile events (see Chapter 11). The wider resilience agenda assumed a softer and subtler approach to embedding security into the broader experience of governance, through stakeholder partnerships for ensuring greater preparedness. Yet there remains an undercurrent of paranoia and suspicion unsuited to idealised liberal democracies that have embedded an institutionalised mistrust of the citizen in state policies. Here, in critical accounts, greater preparedness is often juxtaposed with biopolitics and seen as a strategy for reconciling security and civil liberties (Lentzos and Rose, 2009; Lundborg and Vaughan-Williams, 2011) and internalising emergency within society, through the focuses upon the adaptation of the individual (Duffield, 2011). Emotive and militarised rhetoric which talks not only of the War on Terror, but also a war on drugs, crime, and so on, as well as constant reminders of government threat and risk assessments, reinforces such securitisation. In essence, governments and interest groups played on the whole range of types of fear to justify the intensification of technologically driven control strategies to counter not only terrorism but also anti-social behaviour, democratic protest, to exclude the dangerous 'other' from public space and to introduce identity cards and other systems of surveillance that link citizens to state-held databases.

Of particular concern has been the ways that the security, counter-terrorism and resilience agendas may sacrifice what is supposedly to be safeguarded – the values and freedoms of liberal democracy. The danger comes from the assumption that some civil rights and liberties impede an effective counterterrorist strategy, and that the solution is to find an appropriate 'balance' between the two that is inevitably weighted more towards security than liberty. This, it has been argued, comes from a misconception of security (Lustgarten and Leigh, 1994; Coaffee et al., 2008). Weighing fundamental human rights in a balance against national security is to miss the point that the legitimacy of the nation-state depends on the guaranteeing of those rights and freedoms. Without them, the state ceases to have a purpose beyond its self-perpetuation: it becomes – like Mumford's account of early defended cities – pathological.

Third Way security

In Western states, how resilience policy developed and was transmuted into what was described as 'third way security' (Coaffee and O'Hare, 2011)[22] to manage the complexities of the increasingly insecure world, highlighted an array of interconnected local and global issues, as well as new international security threats from a wide range of sources, not just terrorism. Resilience, as a synonym for effective security governance, was also boosted as a result of the decentralisation of power and responsibility to different tiers of government and was premised upon multilevel working that would provide civic framework where citizens receive a certain level of protection, whist commercial enterprises were made more resistant to events that might stop the orderly flow of commerce. 'Third way security' articulated a new mode of governance and governmentality through the rescaling of the state, an increased emphasis on partnership working and a greater role and reasonability being afforded to civil society for the management and control of risk in their everyday life. This was a political logic of decentralised responsibility rooted in Cold War civil defence programmes – or what Collier and Lakoff (2008) referred to as 'distributed preparedness' – where 'responsibility was delegated to different levels of government, and to both public and private agencies according to their competencies and capacities' (p.128).

The discourse of resilience has further been responsible for a shift from state-level to societal-based understandings of security practices, where the focus becomes building internal capabilities and coping capacities within the wider citizenry to respond to different forms of disruption, rather than national and territorial forms of protection and regulation against specific external security threats (Duffield, 2012; Chandler, 2016). Here, the state's role has been recast as a facilitator, rather than a manager, keen to regulate and direct 'hands-on' responsibility. This for many was seen as an expression of neoliberal governmentality and represented 'not the end, but a transformation of politics, that restructures the power relations in society... between statehood and a new relation between state and civil society actors' (Lemke, 2002, p.58).

Conclusions: Security and counter-terrorism as resilience

In the years and decades following 9/11, security-driven urban resilience rose to prominence as a governing logic and spatial practice to meet the 'new' security and terrorism challenges of the twenty-first century. More critically, the rolling out of such security policy under the aegis of resilience has had significant impacts on the ability to generate effective, transparent and legitimate governance in the face of nationally derived counter-terrorism policy. Resilience framing has refocused security policy on absorbing and rebounding from shocks rather than strictly on the traditional security logics of prevention and deterrence but has often lacked the agility, flexibility and adaptability of approach that they purportedly represent. They are also seen by many as reactionary and governed by a governmental structure that rides roughshod over community concerns and civil liberties.

In policy arenas connected with counter-terrorism, resilience discourse metamorphosed out of a fixation with future security challenges to reduce the exposure of places to terror risk through material interventions and a focus upon pre-emption and new modes of risk scanning. This led to a reappraisal of who, what and where is vulnerable to terrorism and how people, places and processes can be made more resilient (Coaffee, 2020). Whilst national and local political contexts defined the operation of resilience policy directions, consistency was more apparent in the rhetoric and direction underpinning emerging policies. Historically, security and terrorism concerns have generally been referenced to national, transnational or global scales, yet more recently, local responses that require analysis through different frames of reference have emerged as the key focus.

National security has therefore been increasingly played out in the local realm under the rubric of resilience that has placed a particular emphasis upon preparedness and anticipation. In this scenario, resilience was seen as both a collective concern where multiple stakeholders, rather than just the security services alone, were given responsibility for ensuring security, as well as becoming increasingly focused on developing pre-emptive solutions to perceived security threats. This consequently narrowed formerly diverse concerns towards very specific forms of security and sought to draw in of a range of institutional stakeholders in counter-terrorism; Government – at central, regional and local levels, emergency planners, the police and private security professionals and range of private-sector partners, and importantly local communities. In many countries, security therefore became a potent driver and shaper of contemporary resilience practices, whilst, at the same time, security policy adopted the softer language of resilience that provided further strategic direction for developing security so that people can go about their daily lives freely and with confidence.

As a report on *London's Preparedness to Respond to a Major Terrorist Incident* (Harris, 2016) noted, deploying the mixed language of security and resilience and embracing a narrative of shared responsibly:

> [The current terrorist threat] requires that we all acquire a mind-set of community security and resilience...where security and resilience is designed in and is part of the city's fabric, and where everyone who lives and works here sees security and resilience as their responsibility just as much as it is for the emergency services and civic authorities.

Whilst security and counter-terrorism increasingly adopted the language of resilience in the wake of 9/11, in many ways this was only a partial adoption of a broader resilience narrative that sought to prepare populations for future risk and danger, and, in particular, the next imminent catastrophe. For all the talk of preparing for, and anticipating the next attack, how resilience has been drawn into counter-terrorism is largely through command and control strategies that seek to proscribe one-size-fits-all solutions to managing the terrorist threat. Here, it is resilience as bouncing-back or business-as-usual that currently predominates as the overarching philosophy. In many ways, approaches to contemporary security-driven resilience, to date, represent a particularly modernist way of thinking about uncertain and postmodern threats (Coaffee, 2019). These processes further illuminate the particularly important two-part question, long established in critical security studies but only recently gaining prominence in counterpart critiques of resilience: 'what is being made resilience, and for whom?' (Coaffee and Fussey, 2015).

In the following chapter, this discussion will be enhanced by unpacking the communities' role in counter-terrorism through the emergence of resiliency programmes that actively attempted to prevent the radicalisation of individuals as well as government communications that seeks local citizens help identify signs of imminent terrorist attack.

Notes

1 The National Security Strategy also made clear that the 'view of international security had broadened' to encompass not just terrorism, but transnational crime, health pandemics and flooding, 'that were not part of the traditional idea of national security' (Cabinet Office, 2008, p.3).
2 Brown unveils security strategy, *BBC News*, March 19, 2008. Available at http://news.bbc.co.uk/1/hi/uk_politics/7303846.stm.
3 This echoed prior work in critical resilience studies that sees resilience as the art of governance in complex times (Chandler, 2014a, b).
4 The Cold War is seen as the other classic example of macro-securitisation.

5 Bourbeau (2013) noted that political science, International Relations (IR) and particularly security studies were largely absent from these early debates in the 2000s.
6 For example, in the United Kingdom in the early 2000s, there was a sense of fatalism about the likelihood of London being targeted by international terrorists utilising non-traditional methods of attack. Sir John Stevens Commissioner of the Metropolitan Police, speaking in the wake of the 2004 Madrid train attacks noted that there is an inevitability that some sort of attack will get through – see, London terror attack inevitable, *BBC News*, March 16, 2004. http://news.bbc.co.uk/1/hi/uk_politics/3515312.stm.
7 Here, there was further a move away from static risk-based indices that used out-of-date representations of the past to predict the future, and towards new processes that thought through multiple scenarios and undertook simulation modelling and real-time testing. The move towards anticipatory strategies however was not without significant challenges. As Omand (2010, p.12) noted, such an approach was premised on high quality pre-emptive operational intelligence and maintaining community confidence that such intelligence is being used appropriately and not as a 'blunt discriminatory measure' that might alienate sections of society.
8 Exercise Capital Focus in 2003 further tested the revised structures in an exercise designed to trial communication arrangements and information flows between the lead responders and Government.
9 London tests have been an ongoing part of emergency planning for many years. Tests, for instance, on the underground network have been a regular occurrence since the mid-1990s, stimulated by the 1995 Tokyo subway attack using poison gas.
10 See, Anti-terror drill revealed soft targets in London, *The Observer*, July 10, 2005 at http://observer.guardian.co.uk/uk_news/story/0,6903,1525247,00.html.
11 In the United Kingdom this policy review built on what has been referred to anecdotally as the '3 Fs'; the *fuel* protests (blockades of oil refineries, go-slow convoys on motorways), the outbreak of the *Foot and Mouth* Disease and a number of serious *flooding* incidents. The combination of these disaster events led to questions being posed regarding 'who was in charge' of emergency responses, and the need for a meaningful peacetime response to 'civil contingencies', as opposed to the previously over-simple rhetorics of defence and protection.
12 The long-overdue review of emergency planning procedures began in early 2001 and was to be completed by the end of that year, during which time responsibility for civil contingency planning was shifted from the locally fragmented Home Office Emergency Planning Department to the emergent Cabinet Office's national body – the Civil Contingencies Secretariat (CCS) in July 2001 (Smith, 2003).
13 The development of a national counter-terrorism strategy (known in government circles as CONTEST) was developed from 2003, but only published finally in July 2006.
14 Cited in Walker and Broderick (2006, p.46).
15 However, such an appearance of decentralised control was balanced so that executive authority can be manifest during the national or larger scale crisis.
16 Between 2004 and 2010 there was a regional resilience tier established to mediate between local areas and national government.
17 This was seen by many as an exemplar of a 'state of exception' where the rule of law is abandoned (Agamben, 2005).
18 See www.dhs.gov/sites/default/files/publications/2010-qhsr-report.pdf.

19 See www.whitehouse.gov/wp-content/uploads/2017/12/NSS-Final-12-18-2017-0905.pdf.
20 See www.dst.defence.gov.au/sites/default/files/basic_pages/documents/counter-terrorism-white-paper.pdf.
21 Commonwealth of Australia, Australia's Strategy for Protecting Crowded Places from Terrorism, 2017, at www.nationalsecurity.gov.au/Securityandyourcommunity/Pages/australias-strategy-forprotecting-crowdedplaces-from-terrorism.aspx.
22 'Third way' politics – a normative agenda for centre-left politics throughout the Western world – emerged in the 1990s alongside the perceived need to reform public administration and public services in response to the ongoing restructuring of the global economy, and was most notably adopted by the Clinton administration in the U.S. and the Blair Government in the U.K.

9 Everyday terror prevention

Introduction: Community and the War on Terror

In July 2020, a former U.K. Home Secretary, reflecting upon over a decade of anti-radicalisation programmes under the 'Prevent' strand of national counter-terrorism efforts, noted that 'its reputation is so toxic...[and] in danger of being counter-productive, alienating communities and ultimately making the fight against terrorism harder'.[1] But how did such programmes of action become so alienating to large sections of society? In addressing this question, this chapter will highlight a shift in official thinking away from prioritising protective interventions and towards 'softer' awareness raising and preventative measures that sought to deal with the root causes of terrorism through counter-radicalisation programmes. The focus of such programmes was focused on the local and personal enactments of security beyond the representational, state-centred framings of national security; the 'banal terrorism' work of local and everyday security initiatives. As Katz (2007, p.351) noted

> The banality of terrorism and the state of terror it evokes work almost at the capillary level; we've gone from duct tape to the farce of color-coded alerts to talismanic lunacy. I recently saw a license plate that said 'fight terrorism'. As the fight stoops to smiley face tactics, we are urged – everywhere – to 'say something' if we 'see something' ...Banal terrorism is sutured to – and secured in – the performance of security in the everyday environment.

Here, the increasing 'routinization' (ibid., p.360) and performances of security potentially incited personal insecurities and revealed invasive state-citizen relationships that posed fundamental questions of state legitimacy and personal morality (Coaffee et al., 2008).

The majority of post-9/11 security approaches centred upon the technocentric and material manifestations of terror and failed in large part to make connections between the macro-politics and regimes of securitisation and domestic, everyday urban lived experience (Harker, 2014). Such localised work was progressively intensified in the mid-late 2000s and centred upon

DOI: 10.4324/9780429461620-12

Everyday terror prevention 165

understanding the social processes that bring about the awareness and de-escalation of conflict. In seeking to understand the impact of the War on Terror through an analysis of local processes further reintroduced questions raised by de Certeau (1984) regarding the necessity of unpacking the deployment of everyday spatial practices to illuminate 'blind spots' and the 'opaqueness' of city life (p.93). In more contemporary terrorism studies since that emerged after 9/11, there was an upsurge in work looking at everyday, domestic and lived experiences of security as it became re-evaluated and rescaled.

Partly this challenge came from the emerging ideas of 'human security' which, from the 1990s, had tried to wrench security away from its institutional bias, to focus it on the needs of people and populations (Paris, 2001), be it the recognition of the dangers of climate change, or the particular threat of Jihadist terrorism. This increased focus upon localities and communities as an evolution of counter-terrorism towards a broader counterinsurgency strategy (Bell and Evans, 2010), heralded the increasing civilianisation of warfare where certain local areas were identified as 'breeding grounds' for terrorism and where intervention to help vulnerable individuals develop coping capacities to resist radicalisation, was required (Bell, 2011).[2]

As a result, orthodox institutionalised problem-solving approaches to security that sought to explain terrorism from a realist state-centric prospective increasingly became usurped by approaches engaged in a root-cause debate, opening up a social front in the War on Terror (Franks, 2009). In practice, when faced with these new security challenges in the early twenty-first century, many Western governments responded by further collapsing distinctions between internal and external security, raising concerns over 'home grown terrorists', and focusing attention on 'the radicalization of individuals' and their pathway to violent extremism.[3] In line with broader trends in securitisation that saw security increasing articulated through the language of resilience, emerging preventative policy approaches further sought to develop the 'resilience' of places and communities (Coaffee, 2014). This, as Chandler (2016) noted, fomented the 'societalisation of security' that focused upon the proactive engagement with individual citizens and communities to give them the tools (and security responsibilities) to adapt to security risks, and in so doing, 'reduce the problematic of security to the generic or everyday problems of individual behaviour or practices' (p.29). Here the focus was upon how resilience was rescaled from a state-based security practice to a societal understanding that was locally enacted as a form of neoliberal governance (O'Malley, 2010), utilitarian neoliberal citizenship (Neocleous, 2013), or, as a broader form of governmentality.

A corollary of this concerned the manifold and localised ways in which resilience became interpreted and translated into practice locally. This signified a narrowing of the polymorphic range of concerns implied by resilience towards those of security and was underpinned by a localising logic that was directed towards everyday activities. More specifically, the focus and co-option of community-level groups into the provision of urban security focused on preventing future acts of terrorism through anti-radicalisation programmes that become blended with community cohesion policies, risk awareness campaigns and the social control practices of surveillance, that served to the direct use of specific security practices towards pre-emptive and amelioratory ends (Kaplan, 2006).

Within this context, the remainder of this chapter is divided into four main parts. First, a critical interrogation of emerging policy work on the governance of counter-terrorism, and the purported requirement to enhance community resilience to reduce threats from terrorism, is undertaken. Second, emerging anti-radicalisation polices are explored within a number of contexts, with a particular focus upon how building the trust of communities at local levels was activated as a key pillar of national security. Third, recent experiences from major U.K. cities are used to illustrate how counter-terrorist interventions were gradually amalgamated within broader systems of community resilience, and cut across and connect to various other local strategies. In this section, practice vignettes are presented that both illuminate how citizens and, local communities were expected to contribute to counter-terrorism efforts, and, the tensions and resistances this provoked for conventional security practices. Fourth, the implications of the growing importance of community governance in counter-terrorism policy are drawn out and questions raised about what such policies might mean in practice for the 'active' or 'passive' role of citizens in civic life.

Activating community-voice in the War on Terror

In the wake of 9/11, many Western countries established new ways of managing a range of civil contingencies based on a top-down modus operandi under the banner of resilience that was seen as a professional, legal and technical response developed by 'experts' (Chapter 8). Under such new governing structures, there was usually a key responsibility for the local state to develop systems of local communication for 'warning and informing' citizens about the risks they faced, and for enhancing place-based resilience where a well-informed public was seen as better able to respond appropriately in an emergency. Rhetorically, this implied attempts to get citizens to play a role in developing *their own* resilience. However, governance processes that were rapidly established to cope with new terrorist threats, with only a few exceptions, largely excluded citizens from meaningful discussion. The public were thus chiefly *passive* recipients within an increasingly controlled and regulated society, whilst, paradoxically, new policy visions focus for how individuals and local communities might become more responsible for their own risk management were advanced (Coaffee and Rogers, 2008).

In responding to the complex challenges of urban terrorism, the ideas of collective-action governance pervaded debates about the most effective responses, as the focus of security shifted away from external threats towards internal home-grown threats from individuals and certain communities. Such collective-action promoted a focus on the power that communities can exercise in helping the national counter-terrorism effort by strengthening 'bottom-up' approaches and increasing local responsibility and coping capacities. In many countries, this specifically focused on the purported need to build 'community resilience' as a reinforcement of broader national security strategies (Coaffee, 2014).

For example, in the U.K., this policy dynamic generated a shift in security governance, providing a fit with wider government ambitions to create a new, more community-driven social contract between citizens and the state. Here attention focused on local place-based solutions so as to 'reduce the barriers which prevent people from being able to help themselves and to become more resilient to shocks' whilst recognising the importance of anticipatory, holistic and comprehensive approaches to the changing nature of places (HM Government, 2010). Although enhanced institutional and adaptive capacity was expected to drive the move towards improved local resilience, a *Strategic National Framework on Community Resilience* directed it (Cabinet Office, 2011). Here, community resilience was seen through the lens of emergency planning, conflating top-down and bottom-up impulses with 'communities and individuals harnessing local resources and expertise to help themselves in an emergency, in a way that complements the response of the emergency services' (ibid., p.4). Such attempts to enhance community resilience by the sharing of advice and guidance with the public about emergency response, and increasingly at this time about countering radicalisation in certain communities, were seen as measures that would reduce vulnerability to terrorism.

Over time, specific counter-terrorism activities became increasingly focused upon how the public can assist this securitisation process by becoming better prepared and more responsible for their personal risk management in ways that questioned broader issues of citizenship. From a governmentality perspective, this appeared to be an agenda of civil responsibilisation, where rescaled notions of security morphed from one of sovereign and disciplinary power to seeing the population as an urgent political problem that required a focus upon their everyday milieus and behaviours (Foucault, 2003). Such shifting security approaches were further interpreted as attempts at the biopolitical construction of resilient subjects and communities through a range of techniques that sought to change people's behaviour and place the onus upon individuals and communities to self-regulate (Rose, 2000a).[4]

The rolling out of such contentious security policy, from the mid-2000, was to have significant impacts on the ability to generate legitimate community governance in the face of nationally derived counter-terrorism policy. It has additionally had broader implications for the definition and framework of civil liberties and responsibilities within and through citizenship – both of state to citizen and citizen to state – in the context of complex loyalties and hybrid identities for local communities. For others, the recommendation to enhance community resilience served to naturalise particular modes of prescribed behaviour that would, according to Government pronouncements, make them better able to identify radicalising tendencies in fellow citizens, as well as being able to better cope with multiple forms of disruption.

The civilianisation of the War on Terror

The focus of counter-terrorism upon communities, and in particular anti- and deradicalisation programmes, gave the look of a more cultural and social focus to resilience planning for terrorism, as opposed to the highly technical focus of the majority of counter-terrorist work in the early-mid-2000s (Durodie, 2005). In 2008, *Time Magazine* listed deradicalisation as 1 of 10 future revolutions,[5] and since then, deradicalisation programmes have continued to diffuse across the globe as a solution to restricting terrorism by limiting the radicalisation of individuals and thereby reducing the opportunities for 'violent extremism'. Here radicalisation was commonly seen as part of an overall conveyor-belt to terrorism with deradicalisation as a proactive, anticipatory approach that attempted 'to control the future by acting in the present' (Quarashi, 2018), fitting with broader objectives of pre-emptive counter-terrorism policy.

In the wider international community, ideas of countering violent extremism (CVE) were also seen as a form of 'soft power' that could be deployed by states within their own borders to shape the preferences of citizens through appealing to their sense of civic duty, as well as various community outreach activities, including: the establishment of local partnerships between policing and non-policing agencies; messaging and public relations campaigns; and educational and training programs.[6] Such initiatives have taken many forms but most focus upon 'interreligious and intercultural dialogue, inclusion, and the promoting of understanding' (UN, 2020). However, initial CVE approaches tended to be highly, if not exclusively, centred on the monitoring and surveillance of Muslim communities leading to many accusations of Islamophobia (Allen, 2010). Over time, many CVE schemes evolved to also focus upon domestic right wing extremism and more recent concerns regarding other 'radical' groups such as Incel, Antifa or a range of white supremacist networks.[7]

CVE programmes have also advanced in many countries so as to place a legal duty on service providers to report any suspicions they might have about individuals they come into contact with. Such approaches to CVE have developed into wide-ranging strategies that encompass both hard and soft approaches. As the United Nations Secretary-General noted in 2016, when launching their *Plan of Action to Prevent Violent Extremism (PVE),* we need to adopt 'a comprehensive approach...encompassing not only ongoing and essential security-based counter-terrorism measures, but also systematic preventive measures that directly address the drivers of violent extremism at the local, national, regional and global levels'.

In practice, the development of 'hard' technical surveillance systems to monitor communities deemed at risk of radicalisation, in advance of 'soft' interventions, was a common pattern. The latter were a distinct type of surveillance that involved a partnership approach to collecting local level intelligence by police and non-policing agencies, such as schools or social workers, as well as a targeting of those who had yet to break the law. For Kundani and Hayes (2018, p.14), this was a response to the perceived need to 'identify individuals who were in "the pre-criminal space" – the stages in the process of radicalisation before a crime has been committed'. Overall, the definitions and practices of radicalisation and CVE were deeply contested and have become synonymous with terrorism, but normatively, have come to symbolise an expanding set of 'regulatory practices moving from sanctioning the acts of individuals to anticipating those acts in a sweep of pre-emptive criminal regulation around the globe' (Ní Aoláin, 2018, p.2). This has posed fundamental questions for human rights and civil liberties and led to many accusations of the institutionalisation of civil society by the state, to influence communities seen as particularly vulnerable to radicalisation.

U.K. preventative counter-terrorism

Such CVE approaches became most advanced in the United Kingdom. 'Prevent' and the concern with 'the radicalization of individuals' was first introduced to counter-terrorism policy in the 2003 version of CONTEST, as one of the four strands of work, and has often been used as a guide by other countries. Prevent – and the series of specific policies that flowed from it – was seen as a longer term objective where the state and its agencies attempted to tackle the root causes of extremism in a pre-emptive and community-focused way. Although initially a relatively minor area of activity compared to other strands of counter-terrorism work, Prevent became a controversial programme, with emotive language often used to describe it, and accusations of discrimination against Muslim communities. The ambient threat of terrorist attack by radicalised individuals, and its realisation in London on '7/7' 2005, saw Prevent become a dominate feature of U.K. counter-terrorism from 2005, with increased concerns over 'home grown terrorists', and a deeper focus on community action.

There was a refocusing on localised community-based approaches towards counter-terrorism, with an acknowledgment of the need to work in partnership with Muslim communities to prevent (young) people from being radicalised in the first place, and to ensure that communities were resilient enough to respond to, and challenge, extremists from within (Briggs, 2010). In the wake of the 7/7, the U.K. Government immediately set up the Preventing Extremism Together (PET) Taskforce to underpin this effort. In practice, this meant enhanced funding, with delivery, being coordinated by local police forces and local government in conjunction with community organisations. This new approach was less about formal groups, with an 'emphasis on attitudes, mindsets, and dispositions' that attempted to ensure radicalisation processes 'could not capture the minds of the young and make them into violent extremists' (Kundnani and Hayes, 2018, p.7).

Preventing Violent Extremism was writ large in the reworked 2006 CONTEST strategy, leading to a widening of counter-terrorism to target not just terrorism, but also ideology, that some subsequently argued led to a lack of focus (Richards, 2011). This was followed a year later by the publication of a new Government action plan *Preventing Violent Extremism, Winning Hearts and Minds* (DCLG, 2007) in which the Government pledged to step up work with Muslim communities to isolate, prevent and defeat violent extremism. This coalesced quickly into an overarching anti-radicalisation approach, *Preventing Violent Extremism* (HM Government, 2008). This suite of Prevent work continually re-emphasised the dominant notion that ideological radicalisation leads to violent extremism as the primary problematic (Edwards, 2016), even though the policy identified a significant conflation between social cohesion and counter-terrorism, and the fostering of existing divisions (Abbas, 2018). Later, in 2015, Prevent policies became a legal duty for many public-sector institutions, extending its reach deeper into the fabric of society (HM Government, 2015).

Overall, the co-option of community-level groups into the provision of these 'community resilience' practices was to prove highly controversial, amid accusations that such attempts represented a Trojan Horse for coercive state control to become intensified in specific local contexts, and where enhanced surveillance formed an essential feature of preventative approaches (Kundnani, 2009).[8]

Normative understandings of preventing violent extremism

The counter-radicalisation programs implemented in Western countries differ greatly from one another in terms of aims, budget and underlying philosophy. Each experience is deeply shaped by political, cultural and legal elements unique to that country. Nevertheless, the experience to date points to certain key characteristics and challenges common to all Western counter-radicalisation programs.

In particular, between 2005 and 2015, the U.K's approach, with an emphasis on preventative action and ideological dimensions, became the most significant and best funded global referent on how to combat radicalisation. The transference of ideas occurred most rapidly in the European Union who were advancing collective plans for anti-radicalisation and counter-terrorism in the wake of the Madrid train bombings in March 2004. That the U.K. assumed the Presidency of the European Council on July 1, 2005, further catalysed the development of such approaches and led to U.K.-style Prevent policies being incorporated as one of the four stands of the new EU counter-terrorism policy in late 2005.[9] Here, the Prevent strand was seen as stopping people turning to terrorism 'by tackling the root causes which can lead to radicalisation or recruitment' (Council of Europe, 2005, p.3). In time, a range of CVE action plans were produced that cast radicalisation as a wide net and which required the assistance of all social and political institutions to eliminate.[10]

In the U.S., the post-9/11 focus upon home-grown terrorism and recognising signs of violent extremism took time to develop into wide-scale policy programs. In 2006, as a result of home-grown terror attacks in Madrid and London, American Muslims were deemed more of a domestic security threat (Sageman, 2008). Initial work by the FBI mirrored U.K. ideas focused upon the conveyer-belt approach by which individuals went through various stages of radicalisation from citizen to terrorist and in which, subtle behavioural cues could be identified in perpetrators (FBI, 2006). As a result, law enforcement, promoted by the Department of Homeland Security, 'launched intensive surveillance programmes of Muslim populations in the U.S. on the assumption that the indicators of radicalisation described in their analyses could thereby be detected' (Kundnani and Hayes, 2018, p.8). Such 'community policing', combined with enhanced community engagement to counter-radicalisation, was seen as a 'softer' method of counter-terrorism compared to the widespread use of technological surveillance. Concomitantly, though, there were sharp rises in Islamophobic hate crimes documented as a result of approaches that proactively, and publically, identified a threatening segment of the population and targeted it through a variety of policy initiatives (Kaplan, 2006).

As President Obama took office in early 2009 and sought to distance his administration from the Bush War on Terror rhetoric, specific policies aimed at countering radicalisation and violent extremism begun to emerge. This was in large part driven by an increase in home-grown terror cases through 2009–2010, and a refocusing upon domestic radicalisation, where it could no long be assumed that 'American Muslims are immune to radicalization' (Vidino, 2010, p.1). As the 2010 National Security Strategy advocated, 'our best defenses against this threat are well informed and equipped families, local communities, and institutions [and we] will invest in intelligence to understand this threat and expand community engagement and development programs to empower local communities' (The White House, 2010, p.19).

The previous quotation began a further policy brief that became the U.S. Government CVE strategy – *Empowering Local Partners to Prevent Violent Extremism in the United States*, a White House report released in August 2011. This report focused heavily on the concept of community engagement in counter-extremism efforts noting that in prior cases, all community intelligence gathered had been done so *after* radicalisation had taken place. Subsequently, new CVE polices, and a dedicated interagency task force,[11] were established to address the conditions, and reduce the factors, that most likely contribute to recruitment and radicalisation by violent extremists and where possible, 'be incorporated into existing programs related to public safety, resilience, inclusion, and violence prevention'[12] (ibid.).

Similarly, to the U.S. experience, the introduction of community-based preventive initiatives underpinned counter-radicalisation programmes in Australia that were initially showcased in a 2010 counter-terrorism White Paper that first officially acknowledged the threat from home-grown Islamist terrorists (Australian Government, 2010). The Australian counter-terrorism strategy was modelled on the four-pronged U.K. CONTEST strategy, including a dedicated focus upon preventing violent extremism that was called 'Resilience'. This overarching approache sought to 'build social cohesion, harmony and security' at national/Federal level (ibid., p.67), encourage State police to engage with communities to build trust, understanding and co-operation, and for CVE practices to be implemented at local level involving community partners.[13] Here, this local requirement was based on the assumption that 'communities are best placed to develop solutions to local problems and for that reason, consultation will be occurring with a wide variety of community groups and stakeholders' (Attorney General's Department, 2010).

By 2015, the new Australian national counter-terrorism strategy – *Strengthening Our Resilience* – had more explicitly worded strands around 'Challenging Violent Extremist Ideologies' and 'Stopping People becoming Terrorists' but continued to take a community-centric view about engaging with local partners and provided training and resources towards this endeavour. Such a community engagement model included many of the traditional aspects of community policing notably, liaison officers within the Muslim community, widespread consultations, and the seeking of partnerships with the aim of building trust and cooperation (Dunna et al., 2015). Such community-based tasks were, however, made more difficult by anti-terrorism legislation, most notably control orders, that had been expanding in scope since 2002, and starkly exposed 'issues of selectivity and proportionality between preventive measures and forced consideration of the limits of state action to prevent or pre-empt harm' (Tulich, 2012, p.52). The additional focus on CVE in the 2015 counter-terrorism strategy also reflected increased concern about domestic radicalisation, the increased numbers of citizens joining conflicts in Iraq and Syria who were often radicalised online, as well as several successful and foiled attacks that resulted in an elevation to National terror threat levels in 2014 for the first time since 2002.

Community co-option and counter-terrorism

The focus upon better understanding communities so as to intervene early to restrict radicalisation and stop acts of terrorism, and the more general encouragement of citizen involvement in counter-terrorism, is now unpacked through two practice vignettes from the U.K. These practices expose fissures in the attempts to implement top-down policy dynamics in local places and notable forms of community resistance that emerged.

Citizens defeat terrorism

In her 1961 classic work *The Death and Life of Great American Cities,* urbanist Jane Jacobs illuminated the importance of 'eyes on the street' to improve neighbourhood safety (Jacobs, 1961). The 'eyes' she referred to were what she called the 'natural proprietors of the street': people don't watch a street out of duty but because they have common interests and concerns.[14] However, if such community safety initiatives are undertaken without proper consultation with local citizens, they risk turning neighbours into the eyes and ears of the police, actively reinforce fear and violence and turn neighbour against neighbour.

Following the terror attacks in London in July 2005, in early 2007 new regional police teams in England came into operation with an explicit aim of combatting violent extremism and radicalisation.[15] The role of these Counter-Terrorism Units (CTUs) was publicised by a concerted 'Life Savers' media campaign to ensure that *all citizens* understood the threats faced from terrorism and encouraged them to report any suspicious activity – whether in public or private – through an Anti-Terrorism 'tip-off hotline' (with a slogan 'You don't have to be sure. If you suspect it report it').[16] This new campaign sought the public's help and encouraged 'vigilant visualities' and watching out for the 'out of the ordinary' (Amoore, 2006). More critically, 'the citizen detective' was being 'asked not only to be active in civic spaces but also in what might otherwise have been considered domestic spaces...' (Vaughan-Williams, 2009, p.74).

From a grass-root perspective, there was significant concern expressed at such announcements, which suggested that the public be enrolled in the fight against terrorism. This message was reinforced by a series of high-profile advertisements in the media and displays in public places. For example, in a Security Service press release in February 2008 – *Police Launch New Counter-Terrorism Campaign* – it was warned that 'Terrorists live within our communities, making their plans whilst doing everything they can to blend in, and trying not to raise suspicions about their activities' and that 'we want people to look out for the unusual – some activity or behaviour which shrikes them as not quite right and out of place in their normal day-to-day lives'.

One of the initial billboard posters focused upon hostile reconnaissance. Against a background of security cameras, this poster's message asked 'Thousands of people take photos every day. What if one of them seems odd?' A week after, this poster first appeared a further advertisement was launched, focusing upon the potential danger of terrorists living within communities. This time against the backdrop of a residential front door, the poster asked, 'You see hundreds of houses every day. What if one has unusual activity and seems suspicious?' It continued:

> Terrorists live within our communities, planning attacks and storing chemicals, if you're suspicious of a property where there's unusual activity that doesn't fit normal day-day life, we need to know ...

Fast-forward a decade, and in March 2018, following a number of high profile acts of terrorism where the attackers had been radicalised, the U.K. Government launched a reworked public awareness campaign, *Communities Defeat Terrorism,* once again explicitly aimed at encouraging citizens to report suspicious activity that could indicate terrorism was being planned[17]:

> We depend on information from the public. They can be our eyes and ears and help keep themselves, their neighbours and communities safe by looking out for suspicious activity and reporting it to us.

The *Communities Defeat Terrorism* campaign was part of a much broader approach that was initiated in March 2017 called Action Counters Terrorism (ACT)[18] that encouraged 'communities to act on their instincts to help prevent atrocities taking place' – *'don't worry, don't delay, just act'*.[19] It was further highlighted by the National Counter-Terrorism Police that in a third of cases involving the most serious terrorist suspects, we have benefited from information from the public.

Additional guidance about reporting terrorist or violent extremist content online was also produced to encourage the public to report specific types of content they came across.[20] Since the publication of the 2006 CONTEST strategy, the internet has always been viewed as a place 'where many types of radical views are strongly promoted' (U.K. Home Office, 2006), but over time, advances in the use of social media have made it more complex and challenging for the police and security services to identify would-be terrorists. These issues implicated not only the duties and functions of the police, local authorities and citizens, but also the potential role of technology developers and social media providers. Here social media – seen as an echo chamber of extremist views – became a new frontier in preventative counter-terrorism through the policing of online content and the monitoring extremist or terrorist groups who use social media to radicalise and recruit young or vulnerable individuals, and, who have demonstrated a sophisticated understanding of how social networks operate to promote and glorify acts of terror (Briggs and Strugnell, 2011; Thompson, 2011). As a result, in 2010, the Counter-Terrorism Internet Referral Unit (CTIRU) was established in the U.K. to liaise with internet platforms to allow the public identify content which might inspire terrorism and get them voluntarily removed.[21]

Following a 2011 review of the *Prevent* strategy, online radicalisation was identified as a priority area that had 'transformed the extent to which terrorist organizations and their sympathizers can radicalize people in this country and overseas' (U.K. Home Office, 2011). This is very much an ongoing effort. As the British Prime Minister further noted in June 2017, after a year of terror attacks across Europe, 'we cannot allow this ideology the safe space it needs to breed, yet that is precisely what the Internet and the big companies that provide Internet services provide'.[22] Subsequently the U.K. Government collaborated with technology companies to develop new tools that sought to automatically detect terrorist content on any online platforms with a high degree of accuracy (Home Office, 2018).[23]

More critically, the public communication campaigns and preventative approaches noted earlier, that have been orchestrated over the last decade, are clearly aimed at turning citizens into 'detectives', 'spies' and 'sensors' (in the case of social media) as part of a broader rhetoric of advancing responsible and resilient citizens that can help defeat terrorism. Resistance to such intentions has been forthcoming from civil liberty and human rights groups who have voiced concerns about legal powers rolled out under the guises of enrolling communities in the fight against terrorism, and that raise critical questions about how democracies can fight terrorism and still remain orderly? From a state perspective, community is both the object and subject of concern: as object certain communities are problematised and targeted by policies that place national security over community concerns; as subject because the security maxim 'communities defeat terrorism' creates, demands and recognises the active participation of community members in the prevention of terrorism. Further popular resistance has come from the creation and wide-circulation of spoof anti-terrorism hotline posters that provided critical commentary on what many saw as the sinister and pseudo-fascist nature of official political communication. Indeed more recently, posters used as part of the *See it, Say it, Sorted* campaign on the London underground were argued to demonise particular groups and utilised similar iconography to images of Jewish persecution used in Nazi Germany.[24]

Overall though, resistance, or objection, to the various communities' defeat terrorism campaigns of recent years has been largely muted. Where this has occurred, it has largely taken the form of critical media commentary that has meant that the predominant messages being transmitted from top-down approaches have been left largely unchallenged. Despite the rhetoric of community engagement that emanates from such homogenous campaigns, civil society are, however, not engaged on their own terms, or in relation to local issues, but on a very narrow set of national threat priorities that require a unidirectional response. This has done little to pull the bias of counter-terrorism away from 'expert'-driven operations.

The evaporation of community trust

The practices of counter-terrorism and community resilience are fluid and often harbour internal tensions and contradictions as security has shifted from a narrative of national protection to one of localised prevention and self-organised responses. For example, for state actors, security and resilience is predominantly conceived as protection from terrorism, while for the community it involves grass-roots activism and collective efforts against threats (including the state's desire to monitor them). As these diverse approaches and understandings of counter-terrorism and resilience have become operationalised, their discordances have become visible. More specifically, the initial framing of the terror threat as being almost exclusively Islamic in origin, 'afforded a surveillance infrastructure, embedded into Muslim communities, which...securitised relations with local authorities and served to contain and direct Muslim political agency' (Qurashi, 2018, p.1).

It is these tensions that are unpacked in this vignette through an analysis of 'Project Champion' – an attempt by the police in Birmingham, U.K., to install high-resolution surveillance cameras, often invisibly, into areas with predominantly Muslim populations. The aim of this scheme was ostensibly to deliver a range of security and resilience benefits, including protection from crime, radicalisation and international terrorism; in short, surveillance applications with a range of coercive and enforcement-based roles. In practice, these actions captured how the preventative practices of counter-terrorism were drawn into conflict with other policy priorities – specifically to community cohesion and localism – posing a series of questions about social control, citizenship and the ability to construct local community resilience amidst state attempts to label the same areas as 'dangerous' (Coaffee and Fussey, 2015).

In June 2010, the media reported on a security project to install 290 surveillance cameras in Birmingham, paid for through national counter-terrorism funding.[25] Of the surveillance cameras in 'Project Champion', 150 came equipped with Automatic Number Plate Recognition (ANPR) capability, whilst a further 72 covert cameras were camouflaged within street furniture or by other features of the urban landscape. Given the intensification of surveillance practices within the U.K., at first glance, many aspects of this initiative were not particularly novel. What were unusual about the adoption of such practices in this instance were the scale, technological sophistication and location of the operation.

Geographical suspicion was a key driver for the inception and intended installation of Project Champion. In the U.K., counter-terrorism operations have largely concentrated on a small number of high-density urban areas, often with entire security architectures became installed with the focus spilling over from intended subjects and resting on associates, networks and geographies. Project Champion cameras encircled two predominantly Muslim neighbourhoods of the city, using technological perimeters to replace valuable intramural spaces with those of containment and crude categorical suspicion.

The scheme was originally conceived after the (narrowly) failed London nightclub and Glasgow airport bombings of 2007, with the siting of cameras determined by the location of several prior high-profile terrorist plots originating from specific parts of Birmingham, and leading law enforcement to apply ecological perceptions of dangerousness to these parts of the city (Coaffee and Fussey, 2015).[26] These perceptions converged on the neighbourhoods Sparkbrook and Washwood Heath – two residential areas with high Muslim populations and home to 11 people convicted for terrorist-related activity between 2007 and 2011 – that were encircled by Project Champion cameras.[27]

From its inception, Project Champion was intended to institute both obtrusive and unobtrusive monitoring regimes in which 'suspicious' subjects were tracked and monitored 'from a distance', ensuring the safety of police officers and allowing recordings to take place unhindered (Fussey, 2013). Such ambitions to 'police from afar' contrasted with the community engagement remits of the City of Birmingham's municipal crime reduction body and revealed inherent antagonisms between the different logics of security as they were applied in practice. Here, national security agendas become nested within, and abraded with, local community safety concerns and practices. Central and local state responses clashed through this instrumental use of local state community safety assemblages that were used to deploy highly focused coercive counter-terrorism initiatives, ultimately undermining the legitimacy of the former (Birmingham City Council, 2010).

Project Champion was thus detached from other community-focused policing and local authority approaches to building local resilience being undertaken in the area. In particular, local police had established a dedicated department within its CTU to focus on developing successful partnerships with a range of civil society organisations to drive forward the Prevent agenda locally. Notably, dedicated 'Security and Partnerships Officers' were working across key neighbourhoods – in schools, mosques, community centres and sports clubs – to encourage community-wide action to defeat violent extremism. However, it proved problematic to maintain such relationship when the cameras were installed, with the 'embedding' of counter-terrorism police in local services being viewed as a major cause for concern and growing mistrust for Muslim communities (House of Commons, 2010).

Project Champion highlighted a series of fractures amongst the approaches used in the delivery of a nationally important, but locally focused, counter-terrorism initiative, placing community approaches aimed at 'collective resistance' (Aly, 2013) at odds with protective logics of security in a way that effectively stigmatised the area (Isakjee and Allen, 2013). Protests followed at community meetings and public rallies, and a range of websites emerged such as 'Birmingham against Spy Cameras' to gather local opinion and lobby (successfully) for the removal of surveillance architectures. As one local protestor noted:

> Now the truth is out, there's a lot of anger. Certain communities have been ring-fenced and saturated with cameras, making it impossible for you to get in or out without being tracked. What's happening here is the government is spying on its citizens covertly in some cases, without their knowledge or consent, and it's a gross invasion of privacy and civil liberties.[28]

In Birmingham, the advancement of trusting relationships between citizens and officials underpinned the slow and deliberative work that had previously occurred under Prevent-funded programmes. This partnership approach was beginning to bear fruit and enact new governance possibilities to fight the growing threat of radicalisation. However, disconnect between how Prevent and other policing directives were carried out locally destroyed much of this hard earned trust and ultimately mobilised collective community action that saw the 'spy' cameras removed. The collateral damage was an almost permanent breakdown of relations between police and (Muslim) communities in the city.

The rise and fall of Project Champion further served to illuminate tensions associated with operationalising security-driven resilience in situ: civil liberties and the limits of public acceptability; the material visibility of security infrastructure; the modulation of different scales of resilience and how a range of different actors become involved in governance; and the labelling of populations as 'dangerous' through anticipatory means. Surveillance had thus become a visible symbol of a pernicious expression of local and community-centred security-driven resilience. A formal public consultation was forced, which led to 'hoods' being placed over the visible ANPR cameras in July 2010 pending 'further consultation'.[29] The subsequent independent investigation was highly critical of both the Project Champion scheme and local policing, claiming that it had done irreparable harm to community-police relations.[30] In the longer term, the areas concerned, and Birmingham more broadly, would struggle to the shake of the media-portrayal of a city that was a terrorist 'breeding ground', as a number of raids of residences carried out after attacks in London, in 2017, confirmed.[31]

Conclusions: From passive to active and engaged citizenship in counter-terrorism

Progressively over the last 20 years, preventative approaches to counter-terrorism have sought to develop an enhanced dialogue with communities to better understanding radicalisation in situ, and transform how cities and their urban neighbourhoods are perceived, organised and acted upon by policy instruments. This has evolved to focus on preventing radicalised ideologies taking hold in marginal places that have seen much recent immigration – what are often identified as 'breeding grounds' for extremism – and to which are commonly applied spatially targeted state-led approaches. The impact of such focused 'soft power' approaches that seek to 'civilise' the dangerous *terra incognita* has further reinforced the racialised and territorialised stigmatisation, and social segregation, of these areas from the wider city.

More conceptually, this connects the threads of urban geopolitics that have sought to link migration, spatial questions of urban segregation and re-territorialisation, with War on Terror politics (Rokem and Boano, 2017). As Saberi (2019) has further noted, preventing radicalisation as part of a broader counterinsurgency approach is a central urban geopolitical question that goes 'beyond a sole focus on biopolitics and securitization' (p.2). Here 'radicalization prevention strategies increasingly mediate and are mediated by the reterritorialization and re-articulation of neocolonial urban and geopolitical imaginaries of danger in the unevenly developed and racially segregated cities' (ibid.).

Undoubtedly, in more recent years, national and municipal programmes to tackle radicalisation have become far more nuanced, with a focus upon social integration, community cohesion and reducing polarisation, and are often aligned with broader urban policy objectives (CTPN, 2019a). The changing approaches of counter-terrorism and community resilience have further highlighted a number of implications for everyday urban life and the role of citizens in public policy and broader democratic governance, whilst also emphasising that far more needs to be done to engage citizens in such policymaking processes. With few exceptions such, anti-radicalisation initiatives have been linked to encouraging individuals to take greater responsibility for their own risk management and in so doing inculcate and normalise security routines, whilst at the same time policing and security actors are monitoring defined territories from afar.

Preventative counter-terrorism in many local areas further exemplifies the banality of counter-terrorism which has become 'routinized, barely noticed reminders of terror or the threat of an always already presence of terrorism in our midst' (Katz, 2007, p.350). More particularly, such routinisation impacts upon public perceptions of who is, or isn't, a potential terrorist living within plain site and reinforces the fragmentation of urban areas into safe and unsafe zones that restrict an open city and, with surveillance assemblages making 'vigilance in every direction and at all scales the new normal' (ibid., p.356). For example, Heath-Kelly and Strausz (2019) have highlighted the U.K.'s Prevent programme as an example of the 'banality of counter-terrorism' where public-sector workers, such as social care, education and healthcare workers, are now engaged in the prevention of terrorism through their everyday safeguarding roles (p.90).

As underscored through the two vignettes presented in this chapter, the synergies between different approaches to advancing and understanding localised approaches to countering terrorism exist in perpetual tension. This creates a complex and ambiguous situation where, on one hand community resilience is being articulated by the State as something that should be contextual and contingent, and based on deep community engagement, whilst on the other hand, it provides a homogenised imaginary of expert and professional policymakers seeking to enrol citizens and local communities into state-centric security projects that have limited democratic oversight, or local-level scrutiny. Arguably, such systems of governance, based on limited local contingency, and rooted in older systems of national sovereignty, are not adaptable enough to respond effectively to the complex challenges of counter-terrorism. Whilst, for example, in parts of Europe, urban security agendas have been shown to be more divergent and influenced by local politics to a significant degree (Devroe and Edwards, 2017), in the U.K., where detailed counter-terrorism structures have developed over many decades, command and control governance still dominates and remains obdurate.[32]

We are all counter-terrorists now!

The increased emphasis on attempts to raise public awareness of terrorism through 'warning and informing' have increasingly been laminated onto preventive activities whose mission has progressively focused upon issues of religious extremism, 'radicalisation' and community cohesion. These have become increasingly interlinked through centralised rhetoric's of community resilience and ideas of *active citizenship* and self-governance, but have struggled to advance locally nuanced approaches due to top-down driven circuits of power that often lead to mistrust between state and citizens.

Despite the promise of preventative counter-terrorism being centred upon community engagement efforts and citizens' active ability to influence the direction of local policy, such equitable partnership approaches remain questionable in light of an overarching emphasis on expert judgements. Although such dialogue is increasingly seen by local practitioners as a two-way process, much of the work still follows a more 'passive' model of the citizen as a 'subject' to be informed of appropriate actions, rather than a stakeholder, with the same status as the partner agencies engaged in decision-making and response (Coaffee and Rogers, 2008). This is further conflicted by a pervasive community distrust of security agencies and concerns that 'Government appeals made through the discourse of terrorism have sought to harness public anxieties and fears for political ends' (Mythen and Walklate, 2006, p.138). The use of a sense of impending risk and danger to enact new state-driven civic policy, as most recently demonstrated through the discourse of resilience, is not a new political strategy. However, the potential impact and unquantifiable nature of imminent terrorist risks, combined with political leaders' claims of 'unique' and 'classified' knowledge of potential threats, is increasingly used in justifying the implementation of a raft of counter-terrorism 'resilience' policies aimed at citizens but *without* critical civic consultation.

Mirroring the anticipatory turn in social control practices, the prominence of providing counter-terrorism strategies that meet local concerns, is devolved 'down' to lower levels of the state and to non-state actors. However, the central state retains, at the same time, it's 'whip-hand' status, often overriding local concerns, liberties and rights. Politically, what emerges is a standard governance trope of centralised power alongside decentralised responsibility leading to the 'responsibilization' of ever-increasing numbers of local, public-facing individuals and agencies (Garland, 1996). This places an emphasis on citizenship being 'active', with the self-regulation of conduct within communities supplementing more detailed institutional strategies, whist still being governed 'from a distance' by the state.

In the context of the terrorist threat, the strategic development of 'community resilience' has been a prime way achieving this, but this appears to be part of 'a complex of scientifically grounded techniques of the self, necessary to optimize autonomous subjects in an age of high uncertainty' (O'Malley, 2010). This is a far more pervasive and widespread responsibilisation of citizens than that highlighted previously (Dean, 1999) cloaked in the softer and more palatable language of resilience. Such a turn towards localised and individualised resilience has been described – drawing once again on Foucault – as an attempt at the biopolitical construction of resilient subjects and communities that places the onus upon individuals and communities to 'regenerate and reactivate their ethical values' to 'regulate individual conduct' (Rose, 2000, p. 324). As Chandler and Reid (2016, p.1) have further noted,

> the promotion of resilience calls forth a much degraded subject…one that has been taught, and accepted, the lessons concerning the dangers of autonomy and the need to be 'capacity-built' in order to make the 'right choices' in development of sustainable responses to threats and dangers posed by the environment.

Such responsibilisation, in specific relation to preventative counter-terrorism, has meant 'radicalisation has been cast as an omnipresent and omnipotent threat that all of society's institutions have an obligation to counter' (Kundnani and Hayes, 2017, p.19).

In extreme cases, such 'responsible citizenship' can morph into a citizen spying (Kackman, 2005). Informers and spies have a long history as an apparatus for in social control; however, in most cases, spies were state agents. However, recent counter-terrorism communication campaigns, aimed at enhancing responsibility and restricting radicalisation, produce only very limited understanding in the citizen-spy. The implication here is that such approaches must also have broader intentions, that is first, to encourage of a general climate of categorical suspicion (Norris and McCahill, 2006), and second, to generate a further responsibilising movement in instilling the habit of self-surveillance into everyday life (Coaffee and Murakami Wood, 2006). In the U.S. context, as Reeves (2017) argued in *Citizens Spies: The Long Rise of the Surveillance State*, that the post-9/11 surveillance systems established depended largely on habits that were inculcated for a long time, in particular through the Cold War 'red threat'. This meant that the post-9/11 mantra of 'If you see something, say something' that encouraged citizens to look out for threats and the reporting of the suspicious activity of fellow citizens to the correct authorities, became seen as a patriotic duty, potentially turning neighbour against neighbour and stripping away the traditional boundaries between state and citizenry.

Contemporary community resilience campaigns, like their Cold War predecessors, are aimed at *everyone* as part of their supposed *moral duty as a responsible citizen* (Coaffee et al., 2008). Here, the way in which the state communicates risk to citizens has had significant implications for harnessing or allaying fears about the current level of perceived risk from terrorist attack as well as 'inviting us to be involved in managing the terrorist risk as a logical step towards ensuring our own safety' (Mythen and Walklate, 2006, p.133). Put simply, we are all counter-terrorists now! However, the responsibilisation is currently only taken so far. There is at the same time a deliberate curtailing of the role of the citizen-spy to the *duty of reporting* suspicious activity without further judgement or action.

This type of preventive counter-terrorism policy is also emblematic of a shift in focus away from individual offending, towards pre-emptive strategies that aim to identify threats and make interventions before crimes take place (McCulloch and Pickering, 2009). Here, as earlier work noted, 'the post-crime orientation of criminal justice is increasingly overshadowed by the pre-crime logic of security' (Zedner, 2007, p.261–262). Most recently, in 2015, the view that radicalised tendencies emanate in particular types of residential communities has been side-lined by U.K. Government and a new 'big data'-driven Prevent 'duty'[33] advanced to safeguard vulnerable adults across a range of public services (Home Office, 2015). But, as critics have noted, this legal *obligation* has once again 'invoked a nationalized imagination of pre-criminal space [and] applied preventative surveillance *to all citizens*, for their own protection' (Heath-Kelly, 2017, p.297; see also Altermark and Nilsson, 2018).

Such a *duty* to report suspicions is, however, not new to contemporary counter-terrorism campaigns. Over a decade ago, in his 'Statement on Security' in July 2007, the then British Prime Minster, Gordon Brown, emphasised that in thwarting 'radicalisation', '*every institution* in our country have a part to play', and that:

> this requires not just the security measures ... but that we work with all communities and all countries through debate, discussion, dialogue and education as we tackle at root the evils that risk driving people, particularly vulnerable young people, into the hands of violent extremists.[34]

However, increasingly the significance of what has been reported by citizens, public-sector workers or institutions is to be reserved to the expert in terrorist risk; at the moment of judgement, there is a deresponsibilisation. Here, the discourse of radicalisation is important, in that it simultaneously deresponsibilises the individuals and groups involved in specific terrorist acts, portraying them as victims of radicalisation and, further, moves the responsibility for addressing this to institutions and local communities. It is as much as a means of disciplining those institutions, and instilling habits of mutual surveillance as it is about dealing realistically with those who are likely commit terrorist acts. Individuals and institutions are, therefore, being 'captured' within new modes of governmentality and held accountable, or responsible, for managing national security. As Andrejevic (2007) noted in relation to U.S. advertising campaigns that encouraged preparedness and readiness; homeland security is marketed as the latest form of self-help where the public are encouraged to become 'citizen soldiers' required to fight the internal enemy, accept and live with heightened risks, and, quoting the Ready.

Gov website, 'begin the process of learning about threats so we are better prepared to react' (p.167).

In the West, the combination of moralisation and responsibilisation has further enhanced the collective mistrust between Muslim and non-Muslim communities and fuelled Islamophobia and hate speech. For example, Qurashi (2018) in his analysis of U.K. Prevent policies refers to the normalisation of Islamophobia that has been brought about by the historical continuation of targeted policies in certain communities of 'Others' 'informed by the framing of the terror threat as an Islamic threat, which casts all Muslims as potential terrorists that need to be monitored and categorised' (p.11). This, he argued, creates a normalised 'vantage point from which surveillance and counterterrorism is directed, which is racialized and which results in an uneven surveillance gaze... [that] aims to regulate the conduct of Muslims as British citizens with "British values"' (ibid.).[35]

Viewed through the response of public authorities to current terrorist threats, the governmental aim of community-driven preventative counterterrorism can be seen to amount to a generalised form of discipline that becomes part of everyday life. This is not entirely the panoptic discipline that Foucault (1977) identified as being symptomatic of the enlightenment project and flowing through modern life as part of the carceral texture of society. Nor is it entirely the impersonal control of flows identified by Deleuze (1990) in his work on a society of control. It has elements of both, but as it involves the many watching the particular, it can be viewed as strongly *synoptic* and *moral* (Mathlesen, 1997).

Here, new relationships between state and citizen have emerged through security practices where responsibilisation creates a new kind of capacity, in which the labour is undertaken as much by the watched as the watcher in a type of 'lateral' surveillance (Andrejevic, 2005). In this situation, individuals, communities and institutions are encouraged to adopt practices associated with law enforcement to gain information about customers, employees or community members, in ways that emulate and amplify top-down monitoring, and in so doing nurture the internalisation of governmental strategies (Coaffee et al., 2008). Here, we can see contemporary forms community governance and the regulation of morals in action within a climate where everybody is under suspicion and everyone is enrolled in countering terrorism.

Equally, though, this might be about the state's own *agoraphobia* (De Cauter, 2004); its fear of the citizen. This is the paradox that has existed since the creation of the first city walls, which both protected the liberty of the citizen but acted as a means of control. Here, the State is both acknowledging that it cannot trust the citizen and at the same time wanting to make the citizen responsible for self-policing. Today, in one sense, the problem remains the same as in medieval city or the nineteenth-century moral panic over urban disorder: how can one know the good citizen from the bad?

Notes

1. Cited in *The Daily Mail*, July 21 at www.dailymail.co.uk/news/article-8546057/Diane-Abbott-calls-scrapping-Prevent-counter-terror-programme.html.
2. Bell further noted, such counterinsurgency and civilianisation approaches emerged from practices of humanitarianism and peace interventionism since the end of the Cold War, and served to refashion traditional military practices 'towards investment in civilian modes of warfare' and in so doing 'expose[d] the widening indistinction between contemporary modes of peace and those of war in international relations' (2011, p.309).
3. Violent extremism was a term that originated in the United States, finding its way into U.K. policy around 2006.
4. Such a drive towards multilevel action was further located among a number of broader processes aimed at devolving central state functions and responsibility onto the local realm, including responsibilities for emergency planning and terrorism.
5. Future revolutions. 4. Reverse radicalism. *Time,* March 13, p.6.
6. See, for example, UN programmes of action at https://en.unesco.org/preventingviolentextremism.
7. The Incel (short for involuntarily celibate) movement is an online community members of which define themselves by being unable to find a romantic or sexual partner despite desiring one. A number of attacks carried out by members of this movement have been classed as terrorism. See, for example, a machete attack in Toronto in 2020 – https://time.com/5839395/canada-teen-terrorism-incel-attack/. Antifa is a left-wing, anti-fascist and anti-racist political movement in the United States that is increasingly monitored for radical behaviours and has recently been proscribed as a terrorist group in the U.S., the U.K. and across Europe. Most recently, the attack on the Capitol Building in Washington, D.C. on January 6, 2021 was labelled an act of right-wing domestic terrorism and heightened fears that such groups will become increasing active in the near future.
8. After the Coalition government took office in 2010, the Prevent strategy was revised and the term 'violent extremism' less evident (Edwards, 2016).
9. Indeed, it appeared the entire U.K. counter-terrorism policy had been adapted wholesale with only very minor changes (e.g. the Prepare stand was referred to as Respond in the EU version).
10. It is beyond the scope of this chapter to detail all of these interventions. For more detail, see Kundnani and Hayes (2018).
11. It is worth noting that 'task force' is a term derived from military use.
12. See www.dhs.gov/cve/what-is-cve.
13. Such approaches were overseen by the CVE Task Force within the Attorney General's Department.
14. Surveillance here is voluntary and done almost unconsciously as part of everyday life. Communities, if they feel they have a stake in their area and will engage in 'neighbourhood watch' and feed their voice into any collective vision of community safety.
15. In April 2007, four regional CTUs were established, in Greater Manchester, West Yorkshire, the West Midlands and London to work in partnership with the security services, with a focus on intelligence gathering and on tackling 'violent extremism'.

16 See, for example, 'Help us spot the terrorists urge police', *Manchester Evening News*, March 5, 2007, p.1.
17 See www.npcc.police.uk/Counter-Terrorism/Communitiesdefeatterrorism.aspx.
18 See www.gov.uk/government/news/action-counters-terrorism.
19 The broader ACT campaign also included guidance to the public in how to react if they are caught near a firearms or weapons attack – *Run Hide Tell* – that was especially aimed at young people www.theguardian.com/uk-news/2017/sep/28/police-urge-children-to-run-hide-tell-from-terror-not-take-photos.
20 These included: speeches or essays calling for racial or religious violence; videos of violence with messages in praise of terrorists; postings inciting people to commit acts of terrorism or violent extremism; messages intended to stir up hatred against any religious or ethnic group; bomb-making instructions and advice on how to obtain or make weapons.
21 Similarly, the EU Internet Referral Unit (EU IRU) based on Europol's European Counter Terrorism Centre (ECTC) was established in 2015 to detect and investigate malicious content on the internet and in social media. In 2021, in the U.K., the Internet Referral Unit was supplemented by a reporting app – iREPORTit – that was rolled out in London to encourage referrals easily and anonymously following research identifying that four out of five people were unsure how to report extremist material.
22 Cited in 'Theresa May says the internet must now be regulated following London Bridge terror attack', *The Independent*, June 5, at www.independent.co.uk/news/uk/politics/theresa-may-internet-regulated-london-bridge-terror-attack-google-facebook-whatsapp-borough-security-a7771896.html.
23 In addition, social media allows the police to ask for and receive information from citizens instantaneously and provide a monitoring function during live operations (Coaffee, 2017b). Whilst the promise of social media is bi-directional communication, during terrorist incidents communications flows were generally only *to* the public with 'warning and informing', and with citizens asked to and upload any relevant images once the incident had passed. Overall, social media has proved a useful communication tool, it also caused problems for police responding to incidents in terms of having to expend a lot of time and resources quelling rumours whilst events are ongoing.
24 See www.standard.co.uk/news/london/posters-for-new-police-antiterror-initiative-on-trains-spark-racism-row-a3385836.html.
25 See 'Commons motion over Birmingham CCTV cameras', *BBC Online*, June 14 at www.bbc.co.uk/news/10308165.
26 These included the first attempted U.K.-based Al Qaeda plot (during 2000), the arrest of a suspected Taliban 'commander' and, perhaps most famously, 'Operation Gamble', a plot to kidnap and dismember Muslim soldiers serving in the British Army, resulting in five convictions.
27 Sparkbrook and Washwood heath are inner-city neighbourhoods with similar population sizes of just over 30,000 people each. Other shared characteristics include high levels of ethnic diversity, and of unemployment and other socio-economic disadvantage.
28 Cited in 'CCTV cameras in Birmingham are covered with hoods', *BBC Online*, July 1, 2007 at www.bbc.co.uk/news/10477801.
29 Although, at the time, the cameras were not being disabled and the hidden cameras were, in theory, still useable.

30 See report by Thames Valley Police (2010). A similar review was carried out by Birmingham City Council in 2010.
31 See, for example, www.independent.co.uk/news/uk/home-news/london-attacker-khalid-masood-birmingham-uk-terrorists-breeding-ground-a7646536.html.
32 The key challenges of doing this are to effectively engage citizens and include the public(s) in all aspects of counter-terrorism and resilience policy that impact upon community cohesion, especially in multicultural communities.
33 The Prevent duty is the duty in the Counter-Terrorism and Security Act 2015 on specified authorities, in the exercise of their functions, to have due regard to the need to prevent people from being drawn into terrorism.
34 This has led to attempts to enforce this responsibility. For example, in early 2008, the Department for Innovation, Universities and Skills issued consultation guidance to colleges and universities regarding their role in tackling violent extremism in a document entitled *Promoting Freedom of Speech to Achieve Shared Values and Prevent Violent Extremism on Campus*.
35 Others have also argued that such approaches inevitably lead to greater 'insecuritisation' amongst British Muslims (Croft, 2012).

Part 4
The future of urban security

10 Towards impenetrable and smart security

Introduction: Intensified and flexible security

In the post-9/11 city, the intensification of counter-terrorism responses either sought to make built structures and spaces more resilient to diminish the impact of an explosion or incursion attack, or, to enhance the surveillance of the city terrain through the deployment of increasingly sophisticated and interlinked digital technologies.

Whilst post-9/11 anxieties stimulated widespread introspection about worst-case scenario terrorism and the need to anticipate new types of attack, conventional forms of terror continued unabated. Car bombs were persistently detonated in a vicinity of high-profile targets necessitating ever more elaborate territorial security or bunker architecture. For example, in central London, the security services established the Government Security Zone in the mid-2000s to better protect major government assets and public buildings such as the Houses of Parliament, which were embedded with permanent or temporary protective security features, and where major intensification of digital surveillance occurred (Coaffee et al., 2009). Further afield, similar security retrofitting with an emphasis on restricting access and improving surveillance, is currently ongoing in Oslo, Norway, following the targeting of the government quarter by a large vehicle bomb in 2011.[1] Many other city areas throughout the world have also undergone significant security enhancement, with overseas embassies and consulates being most heavily defended as a result of periodic attacks. Most notably, U.S. diplomatic missions around the world have been attacked with large VBIEDs causing significant loss of life in Istanbul, Turkey,[2] and Sana'a, Yeman[3] in 2008, Peshawar, Pakistan in 2010,[4] Benghazi, Libya, in 2012,[5] and Ankara, Turkey,[6] and Heart, Afghanistan[7] in 2013.

Whilst such attacks against such 'fixed' targets continued, less sophisticated but equally well-planned marauding gun attacks became a viable scenario for international terrorists who could utilise a city's mobility corridors to move around the urban terrain and assault multiple targets. Major attacks of this type stimulated instant security responses. In Mumbai, India, in November 2008 a series of pre-selected public and touristic targets were attacked by small coordinated teams of terrorists armed

DOI: 10.4324/9780429461620-14

with grenades and automatic weapons and who used strategies such as mass hostage-taking to kill over 170 and injure more than 300.[8] Seven years later, in November 2015, Paris was attacked by a series of coordinated assaults in the city's northern suburbs. At just after 9 pm, three suicide bombers struck outside the Stade de France stadium, during a football match, followed by several shootings and a suicide bombing at nearby cafés and restaurants. Gunmen then carried out a mass shooting and took hostages during a concert in the Bataclan theatre. The attackers killed 130 people, injuring over 400 more.[9] That same night, President Francois Hollande, declared a *state of emergency* across metropolitan France and ordered the closure of national borders. Across the Paris metro area, Hollande further asserted that movement and circulation of people would be restricted, mass gatherings banned, and that there would also be widespread stop and search procedures in place throughout city. These measures were reinforced by a large presence of armed police and army on the streets and the establishment of protection and security zones (France Diplomacy, 2015). Most recently, in March 2019, a further mass shooting attack occurred at mosques in Christchurch, New Zealand, when a single gunman – a white supremacist and alt-right extremist who livestreamed the first attack on Facebook – killed 51 people and injured over 40 more.[10] The wider impact of this, and other islamophobic attacks, was to restrict access and mobility in the city amongst Muslims who begun to actively avoid certain public places for fear of attack or victimisation.[11]

Hybrid security responses

Counter-responses to conventional and emergent terrorist methods subsequently saw the intensification of number of security elements in 'at-risk' urban areas as well as new approaches emerging for conceptualising counter-terrorist reactions. The application of such ideas to the practices of urban security further drew attention to new neoliberal forms of urban social control that operated according to new risk-based logics applied to it (Amoore and de Goede, 2009). This was especially the case with regard to crowded places, or transport corridors that permit movement through the city, and that became focal points of governmental security intervention given their continually threatened and threatening nature, and their ubiquity in urban areas.

Linking these security approaches, the spatial footprint of which became excessive fortressing or intensified surveillance, is a long-held element of city life – the management of circulation – that has become increasingly militarised and was central to late Foucauldian ideas of techno-urban security apparatuses (Aradau and Van Munster, 2007; Klauser, 2013). More specifically, this was seen as the 'art of governing' and the ability to manage how objects, groups and individuals circulate around the city. As Foucault noted in *Security, Territory, Population:*

[the problem] is no longer that of fixing and demarcating the territory, but of allowing circulations to take place, of controlling them, shifting the good and the bad, ensuring that things are always in movement, constantly moving around, continually going from one point to another, but in such a way that the inherent dangers of this circulation are cancelled out.

(Foucault, 2007, p.65)[12]

Here, Foucault advanced ideas of a softer and more liberal regime of governing, in contrast to the coercive techniques of *Discipline and Punish*, to symbolise how such circulations are increasingly monitored and filtered as people and goods move between fortified places. This work marked a shift in emphasis from territoriality, enclosure, confinement and the imposition of blanket regimes of prohibition (sovereignty) – or ubiquitous micro-level incentives to discipline behaviour (Fussey, 2015) – to new security assemblages that attempted to monitor and assess complex flows (circulations) in the urban milieu, 'maximising the good circulation by diminishing the bad' (Foucault, 2007, p.18). Here, Foucault famously referred to a security *dispositif* as an 'ensemble of discourses, institutions, architectural forms, regulatory decisions, laws, administrative measures, scientific statements, philosophical, moral and philanthropic propositions' (Foucault, 1980, p.194). In advancing his ideas of new security *dispositifs,* and the development of biopolitical techniques for the management of populations, Foucault contrasted the disciplinary apparatus with the emerging security apparatus that organises circulation so that 'security is exercised over the whole population' (ibid.). As Usher (2014) noted, such an approach represented an attempt by Foucault to 'to scale-up his analysis from the human body to the social body, towards political economy, military strategy and the state', and to pose the question 'How should things circulate or not circulate?' (Foucault, 2007, p.64).

In advancing his changing spatial logic, Foucault explicitly drew on the example of town planning[13] to contrast how 'the spatial distribution for sovereignty, discipline, and security is equally important but differently organized' whereby 'discipline operates through the enclosure and circumscription of space, [and] security requires the opening up and release of spaces, to enable circulation and passage' (Elden, 2007, p.564–565). Here Foucault uses a number of examples of European walled cities to demonstrate how system of governance changed as mercantile capital emerged in the eighteenth century, and how the focus of security shifted as boulevard systems were put in place to enable and control the circulation of people and goods. This rendered physical protection and the control of population by territorial means less important, with a priority shifting to monitoring and filtering circulations around the city by new methods of surveillance and control (security).

In summarising this evolution in emphasis, from disciplined space to spaces of security, it becomes clear that both systems of governance coexist in the contemporary city. The most notable difference, noted Foucault, was that the disciplinary apparatus is centripetal and 'concentrates, focuses and encloses space in a protectionist way' (ibid., p.44). By contrast, the security apparatus is of a different spatial order and acts as a centrifugal force with a tendency to expand upon the space and population on which it acts, becoming 'a surface on which authoritarian, but reflected and calculated transformations can get a hold' (ibid., p.75). Here Foucault dismisses the idea of the all-seeing panopticon that individually disciplines, as 'anarchic', arguing that the governance of populations is a completely different exercise of power over the entire social body. Instead, 'security' is concerned with 'complex networked assemblages that connect people, places and things across time and space, through which circulations of all varieties flow' (Hirst, 2014, p.558).

It is in the managing of these variegated models of spatial distribution and control that Foucault drew a further distinction between disciplinary norms and security *normalisation*; the later having with new statistical methods for analysing populations, dealing with aleatory (uncertain) events, filtering-out bad risks, and promoting a social acceptance for imposed interventions. Here 'normalisation' refereed to the statistical norms for the regulation of populations, with power operating both at the level of the individual body and upon the population as a statistical whole (Munro, 2012). It is at this juncture that Foucault broadens out his discussion of security mechanisms to advance the higher level notion of *gouvernementalité* (governmentality), which is intended to capture the set of 'institutions, procedures, analyses, and reflections, the calculations and tactics that make possible the exercise of this power that has as its principal target the population, [and] as its essential technical instrument the dispositifs of security' (Foucault, 2007, p.108).

In attempts to secure the post-9/11 city, we can see the playing out of both disciplinary techniques, and security dispositifs and governmentality, emerging as a commonplace analysis of the governing of space and the willing participation of the governed population more broadly (see also Chapter 8). For example, certain spaces in the city can still be seen as essentially secured by enclosure, whilst a normalised security apparatus surveys and monitors everything that moves, enveloping the city, and controlling circuits and circulations of people and objects.

In line with these conceptual developments, the remainder of this chapter unpacks and connects both territorially focused and city-wide security to counter-terrorism interventions. The first part analyses the evolution of 'fortress' security at specific overseas political missions since 1998, where sophisticated and robust security has been advanced, often mirroring historical castle and citadel architecture. Detailed examples of the construction of new U.S. Embassies in Iraq and the U.K. are used to exemplify these evolving counter-terrorism 'blueprint' designs. The second part of the chapter illuminates the monitoring and filtering of circulating risk through means of digital surveillance. Here increasing sophisticated biometric security cameras and other 'smart' security techniques and surveillance cordons have increasingly facilitated the automatic production of urban space and enabling the infiltration of surveillance devices into buildings and infrastructure, in ways, it is claimed, help track, or even deter, terrorists. Concomitantly, this has also led to the advance of security control rooms that are increasingly able to integrate multiple data sources and make the city more legible and able to be secured.

New-age fortress defences

As the War on Terror progressed, many states such as the U.S. disguised fear with pride and visually exaggerated national security through the 'emblematic' security architectures of overseas embassies and consulates that were increasingly vulnerable to attack by large and destructive vehicle bombs (Boddy, 2007; Coaffee et al., 2009). As a U.K. architectural critic noted, 'The east African embassy bombings of 1998 and the infamous events of September 11 encouraged the US to rebuild its embassies and consulates as castles' (Glancey, 2009).

As illuminated in earlier chapters, such physical responses to safeguarding strategic public buildings are not unique to the post-9/11 context. The symbolism of embassy security has, for a long time, transmitted a message of physical defence from attack amidst attempts at public diplomacy through architecture.[14] It was in the 1980s, that bespoke design guidance was first drawn up in an attempt to mandate the highest levels of security for such sovereign structures in the wake of the 1983 car bombing of the American Embassy in Beirut, Lebanon (Chapter 3). In 1985, the subsequent *Inman report* on embassy security recommended that U.S. embassies occupy a site of 10–15 acres, which posed intractable logistical and financial challenges in larger cities. These first State Department standards for U.S. Embassy planning continue to frame how embassies have been secured ever since. One central recommendation pertained to the 100-foot setback requirement for the treatment of the exterior of the building so as to resist a car bomb attack from this distance. In practice, this meant that buildings could no longer be glass-fronted and in close proximity to city streets as they were in the past. Such polices were controversial, as for many, this reduced the symbolism of the overseas embassy with embassies built as fortresses, walled off from the countries in which diplomacy was to be carried out. This symbolically presented America to the world as defensive and fearful, with political negotiation conducted from the bunker (Coaffee, 2020).

Such standards endured until the end of the 1990s when the U.S. sought an embassy design and construction program that projected a more positive image. Such a realignment was also direct response to new acts of terror against American diplomatic compounds that were, in most cases, open, city-centre designs, with only minimal fortification. On August 7, 1998 two simultaneous embassy bombings occurred in Dar es Salaam, Tanzania and Nairobi, Kenya against targets where it was easy to park outside (see 9/11 Commission report, p.68). These attacks led to passing of the *Secure Embassy Construction and Counter-terrorism Act* of 1999 that sought increasingly fortified embassy designs. The resultant construction program promoted an identikit walled-off design contrasting sharply with 'the boldly individual designs built during the Cold War, when…U.S. embassies were functionally and architecturally open' (Loeffler, 2009).[15]

The 1999 Act set in stone the 'isolated walled compound' with its multiple agencies, setback, perimeter walls and fencing, anti-ram barriers, blast-resistant construction techniques and materials, and controlled access arrangements.[16] The 100-foot setback rule, which until this point had been optional, now became obligatory, necessitating that the location of vulnerable overseas embassies would have to be changed if stringent security requirements couldn't be met.[17] The 1999 Act begun a new phase of embassy construction, with an aim of spending $14 billion to build 140 fortified compounds within 10 years. The key to achieving such an ambition was to advance a standard design that could be constructed in any overseas territory relatively cheaply.[18] This secure coding of urban space became far more urgent after 9/11, with a further tightening of U.S. Embassy security designs focused on the need for impregnability and impermeability. As one review noted, this meant 'spiritless shells' that were 'squat, unremarkable structures surrounded by green lawns; totally anti-urban, and…, totally secure', in essence, 'isolated, pseudo-military structures…emblematic of Bush-era foreign policy'.[19] This blueprint was described by one commentator, in reference to the new Iraqi Embassy in Baghdad, as creating 'artefacts of fear' replete with 'armoured chambers' and 'blastproof hallways'.[20]

The Baghdad bunker

In January 2009, a decade after the double embassy attacks in Kenya and Tanzania, the U.S. officially opened its Iraqi Embassy in Baghdad with one commentator likening it to 'the imperial mother ship dropping into Baghdad, or a Wild East-version of a 7th Cavalry fort, with the Iraqis playing the role of Native Americans' (Glancey, 2009). A feature article in *Foreign Policy* entitled 'Fortress America' gave a detailed account of how the largest and most secure overseas embassy ever built was constructed, noting that: 'encircled by blast walls and cut off from the rest of Baghdad, it stands out like the crusader castles that once dotted the landscape of the Middle East' (Loeffler, 2009). During its construction, others referred to the Embassy plans as 'the mega-bunker of Baghdad' and akin to a prison where 'the U.S. government itself is a prisoner, and all the more tightly held because it engineered the prison where it resides'.[21]

The embassy, located inside the 4-square-mile Green Zone,[22] occupied a massive site of 104 acres[23] and comprised a multi-building compound that was entirely self-sufficient.[24] Perimeter protection was provided by a 9-foot high blast wall made of reinforced concrete strong enough to deflect the blast from mortars, rockets and car bombs, and with five heavily defended entrance gates. Watchtowers and internal security were taken care of by U.S. Marines with their own on-site barracks.[25] At the centre of the compound stood the

Towards impenetrable and smart security 195

Figure 10.1 The new U.S. Embassy in Baghdad.[26]

bunker-style bomb-proof embassy with narrow slit windows, and a state of the art air-conditioning system in case of chemical or biological attacks (Figure 10.1).

To account for obligatory 'setback', the embassy is essentially an 'island of security' breaking with traditional norms of embassy design that sort interaction with local communities to aid diplomacy. As Loeffler (2009) noted, this design

> appears to represent a sea change in U.S. diplomacy. Although U.S. diplomats will technically be "in Iraq," they may as well be in Washington. Judging by the embassy's design, planners were thinking more in terms of a frontier outpost than a facility engaged with its community.

It is as one architectural critic noted the 'architecture of failed diplomacy' (Glancey, 2009).[27]

After the criticism of the fortress-like Iraqi Embassy, the U.S., when designing new diplomatic buildings – such as Embassies in Berlin, Beijing and London – started to look to bespoke, site-specific designs that were centrally located, similar to the Cold War approach of advertising America through design culture. In 2010, the State Department, through the Bureau of Overseas Buildings Operations, launched a new Design Excellence program intended to 'produce diplomatic facilities that are outstanding in all respects including security, architecture, construction, sustainability, operations and maintenance' (U.S. Department of State, 2010). *Guiding Principles of Design*

196 The future of urban security

Excellence in Diplomatic Facilities directed this effort, with importance placed not just upon security, but on environmental efficiency, and how U.S. embassies and consulates could best contribute to the civic and urban fabric of host cities.[28] The document begins with a quotation by Senator Daniel Moynihan, from March 25, 1999, that summed up this new 'open' approach to embassy design:

> Architecture is inescapably a political art, and it reports faithfully for ages to come what the political values of a particular age were. Surely ours must be openness and fearlessness in the face of those who hide in the darkness.

The new London citadel

As the State Department was launching its new architectural guidance, the design for the new London Embassy was being chosen with a focus on the aesthetics of architectural design and the wider urban impact of such structures.[29] In February 2010, amidst some controversy, proposed architectural plans for a new U.S. embassy building on a vacant site in Wandsworth, South West London were unveiled. Building work started in November 2013 and was completed in 2017, at a cost of well over £1 billion. The requirement for a new embassy was deemed vital for 'security purposes', with the existing embassy site seen as vulnerable, and difficult and costly to protect from terrorist attack, given its constrained location. The previous location in Grosvenor Square, central London, had, since 9/11, become a virtual citadel surrounded by residential and commercial premises and had seen much public protest regarding the high fences, concrete barriers, crash-rated steel blockers and armed guards that encircled the site to protect it from vehicle bombing. It was dubbed 'the fortress in the square' and had offended the 'aesthetic sensibilities' of local residents, some of whom have moved away rather than live near a perceived terrorist target (Coaffee et al., 2009). The spacious site for the proposed new embassy would, in contrast, 'provide room for the high walls and layers of security that have turned U.S. embassies around the world into imposing fortresses over the past 10 years'.[30]

The 2010 design for the new embassy, and the rationale for relocation from the current site, incorporated in a singular design a number of the characteristics of contemporary counter-terrorist protective design. Its large, non-constrained, site in south-west London represented a move away from the reclusive siting of other U.S. embassies around the world, with designers seeking to incorporate a number of innovative and 'stealthy' counter-terrorism design features, many of which were reminiscent of medieval stronghold castle design: a protected castle keep surrounded by moats or ditches which could be crossed using ramparts. The lead architect from Pennsylvania firm Kieran Timberlake noted that his designs had been stimulated by European castle architecture and that, in addition to the use of a blast-proof glass facade, he would use landscape features imaginatively as security devices. This was

Figure 10.2 The new U.S. Embassy in London.[31]

to minimise the use of fences and walls to avoid giving a 'fortress feel' to the site. Ponds (essentially a moat) and multilevel gardens were also incorporated as security features to provide a 30-metre protective 'blast zone' around the site. This was encircled with crash-rated bollards that were to be hidden by think hedges. Referring to his largely glass-based design (Figure 10.2), the lead architect further noted the wider diplomatic design brief, in that 'we hope the message everyone will see is that it is open and welcoming' and that 'it is a beacon of democracy – light filled and light emitting'.[32]

Despite these aspirations of architectural diplomacy, many critics commented that the desire for openness and the embrace of the broader urban milieu was swamped by security concerns. The *New York Times* architecture critic, in his review entitled 'A New Fort, er, Embassy', argued that the building struggled with the balancing of a welcoming, democratic image and threat of attack, noting that:

> The project as a whole, however, is a fascinating study in how architecture can be used as a form of camouflage: an eye-opening expression of the irresolvable tensions involved in trying to design an emblem of American values when you know it may become the next terrorist target.[33]

As it finally opened to the public in December 2017, the designers reiterated that security was a major part of the contract to design the most expensive

U.S. building ever constructed beyond its shores, with at least half the $1 billion budget spent on meeting, and exceeding security needs, and making the new embassy arguably the safest building in London.

Overall, the construction of the embassy encapsulated core principles of contemporary protective design: the need to integrate effective security into the design of sites proportionately; the increased importance of utilising a range of built environment professionals such as planners, and architects in security design; and the need to consider the visible impact of security measures and, where appropriate, make these as unobtrusive as possible (Coaffee, 2020).

More generally, over the last 30 years, U.S. embassies, even in the most liberal of cities, have been subject to acute target hardening despite attempts to create a more open development that better integrates with the host city. Visually, what has emerged in most cases is an emblematic counter-terror architecture that can create emotional dis-assurance, particularly for the neighbours. Such places are now often set back from publically accessible roads (if adjacent roads are not permanently closed), surrounded by reinforced steel bollards, walls, gates and guardhouses and structures are (retro)fitted with blast-proof glazing and cladding.

Circulating surveillance and object identification

Surveillance has been a continual feature of human societies stretching back to antiquity, embedded into ancient architectural forms and, later, exercised through the collection of census data for taxation and conscription. Modernity saw important changes in the use of surveillance, because it enabled multiple ordering and organising processes, and operated as a means to make visible a series of variously imagined forms of urban dangerousness, including disease, dissent and destitution (Coaffee and Murakami Wood, 2008). In time, surveillance practices diversified and extended beyond mere observations to become a means to make cities legible through to a range of increasingly intensified surveillance practices that worked to coerce, regulate and order elements of urban life.

The late twentieth century brought rapid changes in the ubiquity, potency and technological sophistication of surveillance practices, with CCTV in particular expanding so that it became normalised as an expected feature of public space. 9/11 further catalysed these developments and shepherded in many new automated analytical applications. Here, attention quickly turned to the enormous data harvesting operations of U.K. and U.S. intelligence agencies sanctioned by licentiously interpreted 9/11-related legislative enablers, such as the U.S. Patriot Act. As David Lyon (2003) noted at the time,

> technologically, the U.S. administration was fairly quick to come up with the astonishingly comprehensive "Total Information Awareness" scheme. The data-mining technologies had been available for some time

in commercial settings, but until 9/11 no plausible reason existed for deploying them…within a national security apparatus.

(p.4–5)[34]

In this context, this section focuses on twenty-first forms of urban surveillance – a far more complex technologically dominated polity than in the early modern period of Foucault's *dispositif panoptique*, fuelled by post-9/11 anxiety – that increasingly sought to monitor the circulation of people and objects in the city, and in so doing, to differentiate good risks from bad. Specifically, this saw the growth of second-generation surveillance technologies designed to organise, filter or elevate noteworthy signals from the white noise of oversupplied surveillance data. Utilising the pervasiveness, ubiquity or ambience in computing further enabled the infiltration of surveillance devices into buildings and security infrastructure, to monitor bodies and everything that moves.

Conceptually, post-9/11, surveillance was increasingly recast away from being viewed in terms of its classical state/society relations, and increasingly as something electronic and remote, and directed towards the tracking of movements, communications and connections. But, as Ceyhan (2012, p.41) noted, 'while aiming at controlling and regulating populations' movements and preventing the emergence of risky features such as "bad circulation," its aim is also reassuring populations in the context of fear and uncertainty created by the 9/11 terrorist attacks' (p.41).

New forms of surveillance increasingly involved biometrics such as facial and iris recognition linked into digital CCTV (Introna and Wood, 2004), that were monitored in state-of-the-art control rooms. At the same time, the surveillance of the body itself was supplemented by the capturing of associated data and surveillance through searchable databases of information, sometimes called 'dataveillance' (Clarke, 1988). Examples of this technology include relatively straightforward applications such as Automatic Number Plate Recognition (ANPR) in place around the perimeter of London's congestion charge zone (Chapter 5), more complex technologies such as Facial Recognition CCTV (FRCCTV), and software that attempted to model human behaviour, such as London Underground's 'Intelligent Passenger Screening' technology.[35] These enhanced security technologies all involved more asocial and automated forms of surveillance, designed to filter, and hence reduce, the volume of images confronting practitioners, with the intention of directing attention to where it is most effectively applied.

Yet the centripetal pull of new forms of surveillance also involved more than observing the bodies of suspects, and was increasingly focused towards the surveillance of *mobilities* and the detection of harmful elements that circulated around the city. Such dispersed and fragmentary information has become as (or more) important than the embodied subject, with computer databases allowing greater integration and automated algorithmic operations performed effectively in real time, without the bodily subject knowing (Graham

200 *The future of urban security*

and Wood, 2003). This increasingly technological politics has seen the local intensification and legitimation of surveillance and is aligned internationally, within the discourse of the Revolution in Military Affairs (Dillon, 2002) and, at the urban scale, with police adopting neo-Victorian notions of threat from 'genetically dangerous' classes of people, instead of criminality as individual 'deviancy' (Rose, 2000b), in attempts to cleanse and purify city spaces (Fussey et al., 2012). In other cases, the deployment of surveillance has been allowed to grow to compensate for inefficiencies in the existing infrastructures that have little to do with terrorism prevention (Wood et al., 2003).

A face in the crowd

In May 2019, legislators in San Francisco voted to ban the use of facial recognition surveillance cameras by public bodies, notably the police, until regulations are in place, becoming the first city to do so in the U.S.[36] Whilst proponents of FRCCTV argued their banning would hinder crime reduction and counter-terrorism efforts, critics argued the controversial technology, in its current form, is unreliable and error prone,[37] and represented an unnecessary infringement on individual privacy and civil liberty (NIST, 2019).[38] In the proceeding months, many civil rights and privacy advocate groups called on the Federal Government to ban facial recognition technology 'pending further review' with the use of the equipment being seen as disproportionate and which could be used to 'control minority populations and limit dissent'.[39] Amnesty International also called for a ban on the use, development, production, sale and export of facial recognition technology for mass surveillance purposes by the police and other U.S. state agencies.[40] Further afield, European politicians also considered banning FRCCTV in public places for 5 years to safeguard individuals rights.[41] At the same time, trials of FRCCTV across the U.K. that had been ongoing since 2016[42] were proving controversial and, in August 2020, were ruled 'unlawful', in a court case taken out against South Wales Police. The adjudication noted that its use breached human rights as biometric data was being analysed without an individual's knowledge or consent.[43]

These rulings on either side of the Atlantic were the latest chapter in the journey of FRCCTV – a military technology – that was initially trailed in the mid-late 1990s in a variety of settings (Davies, 1996; Woodward, 2001; Lyon, 2003).[44] Notably, FRCCTV had also been used since 2000 at NFL Super Bowl's in the U.S. More recently, in Europe, it has been experimented with predominantly in transport systems[45] and for public space surveillance.[46] Further afield, in China facial recognition has been used as part of the extensive surveillance of Muslim Uighurs in Xinjiang province (see Chapter 12). These trails were all conducted in closed and relatively *controlled* spaces.

Perhaps FRCCTV's first deployment in *uncontrolled* spaces occurred in 1998 in the London Borough of Newham – a few years later to become the heart of the 2012 Olympic Games (see Chapter 11). In an area that had historically been unable to escape the label of 'dangerousness', 300 FRCCTV cameras were introduced into the area on a trial basis for 6 months by the Metropolitan Police. The cameras were American military surveillance technology produced by the company Identix (formerly Visionics), and installed by Dectel, using Mandrake software systems. Alongside their deployment, large signs stating 'Criminals Beware, Smart CCTV in operation' were erected.[47] Officially installed to counter crime and Irish Republican terrorism, the cameras became operational during 1998, the same year as the 'Good Friday Agreement' which, effectively, led to the demilitarisation of Provisional IRA. Critics also emphasised the lack of evidence supporting their effectiveness in tackling crime, with technological limitations meaning the trial was soon abandoned (Fussey, 2012).[48] The introduction of the scheme, however, triggered a series of debates about civil liberties, with the U.K. civil rights group Liberty, noting 'a balance needs to be struck between the needs of law enforcement and individual privacy – our view is that the use of this technology strikes the wrong balance'.[49]

After 9/11, national security apparatuses were urgently reassessed resulting in an inclination to 'nurture, mimic, shelter and appropriate surveillance capitalism's emergent capabilities for the sake of total knowledge and its promise of certainty' (Zuboff, 2019, p.9–10). Governmental aims to monitor and track terrorist activity led to much technological innovation being embedded within the urban landscape, chief among them biometric identification technologies to focus on either detecting those engaged in hostile reconnaissance of target sites or identifying those committing acts of terrorism. In particular, prior work in relatively controlled environments such as airports was utilised by counter-terrorism specialists to consider how security experts could position citizens through technological arrangements orientated to hold and monitor individuals in specifically designed spaces.[50] Such a 'securitization of identity' (Rose, 1999, p.240) became a government imperative, and as Gates (2006, p.417) noted from a U.S. perspective, the biometrics industry 'reoriented itself around the new political priorities of "homeland security". The press gave considerable coverage to biometrics and their developers, and awareness of the technologies mushroomed among policy makers and the public'.

Of all the biometric technologies being advanced, it was facial recognition that caught the public and policymakers imagination as a possible silver bullet that could reduce the terror threat. This emergent technology, which had been trialled pre-9/11, now received a different level of interest and funding as 'there seemed no better way to identify these so-called unidentifiable enemies with their distinctive "face of terror" than the high-tech, state-of-the-art technique of computerized facial recognition' (ibid., p.418). Since 2001, facial recognition systems have evolved through enhancements that have updated the scanning of a limited set of facial characteristics[51] to utilise complex mathematical representations and automatic face processing, and as one review noted, the 'dumb' cameras of yesteryear became 'supercharged' into smart devices that were increasingly able to recognise specific people, objects or unusual behaviours 'allowing them to effectively "see"'.[52]

Although facial recognition technology has come a long way and is now used in an increasingly wide array of everyday activities,[53] there is still a need for enhancements to improve accuracy and reliability and to deal effectively with legal and ethical concerns over bias and privacy. Such concerns have been exposed in the most recent adoptions of facial recognition. From their use to monitor protests,[54] to being trailed for everyday use by U.K. police forces in the fight against crime and terrorism, FRCCTV has increasingly been normalised in the civic domain as their use mushrooms. Concomitantly, legal and ethical pushback against such system has also reached a zenith as attempts are made to get the use of FRCCTV banned and/or better regulated.

Recent London trails of FRCCTV exemplify these conflicting trends placing it at the forefront of the battle between intrusive surveillance and human rights. From the first- and second-generation CCTV and ANPR cameras put in around the financial zones of London to protect against IRA attacks, to initial trails of FRCCTV in the late 1990s, London police's surveillance capability has continued to grow as a result of 9/11, the terrorist attacks of July 7, 2005 and the 2012 Olympics, retaining its position as one of the most surveilled cities in the world.[55]

Most recently, between 2016 and 2019, the Metropolitan Police began live trials of FRCCTV across a number of different sites, moving to operational deployments in early 2020. These tests used NEC's NeoFace Live Facial Recognition (LFR) technology to take images and compare them to images of people on the 'watchlist'.[56] A number of these trials were independently assessed and deemed to be methodologically flawed and disproportionately deployed (Fussey and Murray, 2019). This assessment noted that in the thousands of faces scanned by the cameras only 46 potential matches were flagged as being on the watchlist.[57] Further, after police reviews, only eight were demonstrated to be correct identifications, meaning the system was right only 19% of the time. Moreover, whilst the Metropolitan Police did publicise the FRCCTV trials in the locations they were taking place, there was little option for people to give their consent to have their faces scanned.

After these tests, it was reasoned by the Metropolitan Police that such technologies should be used 'to aid policing operations where we have intelligence that supports its use' and to tackle serious crime and terrorism (Metropolitan Police, 2020). The Metropolitan Police, in a court of law, argued that the use of FRCCTV was part of their intrinsic powers, was not 'invasive' technology that would require special authorisation, and as a result, new legislation was not required to permit its use (Fussey and Murray, 2020).[58] More specifically, it was argued that their legal mandate for using live FRCCTV rested on an interpretation of the Human Rights Act that recognises action in the interests of national security, public safety and the prevention of disorder or crime as legitimate aims. Such a stance was seen by others to be legally dubious, 'taking surveillance to a whole new level', with critics arguing that it 'is an invasion of privacy, has spotty accuracy and is being introduced without adequate public discussion'.[59]

As a result, many significant legal and ethical challenges remain unresolved. In October 2019 the Information Commissioner's Office (ICO) report on *The Use of Live Facial Recognition Technology by Law Enforcement in Public Places* gave the opinion that the adoption of such a technology has moved ahead of legal and ethical guidance and that the current laws, codes and practices are insufficient to manage the risks that facial recognition technology presents (ICO, 2019). Following the announcement, by the Metropolitan Police in early 2020 to operationally deploy LFR cameras, the ICO reiterated its call for the U.K. Government to introduce 'a statutory and binding code of practice for LFR as a matter of priority'.[60] Such views are echoed in further international findings, notably a recent report written by UN Special Rapporteurs on countering terrorism on *Use of Biometric Data to Identify Terrorists: Best Practice or Risky Business?*, highlighting that such practices are 'likely to infringe international human rights law standards' (Huszti-Orbán and Aoláin, 2020, p.9).

Rings of surveillance

In 1998, as the Newham FRCCTV trials were ongoing in East London, the City of London Police were embedding ANPR technology in the 'ring of steel' security cordon that encircled the Square Mile (see Chapter 5) and were actively discussing adding biometric tools to this security infrastructure (Coaffee, 2003). Stimulated by a series of terrorist attacks in London and across Western Europe in 2017, and given advancements of technology in the intervening years, the Commissioner of the City of London Police unveiled concrete proposals in March 2018, for facial recognition technology to be integrated into the existing surveillance network. This new twenty-first-century 'ring of steel' he noted, would go one step further and do 'personal surveillance' and would require a 'wholesale remodelling of the CCTV and ANPR' that would support the introduction of 'the most technologically advanced control room in the world [and create a] world leading protective security regime'.[61] It was further argued by the Commissioner of the City Police in mid-2018 that:

> To take the Ring of Steel to the next level we need to introduce a fully digitalised system, not just the cameras but also the network that will need to carry, manage and store the visual data. This is essential if we are to introduce *new analytical systems such as facial recognition, behavioural detection* or any other developments of the future as they come on line. We could also have the *capability of linking up* wholesale with third- party cameras across the City, connected to a *centralised solution* [creating] an entirely *integrated system*.
>
> (City Security, 2018, emphasis added)

204 *The future of urban security*

Figure 10.3 New security cameras and signage installed in Manhattan in 2007.

In the early years of the War on Terror, other urban areas had taken London digital surveillance ring concept and applied it in their own locality. Most notably, after a series of thwarted plots to bomb New York City in 2004 and 2005,[62] a plan for a London-style 'ring of steel' emerged as part of plans to rebuild Lower Manhattan (Mollenkamp and Haughney, 2006; Coaffee, 2009b). In early 2006, wireless CCTV cameras were installed on poles 30 feet in the air – the first of nearly 500 cameras that were to be installed as part of a major drive 'to prevent, deter and respond to acts of terrorism aimed at disrupting the nation's economy [notably] a vehicle-borne improvised explosive device'.[63] A key justification for the scheme was the use made of London's 'panoptical' scheme to track the July 2005 bombers movements (albeit retrospectively) across the city on the day of attack.[64] By the end of 2007, this strategic counter-terrorism surveillance programme had over 100 ANPR cameras monitoring vehicles moving through Lower Manhattan roadblocks at a cost of around $90 million[65] (Figure 10.3).

It was also reported that at this time the scheme would cost around $8 million a year to run, and that 'the police department is still considering whether to use face-recognition technology, an inexact science that matches images against those in an electronic database, or biohazard detectors in its Lower Manhattan network' (Buckley, 2007). This surveillance cordon was supplemented, as in London, by private CCTV, with over 3000 private security cameras surveilling significant elements in the urban environment, and whose dynamic feeds could be accessed by the New York Police Department (NYPD) (Scientific American, 2011).

This overarching security assemblage – the Lower Manhattan Security Initiative (LMSI) – ultimately aimed to create a 'surveillance veil' to 'detect, track and deter terrorists' (Buckley, 2007).[66] In August 2008, the *New York Times* further noted that plans had progressed and that 'the Police Department [was] working on a plan to track every vehicle that enters Manhattan to strengthen the city's guard against a potential terror attack'.[67] The technologically updated proposal – *Operation Sentinel* – would not just detect number plates, like the London scheme, but use integrated layers of technologies, such as sensors to detect the presence of CBRN elements due to concerns over 'dirty bomb' attacks (Figure 10.4). Such technologies were subsequently deployed at traffic 'choke points' entering Manhattan in an attempt to reassure people that Manhattan was a safe and secure business environment.[68] Civil liberty advocates, however, felt misled about this controversial scheme seeing it as disproportionate police monitoring without any public input or outside oversight.

In 2009, the scheme was geographically extended into Midtown Manhattan so that the counter-terrorism apparatus would cover locations such as Grand Central Terminal, Pennsylvania Station and Times Square.[69] Following an attempted car bombing in Times Square in 2010,[70] in 2012, the overarching, and increasingly integrated programme of counter-terrorism security, was further enlarged in cooperation with Microsoft to form was referred to as the 'Domain Awareness System' that covered all five city boroughs. At the time, this formed the largest fully digital and real-time surveillance network in the world, overseen by the New York Counter-Terrorism Bureau, with connection to over 18,000 CCTV cameras (6500 from NYPD cameras) and various city-wide databases. This facilitated the tracking of people and objects through the city streets, allowing a

> deep, granular analysis of crime patterns in real time [with] access to multiple databases belonging to the NYC and other organizations that can bring up a massive personal history – including both criminal and public domain information – from any suspect in a matter of seconds.[71]

Technically, much of the data captured streamed into the $150 million command centre – the Lower Manhattan Security Coordination Center – which opened in 2008 – where trained police aggregated and analysed data from surveillance cameras, environmental sensors, radiation detectors and license plate readers around the clock, on a unified dashboard.[72] Additionally, the command centre, working with IBM, made use of artificial intelligence to integrate and analyse the everyday habit and routines of those it captured on film, allowing police to identify matches as well as generate alerts for suspicious activity, unattended packages or people entering restricted areas.[73]

Figure 10.4 Multipurpose surveillance devices, 2013.

Whilst the command centre doesn't (yet) use LFR software, there have been claims that technology has been developed and trailed by which an 'object identification' search of databases can be done by skin colour leading to questions about bias and the features the software was designed to log.

Although the system was framed as a counter-terrorism measure, it was acknowledged at the time that any data collected could be used for other public safety and law enforcement purposes.[74] As a result, civil liberties groups once again continued to question the proportionality and lack of oversight of the surveillance scheme and took legal action regarding the scope and use made of the information collected, and who the information was shared with. Furthermore, with the case of IBM, civil liberties advocates contended that New Yorkers should have been made aware of the potential use of their physical data for a private company's development of surveillance technology.[75]

In June 2020, after 3 years of action by a coalition of civil society groups, and in the wake of protests about policing injustice and calls to defund the police, New York's City Council passed the Public Oversight of Surveillance Technology (POST) Act that should ensure greater transparency and accountability for the purchase and use of surveillance technologies by NYPD, who are now required to openly publish a use policy for each surveillance technology it intends to use.[76] As New York City Council (2020) noted, this creates civilian oversight of police surveillance and that 'New Yorkers deserve to know the type of surveillance that the NYPD uses and its impacts on communities'. As another council member and Chair of the Committee on Public Safety noted, linking to a central question in Foucauldian notions of the Panopticon, about who is watching the watchers?:

> In 2020, technology is developing faster than ever before and we need to be able to adapt just as quickly to ensure that there are regulations and safeguards to protect our civil liberties. I am proud to pass the POST Act knowing that while Big Brother is watching us, we are watching Big Brother.
>
> (cited in ibid.)

However, notwithstanding new oversight regulations, the intensification of urban surveillance, rationalised on the need to filter out good and bad circulations to enhance security, has effectively been normalised as part of the everyday cityscape.[77]

Conclusion: The intensification and normalisation of security infrastructures

This chapter has unpacked the design of counter-terrorism measures in the post-9/11 world through the amplification of fortress and surveillance-based security. Such designs also provide examples of the failed technocratic approach to the art of governance during the War on Terror, where new methods and technologies are pursued as quick-fix solutions to complex and intractable problems, both conventional and novel. Here 'old' threats from car bombing still permeated risk assessments, quickly being joined by concerns over how the circulation of people, objects and harmful materials might present 'new' urban threats. Over time through, counter-responses to heavily defended compounds or blanket surveillance have meant that national and city governments have increasingly had to balance security concerns with the wider social functioning of the city, and the impact of such emergent security infrastructures on everyday life.

Historically, the intensification of security can be seen as a rhetorical device intended to enhance or restore the legitimacy of governments in the abnormal and exceptional circumstances of war or national emergency (Agamben, 2005). It is through the consideration of exceptionality that we can perhaps understand the return to the wall and fortification (and mass population surveillance) and a shift back to the predominant use of sovereign power in Foucault's triad of governmentality.[78] However, this reliance on the state for security shows up the weakness of the contemporary nation-state in neoliberal capitalism. It might well be able to declare a state of exception, but it cannot sustain its enforcement in the way that a mediaeval city-state could and instead has sought assistance from non-state actors (Coaffee et al., 2008).

The bunker design of contemporary embassies further reflects this protectionist response, echoing Bauman's (2000, p.96) depiction of postmodern urbanism – 'hermetically sealed fortresses/hermitages [which] are in the place but not of it' – and exposing one possible future scenario for how cities will develop. In more recent years, the intention with new types of secure building design has been to not to just add more and more layers of steel and concrete to enhance blast resistance and 'stand-off' – for both protective and deterrence value – but to also incorporate more holistic defences, including, for example, state-of-the-art surveillance, access control measures and redundant design. However, by extension, the construction of a multi-layer counter-terror defence has had significant physical, social and economic impacts on the everyday city. These sometimes crude security measures detract from the aesthetic value of the street and reduce public accessibility around the site while increasing the perceived vulnerability of neighbouring residences and businesses. The long-established danger with such protect-first counter-terror policy is that defended areas become territorialised, disconnected and splintered from the rest of the city. This is in contrast to calls to balance higher levels of security with concerns for the functionality of places where security solutions are seen as proactive and proportionate to the ongoing threat of terrorism, are embedded within increasingly collaborative design and management systems and seek to minimising the negative impact of security upon the civic realm.

Similarly, the intense surveillance uptake after 9/11 in search of enhanced object identification has had dramatic impacts upon urban life and come under scrutiny from privacy advocates and civil libertarians. As Gates (2006, p.422) noted, 'facial recognition and other biometrics represent that latest instantiation of these efforts to develop standardized identification techniques as part of the apparatuses of security that underlie the government of large, mobile populations of otherwise anonymous individuals'. The routinised use of this new range of technologies in the War on Terror has further been subject to criticism regarding issue of privacy and freedom of access and movement, particularly regarding how the data collected through such schemes might form part of wider surveillance databases used for profiling purposes, and to justify pre-emptive policymaking that many see as algorithmically biased and discriminatory.

More recent reports on regulating biometric technologies, like FRCCTV, paint a picture of the unstoppable growth of invasive surveillance into everyday public and private lives to prevent fraud, access smartphones and laptops and, increasingly, to monitor public spaces. Kak (2020, p.9), for example, noted, 'this growth and normalization of biometric recognition technology follows a similar trajectory to the rapid growth of closed-circuit television (CCTV) use through the 2000s, despite no clear evidence that it was effective in controlling crime' (see also Norris et al., 2004). Others have further argued that normalisation of data-driven security solutions also permeate across the nature of policing work where 'blanket data sharing for policing and intelligence agencies is thus readily accepted and normalized as a necessary response to crime and insecurity, subject to privacy balancing intended to curtail its most abusive and authoritarian dimensions' (Goldenfein and Mann, 2020, p.50).

Governing security

In *Security, Territory, Population*, Foucault (2007) argued that security mechanisms have historically revolutionised urban governance and that both enclosure-based and circulatory security coexist in the city and regulate milieu, establish territorial frontiers and control circuits and circulation. In the context of the Western War of Terror, what binds the evolution of fortified compounds and of circulatory surveillance together are synergistic links between military technologies and urban counter-terrorism that have evolved and intensified during the twenty-first century. Where once military innovation led to urban surveillance technologies being developed and deployed in cities (such as military-inspired ANPR technology), this tendency is increasingly two-way with the military looking to technology companies (such as IBM and Microsoft) to trial technologies on the street before being deployed on the frontline or battlefield (Wood et al., 2003).

The rise of this so-called smart surveillance has further enabled the greater monitoring of urban areas to make them legible and readable through biometrics – not just in terms of iris scanning, fingerprint and facial recognition, but also in relation to behavioural patterns (e.g. the cues given off by potential suicide bombers) and gait analysis (walking style). These technologies are well developed in the laboratory, or on the battlefield, and are increasingly ubiquitous on the high street. Moreover, the design excellence principles that now underpin fortified embassies (or other target risk buildings) are now seeking to extend their planning beyond military-grade security and embrace professional principles from architecture, urban design and town planning so as to make secure urban developments both effective and as socially acceptable as possible.

The adoption and progression of such security assemblages are increasingly driven by a set of priorities from not just state security agencies and law enforcement, but also from private corporations unimpeded by the social implications of their impact. This moves well beyond the military-industrial complex that U.S. President Eisenhower warned against in his final broadcast to the nation in January 1961, cautioning against the 'unwarranted influence' of the private sector in the militarisation of the nation. Increasingly, we have seen a security-industrial complex emerge – an amalgamation of public- and private-sector interaction in counter-terrorism and security-related industries, where 'dual-use' military-civilian technologies and materials, increasingly emerge, stimulated by the War on Terror, and fuelled by private sector entrepreneurs and innovators. As Mills (2004) speculated in the years immediately after 9/11, these 'enabling technologies for terror-sensing tools will rapidly migrate to applications in medicine, industry, transportation, telecom and even entertainment, driving a tech boom'. The new security-industrial complex has further resulted in a symbiotic relationship between the state and the private sector, fuelling ever greater levels of spending on security.

Similarly, others have also referred to the surveillance-industrial complex (Ball and Snider, 2013) to refer to 'the intersections of capital and the neo-liberal state in promoting the emergence and growth of the surveillance society' (p.1), providing opportunities for both social control and profit from surveillance applications, and ushering in a new era of security governance. Here conventional ways of governing society by and through the state no longer hold as expert knowledge, practices and technologies of risk are increasingly provided by a range of non-state actors to manage mobility and retain 'zones of safety and affluence' (Dean, 2007, p.196) within the context of exceptionality provided by the declared, and seemingly permanent, War on Terror.

Notes

1 Here a large van bomb exploded within Regjeringskvartalet, the executive government quarter and next to the Prime Ministerial offices, killing eight people, injuring at least 200 and destroying a large tract of urban space. Two hours later, a second marauding gun attack by the far-right extremist Anders Breivik at a summer camp on the island of Utøya killed 69 and injured over 100.
2 On July 9, 2008, a gun attack on the Consulate General of the United States, Istanbul resulted in six deaths.
3 On September 17, 2008, the 2008 U.S. Embassy attack in Sana'a, Yemen was attacked with rocket-propelled grenades, automatic rifles, grenades and car bombs, resulted in 18 deaths despite its in situ defence which comprised a number of security rings. Earlier in 2008 on March 18 missed the embassy and instead hit a nearby school.

4 On April 5, 2010, the U.S. Consulate in Peshawar was attacked by militants and involved a vehicle suicide bomb and attackers who tried to enter the Consulate using grenades and weapons fire. Six people were killed.
5 On September 11 and 12 there was a coordinated attack against two United States government facilities in Benghazi, Libya. On September 11, the American diplomatic compound was attacked with grenades and weapons resulting in the deaths of two people including the U.S. Ambassador to Libya. On September 12, a mortar attack against a CIA annex 1-mile away, killed a further two people.
6 On February 1, 2013, a suicide bomber attacked the U.S. Embassy in Ankara, Turkey killing two people.
7 On September 13, 2013 The U.S. Consulate in Herat, Afghanistan was attacked by a group of Taliban militants with a large truck bomb followed by a minivan carrying an assault team armed with assault rifles and rocket-propelled grenades. 17 people were killed.
8 Often referred to as 'India's 9/11', these attacks were a relatively novel mode of operation and did not necessarily fit the 'pattern' of prior Al-Qaeda attacks of recent years with deep cultural and historic forces at play in terms of target selection (Coaffee, 2009a). As reported in the United Kingdom's U.K.'s *Guardian* newspaper (2008, p.4): 'the targets for the attacks were clearly chosen for their iconic value, whether as symbols of Mumbai's power and wealth, cultural centres associated with western values or places where foreigners gathered'.
9 France had been on high alert since the January 2015 attacks on *Charlie Hebdo* offices and a Jewish supermarket in Paris that killed 17 people and wounded 22, including civilians and police officers.
10 Shortly after the attack, New Zealand Police launched Operation Whakahaumanu designed to both reassure New Zealanders and investigate possible threats who shared a similar ideology to the gunman. The attack was seen as the motivation for a number of further attacks worldwide, notably in August 2019, a gunman killed 23 people in a mass shooting in a supermarket in El Paso, Texas. In a manifesto posted to social media, he expressed support for the Christchurch mosque shootings.
11 See, Christchurch Attacks Strike at the Heart of Muslims' Safe Places from Islamophobia. *The Conversation*, March 28, 2019, at https://theconversation.com/christchurch-attacks-strike-at-the-heart-of-muslims-safe-places-from-islamophobia-113922#.
12 In the previous lectures, *Society Must Be Defended*, Foucault (2003) had already begun to develop the constitutive elements of security mechanisms.
13 He also uses historical examples from vaccination campaigns and food shortages.
14 As Loeffler (1998) highlighted in *The Architecture of Diplomacy,* innovative architectural design was a political process since the inception of the U.S. Embassy building program in 1926.
15 Many of the U.S. embassies designed in the 1950 and 1960s at the height of the Cold War, these were designed by iconic architects of the day. For example, Walter Gropius, founding director of the Bauhaus school of architecture, designed the U.S. Embassy in Athens; Richard and Eero Saarinen, who designed JFK airport's TWA-terminal, designed the U.S. Embassy in London (see Glancey, 2009).
16 In the U.S., this included a reinforcement of federal building standards that were introduced after the Oklahoma bombing in 1995. For example, in 2003 the

212   *The future of urban security*

Department of Defense (DoD) also republished Unified Facilities Criteria entitled "Minimum Antiterrorism (AT) Standards for Buildings."
17 This requirement could only be waived upon the approval of the Secretary of State if it was in the U.S. national interest.
18 Whilst architectural critics deplore the copycat designs, the costs were cheap, ranging from $35 million to $100 million.
19 Fortress America: How the U.S. Designs Its Embassies. *Citylab*, September 17, 2012, at www.bloomberg.com/news/articles/2012-09-17/fortress-america-how-the-u-s-designs-its-embassies.
20 The Mega Bunker of Baghdad. *Vanity Fair*, October 29, 2007, at www.vanityfair.com/news/2007/11/langewiesche200711.
21 As note 19.
22 The Green Zone is a heavily fortified zone in the centre of the Iraqi capital that historically served as the headquarters of successive Iraqi regimes and now as the zone of international presence in the city. By contrast, the parts of Baghdad immediately outside the perimeter were called the Red zone. Both terms originated as military designations.
23 By comparison, this is six times larger than the UN complex in New York and more than 10 times the size of the new U.S. Embassy in Beijing.
24 It had, for example, its own electricity plant, fresh water and sewage treatment facilities, storage warehouses, and maintenance shops.
25 The U.S. Congress appropriated nearly $600 million for the embassy's construction. It was estimated to would cost $1 billion a year to run.
26 U.S. Department of State: Creative Commons CC-BY-SA-4.0.
27 In January 2020, Iraqi militia and their supporters targeted the U.S. Embassy in central Baghdad. Fires were set badly damaged a perimeter gatehouse, and stones were thrown. Damage to the reception area, was some distance from the embassy building itself. During the incident Diplomats inside the embassy stayed in safe rooms.
28 See, for example, Building a Fortress on the Hill: Welcome to the U.S. Embassy in Baghdad (Bumped and Updated). *Wired*, May 31, 2007, at www.wired.com/2007/05/building_a_fort/.
29 The other option that was readily considered for embassies after 9/11 was relocation to out-of-city sites.
30 'Why Is the US Embassy Moving?', *The Guardian*, October 4, 2010, p.40.
31 ©Kieran Timberlake/studio am.
32 Cited in Ambassador, You Are Spoiling Our View of the Thames with This Boring Glass Cube. *The Guardian,* February 24, 2019, p.13.
33 Cited in, A New Fort, er, Embassy, for London. *New York Times*, February 23, at www.nytimes.com/2010/02/24/arts/design/24embassy.html?ref=arts.
34 This project was advanced by the National Security Agency (NSA) through a series of highly sensitive programmes of bulk data collection and the establishment of 'fusion centers', revealed in 2013 by Edward Snowden.
35 On parts of the London Underground in 2004, in response to the Madrid train bombings, a high-tech 'smart' CCTV surveillance software system (Intelligent Pedestrian Surveillance system, IPS), was rolled out. This system, in theory, would automatically alert operators to 'suspicious' behaviour, unattended packages and potential suicide bombing attempts on the Tube system. The system it was claimed

Towards impenetrable and smart security 213

'automatically tracks and integrates 3D images with CCTV video, maps and other real-time information. The implementation of this system followed extensive trials, which initially had little to do with terrorism and predated 9/11. The original intention was to develop a crowd flow monitoring system that morphed into something more as its potential to spot those waiting on platform who were likely to commit suicide was expanded (Coaffee, 2009b).

36 Additionally, any future plans to buy new surveillance technology must be approved by city authorities. They were quickly followed by a number of other cities such as Oakland, Portland and Boston.
37 This is particularly the case when dealing with women or people with darker skin which in some studies have had an error rate of up to 35%. See Study finds gender and skin-type bias in commercial artificial-intelligence systems, *MIT News*, February 11, 2018, at https://news.mit.edu/2018/study-finds-gender-skin-type-bias-artificial-intelligence-systems-0212.
38 As a spokesperson for the American Civil Liberties Union further noted, 'let's just ensure that we put the policy horse before the technology cart and lead with our values so we don't accidentally wake up someday in a dystopian surveillance state…because behind the scenes, police departments and technology companies have created an architecture of oppression that is very difficult to dismantle'. Cited in *WBUR News*, January 24 2020, at www.wbur.org/news/2020/06/23/boston-facial-recognition-ban.
39 See an open letter signed by over 40 groups – https://epic.org/privacy/facerecognition/PCLOB-Letter-FRT-Suspension.pdf. This followed a *New York Times* investigation of a facial recognition service used by more than 600 law enforcement agencies in the United States. The company, Clearview AI, scraped public photographs from Facebook, YouTube, and other websites to create a database of more than three billion images. www.nytimes.com/2020/01/18/technology/clearview-privacy-facial-recognition.html.
40 See www.amnesty.org/en/latest/research/2020/06/amnesty-international-calls-for-ban-on-the-use-of-facial-recognition-technology-for-mass-surveillance/.
41 See www.technologyreview.com/2020/01/17/238092/facial-recognition-european-union-temporary-ban-privacy-ethics-regulation/ and www.theguardian.com/technology/2020/feb/05/european-parliament-insists-it-will-not-use-facial-recognition-tech.
42 In the Metropolitan Police used facial recognition technology to scan people at the Notting Hill carnival since 2016 in London and the South Wales police trialled its use from 2017 in Cardiff.
43 The Judgment was described by one Lawyer as a 'major victory in the fight against discriminatory and oppressive facial recognition', cited in 'Facial recognition use by South Wales Police ruled unlawful', *BBC News*, August 11, 2020, at www.bbc.co.uk/news/uk-wales-53734716.
44 Internationally, examples of its use included, the trialling of a prototype version in 1995 at Maine Road football stadium in Manchester in attempts to thwart football hooliganism, from 1998, the West Virginia Department of Motor Vehicles using the technology to check for duplicate and false driver's license registrations, the Israeli government using facial recognition to automate the border-crossing process for workers entering Israel from Palestine, the Mexican government used a facial recognition system to eliminate duplicate voter registration in the

214   *The future of urban security*

presidential election, its deployment at a range of airports from Reykjavik in Iceland to Logan airport in Boston. FRCCTV has been used since 2000 at NFL Super Bowl's in the U.S. (Chapter 11).

45 For example, it is used to measure the flow of passengers at Rome's Fiumicino airport, while a number of French airports, including Charles de Gaulle in Paris, have installed the 'Parafe' automated passport verification system.
46 For example, during the 2019 Carnival in Nice, France, the local police tested a facial recognition system in one area of the festival grounds.
47 The system worked by triggering an alarm system whenever its network of cameras identifies a known criminal whose image matches a police database.
48 Some evidence suggested crime rates in the borough reduced, although it was possible that the criminals shifted their efforts to other areas.
49 Cited in Face-recognition CCTV launched *The Independent Newspaper*, October 15, 1998, at www.independent.co.uk/news/face-recognition-cctv-launched-1178300.html.
50 See, for example, Her Majesties Government 2007 and 2009.
51 Specifically, the eyes, ears, nose, mouth, jawline and cheek structure.
52 How London Became a Test Case for Using Facial Recognition in Democracies. *Financial Times*, August 1, 2019, at www.ft.com/content/f4779de6-b1e0-11e9-bec9-fdcab53d6959.
53 As the technology has become commercially available in recent years, via companies like Apple and Facebook, it has been adopted by supermarkets, hospital and other public settings that now all have camera systems capable of integrating facial recognition technology.
54 For example, in 2020, the monitoring of protesters using facial recognition occurred during democracy rallies in Hong Kong, political protests in New Delhi, India, and in a number of U.S. cities such as Detroit and Baltimore during Black Lives Matter demonstrations.
55 According to one recent report, London has over 420,000 surveillance camera, making it the number 2 city in the world behind Beijing with 470,000 (West and Bernstein, 2017).
56 Ten trials in a range of environments including at public events and in crowded areas were conducted, by installing temporary cameras (or commonly mounting them on a van) in a particular place such as an Underground station of public space, for an arranged period of time.
57 This research also questions the reason why individuals were placed on any watchlist and which appeared inaccurate and out of date.
58 The Metropolitan Police further claimed that they will take a considerate and transparent approach to future operational deployments of FRCCTV, which will be clearly signposted, for a fixed duration of a few hours at a time, and with information leaflets handed out to the public.
59 London Police Are Taking Surveillance to a Whole New Level. *New York Times*, January 24, 2020, at www.nytimes.com/2020/01/24/business/london-police-facial-recognition.html.
60 See https://ico.org.uk/about-the-ico/news-and-events/news-and-blogs/2020/01/ico-statement-in-response-to-an-announcement-made-by-the-met-police/. Perhaps most importantly, when live deployment of FRCCTV occurred in London at the start of 2020 there was no legal framework to authorise its use with police

Towards impenetrable and smart security 215

forces currently relying on what was referred to as 'a grab-bag of other legislation' that lacks oversight, accountability and necessary safeguards Including, common law, the Human Rights Act 1998, the Protection of Freedoms Act 2012, the Data Protection Act 2018, and the Regulation of Investigatory Powers Act 2000. See 'Facial Recognition is in London. So How Should We Regulate it?' *Wired*, March 16, 2020, at www.wired.co.uk/article/regulate-facial-recognition-laws.

61 Cited in New 'Ring of Steel' Proposed, *Professional Security,* March 28, 2018, at www.professionalsecurity.co.uk/news/interviews/new-ring-of-steel-proposed/. Accessed March 28, 2018. The technology would also link with the Corporation's 'smarter city' programme for management of the environment, such as street lighting.
62 Examples of thwarted terrorism plots against New York City cited in the documents included an alleged 2004 attempt to bomb the Herald Square subway station, an aborted plan to attack the Brooklyn Bridge and the hostile reconnaissance of the financial district by al Qaeda operatives.
63 Department of Homeland Security documents from the Mayor's Office of Management and Budget, cited in Secrecy Shrouds NYPD's Anti-Terror Camera System. *City Limits*, April 26, 2010, at https://citylimits.org/2010/04/26/secrecy-shrouds-nypds-anti-terror-camera-system/. Similar CCTV schemes were later installed in other U.S. cities such as Washington, Chicago and Philadelphia.
64 Such developments were facilitated by visits to London by the Major of New York and law enforcement agencies to view the ANPR technology for themselves.
65 Initially, the NYPD obtained $25 million toward the estimated $90 million cost of the plan ($15 million from the city and $10 million from Homeland Security grants).
66 The cordon also used physical roadblocks to control access and egress.
67 City Would Photograph Every Vehicle Entering Manhattan and Sniff Out Radioactivity, *New York Times,* August 11, 2008, at www.nytimes.com/2008/08/12/nyregion/12cars.html?ref=nyregion.
68 Police Want Tight Security Zone at Ground Zero. *New York Times,* August 11, 2008, at www.nytimes.com/2008/08/12/nyregion/12security.html?ref=nyregion. Accessed September 20, 2008.
69 The Midtown Manhattan Security Initiative (MHSI) was supported by further Homeland Security funding.
70 A crude car bomb of propane, gasoline and fireworks was discovered in a smoking car in the heart of Times Square on May 1.
71 Cited in NYPD, Microsoft Launch All-Seeing "Domain Awareness System" With Real-Time CCTV, "License Plate Monitoring". *Fast Company,* August, 8, 2012, at www.fastcompany.com/3000272/nypd-microsoft-launch-all-seeing-domain-awareness-system-real-time-cctv-license-plate-monito.
72 As of 2014, over 2 million number plates were read each day (Levine and Tisch, 2014).
73 Here, the video analytics software automatically labelled still CCTV images with tags, such as clothing colour, which allowing police quickly search stored videotape. See also: IBM used NYPD surveillance footage to develop technology that lets police search by skin colour. *The Intercept*, September 6, 2008, at https://theintercept.com/2018/09/06/nypd-surveillance-camera-skin-tone-search/. Moreover, work by *The Intercept* and the Investigative Fund published in 2018 highlighted that IBM began developing, refining and testing its object identification

technology using secret access to NYPD camera footage (from 2012) as part of its Domain Awareness System.
74 The scheme supposedly operated according to Public Security Privacy Guidelines that stipulated footage must be stored for no more than 30 days if it is not being used in an investigation (Greenemeier, 2011).
75 As note 67.
76 New York City will join several cities across the country that require their police department to disclose their use of surveillance technology to ensure oversight and transparency.
77 The New York surveillance ring, when it was established, was largely based on the underpinning assumption that the presence of CCTV will in itself reduce crime and terrorism – a concept that has been widely debunked in many studies over the last 30 years.
78 Sovereignty, authority and legitimacy.

11 Pop-up security and the politics of exceptionality

Introduction: Situating event-driven security

In the wake of 9/11, the security deployed for major urban-based events embodied a range of 'new' counter-terrorism practices to secure such 'soft targets' resulting in such events proceeding against the backdrop of 'lockdown', 'total' or 'exceptional' security (Coaffee and Murakami Wood, 2006). Here, planning for the worst through pre-emptive actions were increasingly mobilised with security practices often resembling 'security theatre' – a term coined by Schneier (2003) to refer to the practice of investing in countermeasures intended to provide the feeling of improved security while doing little or nothing to achieve it. This illustrates the powerful symbolic connection between hosting large events with their 'threat-rich' environment and the fear of terrorist violence.[1]

Large-scale events hold significant symbolic value for a diverse range of terrorist actors. However, whilst historically terrorist threats to such events have been normally rooted in the *localised* settings rather than being derived from external 'international' threats,[2] *globalised* models of security increasingly play out at the municipal scale. This has led to questions being raised over the proportionality of security responses, not least in the way 'threat' is characterised as something external and dissident, and something that can be, in large part, resolved through the imposition of exceptional and standardised security models that reveals the uneven geographies that such hyper-carceral security produces (Coaffee et al., 2011).

Increasingly, since 9/11, there has been a progressive global standardisation of mega-event counter-terrorism strategies comprising continually reproduced security *leitmotifs* (Fussey and Coaffee, 2012a). Such orthodoxies have impacted upon the physical, organisational and technological aspects of security at event venues, as well as the urban spaces and communities in which the event venues are located. Here large-scale events are viewed as spectacular terrorist targets, which required defending through highly militarised tactics and detailed and expensive contingency planning, as organisers and security personnel attempt to deliver an event in maximum safety and with minimum disruption to schedule. Such spatialised security is increasingly viewed as an

DOI: 10.4324/9780429461620-15

urban 'battlespace' (Graham, 2010) and 'as terrain in which military tactics and weaponry are necessary to control crowds and prevent and respond to terrorist's attacks' (Schimmel, 2006, p.162). The perceived requirement for event security also serves another purpose; as an ideal urban laboratory for the testing of an array of new technologies, techniques of social control, or security procedures, that are seen as necessary as part of the War on Terror, as well as their *permanent* embedding into the everyday urban landscape.

There is of course nothing new about the deployment of counter-terrorism at major events, particularly sporting ones. The foundations of such practices were laid in the 1970s and 1980s that, in time, would support the architecture of contemporary major event security programmes. Notably, the Black September attack on Israeli athletes at the 1972 Summer Olympics in Munich saw a massive ramping-up of counter-terrorist practices and exponential investment in security infrastructure to surveil and track crowds, the padded bunkers of fortified architecture to protect athletes and spectators, a highly visible military presence to reassure the public, and the development of detailed contingency planning to prepare for every possible threat scenario.

In the post-9/11 context of the War on Terror, large events have evoked increased security concerns. This has led to not only spiralling budgets and enhanced security planning predicated on elevated threat levels, but also to new ways of conceptualising security governance practices that filter broader transnational security process and play out at a metropolitan scale, giving rise to important questions about the balance of security and social functioning. To understand such processes, commentators initially drew on early Foucauldian ideas emphasising how the ubiquity of coercive techniques become normalised through the imposition of event-time security assemblages, where militarised strategies were increasingly embedded within the civic realm and systems of management to better respond to a growing international terrorist threat. Others also drew on later work by Foucault on 'circulatory' models of security concentrating on people and objects on the move and 'to manage connections along the very circuits where groups and individuals circulate' (Klauser, 2013, p.295; see also Chapter 10).

Perhaps most notably through, powerful accounts of the uneven geographies of security and surveillance that emerged at large-scale events drew on Agamben's work on exceptionality, which emphasised the coercive techniques of enclosure, cleansing, incarceration and exclusion that permeate the fabric of the cities before, during and after the event, and attempt to profile and filter risky elements from otherwise safe spaces. Here, security lockdown, urban fragmentation and punitive approaches to control are argued to have become the 'default' option for the host city (Coaffee, 2014). Agamben's work on states/spaces of exception (1998, 2005) illuminated the uneven spatial configurations produced when the rule of law is suspended, facilitating extraordinary social control where citizens can be literally stripped of political rights.[3] As Agamben (2001) noted in the immediate wake of 9/11:

Today we are facing extreme and most dangerous developments of this paradigm of security. In the course of a gradual neutralisation of politics and the progressive surrender of traditional tasks of the state, security imposes itself as the basic principle of state activity [and] becomes the sole criterion of political legitimation. Security reasoning entails an essential risk. A state which has security as its only task and source of legitimacy is a fragile organism; it can always be provoked by terrorism to turn itself terroristic.

This can not only lead to the alteration of the established relationship between the state/sovereign and citizenry within a particular territory, but also to exceptional conditions becoming normalised under attempts to anticipate future risk and threats and in so doing, change the operation of sovereign power (Arias, 2011, p.370).[4] This is best exemplified by President Bush's declaration of a National Emergency on September 14, 2001 which, according to Agamden (2005), meant emergency becomes the rule and by which provisional and exceptional measures become a permanent and normalised technique of government. However, as recent critiques of Agamben have argued, how laws are enacted to deal with exceptionality is both open to human discretion (what becomes seen as exceptional and who decides this), as well an ability to act prior to an event to pre-empt its emergence. As Amoore (2013) has illuminated in an important amendment to Agamben's notion that the exception always becomes the norm;

> the designations and conditions of that exception do not simply *become the norm* (or constitute a new normalcy)....but instead they operate through the norm itself...Far from simply becoming the norm the rapid and fleeting decisions on exceptions is a norm that is always in the process of becoming.
>
> (p.17–18)

In other words, norms are fluid and malleable in relation to what sovereign powers perceive as dangerous.

At event time, the political act of exceptionality spatially manifests itself as exorbitant levels of security and restrictive legal measures that transform the cityscape into a series of temporary 'spaces of exception'. This commonly leads to the displacement of the policing by consent, as special regulatory regimes are brought to bear so as to control behaviour and maintain order. Such security assemblages are easily justified on the basis of post-9/11 anxieties. Whilst event-time security is often highly visible and exceptional, locking down large parts of an urban area for days on end, importantly, the temporary retrofitting of such security 'stage sets' to promote a particular destination as a safe and secure location often leaves a permanent legacy of fixed security infrastructure, or the altered regimes of policing or counter-terrorism (Murakami Wood and Coaffee, 2007).

Drawing on a range of international examples, the remainder of this chapter will unpack how 'exceptional' lockdown security regimes are deployed: as a prerequisite of hosting events; as a testing laboratory for counter-terrorist technologies and procedures; as well as highlighting the wider implications of this for the future city and its citizens. The first section will showcase the rapid expansion of security deployed annually for the U.S. Super Bowl as it moves from city to city on condition that organisers can demonstrate they are security-ready. The second section will detail the 'lockdown' and 'island security' put in place for U.K. political conferences in the wake of 9/11 and demonstrate how military operations to secure the urban terrain became standardised. The third and most substantive section will illuminate how Olympic Games are compelled to put in place ever more exceptional security measures in a bid to deliver a safe and secure event, often leaving a legacy of enhanced security as part of sustainable regeneration planning. The fourth and final section will provide a critique of these emerging pop-up security approaches that provide tangible evidence for the normalising of enhanced security in, and across, urban society.

Testbed counter-terrorism and clean zones

The U.S. Super Bowl is the most watched, single-game, sporting event in America, with the National Football League's (NFL) awarding the hosting of the event only to a 'Super-Bowl-ready' stadium that has stringent security plans in place. As the U.S. House of Representatives (2014) noted, 'the Super Bowl is one of our nation's archetypical mass gatherings. The league sets out to strike an appropriate balance, ensuring that fans enjoy a rich and festive in-stadium experience, while making their safety and security paramount'. As Schimmel (2012) has further highlighted, the 'intersections between the NFL's security practices and the Department of Homeland Security's (DHS) counter-terrorism agenda... [that] render the NFL a uniquely militarized sport association and the annual Super Bowl game a uniquely militarized sport mega-event' (p.338–339). Moreover, since 9/11, having a location that is '"Super-Bowl-ready" has meant shifting from "violence-complacent" to "terrorist-ready"' (Schimmel, 2011, p.3377).

Even before 9/11, the Super Bowl was being used as a testing ground for counter-terrorism and crime reduction technologies notably the much trumpeted use of biometric Facial Recognition CCTV at the XXXV Super Bowl in 2001.[5] At the time, this relatively new and untested technology was used to scan the 100,000 fans, without their knowledge, as they entered the Stadium in Tampa, and matched them against a crime database. In their assessment of the deployment – *Super Bowl Surveillance: Facing Up to Biometrics* – the Rand Corporation noted that facial recognition technologies could provide significant social benefits *if* privacy concerns are taken into account (Woodward, 2001). Less publicly proclaimed were the manifest failures of the system, which was unable to identify anyone engaged in anything more serious than ticket touting, and that occupied operators with repeated false alarms (Stanley and Steihardt, 2002). In terms of post-event legacy, the system was given to Tampa police for a year's trial where it was deployed in the downtown entertainment district.[6] This trial was abandoned after 3 months as the system failed to identify anyone on its database.

Following 9/11, the 2002 Super Bowl in the New Orleans Super Dome was designated by the White House as a 'National Security Special Event' where the Secret Service took a leading role in the provision of unprecedented security. This saw over 2000 federal, state and local law enforcement officers and private security guards, collaborating to ensure safety.[7] According to organisers, 48 agencies were involved in security planning over a 90-day period. The security blanket thrown over the stadium (the hard target) and its surrounds (the soft target) included a no-drive zone around the arena, the use of magnetometers funnelling fans through a single entrance point, snipers on rooftops, hundreds of undercover officers and sniffer dogs doing sweeps of the vicinity, as well as widespread use of facial recognition cameras. As one media report noted, 'the perimeter of the Super Dome has become a fortress. Streets are blocked by concrete barriers and barbed wire. Heavily armed National Guard patrol the city'.[8] One shocked pedestrian additionally told the Associated Press two days before the game that 'Oh my God, it looks like Beirut', as she observed the vast number of tanks and National Guardsmen surrounding the stadium.[9]

Over time, Super Bowl security became a lengthier and more expensive endeavour with the 2006 Super Bowl in Detroit providing perhaps the starkest example of what was referred to as 'supersize security', involving one of the largest security operations in the U.S. history.[10] Such an operation took 18 months of intensive preparation and involved over 50 federal, state and local law enforcement agencies, and resulted in securing the borders of the stadium site with a 300-metre perimeter fence cordon. Inside the secure zone, fans were screened by metal and radiation detectors; SWAT teams aided by digital maps of the stadium terrain, and bomb disposal teams were on standby; computer linked high-resolution CCTV was utilised along with real-time satellite imagery to allow instant response; and, the area was guarded with 10,000 police and private security guards.[11] There was also significant rerouting of traffic, a river exclusion zone patrolled by the U.S. Coast Guard and Navy vessels, and a no-fly zone in operation for a 30-mile radius.

In 2009, the Super Bowl returned to Tampa with the usual theatre of fortress security where the city had spent a number of years honing advanced digital security. The city expanded its use of E-SPONDER and Microsoft Surface technology, originally purchased in 2005 through a DHS grant, to integrate all aspects of Super Bowl security. This involved coordinating multiple agencies and 1500 local personnel, alongside digital maps, radio and voice communication software, to be able to respond effectively and make tactical decisions in real time (Microsoft, 2010). The Tampa Super Bowl also saw the first ever deployment of 'behaviour detection' officers to identify individuals exhibiting

222 *The future of urban security*

suspicious behaviour (Transportation Security Administration, 2009). This event also saw the NFL received official endorsement from the DHS for its security efforts with the award of certification for 'Best Practices' in 'stadium and event security operations', and specifically, 'the NFL's practices of digital surveillance, spectator searches, the enforcement of barricaded zones, threat assessments, and the hiring, vetting, and training of personnel' (Schimmel, 2012, p.350).[12]

In 2011, in Arlington, Texas, and 2012 in Indianapolis, additional elements were added to Super Bowl security through the encouragement of fans to report suspicious activity, inculcating them as 'citizen soldiers' (Schimmel, 2012), reinforcing the notion that 'an alert public plays a critical role in keeping our nation safe' (DHS, 2011b; see also Chapter 9). Here a partnership between the NFL and the DHS actively rolled out the 'If You See Something, Say Something' public awareness campaign (DHS, 2011a). Such messaging appeared on the video board and televisions throughout the stadium on game day, were printed in game programmes, advertised in local airports, hotels, restaurants and bars, and publicised on public transport and in visitor guides in the build-up to the game (DHS, 2012).

In the years after 9/11, a standardised model of Super Bowl security was established and transferred between host cities. Whilst such approaches were dependent on the characteristics of the location, the jurisdictions involved and local law enforcement practices, the standard tropes of these counter-terrorism operations centred upon: interagency coordination and interoperability; high levels of policing and National Guard presence; the use of police dogs for detecting explosives; widespread use of CCTV and other forms of surveillance; the deployment of detectors for CBRN contaminants; snipers; enhanced security on public transport and use of no-fly zones and coast guard patrols dependent on location; extensive road closures; and, in time, increasing use of cybersecurity measures to protect the vast array of interlinked digital technology being used in security planning (U.S. House of Representatives, 2014). For example, for the 2020 Super Bowl in Miami, 5G technology developed by Verizon and AT&T was deployed to boost connectivity between technologies, enhancing the ability of first responders (and drones) to communicate and utilise artificial intelligence (AI). This technology, embedded in the stadium control rooms, provided a tangible legacy that could be used by the local police force for future events, as well as showcasing how it can be transferred to other NFL stadiums to enhance their game day security.[13]

Overall, the development of complex, militarised, and ever more technical, security for the Super Bowl have enabled exceptional measures to be operationalised but with major impacts upon everyday city life. As Schimmel (2012, p.347) noted,

> it alters traffic patterns, restricts movement throughout the city and commerce in NFL 'clean zones' that extend a mile out from the stadium,

and subjects citizens to military operational and security procedures that they do not encounter anywhere else, including at US airports.

These wider social and mobility implications have, like fortress security, become recognised tropes of event hosting during the ongoing War on Terror, be it for a major sporting attraction or, as detailed next, for political conferences.

Conferencing and the development of 'island security'

In the U.K. in the 2000s, given the heightened risk of terrorist attack as a result of the Blair Governments' decisions to join the U.S.-led War on Terror, political party conferences of the ruling Labour Party became large-scale security events, which demonstrated, in practice, the operation of the new security governance infrastructure combined with territorial counter-terrorist security (Coaffee and Rogers, 2008). The conference location, like that of the Super Bowl, was mobile as a variety of the U.K. cities actively competed to host the event, seeing it as a perfect opportunity to boost their local economy and raise their national, or global, profile for business tourism. However, the high-profile counter-terrorism operations that accompanied such events quickly became normalised, becoming a stage-set that was assembled at a given location, and then dismantled, moved on and reassembled at the next chosen site (Coaffee and Murakami Wood, 2006).

At the spring Labour Conference[14] in March 2004 in Manchester, North West England, in the immediate wake of the Madrid train bombings,[15] a 'ring of steel [was] thrown around parts of the city centre to protect the Prime Minister and his government'.[16] This cordon was guarded by armed police and cost in excess of £1 million. Confusion regarding the extent to which this cordon would restrict public access to the city centre led to local concern that the central city would 'be shut' or 'out of bounds', and subsequently resulted in a much lower level of trading than expected, despite only small section of the city being off-limits. Security-wise, the Conference was seen as a success and Manchester was subsequently awarded the larger summer conference for 2006.

During 2005, other intervening conferences also became massive security events. In Gateshead, North East England, in February, a large regenerated urban area was put into 'lockdown' for a fortnight to provide a safe and secure venue at a cost of £3 million. Half of this total was spent on CCTV, radio communications and other technical equipment that was to be made available to local police to use for future major events and in fighting crime (Murakami Wood and Coaffee, 2007). Similarly, in Brighton on the South Coast of England in the summer of 2005, following the devastating 7/7 attacks in London, the conference site was sealed off as police enacted a £3.7 million operation. Here, as the local media reported, secure bridges were built linking the two main conference hotels so that delegates did not even need to leave the secure zone with 'an island site being created around the Brighton Centre... with barriers, fencing and turnstiles to stop possible car bombers'.[17] This was complimented by widespread police 'stop and search', over 1000 police officers and security staff on patrol, and with no-fly zones in operation and the Royal Navy patrolling the sea.

As a result of heightened terror threat levels, in the 2006 conference build-up in Manchester, Greater Manchester Police, other 'blue light' agencies and the Local Resilience Forums organised security preparations up to a year in advance with 'island security' being constructed for the event at an estimated cost of £4.2 million to protect delegates. Pre-planning for the event centred upon a publicly funded flagship regeneration project in central Manchester that had converted a disused railway station into a state-of-the-art conference and events quarter.[18] As well as constructing a control zone around the conference site, procedures to deal with evacuation, contamination and decontamination sites, and major incident access, were considered and role played on tabletop exercise so that decision-making processes could be analysed. Technical information was also scrutinised for all buildings, regarding, for example, structure and supply points for utility provision, fire exits and air conditioning systems, so that any weakness and vulnerabilities could be planned out in advance.

Practically, such an operation – code named *Operation Protector* – was rolled out by Greater Manchester Police and their Counter Terrorism Unit in combination with state security services and private security firms.[19] The security operation was both overt and subtle in orientation. Initially, it began with the closure of public footpaths in the vicinity of the conference venue and the gradual build-up of security personnel. Within the surrounding city centre environment – seen by commentators as symbolising the rebirth of British urban renaissance – an unprecedented 'beautification' campaign was conducted, including an intensification of street cleaning, the promotion of the city through the display on billboards that were used to welcome the Labour Party delegates to Manchester and to advertise the city's growing international reputation as a premier business location.

As the conference approached, the promised 'island security' came into operation as large expanses of steel fencing and concrete blocks surrounded the conference venue creating a hermetically sealed site.[20] This lockdown included not only the immediate conference site, but also severe restrictions on road access, vehicle parking and bus services many hundreds of metres away. Several days before the conference began the police set up what they referred to as a 'buffer zone' in the area immediately outside the 'island site' alongside a significant visible police presence on foot, in cars, on horseback and on motorcycles. This was backed up by the presence of police helicopters that constantly circled overhead (which was blanketed by a no-fly zone) and a troop of mobile CCTV vans with automatic number plate recording (ANPR) capabilities. The stated policing aim was to keep disruption to the general population to a minimum whilst ensuring security was robust and visible.

Pop-up security and exception security 225

Figure 11.1 Policing a protest in Manchester amidst 'island security'.

This siege-like state was also associated with the perceived threat of civil disorder linked to planned protest marches against the incumbent government.[21] The planned marching route symbolically encircled the 'island security' assemblage established around the conference venue, providing a useful test of its resilience[22] (see Figure 11.1). During the conference itself, the delegate hotels were surrounded by armed police (including snipers on the rooftops) and barricaded by 6-foot-high steel fencing, concrete and steel blockers (Figure 11.2), and surveyed by a raft of permanent and temporary CCTV cameras. To enter the conference site, delegates also had to pass through a series of airport-style checkpoints where they were searched and their bags screened.[23]

Overall, despite significant restrictions on public movement and use of public spaces, the event was seen, in marketing terms, as a success in terms of raising the profile of the city and stimulating growth in the local economy. Post-conference it was estimated that the conference brought an extra 17,000 visitors to the city and boosted the local economy by an initial £15 million.[24] In December 2006, it was further announced that the Labour party conference would return to Manchester in 2008 and 2010, as a result of the high-quality facilities in the conference quarter and, perhaps most importantly, the sophisticated security operation that provided an unprecedented feeling

Figure 11.2 Security fences and steel blockers sealing the conference site.

of safety for delegates. Such procedures had now become an almost compulsory element of such event planning that explicitly linked security strategies to competition for footloose political conferences (Coaffee and Murakami Wood, 2006, p.58).[25] This emphasis on safety, however, failed in any significant way to account for the everyday impacts of exceptional security and widespread public unease at having newly regenerated public spaces, paid for by public money, made off-limits for weeks at a time.

Sporting security archipelagos

In recent years, the risk of terrorism has also seen the Olympics overlain by dystopian images of cities under siege as organisers attempt to deliver this mega-sporting event in maximum safety and with minimum disruption to schedule. The Olympics have become an iconic target that must be defended at ever-increasing cost through highly militarised tactics and detailed contingency planning. The approach to security at these multi-site events requires the protecting of both the venues and the crowded places, and transport corridors, of the host city – creating a security archipelago centred on the main stadium, but spreading outwards into the broader urban terrain. This can be equated to Foucault's notion of the 'carceral archipelago'[26] that he used to

Pop-up security and exception security 227

illuminate how penitentiary techniques were increasingly being deployed in public policy programmes to expand disciplinary control over wider society (Foucault, 1977).

Whilst Olympic security programmes might be considered 'exceptional' in terms of its local impact and scale, they also reside within a number of enduring historical, and extraterritorial political, processes (Coaffee et al., 2011). For all the neo-colonialist rhetoric of the International Olympic Committee (IOC), the importation of hardware from multinational security providers, and the desire to set up dislocated and fortified venues that are located *within* a place if not necessarily *of* it, Olympic events are patrolled by domestic police forces with global networks and processes intersecting with, and becoming filtered through, the local. Here, local governance arrangements are subjected to control by international committees (in this case the IOC) that assert an array of security demands upon the municipal organisers, and make clear in guidance to potential host cities that it is *their* responsibility to provide a safe environment for the 'Olympic Family'.

Increasingly, these mandated security features have evolved to represent an Olympic security blueprint that foster 'total' or 'exorbitant' security paradigms that seek to delineate the Games from their contextual milieu (Table 11.1).

Collectively, these components form sanitised Olympic 'spaces of exception' protected by contemporaneously advanced technologies, target hardening and architectures of 'defensible space', metropolitan militarisation, the use of extensive private security personnel and a commitment to zero-tolerance models of policing (Coaffee et al., 2011). Movement across

Table 11.1 Key features of the standardised Olympic security model

Olympic security feature	Operational characteristics
Intense pre-planning for resilience	To enhance the resilience of the venues and surrounds, and the broader host city by technically scrutinising and planning out weaknesses and vulnerabilities well in advance of Games-time
The development of 'island security'	The temporary physical 'lockdown' of the key venues or 'at risk' areas through barrier methods of physical security, advanced surveillance and airport-style checkpoints to screen spectators
The deployment of advanced surveillance	The real-time monitoring of space often involving the trialling of 'new' technologies
The setting up of peripheral buffer zones surrounding key venues	Attempts to territorially control spaces using policing or private security
	Access restrictions such as restricted public access, vehicle no-go areas and no-fly zones
	Methods to monitor and track spectators
Post-event retention of security infrastructures	Retain security systems for crime reduction legacy purposes

the borders of these 'exceptional' and 'purified' spaces is highly regulated and often dependent on (physical or fiscal) entitlement (Fussey et al., 2012).

The hyper-security of the immediate post-9/11 Olympiads

The hosting of the Winter Olympics in Salt Lake City, just months after 9/11, meant that the need for 'total protection' against all possible threats was required. However, despite their undisputed seismic impact on some areas of policing, the 9/11 attacks initially did not drastically change the landscape of Olympic security strategies.[27] Indeed, according to the security coordinator in Salt Lake City, the strategy's form remained remarkably intact with only minor changes made to aviation support and access control (Bellavita, 2007, p.1). Because such security planning began many years before the Games, and as a result of its prior accreditation as National Special Security Event (NSSE) status, 9/11 mostly impacted the scale, rather than the form of the security operation, culminating in a security cost of $310 million. This sum comprised an unprecedented *quarter* of the overall costs of staging the Games but also exceeded the costs of securing any other Winter Games and, also, the Summer Games in Sydney 2 years previously, despite accommodating less than a third of the spectators.

One new component of security planning focused on bioterrorism, leading to the first ever deployment of the now-instituted Biological Aerosol Sentry and Information System to continually monitor the atmosphere across the city for over a month (Heller, 2003). Additionally, the anthrax attacks in New York and Florida during 2001 were evoked following a false anthrax reading that stimulated emergency response teams at Salt Lake City's international airport 4 days after the opening ceremony. Perhaps reflecting the elevated nature of contemporary anxieties, security agencies also contended with 600 reports of suspicious packages during the Games. Other major technological innovations used in Salt Lake City included the deployment of advanced FBI-supplied communications systems (which failed to work correctly in the mountain terrain) (Decker et al., 2005), and biometric scanners.

To ensure security for the first post-9/11 Summer Olympiad, organisers of the 2004 Athens Games set out the most elaborate, extensive security programme ever attempted, at an overall cost of over $1.5 billion (Hinds and Vlachou, 2007) – over five times the amount spent by Sydney in 2000. While partly attributable to a limited extant security infrastructure prior to the Games, much of this cost can be connected to post-9/11 perceptions of vulnerability alongside intensified emphases on technological security. The Greek authorities deployed over 100,000 specially trained police and military personal to patrol the streets alongside NATO troops specialising in weapons of mass destruction. Military hardware utilised included a network of 13,000 surveillance cameras (forming what Samatas, 2007, referred to as an Olympic superpanopticon), mobile surveillance vans, chemical detectors, a number of Patriot antiaircraft missile installations, AWAC early warning surveillance planes, police helicopters, fighter jets, minesweepers and monitoring airships. The main stadium in Athens was particularly heavily fortified and, according to one journalist, was 'supposed to be one of the most secure places on earth, impenetrable to terrorists plotting a possible attack'.[28]

The Olympics forced the Greek authorities to speed up the modernisation of its state security systems, with Athens, for the duration of the games, becoming a 'panoptic fortress' to give assurances to the rest of the world that the city was safe to host the world greatest sporting spectacle (Samatas, 2004, p.115). Because of its complexity, the technological centrepiece of this strategy was the 'C4I' (Command, Control, Coordination, Communication and Integration) system that sought to amalgamate data from 29 different subsystems, but was widely seen a colossal failure.[29] The retrofitting of such security systems was envisioned as a long-term project, which critics at the time argued would become a menace to privacy and civil liberties. The Greek Government, however, saw it as 'an investment for the future' '[where] the special training, technical know-how and ultra-modern equipment will turn the…Police into one of the best and most professional in the world' (Floridis, 2004, p.4).

The continued standardisation of Olympic security continued for the 2008, Beijing Games, albeit significantly filtered by local and national context. Here, China's newly (and partially) liberalised economy impelled the positive branding of Beijing to its global audience. In turn, the country's considerable security apparatus performed a crucial role in preserving the form of these specific images, as articulated by President Hu Jintao's claim that 'without security guarantees there cannot be a successful Olympic Games, and without security guarantees the national image will be lost'.[30] Olympic security standardisation was perhaps to reach its zenith in London in 2012.

Planning for the worst? London 2012

For London 2012, terrorism concerns and the ability to respond played a critical part in the bidding process and the enacted security operation. The pre-existence of a well-defined and tested security infrastructure (see Chapter 5) meant that London was uniquely placed to offer assurances to the IOC over their security concerns with the city authorities and Metropolitan police having decades of experience in both tackling terrorism and hosting major sporting events (London 2012, 2004). Indeed, terrorism dominated media discussion immediately after the host city was announced. On July 7, 2005, the day after the awarding of the Games, a series of coordinated bomb attacks took place on the London transport network, prompting even more detailed security plans that ultimately saw the security bill quadruple from an initial £225 million to over £1 billion (Fussey and Coaffee, 2015).

As it evolved, the 2012 safety and security programme was laminated onto London's pre-existing security and counter-terrorism infrastructure that comprised a number of distinctive features. *First*, a track record in creating urban enclaves that while, not physically gated, were symbolically and technologically demarcated from their surrounding environments to reduce terrorist risk. The most enduring example of such counter-terrorist exceptionality was the city's security cordons and use of ANPR technology (Chapter 5). As the Metropolitan Police highlighted in 2007, the City of London's 'ring of steel' was an exemplary example of the territorialised security they would be trying to enact for the 2012 Games.[31] *Second*, as part of the spread of this surveillance capability, ANPR was deployed in the Olympic boroughs of Hackney and Tower Hamlets supplementing an already existing capacity to monitor and track local populations built up through a long history of piloting advanced surveillance strategies (Facial Recognition CCTV) in the area through the 1990s (Fussey, 2007; Chapter 10). The *third* major area of pre-existing counter-terrorist expertise that had been developed in London was the embedding of principles of resilience into the design and the strategic management of everyday urban spaces. In 2002, in the wake of 9/11, the Metropolitan authorities established a London Resilience Forum (LRF) that subsequently developed strategic emergency plans for a range of risks, including terrorism. This need for managerial resilience corresponded with a further strand of counter-terrorism work around the physical protection of crowded places (see Chapter 7).

In a global city famed for its counter-terrorism assets, Olympic operations represented an apex of security planning. As noted by the Metropolitan Police:

> The 2012 Olympic and Paralympic Games will require the largest security operation ever conducted in the United Kingdom. The success of the Games will be ultimately dependant on the provision of a safe and secure environment free from a major incident resulting in loss of life. The challenge is demanding; the global security situation continues to be characterised by instability with international terrorism and organised crime being a key component.[32]

The spatial imprint of attempts to develop such regimes of 'total security' combined the tactics and techniques of policing, protective counter-terrorism design and technological surveillance, and can be articulated as a series of familiar operational characteristics (see Table 11.2). The security approach for the 2012 Games was at least an 8-year process that followed a standard Olympic security model, although with local differences evident in terms of London's history of dealing with terrorism as well as the emphasis on legacy.

London's overall multi-pronged security approach centred on the main Olympic Park and stadium. This involved the embedding of design features into key venues at the concept stage, such as access control and integrated CCTV, the designing-in of 'stand-off' areas for hostile vehicle mitigation and the use of more resilient building materials. Venue-specific security was strategically aligned with that in the Olympic Park – a process that began

Table 11.2 The spatial imprint of London 2012 security[33]

Security feature	Spatial imprint for London 2012
Intense pre-planning for resilience	The development of detailed pre-emptive security plans by an Olympic Security Directorate in liaison with pre-existing resilience plans, to plan out vulnerabilities in advance
The development of 'island security'	The sealing and securing of the key Olympic sites Pre-games access restrictions and movement control of public and contractors Checkpoint security at Games-time
The deployment of advanced surveillance	Biometric checks, deployment of sensor technologies to scan for explosives, dangerous chemicals and fissile material
The setting up of peripheral buffer zones surrounding key venues	Large-scale access restrictions and control zones Use of legal measures to restrict public activities The use of existing ANPR infrastructures Ticket tracking Deployment of police and other security personnel drawn from across the U.K.
Post-event retention of security infrastructure	The designing-in of permanent security such as CCTV and Secured by Design measures to counter-crime to improve local perceptions of safety and advanced population rebalancing (gentrification)

with territorial enclosure. In July 2007, and with little advanced warning, the Olympic Park was 'sealed' and nearby public footpaths and waterways closed for public access. An 11-mile blue wooden perimeter fence was established for 'health and safety' reasons and likened to the Belfast peace lines[34] (Figure 11.3). This fence was replaced by a £40-million electrified security fence in late 2009s (Figure 11.4) and evolved into the Command Perimeter Security System with advanced CCTV surveillance at its heart (ODA, 2009). Access to the Olympic Park site was limited and closely monitored with biometric checks routinely carried out on construction workers echoing techniques used to secure what are perhaps the most intensely monitored and securitised public spaces: airports.

Approaching Games time, a militarised security force visibly policed and technologically monitored the security cordon encircled the site, whilst inside the cordon, landscaped security and crime reduction features, infrastructure strengthening (e.g. bridges and other structures) and electronic devices that scan for explosives were deployed to 'push' threats away from the main Olympic site.[35] Such counter-terrorism features were simultaneously invested with crime prevention capabilities for the post-games period when the park was to be opened to the public. These security design features were designed to be unobtrusive, providing a safety legacy and deterring activities such as joyriding, ram-raiding, drug dealing, prostitution and general anti social

Figure 11.3 Cordon blue around the Olympic Park, 2007.

behaviour. This was in line with the wider post-Games objective as outlined in the initial *London 2012 Olympic and Paralympic Safety and Security Strategy*, which aimed to host an inspirational, 'safe and inclusive' Games 'and leave a sustainable legacy for London' (Home Office, 2009). The fear of a spatially displaced terrorist attack meant security measures also bleed through the borders of the Olympic Park and saw new forms of technological security permeate across London. Throughout the duration of the Games, the authorities utilised advanced surveillance to track suspects across the city, including London's ever-expanding system of ANPR cameras.[36] Such technological approaches were complemented by highly visibility policing.

In addition to technological and policing solutions, pre-emptive response planning was played out to allow logistics, such as the placement of cordons and evacuation routes, to be pre-planned. Demonstrating the domestic influence on mega-event security planning, an updated *Olympic and Paralympic Safety and Security Strategy* (Home Office, 2011) was developed in March 2011, which was in line with the latest revised the U.K. National Security Strategy (October 2010) and further harmonised with the third iteration of the U.K.'s counter-terrorism strategy, CONTEST (HM Government, 2011). The CONTEST strategy specifically focused on the 2012 Games, noting that the country U.K. had guaranteed to the IOC to 'take all financial, planning

Figure 11.4 Electrified security fences, 2009.

and operational measures necessary to guarantee the safety and the peaceful celebration of the Games' (p.105).

As the preparations for the Games were finalised, a range of diverse agencies became drawn into play. Here, security planning became managed by the U.K. Security Services, the Olympic Security Directorate and multistakeholder LRF who developed detailed pre-emptive security plans to sit alongside pre-existing resilience strategies to plan out vulnerabilities in advance. Here, a premium was placed on enhanced coordination between the various security actors; something that had proved a critical point of failure at other Olympic Games (Fussey et al., 2011). Organisational infrastructure and processes were thus developed to foster coordination and communication and to facilitate appropriate testing.[37]

Five formal testing events took place with the aim of incrementally increasing the stress on the various security systems. Olympic search and screening processes were tested at English Premier League football matches during January 2012, the military undertook additional exercises in London in late 2011 and May 2012, and numerous affiliated events aimed at binding hitherto unconnected organisations also took place to identify the range of risks and threats to the Games. Most notably, in May 2012, 3 months before the Games, *Operation Olympic Guardian* began – a pre-emptive scenario planning exercise intended to test security preparedness ahead of the Games. Militarised features included in this role-play included the testing of air missile defence systems, the responsiveness of Typhoon jet forces and the establishment of 'no-fly' zones over London. As one BBC correspondent noted, such an exercise has the potential both to alarm and reassure in equal measure:

> Exercise Olympic Guardian is an opportunity to fine-tune military plans. But it is also aimed at reassuring the public... The sound of fighter jets and military helicopters, along with the sight of the Royal Navy's largest warship, HMS Ocean, in the Thames may reassure many. But for some, just talk of this military hardware is causing alarm – most notably the plans to station ground-based air defence systems at six sites around the capital.[38]

This again connected with an enduring set of processes by which military – threat – response technologies and procedures are often repurposed for use in the civic realm. The deployment of these militarised techniques into the East London landscape were communicated via a number of mechanisms causing much alarm – notably when leaflets informed residents of Bow Quarter that surface-to-air missiles would be stationed above their housing complex.[39]

As the Games drew near and interest in all aspects of 2012 preparation intensified, security-related stories flooded the national and international media coverage. Particularly notable was the emphasis on the use of military hardware to control city spaces, airspace or transport corridors: 'Ministry of Defence to control London airspace during Games for first time since Second World War'[40]; 'Sonic device deployed in London during Olympics'[41]; and 'Armoured cars drafted in as security tightens ahead of the Olympic Games'.[42] Other reports highlighted a set of issues regarding policing of the Games, often described as an unprecedented U.K. peacetime operation, with up to 12,000 officers from 52 forces deployed at 'peak time', alongside private security staff, and the utilisation of novel security technologies: 'Metropolitan police plastic bullets stockpile up to 10,000 after UK riots – Scotland Yard confirms August unrest has led to increase in stock of baton rounds as security measures upped before Olympics'[43]; 'Metropolitan Police double officers around torch as crowds bigger than predicted'[44]; and 'Metropolitan Police given 350 mobile fingerprint scanners in Olympics policing boost'.[45]

In reality, the 2012 Olympics passed off without any terrorist incidents being reported and with minimum disruption. The visual appearance of militarised security was, in large part, restricted to the entrance of the venues where search procedures were carried out by the British Army.[46] After the Games, missiles were dismantled and troops redeployed, yet less well documented in the coverage of security planning was the post-Games *legacy* that has been materially inscribed on the East London landscape and improved organisational ways of working between the multiple agencies involved in security planning. During the post-Games period, there was little sign that much of the hi-tech equipment purchased and deployed by police forces had been put away. One such example has been the retention of large numbers of mobile ANPR camera units in Newham, one of the five Olympic host boroughs (Pickles, 2014). The security infrastructure embedded within transformative urban regeneration programmes was further promoted as central to long-term community safety. More broadly, it was also hoped that Olympic-related security would assist in developing safer neighbourhoods, through measures such as improved lighting, and lead to a reduction in crime and the fear of crime. For example, both the Olympic Village and the Olympic Park were granted was full 'Secured by Design' status presenting a permanent material security legacy to its residents and users.

The story of securing the London Games did not start on 7/7, nor did it end once the well-protected Olympic flame was extinguished at the closing ceremony. The security legacy in London is the most comprehensive plan seen for urban regeneration *and* security in modern Olympic history (Coaffee, 2013a). Whilst at previous Olympics these security features have largely been temporary and removed in the post-games period, in London *permanent* design and architectural features were embedded within the material landscape. Likewise, experiences of experimenting with surveillance technologies and the development of significant repositories of knowledge and expertise were retained in London-based networks regarding civil contingency planning for coping with an array of disruptive challenges and securitising urban areas at home and abroad. In its development of secure regeneration spaces and security governance, London's security community arguably created a 'blueprint' for knowledge transfer across the globe for when mega-events come to town. Explicit examples of the use of knowledge from London being applied to physical protective security was explicit in plans for the 2014 Commonwealth Games in Glasgow and the 2016 Olympics in Rio de Janeiro (Coaffee, 2014).[47]

A Russian 'ring of steel'

Core elements of the London experience were also replicated, with local differences, at the 2014 Winter Olympics in Sochi, Russia. In Sochi, the risk was framed differently from London, where the main concern was the ethnonational conflict in the Northern Caucasus and threats by Islamic separatists to attack the Games. This fear was heightened in 2011 following the suicide bombing at Moscow's Domodedovo airport. As the Russian Deputy Prime Minister noted at this time 'we expect terrorist activity to increase the closer we get to the Sochi Olympics. That's because the terrorists want to attract as much international attention as they possibly can'.[48] Such attacks starkly illustrated the risks faced in any Olympic city or nation in protecting crowded public spaces from attack, as well as illuminating the inevitable security response to protect the reputation of the host nation and to fulfil IOC security stipulations. The Sochi Candidate File (2009) also made great play of national security competences, particularly emphasising recent investments by the Russian state in the latest counter-terrorism equipment and the training of security personnel (Russian Olympic Committee, 2009, p.25).

As the Games approached, visible security – at perhaps even greater levels than seen in London – was rolled out to make the 2014 Winter Games in Sochi 'the safest Olympics in history'.[49] Such security also had a significant impact on accessibility to the city, and of protestors to lawfully demonstrate. The security deployed included familiar military features, such as air missile defence systems; restricted airspace; tighter national border controls; the nearby stationing of warships and high-speed patrol boats; checkpoints in perimeter fencing with an array of scanning devices for explosives and CBRN material; controlled zones for searching people and their belongings; a plethora of CCTV systems with an estimated 5500 cameras deployed as part of the 'safe Sochi' initiative; a bespoke Olympic CCTV control centre; passenger profiling at Sochi international airport; drones hovering overhead; robotic vehicles for bomb detection; and surface to air missile installations. Alongside this, standardised security operation sat unprecedented monitoring efforts to track telephone and online communications and equipment specifically designed to monitor emotional responses.[50]

Controversially, protests, demonstrations and rallies that were not part of official Olympic activities were also banned in city spaces through the setting up of a so-called forbidden zone (or controlled zones), established by a presidential decree, which argued they were essential to 'guarantee security'. The decree severely restricted access in Sochi and effectively banned all vehicles from the city, with the exception of locally owned or specially accredited vehicles. Human rights activists declared such measures 'unconstitutional', arguing that they amount to 'a state of emergency'[51] where intensive screening and monitoring of people and vehicles will create a safe but 'sterile environment'. In the weeks leading up to the Games the ban on protest rallies was lifted, with protest permitted in specially arranged areas under tight security.[52]

As Games time drew near, the ratcheting up of 'total security' in and around Sochi was further enhanced as a result of two suicide bomb attacks on the southern Russian city of Volgograd in December 2013,[53] a little over a month before the Sochi Winter Games were to begin. Although Volgograd is located 700 kilometre from Sochi, the attacks were widely linked to political instability and anti-Russian sentiment in the Northern Caucuses and prior threats made by Islamic militants to attack the Winter Games with 'maximum force'. These events provided a visible demonstration that crowded public areas in Sochi, and Russia more generally, were at risk of attack with particular concerns over 'black widow' suicide incidents.[54] It was further noted that the police force in Volgograd had recently been reduced, with over 600 officers being redeployed to Sochi, leading to concern that terrorists might decide to attack 'easier' and less defended targets outside of the Olympic city.

The Volgograd bombings also illuminated an unprecedented security operation in Sochi involving the deployment of 42,000 police officers, 10,000 Interior Ministry Troops and 23,000 Ministry of Emergency Situation personnel in and around the city, with thousands more deployed at supposedly vulnerable locations nationwide. The hermetic security cordon that was to surround the city led the IOC, in the wake of the Volgograd attacks, to argue that the Games will be 'safe', noting that 'unfortunately, terrorism is a global phenomenon and no region is exempt, which is why security at the Games is a top priority for the IOC'.[55] These attacks also led to the U.S. Government offering the Russian state full support in its final security preparations. In developing their security strategy, the U.K.'s experiences of securing London 2012 were also explicitly being utilised to boost the security effort and ensure a positive and lasting reputational impact. As Ostapenko (2010, p.60) noted that the Games represent a 'huge international 'comeback opportunity' to present a stronger, better, more glamorous as well as to re-position the country's image globally'.

One month before Games time, a special administration zone was further established for Sochi to enable 'lockdown security' to be fully operationalised.[56] As the BBC noted of military operations, 'Russia [are] pouring in over 37,000 extra troops and police and imposing a 'ring of steel' around the Olympic venue, largely closing it off from public access'.[57] The security zone that encircled Sochi stretched 40-kilometre inland and 100-kilometre along the Black Sea coast. Within the secure zone, over 6000 infrastructure facilities and crowded places received 'special attention', such as bridges, tunnels, hospitals and hotels, as well as the sporting venues. All venues used hi-tech and space-based surveillance equipment, and all security personal, were placed on 'combat alert'. One media report – 'Russia imposes security clampdown in Sochi before Olympics' – painted a picture of exceptional security where long-planned restrictions had come into force, limiting the movements into and out of the city, and the activities of those inside the accredited 'secure zones'.[58] Here armed checkpoints were set up to stop and search all vehicles entering Sochi. In line with Agamben's state of exception thesis, one local resident noted, 'the resort is turning into a sort of concentration camp. Naturally this will deliver a serious blow to tourism and the huge number of people at the Olympics'.[59]

Conclusions: Event security and proportionality

There is now a broadly accepted security blueprint for major events, which has evolved since the 1980s, and that has developed a series of standardised, mobile and transferable features that were intensified by the events of 9/11. Such features include governance and organisational elements that seek to forge relationships between the numerous public safety agencies and the local organising committee, the planned use of police and security personnel and the deployment of counter-terrorism techniques of surveillance and urban design to create island security and lockdown conditions in the host city. The impact of such 'exceptional' security operations often serves to reinforce urban splintering where the spaces utilised for sporting festivals have the potential to become dislocated from the wider geographical contexts of the host city. More broadly, at the urban scale, 'total' security apparatuses and the ability to respond effectively to disruption have become key selling points for would-be hosts wishing to promise safety and security in the hope of boosting immediate and future economic gains. As Boyle and Haggerty (2012, p.241, emphasis added) highlighted, authorities seek to 'sustain the appearance of maximum security in order to maintain rhetorical control over what are deemed to be highly uncertain and insecure situations' and that 'such performances may paradoxically amplify uncertainty, thus recreating the conditions *that foster the ongoing securitization of everyday life*'.

Importantly, the instigation of such 'lockdown security' and punitive controls on the local population further calls into question the uneasy relationship with cities hosting events for the consumption of privileged audiences and transnational elites. This is especially the case where they are tightly secured, with the security operation largely paid for by the public who are more often than not excluded from the 'show', or have individual freedoms and rights restricted (Coaffee and Murakami Wood, 2006). Here, the push for enhanced security becomes a complicated and evermore expensive task. Ideally, it requires politicians and a range of other stakeholders to balance a number of considerations and adopt a proportionate response to minimise disruption to daily activities. As demonstrated in the numerous examples in this chapter, such proportionality is seldom found, with security lockdowns the preferred modus operandi as 'spaces of exception' become the default option as city and national reputations are at stake.

Importantly, though, the temporary retrofitting of such pop-up security 'stage sets' to promote a particular destination as a safe and secure location, often leaving permanent legacy of fixed security infrastructure. Such security legacy is increasingly common, with a similar link between permanent securitisation and the football World Cup in Japan and Korea in 2002 evident through the intensification of CCTV systems as a result of terrorist concerns (Abe, 2004).[60] The same was also true in South Africa, where to be seen as secure enough to host the Olympics (that eventually were awarded to Athens in 2004), extensive security infrastructure was introduced into areas posited as likely venues and visitor accommodation centres, but were ultimately retained when the bid failed (Minnaar, 2006).[61]

Such transmissions – from temporary to permanent, from tactics to strategy, and from technology to technique – invite Foucauldian and post-Foucauldian interpretations. Notably, Agamben's (2005) pioneering work on exceptionality can be utilised to understand these processes where, once established, such temporary states undergo a 'transformation of a provisional and exceptional measure into a technique of government' (2005, p.2). In turn, these techniques realise 'the production of new norms' (ibid., p.28) that become installed in a more permanent 'normalised' sense, and become instituted into the management of both specific spaces and the broader geographies of exception (Fussey, 2015). Viewed through the lens of urban

Pop-up security and exception security 239

security and counter-terrorism, these repeated features of event security strategies coalesce into an overall model that is oriented around a number of core themes related to enhanced urban militarism, private security, integrated surveillance, rebordering the city through design intervention, and the control of behaviour (Coaffee and Fussey, 2012). Whilst variations on these exist, event-based counter-terrorism strategies bear remarkable similarities across time and space. By contrast, terrorist threats at such events are almost always grounded in relation to their local setting. Terrorist threats to events, then, are almost always locally produced, yet the strategies designed to counter them are increasingly imported from global patterns of security governance, creating a profound tension between what is being secured and for whose benefit?

Notes

1 However, high-profile events have remained relatively untouched by international terrorism, although elevated 'security' fears are often a key priority of organising authorities. Exceptions include the pipe bomb attacks at the 1996 Atlanta Olympics and the Boston Marathon bombing in 2013.
2 For example, since the 1980s, terrorist threats to Olympic Games have come from a range of local or national sources – ethno-separatists, state-sponsored proxies, left-wing groups, right-wing extremists, environmentalists, violent jihadi extremists and anarchists, with the vast majority of these occurring either before or after the event. The exception to this was a domestic attack during the 1996s Atlanta Games at the Centennial Olympic Park when a pipe bomb was detonated, killing two people and injuring over 100. This attack was motivated by anti-government protest and in particular abortion laws. This event, coming 15 months after the Oklahoma City bombing, was heavily policed with additional security provided by military personnel (Fussey et al., 2011).
3 The states of exception that emerge were seen to represent an 'ambiguous zone … [a] no-man's land between public law and political fact' (Agamben, 2005, p.1–2).
4 This was most graphically represented by the prisoner or concentration camp in Agamben's original work.
5 The threat of terrorism was central to the deployment of this trial technology, especially given relatively recent attacks in Saudi Arabia in 1996, against U.S. embassies in Kenya and Tanzania in 1998, and on the USS *Cole* in Yemen in 2000.
6 See 'That Time the Super Bowl Secretly Used Facial Recognition Software on Fans'. *Vice*, February 7, 2016, at www.vice.com/en_us/article/kb78de/that-time-the-super-bowl-secretly-used-facial-recognition-software-on-fans.
7 NSSE procedures were established in May 1998 to set out the security roles for federal agencies at major events. These are often commonly referred to as Special Event Activity Rating (SEAR) events which are federal level rating assessments by the DHS on a 1–5 scale (level one being the highest priority with regard to required security). Category 1 was previously reserved almost exclusively for political events such as Presidential inaugurations, Party National Conventions and United Nations Assemblies.
8 Super Bowl Security Stepped Up, *ABC News*, January 7, 2002, at https://abcnews.go.com/WNT/story?id=130515&page=1.

240 *The future of urban security*

9 Cited in 'Big Easy Gets Tough Security for Super Bowl', *CNN News*, February 2, 2002, at http://edition.cnn.com/2002/US/02/02/sb.superbowl.security/index.html.
10 Supersizing Bowl Security for Super Bowl XL. *The Detroit News,* November 17, 2005, p.4.
11 See 'How and Why Detroit Will Become a Fortress for Super Bowl XL', *The Guardian,* February 3, 2006, p.30.
12 In gaining such certification the NFL joined the likes of Boeing and IBM as designated suppliers of anti-terrorism technologies.
13 Super Bowl 2020: How 5G Will Help Keep Fans Safe at the Game. *TechRepublic*, January 31, 2020, at www.techrepublic.com/article/super-bowl-54-how-5g-will-help-keep-fans-safe-at-the-game/.
14 The Labour Party holds two major conferences each year in the spring and summer. The summer conference is the highest profile and is always attended by all senior politicians.
15 A series of bombs in March 2004 on the Madrid transport network killed 191 people and injured hundreds more.
16 Terrorist Alert as Blair and Cabinet Arrive, *Manchester Evening News,* March 12, 2004, p.4.
17 Security Bridge Built for Labour Conference, *The Argus*, September 6, 2005, at www.theargus.co.uk/news/6804424.security-bridge-built-for-labour-conference/.
18 This area was called the Greater Manchester Exhibition Centre (G-MEX). This was renamed The Manchester International Convention Complex (MICC) in January 2007.
19 The operational diagrams for this widespread policing operation resembled the diagrams used for Cold War nuclear attacks planning with a series of concentric circles representing a reduction of security spreading out from the heavily militarised core.
20 This security arrangement was nicknamed 'Tony town' by security experts in reference to the U.K. Prime Minister, Tony Blair.
21 For example, the day before the conference over 30,000 demonstrators from across the United Kingdom descended upon Manchester to protest against a raft of government policies ranging from the War on Terror, hospital closures, the future of nuclear energy production and student tuition fees.
22 During this relatively peaceful protest, 1000 police on foot and horseback surrounded the marchers to ensure no serious breaches of public order.
23 This was a slow process and it often took many hours for delegates to gain entry to the secure island site.
24 It was further estimated that there might be the potential of a regional gain of £100 million per year if high-profile conferencing becomes a regular part of the urban scene. See *Manchester Evening News*, September 29, 2006, p.1.
25 The up-scaled version of the security operations in Manchester were notably advanced for global political meetings such as the annual G20 meetings where venues were hermetically sealed by a literal 'rings of steel' and mass policing to secure the venue from terrorist attack, as well as to keep protestors at bay.
26 Drawing inspiration from Solzhenitsyn's *Gulag Archipelago*.
27 The generation of post-9/11 uncertainties, however, represented an escalation of an existing approach to identifying externalised Olympic threats. For example, in the 6 years prior to the Salt Lake City Olympics, security planning led to an extensive compilation of threats to the Games.

28 'How I Strolled into the Heart of the Games', *The Times*, May 14, 2004, p.30.
29 This system, from the U.S. company Science Applications International, faced insurmountable problems included its inability to host large numbers of potential users, failure to operate to capacity and the providers' failure to establish the system in time for the 2008 Beijing Games (Fussey et al., 2011).
30 Cited in 'China Makes Olympic Security Top Priority', *Reuters*, April 1, 2008, at https://uk.reuters.com/article/uk-olympics/china-makes-olympic-security-top-priority-idUKSP532420080401.
31 Metropolitan Police Service Olympic Programme Update July 20, 2007.
32 As note 30.
33 Adapted from Coaffee et al. (2011).
34 Cordon Blue. *The Guardian*, September 21, 2007, at www.guardian.co.uk/society/2007/sep/21/communities.
35 Likewise, concealment points – areas where explosives might be hidden – were also scrutinised and where possible removed (e.g. bird boxes or litter bins) or sealed (e.g. drains).
36 Other high-tech measures suggested but ultimately not operationalised included a ticket system, which would allow spectators to be tracked from their home as well as advanced screening access points – the so-called tunnel of truth that would be allegedly able to check large numbers of people simultaneously for explosives, weapons and biohazards – and which could utilise face recognition CCTV that can be compared against an image store of known or suspected terrorists (Coaffee, 2009).
37 Whilst, much of the command and control was exercised locally these arrangements were further organised under the National Olympic Security Coordination (NOSC) strategy, which served as a single point of coordination and a means of embedding the National Olympic Safety Security Plan (NOSSP) into local activities.
38 London 2012: Major Olympic Security Test Unveiled, *BBC News*, April 30, 2012, at www.bbc.co.uk/news/uk-17891223. Accessed March 6, 2014.
39 Activist activity intensified and became distinctly focused upon the intensive militarised security measures being ushered into East London. One of the highest profile campaigns was the Stop the Olympic Missiles campaign that led to an unsuccessful yet high-profile high court challenge by residents of Fred Wigg Tower in Leytonstone contesting the Army's right to deploy missiles at their place of residence (see Boykoff and Fussey, 2014).
40 Ministry of Defence to Control London Airspace during Games for First Time Since Second World War, *Daily Telegraph,* May 29, 2012, at www.telegraph.co.uk/sport/olympics/news/9281468/London-2012-Olympics-Ministry-of-Defence-to-control-London-airspace-during-Games-for-first-time-since-Second-World-War.html.
41 Sonic Device Deployed in London during Olympics, *BBC News London*, May 12, 2012, at www.bbc.co.uk/news/uk-england-london-18042528.
42 Armoured Cars Drafted in as Security Tightens Ahead of the Olympic Games, *Daily Mirror,* May 8, 2012, at www.mirror.co.uk/sport/other-sports/london-2012-armoured-cars-drafted-824089.
43 London 2012 Olympics: Metropolitan Police Double Officers Around Torch As Crowds Bigger than Predicted, *Daily Telegraph,* May 29, 2012, at www.telegraph.co.uk/sport/olympics/torch-relay/9280127/London-2012-Olympics-Metropolitan-Police-double-officers-around-torch-as-crowds-bigger-than-predicted.html.

44 Metropolitan Police Plastic Bullets Stockpile up to 10,000 after UK Riots, *The Guardian*, May 3, 2012, at www.theguardian.com/uk/2012/may/03/metropolitan-police-plastic-bullets-stockpile-riots.

45 Metropolitan Police Given 350 Mobile Fingerprint Scanners in Olympics Policing Boost, *V3 News,* May 23, 2012, at www.v3.co.uk/v3-uk/news/2179184/metropolitan-police-350-mobile-fingerprint-scanners-olympics-policing-boost. Yet such urban incursions were not universally welcomed. As the Games approached, the uneven impact both on Londoners and visitors to the capital became highlighted: as a man taking photos of a fish tank was stopped by a security guard for hostile reconnaissance amid pre-Olympics terrorism fears; a Dispersal zone was to be set up at Olympic Park target antisocial behaviour, sex workers and protests; and 'Brand' exclusion zones were to be established so that the Olympic canvas could belong exclusively to key sponsors.

46 This was after private contractor G4S has failed to recruit sufficient personnel to staff the entrances.

47 More recently, many advanced surveillance technologies that made use of facial recognition (and increasingly the internet of things and artificial intelligence and 5G networks) were deployed at the rescheduled Tokyo 2020 Summer Games (held in 2021) for risk assessment and venue security alongside the now obligatory 'fortress' protective security and over 18000 security guards.

48 Cited in (2011). Sochi 2014: Russia's Olympic Security Concerns. *BBC News*, February 22, 2011, at www.bbc.co.uk/news/world-europe-12507067.

49 See, for example, Sochi Chief Vows to Make Games 'Safest in History', *Boston Herald,* April 17, 2013, at http://bostonherald.com/sports/other/olympics/2013/04/sochi_chief_vows_to_make_games_safest_in_history.

50 Heightened Security, Visible and Invisible, Blankets the Olympics, *New York Times,* February 13, 2014, at www.nytimes.com/2014/02/14/sports/olympics/heightened-security-visible-and-invisible-blankets-the-olympics.html?_r=0.

51 Russia Bans Public Protests at 2014 Sochi Winter Olympics, *BBC News*, August 23, 2013, at www.bbc.co.uk/news/world-europe-23819104.

52 However, limits were placed on the number of people allowed to take part in demonstrations, and the 'protest zone' was geographically situated in Khosta about 12 kilometre from the nearest Olympic arenas. International condemnation regarding the lack of demonstrations allowed from groups, such as those campaigning for gay rights and political reform, had clearly been influential in facilitating this change. The easing of restrictions on demonstrations can be viewed as a move to enhance Russia's image in advance of the Games, alongside an amnesty that saw the release from prison of two members of the female punk group Pussy Riot, Greenpeace activists held over a protest against Arctic oil drilling and former oil tycoon and oligarch, Mikhail Khodorkovsky.

53 On December 29, 2013, a person-borne improvised explosive device (suicide bomb) was detonated at the entrance of the main rail station in the southern Russian city of Volgograd (formerly Stalingrad) killing 17 people. The following day a similar device destroyed a trolleybus in the city killing a further 14 people.

54 In reference to the attacks by widows of dead insurgents from the North Caucuses.

55 Cited in Second Deadly Bombing HighLights Risks Ahead of Sochi Games, *The Globe and Mail,* December 30, 2013, at www.theglobeandmail.com/news/world/second-terrorist-act-in-russia-kills-14-on-trolleybus/article16124593/.

56 Russia Begins Lockdown Security, *Al Jazeera,* January 14, 2014, at www.aljazeera.com/news/europe/2014/01/russia-begins-olympic-security-lockdown-20141801345439202.html.
57 Cited in 'Sochi: UK Officials Warn Terror Attacks 'Very Likely'', *BBC News,* January 27, 2014, at www.bbc.co.uk/news/uk-25907140.
58 Russia Imposes Security Clampdown in Sochi before Olympics, *Reuters,* January 7, 2014, at www.reuters.com/article/2014/01/08/us-olympics-russia-security-idUSBREA0606V20140108.
59 As note 56.
60 In the run-up to the World Cup the Japanese government announced 190 CCTV cameras in 10 cities around Japan which were thought to be potentially vulnerable to foreign football hooligans. However, after the event, the cameras were not removed: in contrast some cities, especially Tokyo, extended the systems with the justifications now changed to concerns about terrorism, crime, drugs and people trafficking, all of which were easily linked to the same generically portrayed 'foreign threat' as hooliganism (Murakami Wood et al., 2007).
61 In this case the extensive CCTV was rejustified as part of a general programme to combat crime, to attract tourists, business investors and delegates to international conferences (Coaffee and Murakami Wood, 2007).

12 Conclusions
Normalising urban security

Introduction

Over time, the dynamic nature of the terrorist threat has meant that urban counter-terrorism has remained in flux. Here, cities can be seen as the meeting point of international politics, principles expressed in documents, standards, guidance and regulations and everyday encounters between citizens and material life. Within this context, the upsurge in twenty-first century urban counter-terrorism that has been propelled and sustained by the language and practices of War on Terror is no longer just a police and security services issue. Many professional and practice communities, and the general public, have been, and continue to be, enrolled in terrorism prevention, raising a series moral and ethical issues, as well as a broader, perennial question, of what is 'normal' urban security?

To better understand this central question, the foregoing chapters have drawn on, amongst others, Foucauldian ideas of security normalisation and Agambian notions of exceptionality that become a commonplace form of governmentality amidst rising insecurity. As previously showcased across many Western cities, this has necessitated a move from a predominance of *temporary* and conspicuous security measures, towards counter-terrorism being seen as ever-present and mainstream technology of Government that has been effectively normalised in circumstances where the terror threat levels are 'high', and where states of emergency exist as an almost *permanent* condition. As Michael Sorkin noted (2017, p.76) about the ubiquity of urban security 'if every space is susceptible to attack and every person a potential attacker, then the only recourse is to watch everyone and fortify everyplace. If every communication is potentially a fragment of a conspiracy, then all must be recorded'.

Weaponising everyday life

One situation deemed as requiring exceptional and emergency measures surfaced during the 2010s as the common tactics of terrorists begun to evolve in a new wave of lethal attacks where mundane objects were used by untrained

DOI: 10.4324/9780429461620-16

and often lone-wolf attackers, to weaponise everyday life and target crowded urban spaces. In general terms, such approaches were not a new trend.[1] For example, in the immediate wake of 9/11, much government attention was focused upon the ease by which the hijackers had used household objects (craft knifes) as their weapon of choice, and subsequently, 'the variety of ways in which innovative terrorists might work their destructive alchemy with the raw material of daily life' (Andrejevic, 2007, 167). But, as Sahhar (2017) has more recently noted, the use of banal objects for purposes of terror has intensified over time, with 'western audiences witnessing a transformation of the objects of everyday life into tools of unpredictable violence'. Such low-tech and relatively unsophisticated attack methods, combined with phone-based digital media communication methods, represented a shift away from the comparatively complex plots that characterised many initial post-9/11 terror incidents.

Chief amongst such novel attack methods was the weaponisation of the automobile – not through car-bombing that typified many assaults in the pre-9/11 era – but the advent of so-called vehicle-as-weapon (VAW) attacks where a truck or car is deliberately driven at speed, often along city boulevards and into crowded places. Such attacks surged from 2010, spreading quickly across geographical and ideological divides 'by transforming a bland, everyday object into a lethal, semi-strategic weapon' and 'empower[ing] marginal actors by providing them with the means to strike at the heart of urban centres and sow fear in the wider society' (Miller and Hayward, 2018, p.4). Such attacks were almost impossible to anticipate and prevent without radically altering the character of everyday urban life and have led to an intensification of protective security and digital surveillance as counter-measures (Coaffee, 2019; Chambers and Andrews, 2019). As Sandvik (2019) reflected, 'vehicles have become securitized and reconceived as existential threats through their use in urban terror attacks. Their presence is perceived with suspicion and fear, as urban landscapes are remodelled through bollards and security fencing'.

The initial uptick in VAW (or vehicle-ramming) incidents was linked by many to online terrorist propaganda campaigns that begun in 2010, encouraging such attacks.[2] In proceeding years, VAW attacks became an effective low-tech tactic of 'terrifying simplicity' (Friedman, 2017) for individual attackers or small groups of terrorists, with the FBI (2010) noting that 'vehicle-ramming offers terrorists with limited access to explosives or weapons an opportunity to conduct a homeland attack with minimal prior training or experience'. By the end of 2016, such attacks accounted for almost half the deaths from terrorism in Western countries.[3]

Although vehicle ramming was not a new terrorist attack trajectory per se,[4] using vehicles to target pedestrians, often followed by a secondary gun or knife attack, became increasingly common. Initially, an upsurge in this type of attack occurred in Israel – in Tel Aviv in May[5] and August[6] 2011 – with security experts arguing that its tactical popularity increased due to the success of the security/separation barrier that restricted the number of explosive devices that could be smuggled into the country, meaning that only vehicles and knifes were readily available to use as 'weapons' (Keating, 2014). Arguably, this style of do-it-yourself attack that lacked detailed planning was easily replicated. In the West, the first present-day VAW assault occurred in Quebec City, Canada, in October 2014, when a vehicle was driven directly at two Canadian soldiers near a shopping centre, killing one, in what was considered an ISIS inspired attack.[7]

Soon after this incursion, France became the new epicentre of VAW strikes. On December 21, 2014, a Muslim man in the city of Dijon drove a van into pedestrians in five areas of the city in the space of half an hour, injuring 13 people. A day later, 10 pedestrians suffered non-fatal injuries when a van was driven at a crowded Christmas Market in Nantes. These attacks were seen as the first ISIS-linked attacks in the country and, according to some reports, were inspired by a recent French-language ISIS video calling on French Muslims to attack non-Muslims using vehicles and to 'kill them and spit in their faces and run over them with your cars'.[8]

However, most notable, was an attack 18 months later in Nice, where on the evening of July 14, 2016, a 19-tonne truck was deliberately driven into a crowd celebrating Bastille Day on the Promenade des Anglais. Eighty-six people were killed and over 450 injured, including the lone driver, a Tunisian living in France, who had recently been radicalised online. As ISIS claimed responsibility for the attack, the French President declared an extension to the State of Emergency that had been put in place following the attacks in Paris in November 2015 (see Chapter 9) that saw thousands of extra police and soldiers deployed on the streets of French cities. In the wake of this VAW assault, ISIS doubled-down on the promotion of this modus operandi in the 'Just Terror Tactics' section of its November 2016 *Rumiyah* magazine, featuring images of the Nice attack, and noted that:

> Though being an essential part of modern life, very few actually comprehend the deadly and destructive capability of the motor vehicle and its capacity of reaping large numbers of casualties if used in a premeditated manner.[9]

Subsequent VAW attacks in Berlin (December 2016),[10] Melbourne (January 2017),[11] Stockholm (April 2017),[12] London (March and June 2017),[13] Paris (June 2017),[14] Barcelona (August 2017),[15] New York (October 2017)[16] and elsewhere, led to a re-evaluation of protective security and counter-terrorism measures at crowded locations in many Western cities.

Such incidents further illuminated a set of questions and processes, noted at the start of this book. First, how different acts of urban terrorism illicit distinctive, yet often standardised, counter-responses; second, how a wider array of non-governmental stakeholders are drawn into security governance; and third, how exceptional notions of security become reproduced and normalised in the urban environment, highlighting the increased importance of embodied experience and social and spatial justice considerations within the enactment of urban security.

Within this context, the remainder of this chapter pulls together the key arguments presented in foregoing chapters, and critically analyses how emerging strategies of counter-terrorism are amalgamated to best seek proportionality of security approaches across different urban settings whilst ensuring that social, ethical and legal concerns are properly considered. Proportionality is crucial here given the growing centrality of cities to the rewiring of international affairs, meaning that security measures deployed should be appropriate to the risk faced to minimise disruption to everyday activities and, to the ability of individuals and businesses to carry out their normal social, economic and democratic activities. Proportionality also needs to be balanced with necessity, where considerations of under-reacting or over-reacting, and the uncertain and unknown nature of the threats, need to be accounted for in political calculations. However, this is an inherently difficult balancing act, and, as highlighted in preceding chapters, the perpetual threat from terrorism all too often leads to exceptional security becoming the default option when municipal and national reputations are at stake. Here, the danger terrorism poses for democracy and everyday social and economic life goes beyond political or ideologically inspired violence and penetrates into how society thinks about threats, responds to them and prepares for future attack.

Drawing on the most contemporary examples of counter-terrorism interventions, the following sections showcase this difficult evaluation between individual freedom and collective security through the three lenses of the fortified, the watched and the prepared city, before concluding with a discussion of how the normalisation of urban security becomes manifested and mainstreamed as a result of physical interventions and advanced digital surveillance, to become an accepted and legitimised as part of everyday urban management and regimes of resilience.

The fortified city beyond bollards

Security bollards and barriers have long been a key counter-terrorism measure intended to target harden, restrict access to 'at risk' sites and to provide increased set back to mitigate the impact of blast. In response, to the upsurge in VAW attacks after 2015, cities once again looked to bollards and barriers for protection. As in the wake of 9/11, in many locations these were placed haphazardly around key sites to stop vehicle access or, to reassure the public that the threat of terrorism was being taken seriously. In particular, the 2016 Berlin Christmas market attack led to many cities immediately enhancing protective security through the deployment of concrete blockers and steel barriers to encourage the public that these places were safe to visit. Over time, many of these temporary measures have been retained, becoming part of the everyday streetscape and normal shopping experience. For example, in the

Figure 12.1 Barriers established in December 2016 to restrict vehicle access to the Christmas market in Birmingham.

U.K.'s second city, Birmingham, concrete and steel protective security was installed around the annual Christmas market the day after the Berlin attack (see Figure 12.1), but 4 years later had not been removed, becoming 'permanent' fixtures in the city centre with attempts even made to soften their appearance through the planting of flowers (Figure 12.2).

Similarly, the local and international response to the 2017 Barcelona VAW attack on the La Rambla boulevard elicited an international response, swamping many cities with protective security. Immediately after this incident, hostile-vehicle mitigation measures were fitted to the streetscape, with another iconic landmark – the nearby Sagrada Familia – additionally protected with the widespread introduction of concrete blocks and large plant pots to limit vehicle access.[17]

The Barcelona attacks also reverberated across Europe. Notably, in Italy, where concrete barriers were immediately installed at famous landmarks,

Conclusions: Normalising urban security 249

Figure 12.2 Retained steel blockers planted with flowers to 'soften' their appearance.

important tourist sites and crowded and pedestrianised areas in major cities, to separate vehicles and pedestrians. The imposition of such protective measures within Italian cities also stimulated a national conversation about the balancing of security and accessibility in public places and the importance of the aesthetical quality of the public realm (Coaffee, 2018). Such dialogue was also driven by local protests. For example, in Milan, local artists transformed anti-terrorism barriers into open-air works of art, and in Palermo, the city authorities called on painters, sculptors and designers to produce artworks from the concrete blocks so that the anti-terrorism barriers lost some of their distressing appearance. Throughout Italy, an anti-bollard approach to security took root stimulated by the intervention of world-renowned architect Stefano Boeri, who suggested that European cities be redesigned to include trees within bulky planters, rather than concrete blocks, to prevent vehicles targeting pedestrians, and to stop European cities being 'transformed into war check-points'.[18]

Such an approach to security design that saw attempts to disguise the security intention of physical interventions has slowly been adopted across a number of Italian cities[19] with similar schemes also adopted in other European capitals (Coaffee, 2020). For example, between 2015 and 2019 in Copenhagen,

Denmark, the Christiansborg Palace that houses the Parliament, and the political and Supreme Court, incorporated crash-rated bollards encased in Nordic granite spheres – carved from the same stone as the facade of the palace – in a 'string of pearls' formation into its public space design to restrict access to hostile vehicles. This landscaped design solution replaced roughly cut blocks of stone and large planters that had previously provided protection, creating what was referred to by the designers – GHB Landscape Architects – as 'peacekeeping architecture' (see Figure 12.3).[21]

Such an approach to more integrated design-thinking on urban security was also evident in London. Speaking in the summer of 2018 after a number of terror attacks in 2017, the Major of London advocated the use of creative design to enhance security, highlighting that temporary protections should be replaced with 'barriers which don't look like barriers because they've been designed in a way to look attractive and not unattractive'.[22]

A similar security process played out in Melbourne, Australia, after six pedestrians were killed by a car driven at high speed through the CBD in January 2017 (Coaffee, 2019; Chambers and Andrews, 2019). Initially in June 2017, as a result of a heightened threat from VAW attacks and increased security budgets, over 150 temporary concrete anti-terror blocks were placed in and around key public places in Central Melbourne. As the State premier commented at the time, speed of response was of the essence, despite the ugly appearance of the concrete blockers, noting that 'the threat of terror – the threat of hostile vehicle attacks, the threats to public safety – are all too real' and there is 'no time to be wasted'.[23] Consequently, a counter-protest to the installation of such makeshift security measures was organised, going viral on social media – #bollart – where the concrete blockers were artistically decorated as a reaction against what many saw as an unnecessary eyesore that risked turning the city centre into a fortress rather than the world's premier liveable city (Figure 12.4).

In November 2017, the second phase of a comprehensive security plan to deter high-speed vehicle attacks – commonly equated to the City of London's 'ring of steel' – was unveiled by Melbourne City Council.[24] This overall long-term plan will eventually see the CBD fitted with more bollards of varying designs, 'planters' and special road treatments, such as chicanes, to stop cars mounting kerbs. As Melbourne Lord Major noted: 'we are about to spend money in the city on bollards, and different sorts of obstructions that will change the face of the city, probably forever'.[25]

These emerging approaches further illuminate the power of the secured built environment to shape everyday urban (geo)politics, as well as the balance between security and freedom, and war and peace, and indicate the importance of the involvement of built environment professionals in protective counter-terrorism to ensure security design is integral to overall public realm improvement. Recently, such security-by-design approaches has perhaps reached a new high point in Paris where already installed, and highly visible, protective security[26] is due to be supplemented by a full integration between landscape design and security concerns. In a large-scale urban master plan commissioned in

Conclusions: Normalising urban security 251

Figure 12.3 Granite security outside the Christiansborg Palace, Copenhagen.[20]

Figure 12.4 #Bollart protests in Melbourne.

preparation for welcoming visitors to the 2024 Summer Olympics, a public realm upgrade, which boosts safety, improves the visitor experience as well as creating a unifying green axis centred on the Eiffel Tower, will see counter-terrorism concerns regarding hostile vehicles seamlessly embedded through the undulating landscape. This represents a novel approach where planners are working with security professionals to advance effective and socially and environmentally acceptable, safety solutions that are invisible to the general public (Coaffee, 2020).

Despite the innovation of the Parisian approach, and as highlighted in the earlier examples, bollards and barriers, and other ad hoc security measures, still remain the default option for security enhancement against vehicle-borne threats.[27] The normalcy of such reactive 'lockdown' solutions was further showcased in Washington, D.C. in late 2020 and early 2021 when militarised 'islands of security' comprising unscalable steel fences topped with razor wire, and concrete blockers, were established in scenes resembling the immediate aftermath of 9/11 (see Chapter 6). Such fortress security occurred first around the White House in August 2020, amidst fears of violence from Blacks Lives Matter protests, and which resulted in the city's Mayor asking the U.S. President to withdraw the extra security forces.[28] The second major security enhancement within the 'monumental core' occurred after the storming of the Capitol Building on January 6, 2021.[29] This was widely seen as a right-wing domestic terrorist attack, and prompted fears of further terrorism in the period before the Presidential inauguration, in 2 weeks' time.[30] On both occasions, the city was effectively placed under siege, with security infrastructure staffed by thousands of Metropolitan Police, National Guardsman and military personal, seen as a disproportionate imposition, and regularly likened in the media to the Green Zone in Baghdad.[31] In March 2021, the widespread fencing around the Capitol building was consolidated so as to reduce its spatial footprint that had spread into adjoining residential neighbourhoods, and discussions were ongoing about developing 'permanent and more aesthetically pleasing security due to a concern about the fortress feel around the Capitol'.[32] As these discussions about permanent security were taking place, a VAW attack occurred as a car careered into the two Capitol Police officers, killing one, before crashing into a security barrier. The suspect then existed the vehicle and lunged at other officers with a knife, before being shot and killed. This event added further impetus to call for permanently securitising the area and again raising questions about the impact of this securityscape on the publicness of the city. As the *Washington Post* noted:

> The decisions that legislators and urban planners will make in the coming months about fencing, barriers and security measures could alter the landscape of the District and change the ease with which residents and visitors access public buildings, parks and elected officials.[33]

Overall, advancing proportionate protective security approaches is a difficult balancing act, but there remains an enormous opportunity for the built environment stakeholders to forge new approaches that address security needs within more comprehensive development schemes. Here, particular emphasis should be placed on minimising the anxiety produced by protectionist

Conclusions: Normalising urban security 253

architectures that have been argued, in some cases, to create conditions of 'securitised agoraphobia' – where the public are fearful of visiting crowded locations – and embed subtler forms of security design.[34] History shows that how Western society continues to react to urban terror threats will significantly impact the public realm for many years. Here, the risk to cities comes as much from urban policy responses as the actual act of terrorism, with both having the potential to harm the freedom of movement and expression that define an animated and mobile city. Moreover, experience tells us that once permitted such hyper-security has a tendency to become permanent. In this regard, if we want a vibrant public realm we should not let exceptional protective security become the norm as we seek more proportionate ways of coping with urban terrorism, and increasingly embrace blended security-by-design solutions rather than barrier and bollard solutions by default.[35]

The increasingly automated watchful city

Previous chapters have analysed how surveillance techniques have evolved over time: from walled cities to reinforce the monitoring of populations; the enhanced sightlines provided by the construction of boulevards; early analogue security cameras to surveil risky spaces; and, increasingly, to digital and biometric devices to track and filter the circulation of people and objects. Such 'watching' techniques and technologies have progressively advanced since the initial post-9/11 surveillance surge, are often hidden from public view or embedded in everyday objects such as traffic cones, and have become increasingly automated as part of wider smart and safe city initiatives. Whilst initially deployed out of fear of terrorism, new high-tech devices are also increasing being utilised for minor crimes and misdemeanours in a process of control creep that 'reanimate and reinvigorate critical arguments over the governance, control and selective visions of order that strive to organise the urban realm' (Fussey and Coaffee, 2012b, p.207).

One increasingly common approach, deployed in a number of cities across the globe, is 'smart' street-lamps implanted with an array of sensor technologies to monitor urban phenomenon such as the environmental conditions, license-plate recognition,[36] gunshot detection and continuous audio-visual monitoring. Such initiatives have proved controversial, with data feeds from the embedded sensors increasingly being used by police to monitor street protests as well as for investigating serious crime and terrorism. In response, in one well-publicised incident, democracy protestors in Hong Kong during 2019 demonstrations, deliberately targeted and toppled the city's smart street lamps with electric saws out of fear of Chinese surveillance.[37]

In the U.S., a number of cities have recently adopted such devices. For example, in 2017, over 3000 publically funded smart 'CityIQ' streetlights equipped with an array of video and audio collection sensors were installed in San Diego, 'turning the city into a stealthy laboratory for infrastructure-embedded intelligence'.[38] Here, police requests for access to the data feeds for criminal investigations (including for the examination of civil unrest during Black Lives Matter marches in May and June 2020) sparked calls for new surveillance ordinances[39] and accusations of function creep as streetlights were retooled as surveillance systems, showcasing how 'the capacities of the smart city to do good things can also increase state and police control' (Perry, 2020).

Moreover, at the request of counter-terrorism police and intelligence agencies, such unobtrusive techniques of surveillance are being expanded beyond individual devices towards integrated surveillance webs that watch over entire cities, scouring its digital ecosystem and physical terrain for signals that *might* indicate a terrorist act is imminent.[40] Such systems increasingly utilise forms of artificial intelligence (AI), and specifically, machine learning techniques and algorithms, to facilitate the application of mass surveillance to identify threats.[41] At the urban scale, such techniques are not novel and have been steadily utilised by law enforcement over the last 20 years for crime detection through well publicised programmes of predictive policing (Meijer and Wessels, 2019), social network analysis of urban gangs (Piquette and Papachristos, 2014), biometric identification (Gates, 2011) and the generation of city-wide alert and awareness systems (Levine et al., 2017). Progressively, such state- and city-level programmes are being supplemented by an array of private-sector-developed digital tooling that seek to intervene in a number of practical aspects of crime and counter-terrorism, often with multiple data feeds being integrated in state-of-the-art control rooms such as the IBM-built 'Intelligent Operations Centre' in Rio de Janeiro, Brazil,[42] or the military-inspired C4I4 surveillance control centre in Mexico City built by the Mexican telecoms giant Telex and the French military supplier Thales.[43]

We can also look to China to see the potential and pitfalls of AI technologies to surveil 'suspect communities' and attempt to control all aspects of city life. Here, the process of rapidly expanding state surveillance over the population and visitors was catalysed both by the global War on Terror and the 2008 Olympic Games hosted in Beijing (Chapters 9 and 11) but has also intensified since with the increasing incorporation of technology firms into national security agendas. The governmental aim has been to achieve the blanket coverage of urban spaces with an all-seeing digital panopticon that seeks to identify disruption in real time and identify threats before they become reality. Such systems of 'total surveillance' have been extensively 'trialled' in the north-western territory of Xinjiang. This region is the home of more than 1 million Muslim Uighurs who have, in recent years, been accused of dissident and terrorist acts, including rioting, bombings, person-borne suicide incidents,[44] knife attacks[45] and vehicle rammings,[46] notably, a suspected car suicide attack in 2013 in Tiananmen square, Beijing.[47] Conversely, the Western media and international advocate groups have documented alleged mass surveillance and detention of Muslim Uighars in almost 400 're-education camps'[48] with access controlled by police checkpoints and video and biometric cameras, and guided by sweeping (biometric) data collection, mandated apps to cleanse smartphones of subversive material and use of AI to select huge numbers of the Xinjiang community as candidates for detention based on the use of predictive algorithms.[49]

The systematic repression of the Uighur population dates from the start of China's War on Terror, whereby the internal separatist threat of the 1990s was relabelled and securitised. As Roberts (2018) has documented, it was almost immediately after 9/11 that China decreed that this population represented 'a terrorist threat' which, over the last 20 years, has led to the increased isolation and exclusion of the Uighurs from mainstream life in China in an extreme form of biopolitics. Here, the Uighur people, as a whole, were seen by the State 'to symbolize an almost biological threat to society, akin to a virus that must be eradicated quarantined or cleansed from those it infects through surveillance, punishment, and detention' (p.232–233).

Xinjiang has become an urban laboratory to test the tactics and technologies used in the name of counter-terrorism and control, before expanding its reach across mainland China. Increasingly, such approaches are being rolled-out across entire urban terrains through large-scale AI-powered software systems called 'City Brain'. These total surveillance schemes are focused on cities, where population density makes centralised surveillance simpler. City Brain,[50] hosted on the Alibaba platform, began life in 2016 and is capable of massive multi-source data collection from embedded sensors, enabling new forms of integrated surveillance.[51] As Zhang et al. (2019, p.5) noted 'with the anomaly detection framework, the all-time all-area patrolling and alerting system can detect abnormal events in a variety of scenarios in real time…ensuring the public safety and operational efficiency of a city'.

Internationally, AI and machine learning tools, combined with big data availability, are further impacting Western counter-terrorism operations through the use of automated data analytics and visualisations to prioritise terrorist suspects, provide support for real time operations or assisting with post-event investigations by revealing patterns and linkages that expose terrorist networks and organisations, or suspicious individuals and activities (Van Puyvelde et al., 2017; UN News, 2019). As in China, private-sector companies are driving advances in software and data-fusion technologies, as well as in the analysis of digital information and traces. Notably, social media and web-browsing history can be mined and processed to 'predict' individual's movements and malicious intentions.

Such predictive technology-driven approaches are beginning to change counter-terrorism and intelligence gathering practices, be that in the identification of terrorists or those likely to the radicalised, or predicting the timing and location of attacks (McKendrick, 2019). For example, the U.K., the Ministry of Defence (2018), has recently highlighted how their strategy to use big data approaches for counter-terrorism 'links different behaviours, using data held across multiple disparate systems, and analyses them to identify patterns'. The MoD has engaged with private-sector IT companies and evolved a system to anticipate future threats that allow counter-terrorism forces to more effectively deploy resources. Here, one approach, operationalised under the U.K. Prevent strand of counter-terrorism, uses a POLE-type data model (Person, Object, Location and Event) for the storage and recording of 'incidents and entities' that can be interlinked to build up an integrated profile of monitored subjects, including their network of associations.[52] Whilst at present such models lack precision and accuracy – in part as a result of the low incidence of terrorism – progressive digitisation and the availability of metadata will make such predictive tools faster, more efficient, sophisticated and accurate in the future. This will subsequently allow AI-driven data processing and synthesis systems (often provided by private-security IT firms such as Palantir or Clearview AI) to be connected to huge national databases for the purpose of identifying those suspected of terrorist activity (Ganor, 2019). For example, in a rare published paper on the *Ethics of AI: Pioneering a New National Security* in early 2021, the U.K. signals and intelligence division – GCHQ – argued that such technology will be central to U.K. security in an increasingly complex world enabling the analysis of an ever-increasing volume and complexity of data so as to improve the quality and speed of their decision-making.[53]

Outside of utilising AI for identifying and tracking terrorist suspects, such technologies are further being used in autonomous weapons systems and deployed on the battlefield as part of the ongoing War on Terror. Here, particular interest is being shown in the application of AI in Unmanned Aerial Vehicles (UAVs) and in creating autonomous killer drones or drone swarms.[54] Such developments have further reawakened concerns about how militarily technology, often developed alongside technology firms, can be regulated, but moreover, how such techniques could be redeployed in the homeland. Here, with the advance of AI and machine learning techniques in practices of war and overseas counter-terrorism operations, it appears that 'war is coming home' with the increased deployment of such technologies into everyday life and against citizens. As Pasquale (2020) illuminated:

> The advance of AI use in the military, police, prisons and security services is less a rivalry among great powers than a lucrative global project by corporate and government elites to maintain control over restive populations at home and abroad. Once deployed in distant battles and occupations, military methods tend to find a way back to the home front. They are first deployed against unpopular or relatively powerless minorities, and then spread to other groups.

Such progressions provide an unadorned warning of how militarised and privately developed technologies of mass surveillance can seep into everyday urban life and demand a reconsideration of the trade-offs between national security interests and individual privacy concerns.[55] Decoding this process involves understanding the duel trends of the globalisation of surveillance, often in military arenas, and the domestication of security (Coaffee et al., 2008). Here, the 'new normality' of everyday surveillance in situ occurs through a constant reinforcement by state and private-sector actors, and an inculcation of habits over time, which leads to society accepting evermore intrusive forms of surveillance that are increasingly infiltrating policy arenas at all levels. The normalisation of such new sophisticated technologies follows an almost identical pattern to prior studies of the uncritical adoption of first-generation CCTV systems. Here, Government action sought to shape conditions of acceptance that, over time, became 'normal' and which were maintained through safety and security practices and the ubiquity and affordability of surveillance technologies, so that 'what would in the previous mode of ordering be regarded as temporary or even entirely unacceptable becomes unremarkable, mundane, normal and consequently may not even be challenged' (Murakami Wood and Webster, 2009, p.262–263).

In essence, this is about states legitimising surveillance techniques and technologies to normalise them in everyday life. The emergence and perpetuation of such 'risk-surveillance society' models seek anticipated and pre-managed risk, control and security that are embedded in the norms and institutions of society (Murakami Wood et al., 2006). This provides important lessons for the normalisation of ever advancing technologies, such as AI, or practices such as embedding technologies unobtrusively in everyday objects, that for many are becoming an accepted and necessary response to crime and terrorism regardless of their technical accuracy or ethical management.

The rationale for advanced surveillance in 'new' counter-terrorism was to mitigate human bias in decision-making, and to do more-for-less by making automated behavioural predictions, rather than relying on crude profiling. Only when thoroughly scrutinised do ethical, legal and regulatory concerns emerge around discriminatory targeting, algorithmic bias and other human rights and civil liberty abuses that make society question whether such intensified surveillance is proportionate and appropriate, and whether control or technology creep is occurring where surveillance justified for one reason is inevitably repurposed for other, more everyday, monitoring tasks.

Mainstreaming resilience across the urban terrain

The relationship between security and resilience, and the subsequent linkages to controlling urban terrains, became starkly illuminated in the wake of 9/11 that made traditional security approaches appear inadequate whilst ironically stimulating their growth (Chapter 8). Since 9/11, security policy has evolved to focus on preparedness, anticipation and pre-emption as key underpinning principles in the War of Terror and the production of national and city-based security. Subsequently, the meanings and practices of security have become a potent driver and shaper of contemporary resilience practices in which resilience policy became increasingly driven by security concerns and, at the same time, security policy adopted the softer and more palatable language of resilience (Coaffee and Fussey, 2015).

Over time, the ideas of being constantly prepared to counter 'inevitable' terror attack has emerged as a staple of international security discussions, becoming mainstreamed within numerous government documents, and often updating policy ideas based on risk management. Policies of resilience led to a reappraisal of who, what and where is vulnerable to terrorism and how people, places and processes can be made more resilient and have led to counter-terrorism systematically siphoning up an increasingly large proportion of government emergency budgets, in a process of 'resilience creep' (Walklate and Mythen, 2014, p.144).

The post-9/11 push for resilience increasingly highlighted the importance of localised urban responses to new security challenges that did not rely on centralised command and control, and meta-strategies linked to national security or emergency management. Managing in a resilient way has thus meant redefining protectionist reflexes and going beyond conventional risk management procedures to address the complexities of integrated systems and the uncertainty of future city-based threats. By contrast, at a national level, 'states of emergency' announced by governments in the wake of terror attacks have led to accusations of security-logics unjustly and permanently penetrating everyday life. For example, such a declaration in November 2015 in France, after 130 people were killed in Paris, was in place for nearly 2 years. This was subsequently replaced by far-reaching counter-terrorism laws which gave police more power to fight violent extremism, including the conduction of searchers, closure of religious buildings and placing restrictions on the movement and associations of those with suspected extremist links. Civil liberty and human rights groups condemned these legal measures as establishing 'a permanent state of emergency' that could harm citizens' rights to 'liberty, security, freedom of assembly and freedom of religion' (Amnesty International, 2017). Such declarations, in France and elsewhere, reinforced the Western governmental desire for enhanced (city-based) preparedness to form a background to everyday life, and the encouragement of citizens to internalise survival tactics and coping mechanism and become more resilient.

In practice, such exceptionality has led to many local systems of security being established, underpinned by new security governance arrangements, with the city seen as the site of multiple circulating risks that need to be managed or stabilised (made resilient) through a focusing on the aleatory. Critiquing such contemporary practices of governing moves beyond Foucauldian readings of the dispositif of security as an institutional formation and mode of governmentality, where attempts are made to neutralise risk circulations. Here, post-9/11, the local focus of security was central in taking account of both context and a full spectrum of involved stakeholders and allowing a more nuanced and sociologically informed view of institutions to emerge. This sat in contrast to classic studies of governmentality that can be seen as synchronic and lead to 'to somewhat reified and homogenous accounts of modern power, with little sensitivity to diversity, heterogeneity, and resistance within and over time' (Bevir, 2010, p.424). Such a reimagining of security

Conclusions: Normalising urban security 259

governance further focused on decentred theories of governance that sought to extend political analysis beyond the realm of elected officials and statutory stakeholders to interrogate the possibilities of alternative formations, and in particular, to promote greater community voice and civic resistance to imposed security measures that could have an impact on the ground *and* be incorporated within local security efforts.

As different chapters have illuminated, at various points in time, different stakeholders have been co-opted into national counter-terrorism efforts in ways that effectively normalised their involvement. Whether this is though: planners and architects being encouraged to deploy their spatial, analytical or design skills in retrofitting sites with protective security, or seamlessly incorporating resilient designs into new development proposals (Chapter 7); technology companies and data scientists partnering with national security agencies to advance technical tools and metadata sets that can anticipate terror attack through the comprehensive scanning of suspect individuals and the urban terrain (Chapter 10/11); or the focus upon how the public can assist national security efforts advanced by the War of Terror through engaging with in government-backed community resilience initiatives that encourages a culture of preparedness and the reporting of suspicious activity as the normal, moral obligation of good citizenship (Chapter 9); security governance has become far more pervasive, pluralistic and responsibilising.

The rewiring of security governance, post-9/11, not only drew a wider range of stakeholders into its orbit but also became effective at normalising ideas of anticipation and constant preparedness in everyday governing practices. Therefore, whilst from a security governance perspective we can readily acknowledge that 'the building of urban resilience will be most effective when it involves a mutual and accountable network of civic institutions, agencies and individual citizens working in partnership towards common goals within a common strategy' (Coaffee et al., 2008, p.3), urban authorities have undoubtedly struggled with this objective. In many locations, this is partially a result of restructured risk management processes where terrorism is seen as one of many risks faced within broader regimes of resilience planning, and where partnerships between the police, security services and city managers have required time to establish themselves. For example, London's recently published 'all-risks' *City Resilience Strategy* (Greater London Authority, 2020) prioritises terrorist risk but notes that 'building resilience in London is about building the ability of all Londoners, our businesses and our communities to survive and thrive no matter what kinds of chronic stresses and acute shocks we as a city experience' (p.6). With regard to counter-terrorism, and led by the London Resilience Group, the city has now established a Counter-Terrorism Preparedness Network (CTPN) with a range to global city partners to collaborate and share lessons with regard to how best to prepare and respond to terrorist attacks through a shared peer-peer city learning network. This collaboration complements U.K. and international strategies for countering terrorism, and notably a previous 2016 review into London's preparedness to respond to a major terrorist incident (Harris, 2016). This latter review highlighted that despite great strides made in counter-terrorism in London, 'we should always be prepared for the unexpected [and] why preparedness has to be proactive and...enable all the relevant organisations – along with the business community and the public – to react seamlessly and effectively, whatever the nature of the incident' (p.3). Ultimately, this report concluded that,

> this requires that we all acquire a mind-set of community security and resilience, that London becomes a city … where everyone who lives and works here sees security and resilience as their responsibility just as much as it is for the emergency services and civic authorities.
>
> (ibid., emphasis added)

COVID-19 and the homecoming of resilience

Building a culture of resilience across individuals, households, communities, the city and entire countries as a nationwide political marketing strategy was seen as way of lessening the impact and cost of terror attacks *before they occur,* as well as gaining increased levels of public acceptance for exceptional security policy responses. In Western nations, and especially in its larger cities, whilst the preparation and response to a range of disruptive shocks and stresses have been primarily driven by concerns around terrorism (and climate change), they have more recently been severely stress-tested during the COVID-19 pandemic from early 2020 onwards. Responses have showcased the similarity of government-in-crisis approaches adopted across a number of scales in reaction to different shocks and attempts to control the behaviour and movement of citizens through the use of normalising security and surveillance techniques.

At the level of planning and preparedness, a number of Western nations had gone some way in advancing strategic plans for dealing with health pandemics, long identified as a low-probability, high-impact risk in national risk assessments.[56] However, these were largely left on the shelf, or only partially activated, as it rapidly became clear that most Western nations were woefully underprepared for the emerging crisis.[57] As national governments and city managers attempted to control the spread of COVID-19, militarised rhetoric, all too familiar in the War on Terror, was frequently deployed as pandemic response became securitised with politicians regularly announcing that we were 'at war' with the virus (also often articulated as an invisible killer), reinforcing statist thinking through the use of military language. For example, U.S. President Trump labelled himself a wartime president with extraordinary powers, with others in the U.S. administration referring to this time as 'our Pearl Harbor or 9/11 moment'.[58] Many other countries declared 'states of emergency', 'wartime states' or gave 'special emergency powers', allowing officials greater scope to impose new measures to contain the spread of COVID-19, regardless of how such exceptional actions would normally be considered infringements on liberty.

As with the suspension of government obligations in a time of crisis linked to terrorism, there have been significant implications for everyday life from COVID responses, including local, national or city-level 'lockdowns', that provided new powers to close non-essential businesses, limit public gatherings and restrict people's mobility, liberty, and freedom of movement which, in many cases, were developed and deployed using the military and emergency planning forums.[59] In short, framing health concerns as security issues led to civil liberties being overlooked in the interests of public safety. Importantly, such strategies, as well as enforcing lockdowns, were also required to 'protect' essential circulatory flows and facilitate the selective movement of people and material required to sustain everyday life. Whilst such declared emergency powers were nominally time-limited – from period of weeks to months – we should remember that many of the emergency provisions put in place after 9/11 have never gone away, being legitimised and integrated into everyday life.

The performative acts of public communication surrounding the COVID-19 restrictions also closely resembled counter-terrorism approaches, with a clear goal of such work being to enable citizens to endure the crisis. As with calls to encourage citizens to engage with preventative counter-terrorism and become more resilient, Governmental announcements regarding the easing social distancing restrictions have commonly evoked the mantra of personal responsibility as key to getting back to normality. Moreover, tiered colour-coded alert and monitoring systems to detect future outbreaks, simple messaging asking the public to stay alert to control the virus and the encouragement to report other citizens to public authorities if they were breaking the rules, were reminiscent of responses to terror threats that sought regulate fear and 'trigger' public conformance (Chapter 6).[60]

More generally, the crossover between counter-terrorism and health pandemic playbooks was evidenced in the U.K. where the government followed a similar approach to its four-pronged counter-terrorism strategy CONTEST (Protect, Prevent, Pursue and Prepare) that represented a 'resilience' and multi-agency response. As Malik (2020) has highlighted, the U.K.'s Coronavirus Action Plan of March 2020 'also consisted of four elements (Contain, Delay, Research, and Mitigate)' and focused upon, 'preventing, preparing, and building resilience to future risks of disease'. Moreover, this illuminated

> crossovers between existing apparatuses of security - which operate on the foundation that intervention in the present for an event that may occur in the future is anticipated through pre-emption, preparedness, precaution, and deterrence – applied to preparing for a public health emergency.
>
> (p.49–50)

Additionally, the U.K.'s *Integrated Security Review* published in March 2021 (which was delayed by a year due to the pandemic) gave a commitment to developing a 'comprehensive national resilience strategy' so that 'in the years ahead, agility and speed of action will enable us to deliver for our citizens, enhancing our prosperity and security' (HM Government, 2021, p.3).

Such preparedness has been further elaborated by protective security and enhanced surveillance that drew on conventional and emerging counter-terrorism practices. In some cities, to create temporary pedestrianised zones and enlarge outdoor entertainment and dining spaces in the public realm, protective access systems were deployed to separate the walkable street from the road (also a result of continued security concerns regarding hostile vehicle attacks).[61] In one example, the U.K.'s second city, Birmingham, deployed low-height crash-rated access barriers across a number of sites during weekends that according to the guard developer increased street trading by 50%:

> The barriers are designed to allow people to flow in and out of an area with minimal disruption, preventing the unnecessary build-up of crowds. This makes them ideal for facilitating social distancing, while also providing further protection from vehicle as a weapon attacks.[62]

Advanced surveillance technologies have also been routinely deployed to monitor the circulation of people on the street and to extend governments' monitoring and screening reach. For example, in many parts of urban China, as part of a broader 'robotic restructuring of cities' (Chen et al., 2020), specific COVID-19 pandemic control management strategies, such as the use of facial recognition cameras, have been supplemented with new AI-enabled screening software to detect individuals not wearing face coverings.[63] Handheld thermal imaging technologies in portable thermometers, smart clothing and body-worn equipment such as 'smart' Police helmets with infra-red detection that can detect high body temperature in a 3–5-metre radius have also been deployed in China, and in many European cities, to biometrically screen citizens in real time.[64] In the future, COVID-19 responses will likely have a significant impact on biometric applications for wider security management, with touchless and contactless technologies such as face and iris recognition likely to be readily adapted to meet emerging threats and to evolve existing access control systems.[65]

However, concern has been voiced about the mission creep of legal mechanisms and technological innovations that have been unfurled due to COVID-19, with widespread unease expressed that temporary restrictions could become permanent. Temporary exceptionalism, as many have long warned, can easily follow this trajectory and become a permanent governmental strategy.[66] In the case of pandemic-response technologies, concerns were immediately raised about the personal surveillance and civil liberty implications of contract tracing data, collected by cameras or apps, being stored by the police for security, rather than health-related reasons. As Kitchen

(2020, p.9) noted, while in the present crisis 'control creep' is occurring for health reasons, the 'danger is that its use will normalize government tracking and digital fencing/leashing, with the architectures developed subsequently… pivoting to other issues such as policing, emergency management response, and national security'. For example, it has been reported that location-tracking apps adopted by many Chinese universities at the height of the pandemic will be retained to monitor the movement of students,[67] whilst the Indian Government has made the use named tracking apps mandatory for those living in certain zones, amounting to a form of geofenced quarantining. In both these cases, and many others, this raises fears that their use has become legitimised, accepted and quickly becoming a 'normal' operating procedure.

The concerns with using networked and digital technologies to respond to COVID-19, as with their post-9/11 surge, surround effective oversight and democratic safeguards as society aims to 'bounce forward' and design 'new normal' post-pandemic cities. As Yeung (2020, p.56) has noted 'although the exceptional demands of the pandemic may justify loosening some procedural constraints that otherwise apply to the exercise of governmental authority, it does not dispense with them altogether'. Here proportionality again plays a crucial role in balancing a responsible loss of privacy against national health concerns, but with a danger that 'unfettered surveillance and executive power in the name of emergency response [will lay] the groundwork for infrastructures that will continue to violate privacy well after the pandemic has passed' (Marda, 2020, p.29–30). The danger here is that the pandemic 'will supercharge the solutionist state, as 9/11 did for the surveillance state, creating an excuse to fill the political vacuum with anti-democratic practices, this time in the name of innovation rather than just security' and entrench high-tech solutions 'as the default option for addressing all other existential problems' (Morozov, 2020).

Conclusion: Can we achieve 'proportionate' and 'normal' security?

The goal of achieving proportionate security is writ large in most Western-centred national and international counter-terrorism strategies but has long been seen as impossible to achieve (Neocleous, 2007). The idea of achieving proportionality, however, does importantly make clear that when security implemented as a result of wartime powers are transposed into the civic sphere, government should at least consider its wider impacts on how citizens go about their everyday lives. This is an age-old balancing act between security – the prevention of events yet to happen through anticipation – and freedom, and is commonly informed by the assessment and quantification of future risks and dangers where 'the "balance" between prevention/anticipation and other dimensions becomes central to security thinking' (Tulumello, 2020, p.3).

In particular, ensuring freedom of movement and privacy has become central to balancing individual rights with the need for security, with its numerous budgets, functions, forms and resiliencies. As Simpson et al. (2017, p.11) questioned when considering the rebuilding on Central Oslo after the 2011 terrorist bombing, 'to what extent is the notion of the secure and safe city produced at the cost of the city of freedom, democracy and the right to the city?' All too often, as highlighted in previous chapters, city and security authorities – all with very different histories and ideas and practices of security and counter-terrorism – have enacted similar/standardised programmes of protective security and associated population surveillance in the wake of attack as a demonstration of strong leadership that all-to-often has remained in place for some time, or permanently, given the purported, 'inevitability' of future attack. Such approaches are also typically characterised by the delegation and distribution of responsibility to an array of non-traditional stakeholders, with such obligations often framed by Government as a moral imperative of being a good citizen. Demonstrating the continuation of such approaches that have been well documented since the Cold War (Chapter 2) and increasingly prevalent since 9/11, in February 2021 a U.K.-wide consultation on establishing a 'Protect Duty' was announced that would make it a legal requirement for all owners and managers of public spaces and venues to consider the risk of a terrorist attack and to ensure appropriate and proportionate security was in place, essentially localising and responsibilising the burden of risk through protective security planning and preparedness.[68]

As different types and style of terrorism have evolved, new design approaches and governance processes have emerged as counter-responses, and have thrown up a series of distinctive operational and ethical issues. In analysing such responses as part of how society has become increasingly securitised through the perpetual fear of urban terrorism, this book has charted the surfacing and progression of different waves of terrorism and urban counter-terrorism. It has examined how security practices have been embedded within the material urban landscape and systems of governance that have moved beyond state-centric accounts to focus upon local areas and illuminated the responsibly placed on a wider range of civic stakeholders to both manage their own risk management and contribute to national strategies. This book has further unpacked fundamental political questions of security for whom and by whom, highlighting how effective urban security and socially, legally and ethically acceptable approaches have been traded-off, or balanced, and shone a light on the processes by which exceptional notions of security become reproduced and normalised in the urban environment.

Conceptually, this analysis has been informed by a range of ideas from philosophy, political science and IR, urban geography, sociology, city planning, engineering and architecture, that have been deployed to understand counter-terrorism practices in situ, and their impact on everyday life at particular moments in time. This has been contextualised by responses to particular threats, specific terrorist tactics and the roles and responsibilities assigned to city stakeholders and citizens in security governance. Influential in this analysis has been the work of key scholarship on the historical shift from

Conclusions: Normalising urban security 265

disciplinary control to circulatory security; of the evolution of defensive city designs and their impact upon the social practices and landscapes of everyday life; a range of theorising on 'everyday', 'vernacular', 'material' and 'aesthetic' 'turns'; securitisation studies and critical security and terrorism studies, with a focus upon governmental procedures, language and the processes through which meanings of security are constructed and communicated; more recent critical accounts that saw the city increasingly scrutinised through military perspectives and recast post-Cold War military doctrine; a focus upon the meanings and social impacts of intensified surveillance and fortification practices, often under the guise of the need to improve city resilience; and work that has interrogated the embodied and experiential practices and emotions elicited by security and the creation of everyday 'atmospheres' of counter-terrorism.

Such a focus on the everyday has generated further research questions of critical future importance linked to how urban places are embedded with security designs that manipulate emotions and are affectious (Micieli-Voutsinas and Person, 2021); how mass surveillance permeates the everyday and 'is in the air' (Søilen, 2020); how security is embedded within algorithmic code, offering alternative perspectives on places and practices of security; and leading to a questioning of who constructs these 'normal' feelings of security? It also opens up wider avenues for a focus upon 'feelings' of security and insecurity amidst a predominant framing of responses to terror that emphasises security and identity and pays less attention to 'the improvised, affective ways in which people respond to terror' and creates 'public atmospheres', demonstrating, 'the transient, plural, and everyday ways in which politics is practiced, assembled, and negotiated by different publics in response to terror' (Closs Stephens et al., 2020).

Drawing many of these security and counter-terrorism concepts and practices together has been the notion that there is a tendency to let temporary and exceptional security become permanent and normal. Drawing on Foucault's reading of disciplinary normalisation and governmentality where 'punitive' landscape markers control by filtering the normal and abnormal and selectively ordering the late modern city, Agamben's post-9/11 studies of exceptionality have notably highlighted how the exceptional becomes an institutionalised paradigm of government that can colonise all aspects of everyday life, and where counter-political action is neutered. Here decision-making around security is commonly framed through the relationship between technological, political and social change and, over time, is inevitably forced to 'balance', or perform a trade-off, between security and accountability, democracy, liberty and privacy. However, liberty and egalitarianism often lose out 'because they require constant reference to a state of exception, measures of security work towards the growing depoliticization of society in the long run, they are incompatible with democracy' (Agamben, 2002, p.2). Such ideas can most persuasively been deployed to highlight how 'lockdown' security often becomes the 'normal' option for cities, seen as being on the frontline in the War on Terror, and how a range of uneven geographies emerge and are sustained in such locations on a permanent basis, as a result. Exceptionalism here, which might have been considered at one time to be acceptable or temporary, has become reproduced, permanent, everyday and unchallenged (normalised) in particular spatial contexts. In other words, such measures cease to be extraordinary, time limited and deployed for specific threat-reduction purposes, but rather, have been validated as part of normal life.

Viewed through this lens, we can see how the various spatial security strategies and legal measures have emerged from new conceptualisations and practices of urban security and counter-terrorism, where the exceptional and the normal are blurred as a result of a disposition of states to act prior to a risk event to pre-empt its emergence through preparedness and enhanced resiliency. These are political power plays that are operationalised to both ensure cities and nations, and more particularly their economies, can 'bounce back' to full functioning as quickly as possible. Moreover, such strategies also seek inculcate an acceptance of heightened security and the moral obligation of citizens contributing to it habitually, and where the adoption of such 'acceptable' security levels, and the decentralisation of responsibilities across civil society, becomes an established part of everyday life. In this sense, risks are little more than social constructions informed by expert systems that assesses levels of threat, where 'an acceptable risk is an accepted risk' that becomes routinised (Beck, 1995, p.92) and changes the relationship of security to the future by pre-emptively seeking to control impending threats (Aradau and van Munster, 2008). Probabilistic risk assessment further informs security decision-making by creating zones of different exposures to risk, be that in alert level systems, vulnerability calculation of crowded places or the increased use of quantitative measures of AI to identify suspect individuals or communities and to 'predict' the occurrence of terror attacks. On the ground, the spatial and material imprints of such calculative rationality represent the normalisation of urban security during the War on Terror, where the spaces that are secured, and their social and material effect on adjacent areas, or the wider nation, have become centrally relevant to the remapping of the growing interdisciplinary scholarship on the geopolitical and everyday impacts of the terror and (in)security.

Notes

1 The modus operandi used by terrorists has a tendency to go in 'waves' with their own distinct energy, temporal clustering, territorial imprint and communication method (Rapoport, 2001; Kaplan, 2007; Simon, 2011; Radil and Pinos, 2019).
2 In 2010, an article entitled 'The ultimate mowing machine' appeared in *Inspire*, the online, English-language magazine produced by Al Qaeda, urging their followers to 'achieve maximum carnage' through VAW attacks (cited in Keating, 2014) and encouraged the use of knifes that could be easily obtained from local hardware stores.

3 Vehicles as Weapons of Terror: US Cities on Alert as Attacks Hit the West. *Stars and Stripes*, July 9, 2017, at www.stripes.com/news/us/vehicles-as-weapons-of-terror-us-cities-on-alert-as-attacks-hit-the-west-1.477364.
4 Using vehicle ramming to target-specific buildings was a regular tactic of terror in the 1980s (or example in Lebanon – Chapter 4), but it wasn't until 2001 that people were commonly the main target. One early attack occurred in Azor, Israel, in February 2001, when a Palestinian drove a bus into a group of Israeli soldiers who stood at a bus stop killing eight people. The Islamist resistance movement, Hamas, claimed responsibility for the attack.
5 On May 15, 2011, in Tel Aviv a truck was deliberately rammed into cars and pedestrians killing 1 person and injuring 17 others.
6 On August 29, 2011, a popular Tel Aviv nightclub was attacked when a police checkpoint guarding it was rammed by a vehicle followed by a knife stabbing attack, injuring nine people.
7 After the vehicle ramming, the suspect's car crashed and he then attacked a police officer with a knife and was shot dead. It later emerged that the attacker was under police surveillance due to fears of him being radicalised.
8 Cited in, History of Lone-Wolf Vehicle Attacks Suggests Risk of Emulation is Very Real, *The Globe and Mail*, July 15, 2016, at www.theglobeandmail.com/news/world/history-of-lone-wolf-vehicle-attacks-suggests-risk-of-emulation-is-very-real/article30933070/. These vehicle attacks were preceded by a knife attack on police in Tours on December 20.
9 Cited in, The Terrifying Simplicity of the Stockholm Attack. *The Atlantic*, April 7, at www.theatlantic.com/international/archive/2017/04/stockholm-truck-attack/511364/. A similar article appeared in the May 2017 issue. Whilst such articles are clearly a factor driving the copy-cat attacks across Western cities, their publication dates mean that they should not be seen as causal (Miller and Hayward, 2017).
10 On December 19, 2016, a truck was deliberately driven into the Christmas market at Breitscheidplatz in Berlin, leaving 12 people dead and 56 others injured. Four days after the attack, he was killed in a shootout with police near Milan, Italy.
11 On January 20, 2017, a car was deliberately driven into pedestrians in Central Melbourne, Australia. Six people were killed and 27 were seriously injured. According to subsequent court reports, this was not considered an act of terrorism as the driver was suffering a drug-induced psychosis. It was, however, treated as a terrorist attack in the immediate aftermath.
12 On April 7, 2017, a truck attack in the Swedish capital, Stockholm killed 5 people, and injured 15 more.
13 A number of major attacks occurred in London in early-mid-2017. On Westminster Bridge on March 22, outside the Houses of Parliament, when a car was driven at pedestrians on the bridge pavement before the lone attacker exited and began a knife attack. Six people were killed, including the attacker, and over 50 were injured. On June 3, a similar terrorist vehicle-ramming and stabbing took place on London Bridge. A van was deliberately driven into pedestrians, where its three occupants then ran into the nearby Borough Market area and began stabbing people. Eight people were killed and 48 were injured. A third major vehicle as weapon attack occurred a few weeks later in apparent far right 'retaliation' for the two previous ISIS-inspired Bridge attacks. On June 19, a van was driven into pedestrians in Finsbury Park, near a large Mosque, killing one person and injuring a number of others.

14 On June 19, a car packed with guns and explosives was rammed into a convoy of Police vehicles on the Champs-Élysées in Paris, France, killing the attacker.
15 In the afternoon of August 17, 2017, a van was deliberately driven into pedestrians on the La Rambla in Barcelona, Spain, killing 13 people and injuring at least 130 others.
16 On October 31, 2017, a rented truck was deliberately driven into cyclists and runners for about 1 mile of a bike path in Lower Manhattan, New York, killing eight people. After the truck came to a standstill, the attacker exited the vehicle with two guns (later found to be a paintball and pellet gun) and was shot.
17 A later attack in the nearby resort of Cambrils led to one person being killed when a car was driven into pedestrians. Five suspected terrorists were killed at the scene by police.
18 Cited in Dezeen, August 24, 2017, at www.dezeen.com/2017/08/24/stefano-boeri-treebarriersprevent-vehicle-terror-attacks-news/. Boeri further highlighted that bespoke 'hardened' street furniture could also be utilised to provide barriers to vehicle-led attacks whilst also improving the functionality of public spaces in the city. Whilst such an approach has been considered by counter-terrorism experts for over 20 years, in most cases they are dismissed as too costly and not robust enough.
19 For example, in Rome, 40 large pots containing oleander flowers were placed around the perimeter of Piazza del Quirinale in Rome, an official residence of the Italian president.
20 Image from Matthias Schalk under the 'CC-BY-SA-4.0' Creative Commons in Wikimedia Commons.
21 The stone spheres were 100 centimetre in diameter and had a small number of retractable bollards placed amongst them to allow access to official vehicles. This scheme won the Danish Landscape Architecture Award for 2019.
22 Cited in the *Daily Telegraph* online August 15, 2018, at www.telegraph.co.uk/news/2018/08/15/parliament-square-cars-could-banned-says-uks-senior-police-officer/.
23 Cited in 'Bollard Bid to Protect Melbourne's CBD from Terrorist Attacks', *The Herald Sun*, October 27, 2017, at www.heraldsun.com.au/news/victoria/bollardbidto-protect-melbournes-cbdfrom-terrorist-attacks/news-story/3481de5986df7fe027ad2e417fee1d9e.
24 On November 27, 2017, an Australian man of Somali heritage was arrested for plotting a mass shooting terrorist attack in Federation Square, Melbourne, on New Year's Eve.
25 As note 21. The scheme currently being put in place was seen to meet the expected standards of security in terms of crash ratings whilst ensuring the best visual outcome with long-term plans looking to use unobtrusive security measures where appropriate. The visible enhancement of security in downtown Melbourne was given further impetus in early November 2018 where an attacker whet on a rampage with a knife after the vehicle he was travelling, and which was packed with 'barbecue-style' gas cylinders, crashed and caught fire.
26 Given increased security concerns, in June 2018, Paris unveiled a 'ring of steel' for the Eiffel Tower. Concrete and steel blockers that had encircled the tower since 2016 were replaced by a tall and an apparently impregnatable security belt at a cost of nearly €35 million ($40.1 million). This consisted of 2.5-inch bulletproof glass walls on two sides of a security square, with the other two blocked off with 10.5-foot high steel barriers formed from curved prongs in the form of the tower itself.

Conclusions: Normalising urban security 269

27 Most recently, in the wake of a vehicle bomb that exploded in the U.S. city of Nashville on Christmas day 2020 – devastating multiple buildings, injuring eight people and killing the alleged perpetrator, there were immediate calls for the city's infrastructure to be securitised and made more resilient.
28 The Mayor also dispatched city workers to paint Black Lives Matter in giant yellow letters covering two blocks visible from the White House – see Security Concerns Give the White House a Fortified New Look, *New York Times*, June 5, 2020 at www.nytimes.com/2020/06/05/us/politics/white-house-security.html. Further, protesters turned the White House security fence into a living memorial to racial justice by affixing the signs they carried during demonstrations.
29 The storming of the U.S. Capitol was a riot and violent attack against the 117th U.S. Congress carried out by a group of supporters of U.S. President Donald Trump in an attempt to overturn his defeat in the 2020 presidential election.
30 The Presidential inauguration is always designated as a National Special Security Events, where the secret service takes responsibility for security planning (see Chapter 11).
31 Police vehicles sealed off a huge area of downtown creating a restricted security zone in which car parks were closed, Metro stations shut and residents told to avoid the area. See, for example, National Guard Troops Flooding in as Washington Locks Down. *Associated Press*, January 14, 2021, at https://apnews.com/article/biden-inauguration-dc-lockdown-4d8ddcb1530851c6721b9301e455e39a.
32 Interview with a senior member of the Homeland Security and Emergency Management Agency, March 31, 2021.
33 See An Increasingly Fortified Federal City: After Deadly Capitol Attacks, Lawmakers Consider What Fences Should Stay or Go. *Washington Post*, April 13, 2021, at www.washingtonpost.com/dc-md-va/interactive/2021/us-capitol-fencing/.
34 Urban Terrorism Isn't Going to Stop. Can City Planners Help Reduce Its Lethal Impact? *The Washington Post*, June 22, 2017, at www.washingtonpost.com/news/posteverything/wp/2017/06/22/urban-terrorism-isnt-going-to-stop-can-city-planners-help-reduce-its-lethal-impact/?utm_term=.b1e62fb04d83.
35 Beyond Bollards: Protecting Crowded Places Means Not Letting the Exceptional Become the Norm. *The Conversation (Australia)*, August 22, 2017, at http://theconversation.com/beyond-bollards-protecting-crowded-places-means-not-letting-the-exceptional-become-the-norm-82755.
36 Separately, a little known company called Flock has steadily rolled out AI-enabled automatic number plate recognition cameras through their TALON programme creating a smart camera network across the United States that is utilised by the police. See, for example, Inside 'TALON', the Nationwide Network of AI-Enabled Surveillance Cameras. *Vice*, March 3, 2021 at www.vice.com/en/article/bvx4bq/talon-flock-safety-cameras-police-license-plate-reader.
37 See, for example, Why Hong Kongers Are Toppling Lampposts. *The Atlantic*, August 30, 2019, at www.theatlantic.com/technology/archive/2019/08/why-hong-kong-protesters-are-cutting-down-lampposts/597145/.
38 Cited in San Diego's Street Lights That Spy. *San Diego Reader*. February 20, 2020, at hwww.sandiegoreader.com/news/2019/feb/20/san-diegos-street-lights-spy/.
39 Currently such oversight comes from the police themselves through published policies for the use of streetlamp data published in March 2019. In July 2020, the City Council approved two proposed ordinances linked to the use and privacy

270 *The future of urban security*

implications of streetlight data and in August the Major ordered that the streetlight sensors be turned off until voted upon.
40   Notably, Governments around the world have sort to develop automated systems for the bulk collection (notably from communications infrastructure) and evaluation of metadata, in efforts to ensure national security. The U.S. National Security Administration's (NSA) PRISM and SKYNET programs, exposed by Edward Snowden in 2013, are two of many examples of where state-led and nationwide data surveillance programmes have been set in train to detect suspicious behaviour within the wider population.
41   This has been facilitated by the capture and utilisation of evermore detailed personal data to 'train' algorithms to detect patterns and occurrence in large data sets and consequently label them as 'threats'.
42   This centre opened in 2010 and now integrates over 20 city departments to improve emergency response management and collaboration across the city using predictive analytics.
43   This centre, built in 2011, amalgamates the data feeds from up to 47 municipal agencies and has the capability to monitor the cities thousands of surveillance cameras to assess crowd density and movements as well track vehicles in the city's main streets thanks to automatic number plate recognition technology (Mushkin, 2016).
44   On February 25, 1997, three bombs exploded on three buses in Ürümqi, Xinjiang, killing nine people. Another two devices in the city's main railway station failed to explode.
45   On July 18, 2011 in Hotan, Xinjiang, a bomb and knife attack was carried out by 18 young Uyghur men who then occupied a police station and took hostages. Fourteen of the attackers and two of the hostages were killed.
46   On May 22, 2014, two SUVs were driven at speed into a busy street market in Ürümqi, Xinjiang, and explosives were thrown out of the windows at shoppers. After the vehicles had hit pedestrians, they collided with each other and exploded. Over 40 people were killed and around 100 injured.
47   On October 28, 2013, a car crashed outside of the Gate of Heavenly Peace on Tiananmen Square in what was seen as a terrorist suicide attack. This represented the first terrorist attack in Beijing's recent history. Five people were killed, including 3 inside the vehicle, and a further 38 were injured.
48   China has Built 380 Internment Camps in Xinjiang, Study Finds. *The Guardian*, September 24, 2020, at www.theguardian.com/world/2020/sep/24/china-has-built-380-internment-camps-in-xinjiang-study-finds?CMP=Share_iOSApp_Other.
49   China Cables: Who Are the Uighurs and Why Mass Detention? *International Consortium of Investigative Journalists'*, November 24, 2019, at www.icij.org/investigations/china-cables/china-cables-who-are-the-uighurs-and-why-mass-detention/. There was also condemnation at the 41st United Nations Human Rights Council (UNHRC) in July 2019 where dozens of mainly Western countries complained about China's treatment of Uighurs in Xinjiang. Conversely, a group of 37 nations issued a competing letter to the UNHRC, defending China's actions.
50   The concept of 'City Brain' was formally proposed in 2016 as a new infrastructure built on big data, which utilises AI to solve urban governance and development issues. In November 2017, Alibaba Cloud ET City Brain was selected as one of the first four AI innovation platforms by the Chinese Ministry of Science and

Conclusions: Normalising urban security 271

Technology (Zhang et al., 2019). Such systems are still in development and are not fully integrated at the time of writing. That said, the private-sector technologies underpinning it are being transferred overseas and embedded in cities globally.
51 Whilst such systems are multipurpose and focus upon optimising urban operations, City Brain has a particular focus upon safety and security, with the ability to detect objects in motion and track them across the city to predict unusual events using. For example, it can integrate footage from a plethora facial recognition cameras and an array of surveillance deceives embedded in everyday objects such as lampposts and traffic cones.
52 Whilst terrorist identification in advance of attacks remains the holy grail of counter-terrorism, it is currently more a possibility rather than a reality. The limited trails of such quantitative methods that have been conducted, such as the U.S. NSA's SKYNET system tested in Pakistan, have been relatively inaccurate due to deficiencies of available datasets (Ganor, 2019).
53 See Government Communications Headquarters, www.gchq.gov.uk/news/artificial-intelligence, published February 25, 2021.
54 Are Drone Swarms the Future of Aerial Warfare? *The Guardian*, December 4, 2019, at www.theguardian.com/news/2019/dec/04/are-drone-swarms-the-future-of-aerial-warfare.
55 This would especially apply to issues of informed consent, bulk data collection and the weakly regulated role of the private sector in the development of such technologies.
56 Most notably, before the pandemic struck, both the United States and the United Kingdom, though the DHS and Civil Contingency Secretariat, respectively, had developed holistic playbooks that covered responses to all aspects of a pandemic.
57 Some countries supplemented their strategic plans with data and lessons drawn from emergency 'resilience' exercising most commonly used to prepare for terrorist attacks. For example, in the United Kingdom, Cygnus, a 3-day simulation exercise in 2016 involving 950 people, assessed the United Kingdom's ability to cope with a large-scale influenza pandemic. According to an exercise summary, 'the aim was to test systems to the extreme, to identify strengths and weaknesses in the U.K.'s response plans, which would then inform improvements in our resilience' (Department of Health of Social Care, 2020). The exercise assessment concluded that the United Kingdom, and in particular its health infrastructure, was underprepared for such a catastrophe. The result of this exercise became subject to a freedom of information request in the summer of 2020 when Government refused to release its detailed findings amidst speculation that it had failed to learn the lessons from its own exercise.
58 Are We at 'War' with Coronavirus? *The Washington Post*, April 6, 2020, at www.washingtonpost.com/world/2020/04/06/are-we-war-with-coronavirus/. It is worth noting that the new U.S. President, Joe Biden, on taking office in early 2021, also referred to being 'at war' with the virus.
59 Such pandemic-linked 'lockdowns' are of course not a new phenomenon and inspired the term *cordon sanitaire* that dates from 1821, when French troops were deployed on the border between France and Spain to prevent yellow fever from spreading into France (Taylor, 1882) – and has been regularly used to refer to protective security cordons to counter-terrorism in the late twentieth and early twenty-first centuries (Coaffee, 1997, 2003).

60 This includes concerns over how limitations of the right to protest during lockdown will be retained, with police-granted greater powers to limit and control demonstrations once the COVID restrictions are removed.
61 Some security and terrorism experts argued that the pandemic could leads to new waves of terrorism – away from a focus upon attacking crowded places (although this is still a high priority threat – see Booth et al., 2020) and towards cyberterrorism and online radicalisation. In a warning to security services that more conventional threats were still elevated, three people were killed in a knife attack at a church in Nice, France, on October 29, 2020, which was seen as Islamic terrorism. The attack coincided with urban areas entering entered a second COVID lockdown and led to France raising its national security alert to its highest level, with an extra 4000 troops being deployed to protect churches and schools. Three days alter days later on November 2, a lone gunman with ISIS sympathies, and who was categorised as at high risk to radicalisation by the authorities, opened fire with a rifle in Vienna's inner district, amidst restaurants and shopping streets. The attacker was killed by police. The shooting took place 4 hours before the midnight start of an Austrian nationwide pandemic lockdown, where crowds in bars and restaurants were enjoying one last evening out.
62 ATG Access' Surface Guard system provides Birmingham's bars and restaurants a much needed boost post COVID-19 break September 5, 2020, at www.sourcesecurity.com/news/atg-access-surface-guard-system-birmingham-co-197-ga-co-1559113753-ga.1602682068.html.
63 Even Mask-Wearers Can Be ID'd, China Facial Recognition Firm Says. *Reuters*, March 9, 2020, at www.reuters.com/article/us-health-coronavirus-facial-recognition-idUSKBN20W0WL.
64 Police Use 'Smart Helmets' to Detect People with Coronavirus, *Police Professional*, May 26, 2020, at www.policeprofessional.com/news/police-use-smart-helmets-to-detect-people-with-coronavirus/. In the United Kingdom, a number of cities also deployed AI sensors – initially developed to track the flow of traffic, cyclists and pedestrian movement – to monitor social distancing – see, AI Cameras Introduced in London to Monitor Social Distancing and Lockdown Restrictions. *Evening Standard*, October 8, 2020, at www.standard.co.uk/news/uk/ai-cameras-london-social-distancing-rules-a4566446.html.
65 The Role of Biometrics in a Post COVID-19 World. *Security info watch*, July 7, 2020, at www.securityinfowatch.com/access-identity/biometrics/article/21143152/the-role-of-biometrics-in-a-post-covid19-world.
66 We only have to look to the U.S. Patriot Act that was supposed to expire in 2005 but is still in force to see how easily such legal regimes can become accepted and normalised.
67 Privacy Fears as China Keeps Tracking Student Locations, *Times Higher Education*, December 21, 2020, at www.timeshighereducation.com/news/privacy-fears-china-keeps-tracking-student-locations.
68 See www.gov.uk/government/consultations/protect-duty. This follows a campaign by Figen Murray, mother of Martyn Hett who died in the 2017 Manchester Arena terrorist attack and is often referred to as Martyn's law. Currently, owners of venues and sites are not obliged to act on advice about threats of a terrorist attack and how to mitigate the risk.

References

Abbas, T. (2018). Implementing 'prevent' in countering violent extremism in the UK. *Critical Social Policy*, 39(3), pp.396–412.
Adey, P. and Anderson, B. (2012). Anticipating emergencies: technologies of preparedness and the matter of security. *Security Dialogue*, 43, pp.99–117.
Adey, P., Brayer, L., Masson, D., Murphy, P., Simpson, P., Tixier, N. (2013). Pour votre tranquillité, ambiance, atmosphere, and surveillance. *Geoforum*, 49, pp.299–309.
Agamben, G. (1998). *Homo Sacer*. Redwood City (CA): Stanford University Press.
Agamben, G. (2001). Security and terror. *Theory & Event* 5(4), pp.1–2.
Agamben, G. (2005). *State of Exception*. Chicago (IL): University of Chicago Press.
Agnew, J. (1994). The territorial trap: the geographical assumptions of international relations theory. *Review of International Political Economy*, 1, pp.53–80.
Agnew, J. (2005). Sovereignty regimes: territoriality and state authority in contemporary world politics. *Annals of the Association of American Geographers*, 95, pp.437–461.
Alexander, D. (2002). From civil defence to civil protection and back again. *Disaster Prevention and Management*, 1(3), pp.209–213.
Allen, C. (2010). *Islamophobia*. Farnham: Ashgate.
Altermark, N. and Nilsson, H. (2018). Crafting the 'well-rounded citizen': empowerment and the government of counterradicalization. *International Political Sociology*, 12(1), pp.53–69.
Aly, A. (2013). The policy response to home-grown terrorism: reconceptualising prevent and resilience as collective resistance. *Journal of Policing, Intelligence and Counter Terrorism* 8(1), pp.2–18.
Aly, A. and Green, L. (2010). Fear, anxiety and the state of terror. *Studies in Conflict and Terrorism*, 33(3), pp.268–281.
American Planning Association (APA) (2005). *Policy Guide on Security*. Washington (DC): American Planning Association.
Amnesty International (2017). France's Permanent State of Emergency, September 26. Available at www.amnesty.org/en/latest/news/2017/09/a-permanent-state-of-emergency-in-france/. Accessed June 2, 2018.
Amoore, L. (2006). Vigilant visualities: the watchful politics of the war on terror. *Security Dialogue,* 38(2), pp.215–232.
Amoore, L (2013). *The Politics of Possibility: Risk and Security Beyond Probability*. Durham: Duke University Press.

References

Amoore, L. and De Goede, M. (eds.) (2008). *Risk and the War on Terror*. London: Routledge.

Anderson, B. (2010). Preemption, precaution, preparedness: anticipatory action and future geographies. *Progress in Human Geography*, 34(6), pp.777–798.

Anderson, B. and Adey, P. (2011). Affect and security: exercising emergency in UK Civil Contingencies. *Environment and Planning D: Society and Space*, 29(6), pp.1092–1109.

Andrejevic, M. (2005). The work of watching one another: lateral surveillance, risk, and governance. *Surveillance and Society*, 2(4), pp.479–497.

Andrejevic, M. (2007). *iSpy: Surveillance and Power in the Interactive Era*. Lawrence (KS): University Press of Kansas.

Aradau, C. (2015). Crowded places are everywhere we go: crowds, emergency, politics. *Theory, Culture & Society*, 32, pp.155–175.

Aradau, C. and van Munster, R. (2007). Governing terrorism through risk: taking precautions, (un)knowing the future. *European Journal of International Relations*, 13, pp.89–115.

Aradau, C. and van Munster, R. (2008). Taming the future: the dispositive of risk in the war on terror. In: Amoore, L. and De Goede, M. (eds.), *Risk and the War on Terror*. London: Routledge, pp.23–40.

Aradau, C. and van Munster, R. (2009). Exceptionalism and the 'war on terror': criminology meets international relations. *The British Journal of Criminology*, 49(5), pp.686–701.

Arias, G. (2011). The normalisation of exception in the biopolitical security dispositive. *International Social Science Journal*, 62, pp.363–375.

Attorney General's Department (2010). Countering Violent Extremism', Attorney-General's Department, 17/2/2010. Available at www.ag.gov.au/www/agd/agd.nsf/Page/National_securityCountering_Violent_Extremism. Accessed February 26, 2011.

Australian Government (2010). *Counter-Terrorism White Paper-Securing Australia, Protecting Our Community*. Canberra: Commonwealth of Australia.

Azaryahu, M. (2000). Israeli securityscapes. In: Gold, J. and Revill, G. (eds.), *Landscapes of Defence*, London: Prentice Hall, pp.102–113.

Baer, M., Heron, K., Morton, O. and Ratliff, E. (2005). *Safe: The Race to Protect Ourselves in a Newly Dangerous World*. New York (NY): Harper Collins.

Ball, K. and Snider, L. (eds.) (2013). *The Surveillance-Industrial Complex: A Political Economy of Surveillance*. London: Routledge.

Balzacq, T. (ed.) (2011). *Securitization Theory: How Security Problems Emerge and Dissolve*. Oxford: Routledge.

Barkun, M. (2011). *Chasing Phantoms: Reality, Imagination and Homeland Security Since 9/11*. Chapel Hill (NC): University of North Carolina Press.

Barnes, T. and Duncan J. (eds.) (1991). *Writing Worlds: Discourse, Text and Metaphor in the Representation of Landscape*. London: Routledge.

Barry, A. (2013). *Material Politics: Disputes Along the Pipeline*. Oxford: Wiley/Blackwell.

Bauman, Z. (2000). *Liquid Modernity*. Cambridge: Polity Press.

Bauman, Z. (2002). Reconnaissance wars of the planetary frontierland. *Theory, Culture and Society*, 19(4), pp.81–90.

Beck, U. (1995). *Ecological Politics in an Age of Risk*. Cambridge: Polity Press.

Beck, U. (1999). *World Risk Society*. Cambridge: Polity Press.

References

Beck, U. (2002). The terrorist threat: world risk society revisited. *Theory, Culture and Society*, 19(4), pp.39–55.
Bell, C. (2011). Civilianising warfare: ways of war and peace in modern counter-insurgency. *Journal of International Relations and Development*, 14, pp.309–332.
Bell, C. and Evans, B. (2010). Terrorism to insurgency: mapping the post-intervention security terrain. *Journal of Intervention and Statebuilding*, 4(4), pp.371–390.
Bellavita, C. (2007). Changing homeland security: a strategic logic of special event security. *Homeland Security Affairs*, 3, pp.1–23.
Benton-Short, L. (2007). Bollards, bunkers, and barriers: securing the National Mall in Washington, DC. *Environment and Planning D: Society and Space*, 25(3), pp.51–65.
Berman, M. (1987). Among the ruins. *The New Internationalist*, 178, pp.8–9.
Bernazzoli, R., and Flint, C. (2009). Power, place and militarism: toward a comparative geographic analysis of militarization. *Geography Compass*, 3, pp.393–411.
Betz, D. (2016). Webs, walls and wars. *Global Crime*, 17(3–4), pp.296–313.
Betz, D. (2019). Citadels and marching forts: how non-technological drivers are pointing future warfare towards techniques from the past. *Scandinavian Journal of Military Studies*, 2(1), pp.30–41.
Bevir, M. (2010). Rethinking governmentality: towards genealogies of governance. *European Journal of Social Theory*, 13(4), pp.423–441.
Bigo, D. (2002). Security and immigration: toward a critique of the governmentality of unease. *Alternatives: Global, Local Political*, 27(1), pp.63–92.
Bigo, D. and Tsoukala, A. (eds.) (2008). *Terror, Insecurity, and Liberty: Illiberal Practices of Liberal Regimes After 9/11*. Oxford: Routledge.
Birmingham City Council (2010). *Project Champion: Scrutiny Review into ANPR and CCTV Cameras*. Birmingham: Birmingham City Council.
Bishop, P. and Mallie, E. (1987). *The Provisional IRA*. London: Corgi.
Bishop, R. and Clancey, G. (2004). The city-as-target, or perpetuation and death. In: Graham, S. (ed.), *Cities, War and Terrorism*. Oxford: Blackwell, pp.54–78.
Bishop, R. and Phillips, J. (2002). Manufacturing emergencies. *Theory, Culture and Society*, 19(4), pp.91–102.
Blakely, E.J. and Snyder M.G. (1995). *Fortress America: Gated and Walled Communities in the US*. Cambridge (MA): Lincoln Institute of Land Policy Working Papers.
Bleiker, R. (2000). *Popular Dissent, Human Agency and Global Politics*. Cambridge: Cambridge University Press.
Bleiker, R. (2006). Art after 9/11. *Alternatives*, 31(1), pp.77–99.
Bleiker, R. and Hutchinson, E. (2008). Fear no more: emotions and world politics. *Review of International Studies*, 34(1), pp.115–135.
Boal, F.W. (1969). Territoriality on the shankhill-falls divide, Belfast. *Irish Geography*, 6, pp.30–50.
Boal, F.W. (1971). Territoriality and class: a study of two residential areas in Belfast. *Irish Geography*, 6, pp.229–248.
Boal, F.W. (1975). Belfast 1980: a segregated city? *Graticule*. Belfast: Department of Geography, Queens University.
Boal, F.W. (1995). *Shaping a City – Belfast in the Late Twentieth Century*. Belfast: Institute of Irish Studies.
Boddy, T (2007). Architecture emblematic: hardened sites and softened symbols. In: Sorkin, M (ed.), *Indefensible Space*. Abingdon: Routledge, pp.277–304.
Bollens, S. (2011). *City and Soul in Divided Societies*. New York (NY): Routledge.

Booth, A., Chmutina, K. and Bosher, L. (2020). Protecting crowded places: challenges and drivers to implementing protective security measures in the built environment. *Cities*, 107, doi.org/10.1016/j.cities.2020.102891.
Booth, K. (ed.) (1997). *Critical Security Studies*. London: Wiley Blackwell.
Booth, K. (2004). Realities of security. *International Relations*, 18(1), pp.5–8.
Bourbeau, P. (2013). Resiliencism: premises and promises in securitisation research. *Resilience*, 1(1), pp.3–17.
Boykoff, J. and Fussey, P. (2014). London's shadow legacies: security and activism at the 2012 Olympics. *Contemporary Social Science*, 9:2, pp.253–270.
Boyle, P. and Haggerty, K. (2009). Spectacular security: mega-events and the security complex. *International Political Sociology*, 3, pp.257–274.
Boyle, P. and Haggerty, K. (2012). Planning for the worst: risk, uncertainty, and the Olympic Games. *British Journal of Sociology*, 63, pp.241–259.
Brand, R. and Fregonese, S. (2013). *The Radicals' City; Urban Environment, Polarisation, Cohesion*. Farnham: Ashgate.
Brassett, J. and Vaughan-Williams, N. (2015). Security and the performative politics of resilience. *Security Dialogue*, 46, pp.32–50.
Briggs, R. (2005). Introduction. In: Briggs, R. (ed.), *Joining Forces: From National Security to Networked Security*. London: Demos, pp.9–26.
Briggs, R. (2010). Community engagement for counter-terrorism: lessons from the United Kingdom. *International Affairs* 86(4), pp.971–981.
Briggs, R. and Strugnell, A. (2011). *Radicalisation: The Role of the Internet (Policy Planners' Network Working Paper)*. London: Institute for Strategic Dialogue.
Brown, G. (2007a). Statement on Security. Available at www.number10.gov.uk/output/Page12675.asp. Accessed July 25, 2007.
Brown, G. (2007b). House of Commons Debate, November 14, Col. 667.
Brown, P.L. (1995). Designs in a land of bombs and guns. *New York Times*, May 28, p.10.
Brown, S. (1985). Central Belfast's security segment: an urban phenomenon. *Area*, 17(1), pp.1–8.
Brown, W. (2010). *Walled States, Waning Sovereignty*. New York (NY): Zone.
Bucholz, A. (1999). Militarism. In: Kurtz, L. (ed.), *Encyclopaedia of Peace and Conflict*. New York (NY): Academic Press, p.423.
Buckley, C. (2007). New York plans surveillance veil for downtown. New York Times, July 9. Available at www.nytimes.com/2007/07/09/nyregion/09ring.html?ex=1341633600&en=2644be97bd9577f9&ei=5088&partner=rssnyt&. Accessed September 12, 2007.
Buzan, B. (2006). Will the 'global war on terrorism' be the new cold war? *International Affairs*, 82(6), pp.1101–1118.
Buzan, B. (2008). A leader without followers? The United States in World Politics after Bush. *International Politics*, 45(5), pp.554–570.
Buzan, B. and Wæver, O. (2009). Macrosecuritisation and security constellations: reconsidering scale in securitisation theory. *Review of International Studies*, 35(2), pp.253–276.
Buzan, B., Wæver, O. and de Wilde, J. (1998). *Security: A New Framework for Analysis*. Boulder (CO): Lynne Rienner Publishers.
Cabinet Office (2003). *Dealing with Disaster (Revised Third Edition)*. London: Cabinet Office.

Cabinet Office (2008). *The National Security Strategy of the United Kingdom: Security in an Interdependent World*. London: The Stationary Office.
Cabinet Office (2011). *Strategic National Framework on Community Resilience*. London: Cabinet Office.
Campbell, B. (2002). *War and Society in Imperial Rome*. London: Routledge.
Campbell, D. (1982). *War Plan UK: The Truth About Civil Defence in Britain*. London: Burnett Books.
Campbell, D. (2003). Cultural governance and pictorial resistance: reflections on the imaging of war. *Review of International Studies*, 29, pp.57–73.
Campbell, D., Graham, S. and Monk, D.B. (2007). Introduction to urbicide: the killing of cities. *Theory & Event,* 10(2). Available at https://muse.jhu.edu/article/218080. Accessed March 3, 2018.
Campbell, D. and Shapiro, M. (2007). Guest editors' introduction. *Security Dialogue*, 38(2), pp.131–137.
Carter, A.B., Deutch, J. and Zelikow, P. (1998). Catastrophic terrorism: tackling the new danger. *Foreign Affairs*, 77(6), pp.80–94.
Catterall, B. (2001). Cities under siege: September 11th and after. *City*, 5(3), p.383.
Centre for the Protection of National Infrastructure (2011). *Integrated Security: A Public Realm Design Guide for Hostile Vehicle Mitigation*.
Ceyhan, A. (2012). Surveillance as biopower. In: Ball, K., Haggerty, K. and Lyon, D. (eds.), *Routledge Handbook of Surveillance Studies*. London: Routledge, pp.38–45.
Chambers, P. and Andrews, T. (2019). Never mind the bollards: the politics of policing car attacks through the securitisation of crowded urban places. *Environment and Planning D: Society and Space*, 37, pp.1025–1044.
Chandler, D. (2012). Resilience and human security: the post-interventionist paradigm. *Security Dialogue*, 43(3), pp.213–229.
Chandler, D. (2014a). Beyond neoliberalism: resilience, the new art of governing complexity. *Resilience,* 2, pp.47–63.
Chandler, D. (2014b). *Resilience: The Governance of Complexity*. London: Routledge.
Chandler, D. (2016). The socialisation of security. In: Chandler, D. and Reid, J. *The Neoliberal Subject: Resilience, Adaptation and Vulnerability*. London: Rowman and Littlefield, pp.27–50.
Chandler, D and Coaffee, J. (eds.) (2016). *The Routledge Handbook of International Resilience*. London: Routledge.
Chang, N. (2002). *The Silencing of Political Dissent: How the USA Patriot Act Undermines the Constitution*. New York (NY): Seven Springs.
Chen B., Marvin S. and While A. (2020). Containing COVID-19 in China: AI and the robotic restructuring of future cities. *Dialogues in Human Geography*. 10(2), pp.238–241.
Chiodelli, F. (2012). The Jerusalem master plan: planning into the conflict. *Jerusalem Quarterly*, 51, pp.5–20.
City of London Police (2002). *Annual Report for 2001/02*. London: City of London Police
City Security (2018). City of London's Ring of Steel Security, July. Available at https://citysecuritymagazine.com/police-partnerships/city-of-london-police-ring-of-steel/. Accessed March 28, 2018.
Clausewitz, C. (1873 [1984]). *On War*. (Trans. Howard, M. and Paret, P.) Princeton (NJ): Princeton University Press.

References

Clay, G. (1973). *Close-up: How to Read the American City*, London; Pall Mall.

Closs Stephens, A., Coward, M., Merrill, S. and Sumartojo, S. (2020). Affect and the response to terror: commemoration and communities of sense. *International Political Sociology* https://doi.org/10.1093/ips/olaa020.

Coaffee, J. (1996a). Terrorism, insurance rhetoric and the City of London. *Association of American Geographers Annual Meeting, Charlotte, North Carolina, April 9–13*.

Coaffee, J. (1996b). Creating images of risk and security in Belfast and London. *Annual Meeting of the Society for Risk Analysis-Europe – Risk in a Modern Society: Lessons from Europe, University of Surrey, Guildford, June 3–5*.

Coaffee, J. (1997). The City of London's ring of steel – panacea or placebo. *Fourth International Seminar on Urban Form*, University of Birmingham, July 10.

Coaffee, J. (2000). Fortification, fragmentation and the threat of terrorism in the City of London. In: Gold, J.R. and Revill, G. (eds.), *Landscapes of Defence*. London: Addison Wesley Longman, pp.114–129.

Coaffee, J. (2003). *Terrorism, Risk and the City*. Aldershot: Ashgate.

Coaffee, J. (2004a). Rings of steel, rings of concrete and rings of confidence: designing out terrorism in central London pre and post 9/11. *International Journal of Urban and Regional Research*, 28, pp.201–211.

Coaffee, J. (2004b). Recasting the 'ring of steel'. In: Graham, S. (ed.), *Cities, War and Terrorism: Towards an Urban Geopolitics*. Oxford: Blackwell, pp.276–296.

Coaffee, J. (2005). Urban renaissance in the age of terrorism – revanchism, social control or the end of reflection? *International Journal of Urban and Regional Research*, 29(2), 447–454.

Coaffee, J. (2006). From counter-terrorism to resilience. *European Legacy – Journal of the International Society for the study of European Ideas*, 11(4), pp.389–403.

Coaffee, J. (2008). Redesigning counter-terrorism for soft targets, Royal United Services Institute (RUSI). *Homeland Security and Resilience Monitor*, 7(2), pp.16–17.

Coaffee, J. (2009a). Protecting the urban: the dangers of planning for terrorism. *Theory, Culture & Society*, 26(7–8), pp.343–355.

Coaffee, J. (2009b). *Terrorism, Risk and the Global City: Towards Urban Resilience*. Farnham: Ashgate.

Coaffee, J. (2010). Protecting vulnerable cities: the UK resilience response to defending everyday urban infrastructure. *International Affairs*, 86(4), pp.939–954.

Coaffee, J. (2013a). Policy transfer, legacy and major sporting events: lessons for London 2012 and beyond. *International Journal of Sports Policy and Politics*, 5, pp.295–312.

Coaffee, J. (2013b). Rescaling and responsibilising the politics of urban resilience: from National Security to Local Place-Making, *Politics*, 33(4), pp.240–252.

Coaffee, J. (2014). The uneven geographies of the Olympic carceral: from exceptionalism to normalisation. *The Geographical Journal*, 3, pp.199–211.

Coaffee, J. (2017a). Urban terrorism isn't going to stop. Can city planners help reduce its lethal impact?, *The Washington Post*, June 22 at www.washingtonpost.com/news/posteverything/wp/2017/06/22/urbanterrorismisnt-going-to-stop-can-city-planners-help-reduce-its-lethalimpact/?utm_term=.b1e62fb04d83.

Coaffee, J. (2017b). Social media and the protection of crowded places. Counter-Terrorism Business, February, pp.83–85.

Coaffee, J. (2018). Introduction. In: *Beyond Concrete Barriers Innovation in Urban Furniture and Security in Public Space*. Available at https://gcdn.net/wp-content/uploads/2018/01/GCDN-Urban-Furniture-Study-A4-FINAL-highres_web.pdf.

Coaffee, J. (2019). *Futureproof: How to Build Resilience in An Uncertain World*. London: Yale University Press.
Coaffee, J. (2020). *Security, Resilience and Planning: Planning's Role in Countering Terrorism*. London: Lund Humphries.
Coaffee, J. and Bosher, L. (2008). Integrating counter-terrorist resilience into sustainability. *Proceedings of the Institution of Civil Engineers Urban Design and Planning*, 161(2), pp.75–83.
Coaffee, J. and Clarke, J. (2016). Critical infrastructure lifelines and the politics of anthropocentric resilience. *Resilience*, 5(3), pp.1–21.
Coaffee, J. and Fussey, P. (2012). Securing the games. In: Girginov, V. (ed.), *Bidding, Delivering and Engaging With the Olympics*. London: Routledge, pp.99–113.
Coaffee, J. and Murakami Wood, D. (2006). Security is coming home – rethinking scale and constructing resilience in the global urban response to terrorist risk. *International Relations*, 20(4), pp.503–517.
Coaffee, J. and Murakami Wood, D. (2008). Terrorism and surveillance. In: Hall, T, (ed.), *The SAGE Companion to the City*. London: Sage, pp.352–372.
Coaffee, J. and O'Hare, P. (2008). Urban resilience and national security: the role for planners. *Proceeding of the Institute of Civil Engineers: Urban Design and Planning*, 161(DP4), pp.171–182.
Coaffee, J. and O'Hare, P. (2011). Co-opting urban planners into the 'war on terror": a "balanced way" for domestic security. *International Studies Review*, 13(2), pp.376–385.
Coaffee, J. and Rogers, P. (2008). Rebordering the city for new security challenges: from counter terrorism to community resilience. *Space and Polity*, 12(2), pp.101–118.
Coaffee, J., and Fussey, P. (2015). Constructing resilience through security and surveillance: the practices and tensions of security-driven resilience. *Security Dialogue*, 46(1), pp.86–105.
Coaffee, J., Clarke, J. and. Davis, P. (2016). A HARMONISE'd approach to building security-driven urban resilience. *Journal of Financial Management of Property and Construction*, 21(1), pp.73–80.
Coaffee, J., Fussey, P. and Moore, C. (2011). Laminating security for London 2012: enhancing security infrastructures to defend mega-sporting events. *Urban Studies*, 48, pp.3311–3328.
Coaffee, J., Moore, C., Fletcher, D. and Bosher, L. (2008a). Resilient design for community safety & terror-resistant cities. *Proceedings of the Institute of Civil Engineers: Municipal Engineer*, 161(2), pp.103–110.
Coaffee, J., Murakami Wood, D. and Rogers, P. (2008b). *The Everyday Resilience of the City: How Cities Respond to Terrorism and Disaster*, London: Palgrave/Macmillan.
Coaffee, J., O'Hare, P. and Hawkesworth, M. (2009). The visibility of (in)security: the aesthetics of planning urban defences against terrorism, *Security Dialogue*, 40, pp.489–511.
Collier, S. and Lakoff, A. (2008). Distributed preparedness: space, security and citizenship in the United States. In: Cowen, D. and Gilbert, E. (eds.), *War, Citizenship, Territory*, New York (NY): Routledge, pp.119–146.
Corn, J. and Horrigan, B. (1984). *Yesterday's Tomorrow: Past Visions of the American Future*. New York (NY): Summit books.
Cornell, T.J. (2000). The city-states in Latium. In: Hansen, M. (ed.), *A Comparative Study of Thirty City-State Cultures*. Copenhagen: Kgl. Danske Videnskabernes Selskab, pp.209–228.

Corporation of London (1993a). *The Way Ahead – Traffic and the Environment, Draft Consultation Paper*. London: Corporation of London.
Corporation of London (1993b). *Security Initiatives, Draft Consultation Paper*. London: Corporation of London.
Cosgrove, D. and Daniels, S. (1988). *The Iconography of Landscape*. Cambridge: Cambridge University Press.
Counter Terrorism Preparedness Network (CTPN) (2019a). *Anti-Radicalisation Report*. London: London Resilience.
Counter Terrorism Preparedness Network (CTPN) (2019b). *Report of Strategic Coordination*. CTPN, London.
Coward, M. (2006a). Against anthropocentrism: the destruction of the built environment as a distinct form of political violence. *Review of International Studies*, 32, pp.419–437.
Coward, M. (2006b). International relations in the post-globalisation era. *Politics*, 26(1), pp.54–61.
Coward, M. (2008). *Urbicide: The Politics of Urban Destruction*. Oxford: Routledge.
Cresswell, T. (2006). *On the Move: Mobility in the Modern West*. London: Routledge.
Croft, S. (2006). *Culture, Crisis and America's War on Terror*. Cambridge: Cambridge University Press.
Croft, S. (2012). Constructing ontological insecurity: the insecuritization of Britain's muslims. *Contemporary Security Policy*, 33(2), pp.219–235.
Cross, N. (2008). *Designerly Ways of Knowing*. Basel: Birkhauser.
Cuff, D. (2003). Immanent domain: pervasive computing and public realm. *Journal of Architectural Education*, 57(1), pp.43–49.
Dalgaard-Nielsen, A., Laisen, J. and Wandorf, C. (2016). Visible counter-terrorism measures in urban spaces – fear-inducing or not? *Terrorism and Political Violence*, 28(4), pp.692–712.
Daniels, S. (1993). *Fields of Vision: Landscape Imagery and National Identity in England and the United States*. Princeton (NJ): Princeton University Press.
Davies, S. (1996a). *Big Brother – Britain's Web of Surveillance and the New Technological Order*. London: Pan Books.
Davies, S. (1996b). The case against: CCTV should not be introduced. *International Journal of Risk, Security and Crime Prevention*, 1(4), pp.327–331.
Davis, M. (1990). *City of Quartz – Excavating the Future of Los Angeles*. London: Verso.
Davis, M. (1998). *Ecology of Fear: Los Angeles and the Imagination of Disaster*. New York (NY): Metropolitan Books.
Davis, M. (2007). *Buda's Wagon: A Brief History of the Car Bomb*. London: Verso.
De Cauter, L. (2004). *The Capsular Civilization. On the City in the Age of Fear*. Rotterdam: NAi Publishers.
de Certeau, M. (1984). *The Practice of Everyday Life*. Berkeley: University of California.
De Goede, M. and Randalls, S. (2009). Precaution, preemption: arts and technologies of the actionable future. *Environment and Planning D: Society and Space*, 27(5), pp.859–878.
De la Croix, H. (1963). The literature on fortification in renaissance Italy. *Technology and Culture*, 4(1), pp.30–50.
Dean, M. (1999). *Governmentality: Power and Rule in Modern Society*. Thousand Oaks (CA): Sage.

Dean, M. (2007). *Governing Societies: Political Perspectives on Domestic and International Rule*. Milton Keynes: Open University Press.
Dear, M. (1999). *The Postmodern Urban Condition*. Oxford: Blackwell.
Dear, M. and Flusty, S. (1998). Postmodern urbanism. *Annals of the Association of American Geographers*, 88(1), pp.50–72.
Decker, S., Greene, J., Webb, V, Rojeck, J., McDevitt, J., Bynum, T., Varano, S. and Manning, P. (2005). Safety and security at special events: the case of the Salt Lake City Olympic Games. *Security Journal*, 18(4), pp.65–75.
DeLanda, M. (1991). *War in the Age of Intelligent Machines*. New York (NY): Zone.
Deleuze, G. (1992). Postscript on the societies of control. *October*, 59, pp.3–7.
Denman, D. (2020). On fortification: military architecture, geometric power, and defensive design. *Security Dialogue*, 51(2–3), pp.231–247.
Department of Homeland Security (DHS) (2011a). *Secretary Napolitano announces, 'If you see something, say something,' campaign at Super Bowl XLV*. Office of the Press Secretary, January 31. Available at www.dhs.gov/ynews/releases/pr_1296509083464.shtm. Accessed April 12, 2011.
Department of Homeland Security (DHS) (2011b). *If You See Something, Say Something Campaign: Report Suspicious Activity to Local Law Enforcement or Call 911*, March 29. Available at www.dhs.gov/files/reportincidents/see-something-say-something.shtm. Accessed April 14, 2011.
Department of Homeland Security (DHS) (2012). Super Bowl XLVI: "If You See Something, Say Something", Available at www.dhs.gov/blog/2012/02/02/super-bowl-xlvi-if-you-see-something-say-something. Accessed March 6, 2006.
Department of Justice (1995). *Vulnerability Assessment of Federal Facilities*. Washington (DC): Department of Justice, June 28.
Devroe, E., Edwards, A. and Ponsaers, P. (eds.) (2017). *Policing European Metropolises: The Politics of Security in City-Regions* London: Routledge.
Dillon, M. (1994). *25 Years of Terror – The Ira's War Against The British*. London: Bantam Books.
Dillon, M. (2002). Network society, network-centric warfare and the state of emergency. *Theory Culture & Society*, 19(4), pp.71–79.
Dillon, M. and Reid, J. (2001). Global liberal governance: biopolitics, security and war. *Millennium*, 30(1), pp.41–66.
Doherty, F., Hurwitz, K., Massimino, E., McClintock, M., Purohit, R., Smith, C. and Thornton, R. (2005). *Imbalance of Powers: How Changes to U.S. Law and Policy Since 9-11 Erode Human Rights and Civil Liberties*. Washington (DC): Lawyers Committee for Human Rights.
Domosh, M. (1989). A method for interpreting landscape: a case study of the New York World Building. *Area*, 21, pp.347–355.
Duffield, M. (2012). Challenging environments: danger, resilience and the aid industry. *Security Dialogue*,43(5), pp.475–492.
Duineveld, M., Van Assche, K. and Beunen, R. (2017). Re-conceptualising political landscapes after the material turn: a typology of material events. *Landscape Research*, 42(4), pp.375–384.
Duncan, J. (1995). Landscape geography, 1993–1994. *Progress in Human Geography*, 19(3), pp.414–422.
Duncan, J. and Duncan, N. (2004). *Landscapes of Privilege: The Politics of the Aesthetic in an American Suburb*. London: Routledge.

Durodie, B. (2005). Terrorism and community resilience: a UK perspective. *Chatham House – NSC Briefing Paper 05/01*, pp.4–5.
Edwards, P. (2016). Closure through resilience: the case of prevent. *Studies in Conflict and Terrorism,* 39(4), pp.292–307.
Ek, R. (2000). A revolution in military geopolitics? *Political Geography*, 19, pp.841–874.
Elden, S. (2007). Governmentality, calculation, territory. *Environment and Planning D: Society and Space*, 25(3), pp.562–580.
Elden, S. (2010). Land, terrain, territory. *Progress in Human Geography* 34(6), pp.799–817.
Elden, S. (2013). *The Birth of Territory*. Chicago (IL): University of Chicago Press.
Ellin, N. (1996). *Postmodern Urbanism*. Oxford: Blackwell.
Ellin, N. (ed.) (1997). *Architecture of Fear*. Princeton (NJ): Architectural Press.
Elmer, G. and Opel, A. (2006). Surviving the inevitable future: preemption in the age of faulty intelligence. *Cultural Studies*, 20(4/5), pp.447–492.
Ericson, R. (2008). The state of preemption: In: Amoore, L. and De Goede, M. (eds.), *Risk and the War on Terror*. London: Routledge, pp.57–76.
Eriksen, E.G. (1980). *The Territorial Experience: Human Ecology as Symbolic Interaction*, University of Texas Press, Austin (TX).
Eriksson, J. (ed.) (2001). *Threat Politics: New Perspectives on Security, Risk and Crisis Management*. Aldershot: Ashgate.
Erlenbusch-Anderson, V. (2018). *Genealogies of Terrorism: Revolution, State Violence, Empire*. New York (NY): Columbia University Press.
European Council (2003). *European Security Strategy: A Secure Europe in a Better World*. Brussels: European Council.
European Council (2004). *Declaration on Combating Terrorism*. Brussels: European Council (25 March).
European Union (2001). *Joint Declaration by the Heads of States and Government of the European Union*. Brussels: European Union, September 14, DOC/01/12.
Evans, M. (2007). *City Without Joy: Urban Military Operations into the 21st Century. Australian Defence College Occasional Paper No. 2*. Canberra: Department of Defence.
Farish, M. (2004). Another anxious urbanism: simulating defense and disaster in cold War America. In: Graham, S. (ed.), *Cites War and Terrorism: Towards an Urban Geopolitics*. Oxford: Blackwell, pp.93–109.
Farish, M. (2007). Panic, civility, and the homeland. In: Cowen, D. and Gilbert, E (eds.), *War, Citizenship, Territory*, New York (NY): Routledge, pp.97–118.
FBI (1999). *Terrorism in 1999, A Special 30 Years of Terrorism – A Special Retrospective Edition*. Washington (DC): Department of Justice
FBI (2006). *The Radicalization Process: From Conversion to Jihad*. Washington (DC): FBI Counter-terrorism Division, May.
FBI (2010). Department of Homeland Security-FBI Warning: Terrorist Use of Vehicle Ramming Tactics. December 13. Available at https://info.publicintelligence.net/DHS-TerroristRamming.pdf. Accessed June 4, 2017.
Federal Emergency Management Authority (FEMA) (2007). *Site and Urban Design for Security: Guidance Against Potential Terrorist Attacks*. Washington (DC): FEMA.
Fedosuk, Y.A. (2009). *Moscow in Sadovoye Rings*. Moscow: AST Publishing House.
Flaschsbart, P.G. (1969). Urban territorial behaviour. *Journal of the American Institute of Planning*, 35, pp.412–416.

Floridis, G. (2004). Security for the 2004 Athens Olympic games *Mediterranean Quarterly*, 15(2), pp.1–5, p4.
Flusty, S. (1994). *Building Paranoia – the Proliferation of Interdictory Space and the Erosion of Spatial Justice.* Los Angeles (CA): Los Angeles Forum for Architecture and Urban Design, p.11.
Flynn, S. (2007). *The Edge of Disaster: Rebuilding a Resilient Nation.* New York (NY): Random House.
Forbes, R.J. (1965). *Irrigation and Power.* Leiden: Bull.
Foucault, M. (1976/2003). *Society Must Be Defended: Lectures at the College de France,* (trans. Macey, D.), New York (NY): Picador.
Foucault, M. (1977). *Discipline and Punish: The Birth of The Prison.* New York (NY): Pantheon.
Foucault, M. (1980). The confession of the flesh. In: Gordon, C (ed.), *Power/Knowledge: Selected Interviews and Other Writings 1972–1977.* New York (NY): Pantheon, pp.194–228.
Foucault, M. (2007). *Security, Territory, Population, Lectures at the Collège de France, 1977-78.* London: Palgrave Macmillan.
France Diplomacy (2015). Paris Attacks – Statement by President François Hollande, November 14. Available at www.diplomatie.gouv.fr/en/french-foreign-policy/security-disarmament-and-non-proliferation/news/news-about-defence-and-security/article/paris-attacks-statement-by-president-francois-hollande. Accessed November 15, 2015.
Franks, J. (2009). Rethinking the roots of terrorism: beyond orthodox terrorism theory – a critical research agenda. *Global Society*, 23:2, pp.153–176.
Freedman, L. (2008). *A Choice of Enemies: America Confronts the Middle East.* New York (NY): Public Affairs.
Fregonese, S. (2012). Beyond the "weak state": hybrid sovereignties in Beirut. *Environment and Planning D: Society and Space*, 30(4), pp.655–674.
Fregonese, S. (2017). Affective atmospheres, urban geopolitics and conflict (de)escalation in Beirut. *Political Geography*, 61, pp.1–10.
Freidman, T. (1983). Living with the violence of Beirut. *New York Times*, July 17, Section 6, p.12.
Friedman, T. (1984). America's failure in Lebanon, *New York Times*, April 8, Section 6, p.32.
Friedman, T. (1989). *From Beirut to Jerusalem.* New York (NY): Ferrar Strus.
Fumagalli, V. (1994). *Landscapes of Fear: Perceptions of Nature and the City in the Middle Ages* (Trans. by Mitchell, S.), Cambridge: Polity Press.
Furedi, F. (2006). *Culture of Fear Revisited*, 4th ed. Trowbridge: Continuum.
Fussey, P. (2007). Observing potentiality in the global city: surveillance and counter-terrorism in London. *International Criminal Justice Review*, 17(3), pp.171–192.
Fussey, P. (2012). Eastern promise? East London transformations and the state of surveillance. *Information Polity*, 17(1), pp.21–34.
Fussey, P. (2013). Contested topologies of UK counter-terrorist surveillance: the rise and fall of project champion. *Critical Studies on Terrorism*, 6(3), pp.351–370.
Fussey, P. (2015). Command, control and contestation: negotiating security at the London 2012 Olympics. *Geographical Journal*, 181(3), pp.212–223.
Fussey, P. and Coaffee, J. (2012a). Balancing local and global security leitmotifs: counter-terrorism and the spectacle of mega-sport events. *International Review of Sociology of Sport*, 47(3), pp.268–285.

Fussey, P. and Coaffee, J. (2012b). Urban spaces of surveillance, *International Handbook of Surveillance Studies*, Ball, K., Haggerty, K. and Lyon, D. (eds.), London: Routledge, pp.201–208.

Fussey, P., Coaffee, J., Armstrong, G. and Hobbs, R. (2011). *Sustaining and Securing the Olympic City: Reconfiguring London for 2012 and Beyond.* Farnham: Ashgate.

Fussey, P., Coaffee J., Armstrong, G. and Hobbs, R. (2012). The regeneration games: purity and security in the Olympic city. *British Journal of Sociology*, 63, pp.260–284.

Fussey P. and Murray, D. (2019). Independent Report on the London Metropolitan Police Service's Trial of Live Facial Recognition Technology, July. Available at www.hrbdt.ac.uk/download/independent-report-on-the-london-metropolitan-police-services-trial-of-live-facial-recognition-technology/. Accessed August 1, 2019.

Fussey, P. and Murray, D. (2020). Policing uses of live facial recognition in the United Kingdom. In: Kak, A. (ed.), *Regulating Biometrics: Global Approaches and Urgent Questions*. AI Now Institute, pp.78–85.

Fyfe, N.R and Bannister, J. (1996). City watching: close circuit television surveillance in public spaces. *Area*, 28(1), pp.37–46.

Ganor, B. (2019). Artificial or human: a new era of counter-terrorism intelligence? *Studies in Conflict & Terrorism*, 42(1–2), 1–20.

Gardner, D. (2009). *Risk: The Science and Politics of Fear.* London: Virgin Books.

Garland, D. (1996). The limits of the sovereign state: Strategies of crime control in contemporary society. *British Journal of Criminology*, 36(4), pp.445–471.

Gates, K. (2006). Identifying the 9/11 'faces of terror'. *Cultural Studies*, 20(4-5), pp.417–440,

Gates, K. (2011). *Our Biometric Future: Facial Recognition Technology and the Culture of Surveillance.* New York (NY): NYU Press.

General Services Administration (GSA) (1997). *Security Criteria and Standards.* Washington (DC): General Services Administration.

General Services Administration (GSA) (1999a). *Balancing Security and Openness: A Thematic Summary of a Symposium on Security and the Design of Public Buildings.* Washington (DC): General Services Administration.

General Services Administration (GSA) (1999b). *Urban Design Guidelines for Physical Perimeter Entrance Security: An Overlay to the Master Plan for the Federal Triangle.* Washington (DC): General Services Administration.

Ghertner, D. (2010). Calculating without numbers: aesthetic governmentality in Delhi's slums. *Economy and Society*, 39(2), pp.185–217.

Giedion, S. (1941). *Space, Time and Architecture.* Cambridge: Harvard University Press.

Gillespie, M. and O'Loughlin, B. (2009). News media, threats and insecurities: an ethnographic approach. *Cambridge Review of International Affairs*, 22(4), pp.667–685.

Glancey, J. (2009). The architecture of diplomacy, *The Guardian*, January 9. Available at www.theguardian.com/artanddesign/2009/jan/09/embassy-iraq-us-architecture. Accessed December 5, 2009.

Gold, R. (1970). Urban violence and contemporary defensive cities. *Journal of the American Institute of Planning*, 36, pp.146–159.

Gold, J.R. (1982). Territoriality and human spatial behaviour. *Progress in Human Geography*, 6, pp.44–67.

Gold, J.R. and Revill, G. (1999). Landscapes of defence. *Landscape Research*, 24(3), pp.229–239.

Goldenfein, J. and Mann, M. (2020). Australian identity-matching services bill. In: Kak, A. (ed.), *Regulating Biometrics: Global Approaches and Urgent Questions*. AI Now Institute, September 1. Available at https://ainowinstitute.org/regulatingbiometrics.html, pp.44–51.
Graham, S. (1999). The eyes have it – CCTV as the fifth utility. *Town and Country Planning*, 68(10), pp.312–315.
Graham, S. (2001). In a moment: on global mobilities and the terrorised city. *City*, 5(3), pp.411–415.
Graham, S. (2002a). Clean territory': urbicide in the West Bank. *Open Democracy*. Available at www.opendemocracy.net/en/article_241jsp/. Accessed March 4, 2003.
Graham, S. (2002b). Special collection: reflections on Cities. September 11th and the 'war on terrorism' – one year on. *International Journal of Urban and Regional Research*, 26(3), pp.589–590.
Graham, S. (2004). *Cities, War and Terrorism: Towards an Urban Geopolitics*. Oxford: Blackwell.
Graham, S. (2006). Cities and the "War on Terror". *International Journal of Urban and Regional Research*, 30(2), pp.255–276.
Graham, S. (2010). *Cities Under Siege: The New Military Urbanism*. London: Verso.
Graham, S. and Marvin, S. (2001). *Splintering Urbanism – Networked Infrastructures, Technological Mobilities and the Urban Condition*. London: Routledge.
Graham, S. and Wood, D. (2003). Digitizing surveillance: categorization, space, inequality. *Critical Social Policy*, 23(2), pp.227–248.
Grant, M. (2010). *After the Bomb: Civil Defence and Nuclear War in Britain*. Basingstoke: Palgrave.
Greater London Authority (2020). *London City Resilience Strategy*. London: GLA.
Greene, A. (2018). *Permanent States of Emergency and the Rule of Law: Constitutions in an Age of Crisis*. London: Bloomsbury.
Greenemeier, L. (2011). The Apple of Its Eye: Security and Surveillance Pervades Post-9/11 New York City. *Scientific American*, September 9. Available at www.scientificamerican.com/article/post-911-nyc-video-surveillance/. Accessed October 6, 2013.
Gregory, F. (2007). UK Draft Civil Contingencies Bill 2003 and the subsequent act: building block for homeland security? In: Wilkinson, P. (ed.), *Homeland Security: Future Preparations for Terrorist Attack since 9/11*. London: Routledge, pp.333–342.
Gregory, D. (2010). War and peace. *Transactions of the Institute of British Geographers*, 35(2), pp.154–186.
Gregory, D. and Pred, A. (eds.) (2007). *Violent Geographies*. London: Routledge.
Grosskopf, K. (2006). Evaluating the societal response to antiterrorism measures. *Journal of Homeland Security and Emergency Management*, 3(2), pp.1–9.
Grove, K. (2018). *Resilience*. London: Routledge.
Guillaume, X, and Huysmans, J. (eds.) (2013). *Citizenship and Security: The Constitution of Political Being*. London: Routledge.
Gunning, J. (2007). A case for critical terrorism studies? *Government and Opposition*, 42(3), pp.363–393.
Hall, P. (2001). The unthinkable event that may doom high-rise. *Regeneration and Renewal*, September 21, p.14.
Hansen, M.H. (ed.) (2000). *A Comparative Study of Thirty City-State Cultures 9*. Copenhagen: Kgl. Danske Videnskabernes Selskab.

Hardt, M. and Negri A. (2002). *Empire*. Cambridge (MA): Harvard University Press.
Harker, C. (2014). The only way is up? Ordinary topologies of Ramallah: ordinary topologies of Ramallah. *International Journal of Urban and Regional Research*, 38(1), pp.318–335.
Harris, T. (2016). An Independent Review of London's Preparedness to Respond to a Major Terrorist Incident. Available at www.london.gov.uk/sites/default/files/londons_preparedness_to_respond_to_a_major_terrorist_incident_-_independent_review_oct_2016.pdf. Accessed December 3, 2019.
Harvey, D. (1990). *The Condition of Postmodernity: an Enquiry into the Origins of Cultural Change*. Oxford: Blackwell.
Hawkins, Harriet and Straughan, Elizabeth (eds.) (2016). *Geographical Aesthetics: Imagining Space, Staging Encounters*. London: Routledge.
Haywood, K.J. (2004). *City Limits: Crime, Consumer Culture and the Urban Experience*. London: Glasshouse Press.
Heath-Kelly, C. (2017). The geography of pre-criminal space: epidemiological imaginations of radicalisation risk in the UK Prevent Strategy, 2007–2017. *Critical Studies on Terrorism,* 10(2), pp.297–319.
Heath-Kelly, C. and Strausz, E. (2019). The banality of counter-terrorism "after, after 9/11"? Perspectives on the prevent duty from the UK health care sector. *Critical Studies on Terrorism*, 12:1, pp.89–109,
Heller, A. (2003). BASIS counters airborne bioterrorism. *Science and Technology Review*, October, pp.6–8.
Herbert, S. (1997). *Policing Space: Territoriality and the Los Angeles Police Department*. Minneapolis (MN): University of Minnesota Press.
Hewitt, C. (2003). *Understanding Terrorism in America: from the Klan to al Qaeda*. London: Routledge.
Hinds, A., and Vlachou, E. (2007). Fortress Olympics: counting the cost of major event security. *Janes' Intelligence Review*, 19(5), pp.20–26.
Hinman, E. and Hammond D.J. (1997). *Lessons from the Oklahoma City Bombing: Defensive Design Techniques*. Reston (VA): American Society of Civil Engineers.
Hinman, E. and Levy, M. (1993). Protecting buildings against terrorism. In: *US Fire Administration/Technical Report Series USFA-TR-076/February 1993: The World Trade Center Bombing: Report and Analysis*. New York: New York City, pp.109–112.
HM Government (2021). *Global Britain in a Competitive Age The Integrated Review of Security, Defence, Development and Foreign Policy*. London: TSO
HM Government (2006). *Countering International Terrorism: The United Kingdom's Strategy*, CM 688. London: HMSO.
HM Government (2008). *Preventing Violent Extremism: A Strategy for Delivery*. London: The Stationery Office.
HM Government (2011). *CONTEST: The United Kingdom Strategy for Countering Terrorism*. London: TSO.
HM Government (2015). *Prevent Duty Guidance: For England and Wales*. London: TSO.
Hobbes, T. (1651[2017]). *Leviathan*. London: Penguin Classics.
Hoffman, B. (1998). *Inside Terrorism*. London: Indigo.
Hoffman, B. (1999). Terrorism trends and prospects. In: Lesser, I., Hoffman, B., Arquilla, J., Ronfeldt, D. and Zanaini, M (eds.), *Countering the New Terrorism*. Santa Monica (CA): Rand Corporation, pp.7–35.
Hollander, J.B. and Whitfield, C. (2005). The appearance of security zones in US cities after 9/11. *Property Management*, 23(4), pp.244–256.

Home Office (2009). *London 2012 Olympic and Paralympic Safety and Security Strategy*. London: TSO.
Home Office (2010a). *Working Together to Protect Crowded Places*. London: Home Office.
Home Office (2010b). *Crowded Places: The Planning System and Counter-Terrorism*. London: Home Office.
Home Office (2010c). *Protecting Crowded Places: Design and Technical Issues*. London: Home Office.
Home Office (2011). *Prevent Strategy*. London: Home Office.
Home Office (2015). *Revised Prevent Duty Guidance for England and Wales*. London: HM Government.
House of Commons (2010). *Communities and Local Government Committee: Preventing Violent Extremism, Sixth Report of Session 2009–10*. March 6. London: HMSO.
Howell, S. and Shryock, A. (2003). Cracking down on Diaspora: Arab Detroit and America's 'War on Terror'. *Anthropology Quarterly*, 76, pp.443–462.
Huber, P. and Mills M. (2002). How technology will defeat terrorism. *City Journal*, 12(1), pp.24–34.
Huszti-Orbán, K. and Ní Aoláin, F. (2020). Use of Biometric Data to Identify Terrorists. Available at www.law.umn.edu/sites/law.umn.edu/files/2020/07/21/hrc-biometrics-report-july2020.pdf. Accessed September 5, 2020.
Huysmans, J. (2014). *Security Unbound: Enacting Democratic Limits*. London: Routledge.
Information Commissioner's Office (ICO) (2019). The Use of Live Facial Recognition Technology by Law Enforcement in Public Places. Available at https://ico.org.uk/media/about-the-ico/documents/2616184/live-frt-law-enforcement-opinion-20191031.pdf. Accessed December 18, 2019.
Introna, L. and Wood, D. (2004). Picturing algorithmic surveillance: the politics of facial recognition systems. *Surveillance and Society*, 2(2/3), pp.177–198.
Isakjee, A. and Allen, C. (2013). A catastrophic lack of inquisitiveness: A critical study of the impact and narrative of the Project Champion surveillance project in Birmingham. *Ethnicities* 13(6), pp.751–770.
Jackson, P. (2000). Rematerializing social and cultural geography. *Social and Cultural Geography*, 1, pp.9–14.
Jackson, R. (2005). *Writing the War on Terror: Language, Politics and Counter-Terrorism*. Manchester: Manchester University Press.
Jackson, R. (2007a). An analysis of EU counter-terrorism discourse post-September 11. *Cambridge Review of International Affairs*, 20(2), pp.233–247.
Jackson, R. (2007b). Introduction: the case for critical terrorism studies. *European Political Sciences*, 6, pp.225–227.
Jackson, R. (2009). Knowledge, power and politics in the study of political terrorism. In: Jackson, R., Smyth, M. and. Gunning, J. (eds.), *Critical Terrorism Studies: a New Research Agenda*. London: Routledge, pp.66–84.
Jacobs, J. (1961). *The Death and Life of Great American Cities*. New York (NY): Random House.
Janz, B. (2008). The terror of place: anxieties of place and the cultural narrative of terrorism. *Ethics, Place and Environment*, 11(2), pp.191–203;
Jarman, N. (1993). Intersecting Belfast. In: Bender B. (ed.), *Landscape—Politics and Perspectives*. Oxford: Berg, pp.107–138.

Jarvis, L. and Lister, M. (2013). Vernacular securities and their study: A qualitative analysis and research agenda. *International Relations,* 27(2), pp.158–179.

Jeffery, C. Ray (1971). *Crime Prevention through Environmental Design.* Beverly Hills (CA): Sage.

Jenkins, S. (2006). Not totalitarianism – but guilty of creeping authoritarianism. *The Guardian*, April 26, p.19.

Jones, M.C. and Lowrey, K.J. (1995). Street barriers in American cities. *Urban Geography,* 16(2), pp.112–122.

Joseph, J. and Juncos, A. (2019). Resilience as an emergent European Project? The EU's place in the resilience turn. 2019 *Journal of Common Market Studies*, 57(5), pp.995–1012.

Kackman, M. (2005). *Citizen Spy: Television, Espionage, and Cold War Culture.* Minneapolis (MN): University of Minnesota Press.

Kak, A. (ed.) (2020). Regulating Biometrics: Global Approaches and Urgent Questions. AI NowInstitute, September 1. Available at https://ainowinstitute.org/regulatingbiometrics.html. Accessed September 2, 2020.

Kaplan, J. (2006). Islamaphobia in America? September 11 and Islamophobic hate crime. *Terrorism and Political Violence,* 18(1), pp.1–33.

Kaplan, J. (2007). The fifth wave: the new tribalism? *Terrorism and Political Violence,* 19(4), pp.545–570.

Katz, C. (2007). Banal terrorism: spatial fetishism and everyday insecurity. In: Gregory, D. and Pred, A. (eds.), *Violent Geographies: Fear, Terror, and Political Violence.* London: Routledge, pp.349–361.

Kaunert, C. and Leonard, S. (2019). The collective securitisation of terrorism in the European Union. *West European Politics*, 42(2), pp.261–277.

Keating, J. (2014). Why terrorists use vehicles as weapons. Slate, November 5. Available at https://slate.com/news-and-politics/2014/11/car-attack-in-jerusalem-why-are-terrorists-ramming-vehicles-into-crowds-of-people.html. Accessed November 6, 2014.

Keegan, J. (1993). *A History of Warfare.* London: Hutchinson.

Kelly, O. (1994a). By all means necessary. *Police Review*, April 15, pp.14–16.

Kelly, O. (1994b). The IRA threat to the City of London. *Policing*, 10. pp.1–2.

Khalidi, R (1986). *Under Siege: PLO Decision Making During the 1982 War*. New York (NY): Columbia University Press.

Kitchin, R. (2020). Civil liberties or public health, or civil liberties and public health? Using surveillance technologies to tackle the spread of COVID-19. *Space and Polity*, DOI: 10.1080/13562576.2020.1770587.

Klauser, F. (2013). Spatialities of security and surveillance: managing spaces, separations and circulations at sport mega events. *Geoforum*, 49, pp.289–298.

Knox, P, (1989). *Urban Social Geography – An Introduction.* London: Longman Group.

Kraftl, P. (2010). Geographies of architecture: the multiple lives of buildings. *Geography Compass*, 4(5), pp.402–415.

Krause, K. and Williams, M.C. (eds.) (1997). *Critical Security Studies: Concepts and Cases.* Minneapolis (MN): University of Minnesota Press.

Krohe, J. (1993). The man with a plan. Chicago Reader, June 17. Available at www.chicagoreader.com/chicago/the-man-with-the-plan/Content?oid=882168. Accessed June 3, 2018.

Kundnani, A. (2009). *Spooked: How Not to Prevent Violent Extremism.* London: Institute of Race Relations.

Kundnani, A. and Hayes, B. (2018). *The Globalisation of Countering Violent Extremism Policies. Undermining Human Rights, Instrumentalising Civil Society.* Societal Security Network.
Kunstler, J. and Salingaros, N.A. (2001). The end of tall buildings. *PLANetizen*, September 17. Available at www.planetizen.com/. Accessed February 12, 2002.
Lance, P. (2004). *1000 Years for Revenge: International Terrorism and the FBI – the Untold Story.* New York (NY): Regan Books.
Lanciani, R. (1897). *The Ruins and Excavations of Ancient Rome.* Houghton: Mifflin and Company.
Laqueur, W. (1996). Post-modern terrorism. *Foreign Affairs*, 75(5), pp.24–36.
Laqueur, W. (1999). *The New Terrorism: Fanaticism and the Arms of Mass Destruction.* Oxford: Oxford University Press.
Laqueur, W. (2004). *No End to war: Terrorism in the Twenty-First Century.* New York (NY): Continuum.
Latour, B. (1992). Where are the missing masses? – The sociology of a few mundane artefacts. In: Bijker, W.E. and Law, J. (eds.), *Shaping Technology/Building Society.* Cambridge (MA): MIT Press, pp.225–258.
Laurie, P. (1979). *Beneath the City Streets.* London: HarperCollins.
Law, J. and Mol, A. (1995). Notes on materiality and sociality. *The Sociological Review*, 43, pp.274–294.
Lees, L. (1997). Ageographia, heterotopia, and Vancouver's new public library. *Environment and Planning D: Society and Space*, 15, pp.321–347.
Lefebvre, H. (1991 [1974]). *The Production of Space.* Oxford: Blackwell.
Lemke, T. (2002). Foucault, governmentality, and critique. *Rethinking Marxism*, 14(3), pp.49–64.
Lentzos, F and Rose, N (2009). Governing insecurity: contingency planning, protection, resilience. *Economy and Society*, 38(2), pp.230–254.
Lesser, I., Hoffman, B., Arquilla, J., Ronfedt, D., Zanini, M. and Jenkins, M. (1999). *Countering the New Terrorism.* Santa Monica (CA): Rand Corporation.
Levine, E.S. and Tisch, J.S. (2014). Analytics in action at the New York City Police Department's Counter-terrorism Bureau. *Military Operations Research*, 19(4), pp.5–14.
Levine, E.S., Tisch, J., Tasso, A. and Joy, M. (2017). The New York City Police Department's Domain Awareness System. *Interfaces*, 47(1), pp.70–84.
Levy, M. and Salandori, M. (1992). *Why Buildings Fall Down: Why Structures Fail.* New York (NY): W.W. Norton and Company.
Leydenfrsot, A. (1950). Cities vs A bombs. *Life Magazine*, December18, pp.76–80.
Lianos, M. and Douglas, M. (2000). Dangerization and the end of deviance: the institutional environment. *British Journal of Criminology*, 40, pp.261–278.
Light, J. (2002). Urban security from warfare to welfare. *International Journal of Urban and Regional Research*, 26(3), pp.607–613.
Linenthal, E. (2003). *The Unfinished Bombing: Oklahoma City in American Memory.* Oxford: Oxford University Press.
Loeffler, J. (1998). *The Architecture of Diplomacy: Building America's Embassies* Princeton (NJ): Princeton Architectural Press.
Loeffler, J. (2009). Fortress America. Foreign Policy, October 12. Available at https://foreignpolicy.com/2009/10/12/fortress-america-3/. Accessed December 5, 2018.
London Prepared (2006). London Exercises', Available at www.londonprepared.gov.uk/londonsplans/londonexercises/. Accessed December 2, 2006.

Lowenthal, D. (1992). The death of the future. In: Wallman, S. (ed.), *Contemporary Futures: Perspectives from Social Anthropology*. London: Routledge, pp.23–35.

Lustgarten, L. and Leigh, I. (1994). *In from the Cold: National Security and Parliamentary Democracy*. Oxford: Clarendon Press.

Lyon, D. (1994). *The Electronic Eye – The Rise of Surveillance Society*. Cambridge: Polity Press.

Lyon, D. (2002). Everyday surveillance: personal data and social classifications. *Information, Communication & Society*, 5(2), pp.242–257.

Lyon D. (2003). *Surveillance after September 11*. Cambridge: Polity Press.

Maier, C. (2016). *Once Within Borders: Territories of Power, Wealth, and Belonging Since 1500*. Cambridge (MA): Harvard University Press.

Malik, N. (2020). Pandemic preparedness: a U.K. perspective on overlaps with countering terrorism, *CTC Sentinel*, 13(6), pp.49–54.

Marcuse, P. (1993). What's so new about divided cities. *International Journal of Urban and Regional Research*, 17, pp.353–365.

Marcuse, P. (2001). Reflections on the events. *City*, 5(3), pp.394–397.

Marcuse, P. (2002a). Afterword. In: Marcuse P. and van Kempen, R. (eds.), *Of States and Cities: The Partitioning of Urban Space*. Oxford: Oxford University Press, pp.269–282.

Marcuse, P. (2002b). Urban form and globalization after September 11th: the view from New York. *International Journal of Urban and Regional Research*, 26(3), pp.596–606.

Marcuse, P. (2006). Security or safety in cities? The threat of terrorism after 9/11. *International Journal of Urban and Regional Research*, 30(4), pp.919–929.

Marda, V. (2020). Papering over the cracks: on privacy versus health. In: Taylor, L. Martin, A. Sharma, G. and Jameson, S. (eds.), *Data Justice and COVID-19: Global Perspectives*. London: Meatspace Press, pp.29–33.

Marvin J., Montefrio, F., Lee, X. and Lim, E. (2020). *Aesthetic Politics and Community Gardens in Singapore. Urban Geography*, DOI: 10.1080/02723638.2020.1788304.

Massumi, B. (ed.) (1993). *The Everyday Politics of Fear*. Minneapolis (MN): University of Minnesota Press.

Massumi, B. (2005). Fear (the spectrum said). *Positions*, 13:1, pp.31–48.

McCulloch, J. and Pickering, S. (2009). Pre-crime and counter-terrorism: imagining future crime in the 'War on Terror. *British Journal of Criminology*, 49, pp.628–645.

McDonald, M. (2005). Constructing insecurity: Australian security discourse and policy post-2001. *International Relations*, 19(3), pp.297–320.

McDonald, M. (2008). Securitization and the construction of security. *European Journal of International Relations*, 14(4), pp.563–587.

McKendrick, K. (2019). *Artificial Intelligence Prediction and Counter-terrorism*, London: Chatham House

Meijer, A. and Wessels, M. (2019). Predictive policing: review of benefits and drawbacks. *International Journal of Public Administration*, 42(12), pp.1031–1039.

Metropolitan Police (2020). Live Facial Recognition. Available at www.met.police.uk/advice/advice-and-information/facial-recognition/live-facial-recognition/. Accessed January 29.

Meyer C. (2009). International terrorism as a force of homogenization? A constructivist approach to understanding cross-national threat perceptions and responses. *Cambridge Review of International Affairs*, 22(4), pp.647–666.

Michel, T. and Richards, A. (2009). False dawns or new horizons? Further issues and challenges for critical terrorism studies. *Critical Studies on Terrorism*, 2(3), pp.399–413.
Micieli-Voutsinas, J. and Person, A. (eds.) (2021). *Affective Architectures: More-Than-Representational Geographies of Heritage*. London: Routledge.
Microsoft (2010). E•SPONDER and Microsoft Move Public Safety into the 21st Century. Available at https://news.microsoft.com/2010/01/26/e•sponder-and-microsoft-move-public-safety-into-the-21st-century/. Accessed March 6, 2011.
Miller, D. (1998). *Material Cultures: Why Some Things Matter*. Chicago (IL): University of Chicago Press.
Miller, V., and Hayward, K.J. (2018). 'I did my bit': terrorism, tarde and the vehicle ramming attack as an imitative event. *The British Journal of Criminology*, 59(1), pp.1–23.
Mills, M. (2004). The Security-Industrial Complex. *Forbes*. Available at www.forbes.com/forbes/2004/1129/044.html#6024d7b24dd9. Accessed September 5, 2018.
Minca, C. (2006). Giorgio Agamben and the New Biopolitical Nomos. *Geografiska Annaler B*, 88(4), pp. 387–403.
Minnaar, A. (2006). Crime Prevention/Crime Control Surveillance: Public Closed Circuit Television (CCTV) in South African Central Business Districts (CBDs). *Paper Presented at the Crime, Justice and Surveillance Conference, Sheffield, April 5–6.*
Misselwitz, P. and Weizman, E. (2003). Military operations as urban planning. In: Franke, A. (ed.), *Territories*. Berlin: KW Institute for Contemporary Art, pp.272–285.
Mitchell, K. (2010). Ungoverned space: global security and the geopolitics of broken windows *Political Geography*, 29, pp.289–297.
Mlakar, P., Corley, W., Mete A. and Thornton, C. (1998). The Oklahoma City bombing: analysis of blast damage to the Murrah Building. *Journal of Performance of Constructed Facilities*. 12(3), pp.113–119.
Mollenkamp, C. and Haughney, C. (2006a). A ring of steel for New York to protect Lower Manhattan. Wall Street Journal, January 25. Available at www.mindfully.org/Reform/2006/N-Ring-Of-Steel25jan06.htm. Accessed January 30, 2006.
Möller, F. (2007). Photographic interventions in the post-9/11 security policy. *Security Dialogue*, 38(2), pp.179–196.
Moloney, E, (2002). *A Secret History of the IRA*. New York (NY): W.W Norton and Company.
Moltoch, H. (2012). *Against Security*. Princeton (NJ): Princeton University Press.
Monroe, K. (2016). *The Insecure City: Space, Power, and Mobility in Beirut*. New Brunswick (NJ): Rutgers University Press.
Moore, C. (2006). Reading the hermeneutics of violence: the literary turn and Chechnya. *Global Society*, 20(2), pp.179–198.
Morozov, E. (2020). The tech 'solutions' for coronavirus take the surveillance state to the next level. The Guardian (Opinion), April 15, 2020. Available at www.theguardian.com/commentisfree/2020/apr/15/tech-coronavirus-surveillance-state-digital-disrupt. Accessed April 16, 2020.
Morris, A.E.J. (1994). *History of Urban Form – Before the Industrial Revolution*, 3rd ed. London: Longman.

Mumford, L. (1961). *The City in History: Its Origins, Its Transformations, and Its Prospects*. London: Penguin.
Munro, I. (2012). The management of circulations: biopolitical variations after foucault. *International Journal of Management Reviews*, 14, pp.345–362.
Murakami Wood, D., Ball, K., Lyon, D., Norris, C. and Raab, C. (2006). *A Report on the Surveillance Society*. Wilmslow: Office of the Information Commissioner.
Murakami Wood, D. and Coaffee, J. (2007). 'Lockdown! Resilience, resurgence and the stage-set city. In: R. Atkinson, R. and Helms, G. (ed.), *Securing the Urban Renaissance*. Bristol: Policy Press, pp.91–106.
Murakami Wood, D., Lyon, D. and Abe, K. (2007). Surveillance in Urban Japan: a critical introduction. *Urban Studies*, 44(3), pp.551–568.
Murakami Wood, D. and Webster, C.W.R. (2009). Living in surveillance societies: the normalisation of surveillance in Europe and the threat of Britain's bad example. *Journal of Contemporary European Research*, 5(2), pp.25–273.
Murray, R (1982). Political violence in Northern Ireland 1969–1977. In: Boal, F.W and Douglas, J.N.H. (eds.), *Integration and Division: Geographical Perspectives on the Northern Ireland problem*. London: Academic Press, pp.309–331.
Mushkin, H. (2016). Reconnaissance: inside the panopticon: a low-tech visit to Mexico City's high-tech urban surveillance center. *Places Journal*, February. Available at https://placesjournal.org/article/inside-mexico-citys-c4i4-surveillance-center/?cn-reloaded=1.
Mythen, G. and Walklate, S. (2006). Communicating the terrorist risk: harnessing a culture of fear. *Crime, Media and Culture*, 2(2), pp.123–144.
Nadel, B.A. (2007). Oklahoma City: security civics lessons. *Buildings.com*. December 15, 2007. Accessed June 5, 2019.
Nasrallah R. (2014). Planning the divide: Israel's 2020 Master Plan and its impact on East Jerusalem. In: Turner M., Shweiki O. (eds.), *Decolonizing Palestinian Political Economy*. London: Palgrave Macmillan, pp.158–175.
National Capital Planning Commission (2001). *Designing for Security in the Nation's Capital*. Washington (DC): NCPC.
National Capital Planning Commission (2002). *The National Capital Urban Design and Security Plan*. Washington (DC): NCPC.
National Capital Planning Commission (2004). *The National Capital Urban Design and Security Plan*. Washington (DC): NCPC.
Neill, W. (1992). Re-imaging Belfast. *The Planner*, pp.8–10.
Nemeth, J. and Hollander, J. (2010). Security zones and New York City's shrinking public space. *International Journal of Urban and Regional Research*, 34(1), pp.20–34.
Németh, J. and Schmidt, S. (2007). Toward a methodology for measuring the security of publicly accessible spaces. *Journal of the American Planning Association*, 73(3), pp.283–297.
Neocleous, M. (2007). Security, liberty and the myth of balance: towards a critique of security politics. *Contemporary Political Theory* 6(2), pp.131–149.
Neocleous, M. (2013). Resisting resilience. *Radical Philosophy*, 178, pp.2–7.
Neumann, P. (2009). *Old and New Terrorism*. Cambridge: Polity Press.
Neumann, P. and Smith M. (2008). *The Strategy of Terrorism: How It Works and Why It Fails*. London: Routledge.
New York City Council (2020). City Council Plans Vote on POST Act, Creating Civilian Oversight of Police Surveillance, June 16. Available at https://council.nyc.gov/press/2020/06/16/1984/. Accessed June 16, 2020.

Newman, O. (1972). *Defensible Space: Crime Prevention through Urban Design*. New York (NY): Macmillan.

Newman, O. (1996). *Creating Defensible Space*. Washington (DC): U.S. Dept. of Housing and Urban Development, Office of Policy Development and Research.

Ní Aoláin, F. (2018). Forward. In: Kundnani, A. and Hayes, B. *The Globalisation of Countering Violent Extremism Policies. Undermining Human Rights, Instrumentalising Civil Society*. Societal Security Network.

Nitzan-Shiftan, A. (2005). Capital city or spiritual center? The politics of architecture in post-1967 Jerusalem. *Cities*, 22(3), pp.229–240.

Norris, C. ad Armstrong, G. (1999). *The Maximum Surveillance Society*. Oxford: Berg.

Norris, C. and McCahill, M. (2006). CCTV: beyond penal modernism? *British Journal of Criminology*, 46(1), pp.97–118.

Norris, C., McCahill, M. and Wood, D. (2004). The growth of CCTV: a global perspective on the international diffusion of video surveillance in publicly accessible space. *Surveillance & Society*, 2(2/3), pp.110–125.

O'Brien, B. (1995). *The Long War – The IRA and Sinn Féin*. Belfast: The O'Brien Press.

O' Malley, P. (2004). *Risk, Uncertainty and Government*. London: Cavendish Press.

Oakes G. (1999). The family under nuclear attack: American Civil Defence Propaganda in the 1950s. In: Rawnsley G.D. (eds.), *Cold-War Propaganda in the 1950s*. Basingsoke: Palgrave Macmillan, pp.67–83.

Olympic Delivery Authority (ODA) (2009). *Olympic Park CCTV Code of Practice*, London: ODA.

Omand, D. (2010). *Securing the state*. London: Hurst and Co.

Osbourne, T. and Rose, N. (1999). Governing cities: notes on the spatialization of virtue. *Environmental and Planning D: Society and Space*, 17, pp.737–760.

Ostapenko, N. (2010). Nation branding of Russia through the Sochi Olympic Games of 2014. *Journal of Management Policy and Practice*, 11, pp.60–63.

Owens, E.J. (1999). *The City in the Greek and Roman World*. London: Routledge.

Parker, G. (1996). *The Military Revolution, 1500–1800: Military Innovation and the Rise of the West*, 2nd ed. New York (NY): Cambridge University Press.

Pasquale, F. (2020). Machines set loose to slaughter': the dangerous rise of military AI. The Guardian, October 15. Available at www.theguardian.com/news/2020/oct/15/dangerous-rise-of-military-ai-drone-swarm-autonomous-weapons. Accessed October 16, 2020.

Pavitt, J. (2008). The bomb and the brain. In: Crowley, D and Pavitt, J. (eds.), *Cold War Modern Design 1945-1970*. London: V&A publishing, pp.101–121.

Pawley, M. (1998). *Terminal Architecture*. London: Reaktion.

Pelling, M. (2003). *The Vulnerability of Cities: Natural Disasters and Social Resilience*. London: Earthscan.

Peoples, C. and Vaughan-Williams, N. (2010). *Critical Security Studies: An Introduction*. London: Routledge.

Pepper, S. (2000). Siege law, siege ritual, and the symbolism of city walls in Renaissance Europe. In: Tracy, J. (ed.), *City Walls: The Urban Enceinte in Global Perspective*. Cambridge: Cambridge University Press, pp.573–604.

Perelman, L.J. (2007). *Shifting Security Paradigms: Toward Resilience. Critical Thinking: Moving from Infrastructure Protection to Infrastructure Resilience*. George Mason University, pp.23–48.

Perry, T (2020). Cops tap smart streetlights sparking controversy and legislation. IEEE Spectrum, August 8. Available at https://spectrum.ieee.org/view-from-the-valley/sensors/remote-sensing/cops-smart-street-lights. Accessed September 5, 2020.

Pickles, N. (2014). Automatic number plate recognition. Paper Presented at the Computers. Data Protection and Privacy Conference, Brussels, January 23.

Piquette J.C., Smith C.M., Papachristos A.V. (2014). Social network analysis of urban street gangs. In: Bruinsma G., Weisburd D. (eds.), *Encyclopedia of Criminology and Criminal Justice*. New York (NY): Springer, p.240.

Pollak, M. (2010). *Cities at War in Early Modern Europe*. Cambridge: Cambridge University Press.

Postgate, J.N. (1992). *Early Mesopotamia*. London: Routledge.

Poyner, B. (1983). *Design Against Crime – Beyond Defensible Space*. London: Butterworths.

Pratt, K. (1993). The fate of Pool Re. *The CII Journal, September* 20, p.5.

Predmore, C.E., Rovenpor, J., Manduley, A. and Radin, T. (2007). Shopping in an age of terrorism. *Competitive Review: An International Business Journal*, 17(3), pp.170–180.

Preston, J., Binner, J., Branicki, L., Galla, T., Jones, N., King, J., Kolokitha, M. and Smyrnakis, M. (2015). *City Evacuations: An Interdisciplinary Approach*. London: Spinger.

Pullan, W. (2007). Contested mobilities and a new spatial topography of Jerusalem. In: Purbrick, L., Aulich, J. and Dawson, G. (eds.), *Contested Spaces: Representation and the Histories of Conflict*. London: Palgrave. pp.49–73.

Pullan, W., Misselwitz, P., Nasrallah, R. and Yacobi, H. (2007). Jerusalem's road 1. *City*, 11(2), pp.176–198.

Qurashi, F. (2018). The prevent strategy and the UK 'war on terror': embedding infrastructures of surveillance in Muslim communities. *Palgrave Commun*, 4, 17, pp.1–11.

Radil, S. and Pinos, J. (2019). Reexamining the four waves of modern terrorism: a territorial interpretation. *Studies in Conflict & Terrorism*, DOI: 10.1080/1057610X.2019.1657310.

Rancière, J. (2004a). *Dissensus: On Politics and Aesthetics*. London: Continuum.

Rancière, J. (2004b). *The Politics of Aesthetics: The Distribution of the Sensible*. London: Continuum.

Rapoport, D.C. (2001). The fourth wave: September 11 in the history of terrorism. *Current History*, 100, p.419.

Raposo, R. (2006). Gated communities, commodification and aestheticization: the case of the Lisbon metropolitan area. *GeoJournal*, 66(1–2), pp.43–56.

Redhead, S. (2006). The art of the accident: Paul Virilio and accelerated modernity. *Fast Capitalism*, 2(1), pp.11–18.

Reeves, J. (2017). *Citizen Spies: The Long Rise of America's Surveillance Society*. New York (NY): NYU Press.

Reid, J (2003). Foucault on Clausewitz: conceptualizing the relationship between war and power. *Alternatives* 28(1), 1–28.

Richards, A. (2011). From terrorism to "radicalization" to "extremism": counter-terrorism imperative or loss of focus? *International Affairs*, 91(2), pp.371–380.

Roberts, S. (2018). The biopolitics of China's "war on terror" and the exclusion of the Uyghurs. *Critical Asian Studies*, 50(2), pp.232–258.

Roe, P. (2008). Actor, audience(s) and emergency measures: securitization and the UK's decision to invade Iraq. *Security Dialogue*, 39(6), pp.615–635.

Rogers, P. (1996). *Economic Targeting and Provisional IRA Strategy*, University of Bradford, Department of Peace Studies, Paper 96.1.

Rogers, P. (2002). *Losing Control: Global Security in the Twenty-First Century*. London: Pluto Press.

Rokem, J. and Boano, C. (eds.) (2017). *Urban Geopolitics: Rethinking Planning in Contested Cities*. London: Taylor & Francis.

Rose, N. (1999). *Powers of Freedom*. Cambridge: Cambridge University Press.

Rose, N. (2000a). Government and control, *British Journal of Criminology*, 40, pp.321–339.

Rose, N. (2000b). The biology of culpability: pathological identity and crime control in a biological culture. *Theoretical Criminology*, 4(1), pp.5–34.

Rosen, B. (2001). A cautionary tale for a new age of surveillance. *New York Times*, October 7, p.11.

Royal Institute of British Architects (RIBA) (2010). *Guidance on Designing for Counter-Terrorism*. London: RIBA.

Russian Olympic Committee (2009). Gateway to the future. *Sochi candidate file 2009*, chapter 12, Security.

Saberi, P. (2019). Preventing radicalization in European cities: an urban geopolitical question. *Political Geography*, 74, pp.1–10.

Sack, R. (1986). *Human Territoriality: Its Theory and History*. Cambridge: Cambridge University Press.

Sageman, M. (2008). The next generation of terror. *Foreign Policy*, 168, pp.36–42.

Sahhar, M. (2017). This is not a truck: Misapprehending terror, recognising resistance. *Arena Magazine*, Issue 146 (February). Available at https://search.informit.com.au/documentSummary;dn=710399106415730;res=IELHSS. Accessed March 3, 2018.

Samatas, M. (2004). *Surveillance in Greece: From Anticommunist to Consumer Surveillance*. New York (NY): Pella.

Samatas, M. (2007). Security and surveillance in the Athens 2004 Olympics: some lessons from a troubled story. *International Criminal Justice Review*, 17, pp.220–238.

Sandvik, K.B. (2019). The Weaponization of Killer Trucks: Vehicular Terror and Vehicular Crypts. Available at www.law.ox.ac.uk/research-subject-groups/centre-criminology/centreborder-criminologies/blog/2019/11/weaponization. Accessed December 6, 2019.

Sauer, C. (1963). The morphology of landscape. In: Leighly, J. (ed.), *Land and Life*. Berkeley: University of California Press, pp.315–351.

Saurette, P. (2006). You Dissin Me? Humiliation and post 9/11 global politics. *Review of International Studies*, 32(3), pp.495–522.

Savitch, H.V. (2005). An anatomy of urban terror: lessons from Jerusalem and elsewhere. *Urban Studies*, 42(3), pp.361–395.

Savitch, H.V. (2008). *Cities in a Time of Terror: Space, Territory and Local Resilience*. New York (NY): M.E. Sharpe.

Schimmel K.S. (2006). Deep play: sports mega-events and urban social conditions in the USA. *Sociological Review* 54(s2), pp.160–174.

Schimmel K.S. (2011). From 'violence-complacent' to 'terrorist-ready': post-9/11 framing of the US Super Bowl. *Urban Studies*, 48(15), pp.3277–3291.

Schimmel, K.S. (2012). Protecting the NFL/militarizing the homeland: citizen soldiers and urban resilience in post-9/11 America. *International Review for the Sociology of Sport*, 47(3), pp.338–357.

Schindler, S. (2015). Architectural exclusion: discrimination and segregation through physical design of the built environment. *The Yale Law Journal*, 124, pp.1937–2024.

Schneier, B. (2003). *Beyond Fear: Thinking Sensibly About Security in an Uncertain World*. Front Cover. Bruce (NY): Copernicus Books.

Scientific American (2011). New York City's hidden surveillance network Part 1. *September 16*. Available at www.youtube.com/watch?v=2NnBK21QELo. Accessed September 15, 2017.

Security Service (MI5) (2006). *Protecting Against Terrorism*. London: TSO.

Šego, K, (1992). *Mostar '92 Urbicid*. Mostar: Croatian Defense Council.

Sennett, R. (1994). *Flesh and Stone: The Body and the City in Western Civilization*. New York (NY), W.W. Norton & Company.

Shaw, M. (2004). New Wars of the City: 'Urbicide' and 'Genocide. In: Graham, S. (ed.), *Cities, War, and Terrorism: Towards an Urban Geopolitics*. London: Blackwell, pp.141–153.

Shirlow, P. and Murtagh, B. (2006). *Belfast: Segregation, Violence and the City*. London: Pluto Press.

Silke, A. (ed.) (2004). *Research on Terrorism: Trends, Achievements and Failures*. London: Frank Cass.

Simiand, F. (1906). La causalité en histoire. *Bulletin de la Société française de philosophie*, 6, pp.245–272.

Simon J.D. (2011). Technology and lone operator terrorism: prospects for a fifth wave of global terrorism. In: Rosenfeld, J. (ed.), *Terrorism, Identity and Legacy*. London: Routledge.

Sims, B. (2017). Resilience and homeland security: patriotism, anxiety, and complex system dynamics. *Limn*, 1(1), pp.6–8.

Sjoberg, G. (1960). *The Pre-Industrial City: Past and Present*. Glencoe: Free Press.

Smith, J. (2003). Civil contingencies planning in government. *Parliamentary Affairs*, 56, pp.410–422.

Smyth, M. (2004). The process of demilitarization and the reversibility of the peace process in Northern Ireland. *Terrorism and Political Violence*, 16(3), pp.544–566.

Smyth, M. (2007). A critical research agenda for the study of political terror. *European Political Sciences*, 6, pp.260–267.

Sniffen, M.J. (2003). DOD mulls citywide tracking system – Pentagon says program would be for foreign combat use. *MSNBC News*. Available at www.msnbc.com/news/933707.asp?0dm=N12MT&cp1=1. Accessed July 3, 2003.

Soffer A. and Minghi, J.V. (1986). Israel's security landscapes: the impact of military considerations on land-use. *Political Geographer*, 38(1), pp.28–41.

Søilen K. (2020). Safe is a wonderful feeling: atmospheres of surveillance and contemporary art. *Surveillance & Society,* 18(2), doi.org/10.24908/ss.v18i2.12756.

Soja, E. (1989). *Postmodern Geographies: The Reassertion of Space in Critical Social Theory*. London: Verso.

Soja, E. (1995). Postmodern urbanization: the six restructurings of Los Angeles. In: Watson, S. and Gibson, K. (eds.), *Postmodern Cities and Spaces*. Oxford: Blackwell, pp.125–137.

Soja, E. (2003). Writing the city spatially. *City*. 7(3), pp.269–280.

Sorkin, M. (ed.) (1995). *Variations on a Theme Park – The New American City and the End of Public Space*. New York (NY): Hill and Wang.
Sorkin, M. (2017). The fear factor. In: Simpson, D., Jensen, V and Rubing, A. (eds.), *The City Between Freedom and Security*. Basel, Birkhäuser Verlag, pp.56–76.
Sperling, J. and Webber, M. (2018). The European Union: security governance and collective securitization. *West European Politics*, 42(2), pp.228–260.
Stanley, J. and B. Steihardt (2002). *Drawing a Black: The Failure of Facial Recognition in Tampa, Florida*. Washington (DC): ACLU.
Sternberg, E. and Lee, G. (2006). Meeting the challenge of facility protection for homeland security. *Journal of Homeland Security and Emergency Management* 3(1), pp.1–19.
Swanstrom, T. (2002). Are fear and urbanism at war? *Urban Affairs Review*, 38(1), pp.135–140.
Taylor, J. (1882). *The Age We Live in: A History of the Nineteenth Century*. Oxford University.
Thames Valley Police (2010). *Project Champion Review*. London: Thames Valley Police.
The White House (2010). *National Security Strategy, May*. Washington (DC): The White House.
The White House (2011). *Empowering Local Partners to Prevent Violent Extremism in the United States. August*. Washington (DC): The White House.
Thompson, R. (2011). Radicalization and the use of social media. *Journal of Strategic Security*, 4(4), pp.167–190.
Thrift, N. and French, S. (2002). The automatic production of space. *Transactions of the Institute of British Geographers*, 27(4), pp.309–335.
Townsend, M. and Harris, P. (2003). Security role for traffic cameras. *The Observer*, February 9, p.25.
Transportation Security Administration (TSA) (2009). TSA Teams with Law Enforcement to Keep Super Bowl Fans Safe, February 2. Available at www.tsa.gov/news/press/2009/02/02/tsa-teams-law-enforcement-keep-super-bowl-fans-safe. Accessed April 4, 2010.
Tulich, T. (2012). Prevention and pre-emption in Australia's domestic anti-terrorism legislation. *International Journal for Crime and Justice*, 1(1), pp.52–64.
Tulumello, S. (2020). Agonistic security: transcending (de/re)constructive divides in critical security studies. *Security Dialogue*. doi:10.1177/0967010620945081.
U.S. Department of State (2010). Bureau of Overseas Buildings Operations Launches Design Excellence Program During National Architecture Week. Media Note. Office of the Spokesman, Washington, DC April 14. Available at https://2009-2017.state.gov/r/pa/prs/ps/2010/04/140238.htm. Accessed December 5, 2010.
U.S. Government (2004). *The 9/11 Commission Report: Final Report of the National Commission on Terrorist Attacks Upon the United States*. Washington DC
U.K. Home Office (2018). New Technology Revealed to Help Fight Terrorist Content Online. Available at www.gov.uk/government/news/new-technology-revealed-to-help-fight-terrorist-content-online. Accessed on February 13, 2018.
UN (2020). Security Council: Counter Terrorism Committee: Countering Violent Extremism. Available at www.un.org/sc/ctc/focus-areas/countering-violent-extremism/. Accessed September 1, 2020.
UN General Assembly (2006). GA/PAL/1031, December 18. Available at https://unispal.un.org/DPA/DPR/unispal.nsf/0/F230789778BF43CA85257249004DECEB. Accessed March 23, 2019.

References

UN News (2019). New Technologies, Artificial Intelligence Aid Fight Against Global Terrorism, September 4. Available at https://news.un.org/en/story/2019/09/1045562. Accessed March 4, 2020.

United States House of Representatives (2014). Mass Gathering Security: A Look at the Coordinated Approach to Super Bowl XLVIII in New Jersey and Other Large Scale Events. June 23. Available at https://web.archive.org/web/20141206230521/http://chsdemocrats.house.gov/SiteDocuments/20140623094446-10021.pdf#page2. Accessed June 1, 2017.

U.S. House of Representatives (2006). *A Failure of Initiative: Final Report of the Select Bipartisan Committee to Investigate the Preparation for and Response to Hurricane Katrina.* Washington (DC): Government Printing Office.

Usher, M. (2014). Veins of concrete, cities of flow: reasserting the centrality of circulation in Foucault's analytics of government. *Mobilities*, 9(4), pp.550–569.

Vale, L.J. (1987). *The Limits of Civil Defense in the USA, Switzerland, Britain and the Soviet Union.* London: Mcmillian.

Vale, J.L. and Campanella, J.T. (eds.) (2005). *The Resilient City: How Modern Cities Recover from Disaster.* Oxford: Oxford University Press.

Van Puyvelde, D., Coulthart, S. and Hossain, M.S. (2017). Beyond the Buzzword: big data and national security decision-making. *International Affairs*, 93(26), pp.1397–1416.

Vanderbilt, T. (2002). *Survival City: Adventures Among the Ruins of Atomic America.* Princeton (NJ): Princeton University Press

Vaughan-Williams, N. (2009). 'Borderwork beyond inside/outside? Frontex, the citizen detective and the War on Terror'. In: Rumsford, C. (ed.), *Citizens and Borderwork in Contemporary Europe.* London: Routledge, pp.63–80.

Vaughan-Williams, N. and Stevens, D. (2016). Vernacular theories of everyday (in)security: The disruptive potential of non-elite knowledge. *Security Dialogue,* 47(1), pp.40–58.

Vidina, L. (2010). *Countering Radicalization in America Lessons from Europe.* Washington (DC): United States Institute of Peace.

Vidler, A. (2001a). Aftermath: The city transformed: designing defensible space. New York Times, September 23. Available at http://query.nytimes.com/gst/fullpage.html?res=9502E4DB163AF930A1575AC0A9679C8B6. Accessed September 24, 2001.

Vidler, A. (2001b). *Lecture to the American Collegiate Schools of Architecture Admissions Conference, November 7, New York.*

Virilio, P. (2000). *A Landscape of Events.* Cambridge (MA): MIT Press.

Virilio, P. (2002b). *Desert Screen: War at the Speed of Light.* London: Continuum.

Virilio, P. (2002a). *Ground Zero.* London: Verso.

Virilio, P. and Lotringer, S. (2008). *Pure War* (Trans. Polizzotti, M.), New York (NY): Semiotext(e).

Walker, C. and Broderick, J. (2006). *The Civil Contingencies Act 2004: Risk Resilience, and the Law in the United Kingdom.* Oxford: Oxford University Press.

Walklate, S. and Mythen, G. (2014). *Contradictions of Terrorism: Security, Risk and Resilience.* London: Routledge.

Warren, R. (2002). Situating the City and September 11th: military urban doctrine, "Pop-up" armies and spatial chess. *International Journal of Urban and Regional Research, 26*(3), pp.614–619.

Warren, R. (2004). City street – the war zones of globalization: democracy and military operations on urban terrain in the early twenty-first century. In: Graham, S. (ed.), *Cities, War and Terrorism: Towards an Urban Geopolitics*. Oxford: Blackwell, pp.214–230.
Weber, M. (1996 [1921]). *The City*. New York (NY): Free Press.
Weber, S. (2004). Targets of opportunity: networks, netwar, and narratives. *Grey Room* 15(1), pp.6–27.
Weizman, E. (2004). Strategic points, flexible lines, tense surfaces, and political volumes: Ariel Sharon and the geometry of occupation. In: Graham, S. (ed.), *Cities, War, and Terrorism: Towards an Urban Geopolitics*. Oxford: Blackwell, pp.172–191.
Weizman, E. (2006). Temporary facts, flexible lines: the concept of security in Israeli territorial design, In: in Igmade, G., Bruyn, D. and Hundsdorfer, D. (eds.), *5 Codes: Architecture, Paranoia and Risk in Times of Terror*. Berlin: Birkhauser, pp.160–175.
Weizman, E. (2007). *Hollow Land: Israel's Architecture of Occupation*. London: Verso.
Wekerle, G. and Whitzman, C. (1995). *Safe Cities – Guidelines for Planning, Design, and Management*. London: International Thompson Publishing Europe.
West, D. and Bernstein, D. (2017). *Benefits and Best Practices of Safe City Innovation*. Washington (DC): Brookings Institute. Available at www.brookings.edu/wp-content/uploads/2017/10/safe-city-innovation_final.pdf.
Whitehead, A. (1985). *Science and the Modern world*. London: Free Association Books.
Wilkinson, P (1996). Blood is spilling over the map. *The Observer*, July 21, p.6.
Williams, G. (2003). *The Enterprising City Centre: Manchester's Development Challenge*. London: Spon Press.
Williams, K. and Johnstone, C. (2000). The politics of the selective gaze: closed circuit television and the policing of public space. *Crime, Law, and Social Change* 34(2), pp.183–210.
Williams, M. (2011). The continuing evolution of securitization theory. In: Balzacq, T (ed.), *Securitization Theory: How Security Problems Emerge and Dissolve*. London: Routledge, pp.212–222.
Wolfendale, J. (2007). Terrorism, security and the threat of counter-terrorism. *Studies in Conflict and Terrorism*, 29, pp.753–770.
Wood, D., Konvitz, E. and Ball, K. (2003). The constant state of emergency: surveillance after 9/11. In: Ball, K. and Webster, F. (eds.), *The Intensification of Surveillance: Crime, Terror and Warfare in the Information Era*. London: Pluto Press, pp.137–150.
Woodward, J. (2001). *Super Bowl Surveillance: Facing Up to Biometrics*. Santa Monica (CA): RAND Arroyo Center.
Woodward, R. (2004). *Military Geographies*. Malden (MA): Blackwell Publishers.
Yeung, K. (2020). Pandemic governance. In: Taylor, L. Martin, A. Sharma, G. and Jameson, S. (eds.), *Data Justice and COVID-19: Global Perspectives*. London: Meatspace Press, pp.51–57.
Yiftachel, O. (1998). Planning and social control: exploring the 'dark side'. *Journal of Planning Literature,* 12, pp.397.
Youseff, O. (2011). Jerusalem: Palestinian space, behaviors and attitudes. *The Palestine-Israel Journal,* 17(1). Available at http://pij.org/app.php/articles/1284. Accessed February 1, 2019.

Zedner, L. (2007). Pre-crime and post-criminology? *Theoretical Criminology*, 11, pp.261–281.
Zelinka, A., and Brennanm D. (2001). *SafeScape: Creating Safer, More Livable Communities Through Planning and Design*. Chicago (IL): APA Planners Press.
Zhang, J., Hua, X., Huang, J., Shen, X., Chen, J., Zhou, Q., Fu, Z. and Zhao, Y. (2019). City brain: practice of large-scale artificial intelligence in the real world. *IET Smart Cities*, 1(1), pp.1–10.
Zucker, P. (1955). Space and movement in high Baroque City planning. *Journal of the Society of Architectural Historians*, 14(1), pp.8–13.
Zulaika, J. and Douglass, W.A. (1996). *Terror and Taboo: The Follies, Fables and Faces of Terrorism*. New York (NY): Routledge.

Index

9/11 4, 9–18, 28, 33–34, 53, 55, 69, 94, 98–116, 119–120, 122–126, 129, 131, 132, 142–143, 145–155, 157, 160–161, 164, 166, 171, 181, 189, 192–194, 196, 198–202, 207–208, 210, 212, 217–222, 228, 230, 237, 240, 245, 247, 252–253, 255, 257–261, 263–265

acceptability 120, 128, 133, 138, 178
accessibility 39, 77, 108–9, 112, 124–125, 208, 236, 249
adapt 62, 148, 165; adaptive capacity 167
Adey, P. 14, 149–150, 273–274
aesthetics 8, 13, 26, 55, 71, 80, 91, 101–102, 122, 127–140, 196, 208, 249, 252, 265
Agamben, G. 10, 158, 162, 208, 218–219, 237–239, 265, 273
agora 5, 23
agoraphobia 132, 183, 253
Al-Qaida 141, 147, 211
Amnesty International 200, 213, 242, 258, 273
Amoore, L. 10, 106, 114, 173, 190, 219, 273–274, 282
Anderson, B. 116, 149–150, 273–274
Andrejevic, M. 182–183, 245, 274
anticipation 101, 112, 143, 145, 147, 149, 152, 154, 157, 160, 257, 259, 263
anti-terrorism 41, 43, 52–53, 60, 65, 69, 73, 87, 91, 101–102, 107–108, 119, 124, 135, 146, 158, 162, 172–175, 185, 212, 215, 240, 249–250
Aradau, C. 119, 145–146, 190, 266, 274
architecture 7, 14, 21, 23–24, 28, 34, 39–42, 44, 48–49, 52–54, 61–65, 68, 73, 76, 79–81, 90, 93, 107, 112, 119–142, 189, 191, 198, 209, 211–213, 218, 227, 235, 249–250, 253, 259, 264

artificial Intelligence (AI) 205, 213, 222, 242, 254, 271, 290, 298, 300
armed guards 87, 90–91, 102, 196
Athens (Greece) 211, 228–229, 238
Australia 139, 141, 145, 155–156, 158, 163, 172, 250, 267–269, 274
automatic Number Plate Recognition (ANPR) 14, 91, 94, 176–178, 199, 202–204, 209, 215, 224, 230–235, 241, 269–270

Baer, M. 62, 71, 274
Baghdad (Iraq) 194–195, 252
banal terrorism 13, 107, 164, 179, 245, 288
barbed wire/razor wire 43–44, 94, 221, 252
Barcelona (Spain) 6, 17, 246, 248, 268
barriers/Jersey barriers 16, 19, 25, 37, 40–44, 51–54, 59, 68–70, 76–79, 83, 87, 94, 102, 109, 119–124, 133–135, 142, 167, 194, 196, 221, 224, 247–52, 262, 268
Beck, U. 13, 78, 100, 113, 266, 274
behaviour 6, 11, 34, 37–41, 43, 48, 54, 61, 79, 110–111, 131–132, 158, 165, 167–168, 171, 173, 184, 191, 199, 202–203, 209, 212, 219, 221, 232, 239, 242, 255, 257, 260, 270
Beijing (China) 195, 212, 229, 241, 254, 270
Beirut (Lebanon) 42, 49–59, 65, 72, 77, 193, 221
Belfast (Northern Ireland) 42, 43–47, 49, 53–55, 74, 76, 82, 85, 87, 101, 231
benches 35, 121–122, 135
Benton-Short, L. 112, 275
Berlin (Germany) 15, 144, 195, 246–148, 267

Index

Betz, D. 20–21, 33, 116, 275
Bevir, M. 15, 258, 275
biometric technology 15, 110, 192, 199–201, 203, 208–209, 220, 228, 231, 253–254, 262, 272
biopolitics 17, 114, 129, 142, 158, 167, 178, 181, 191, 255
Birmingham (U.K.) 176–178, 185, 248, 262, 272
blast-proof 196, 198
blast resistant 63, 68, 71, 73, 126, 194, 208; Bleiker, R. 129, 275
blockers 102, 120–121, 196, 225–226, 247, 249–250, 252, 268
Boal, F. 43, 275
Boddy, T. 132, 134, 136, 193, 275
bollards 68, 71, 90, 93, 102, 109, 119–126, 131, 134–135, 139–142, 197–198, 245, 247–252, 267–268
bomb-proofing 28, 194
Bombay (India) 61, 77; Mumbai 15, 123, 141, 189, 211
Boston (U.S.) 15, 135, 138, 213–214, 239, 242
boulevards 5, 6, 20, 24–27, 32, 35–36, 42, 47–48, 52, 191, 245, 248, 253
Briggs, R. 113, 120, 169, 174, 276
Brighton (U.K.) 80, 95, 223–234
Brown, G. 126–127, 161, 182, 276
Brown, S. 38, 44, 276
Brown, P.L. 68, 276
Brussels (Belgium) 15, 24
bunker 28–29, 32, 34, 52, 54, 59–76, 102, 189, 193–194, 208, 212, 218
Buzan, B. 11, 146, 276

cameras 64, 68, 78–80, 83, 85, 89–91, 94, 110–111, 116, 173, 176–178, 185, 192, 200–205, 214, 221, 225, 228, 232, 236, 243, 253–254, 262, 269–275; *see also* CCTV
camouflaged 168, 120, 131, 133, 176, 197
Canary Wharf 83, 97; *see also* London Docklands 61, 83, 91, 94
car bomb 34, 49, 52, 245, 6, 36, 42–46, 49–53, 59, 63, 74, 77, 83, 102, 121, 126, 141–142, 189, 193–194, 205, 207, 210, 215, 224, 245; *see also* vehicle bombs
carceral 3, 8, 65, 80, 183, 217, 226
CCTV 41, 70, 77, 80, 83, 85, 89, 91, 95, 109–112, 185, 198, 201–205, 209, 212, 214–216, 221–225, 230–231, 236, 238, 241, 243, 257
Chandler, D. 4, 144–145, 148, 159, 161, 165, 181, 277
checkpoint 37–38, 43–44, 47, 52, 76, 85, 87, 90–91, 94, 96, 102, 132, 225, 227, 237, 254, 267
China 200, 229, 241, 254–255, 262, 270, 272
Christchurch (New Zealand) 190, 211
circulation 25, 28, 68, 175, 190–192, 199, 207, 209, 253, 258, 262
citadel 21–23, 27, 44, 102, 108, 111, 192, 198
citizenship 18, 29–30, 132, 165, 167, 176, 178, 180–181, 259
City of London (or Square Mile) 77–78, 81–97
civil contingencies 143, 151, 153, 156–157, 162, 166, 235, 271
Civil contingencies act 151
civil defence 11, 19–20, 27, 29–33, 104, 143, 148, 151, 159
civil liberties 10, 15, 95, 107, 109–111, 115, 145, 153, 157–158, 160, 167, 169, 175, 178, 200–201, 205, 207–208, 213, 229, 257–258, 261–262
Cold War 6, 13–14, 17, 20, 27, 30–34, 42, 60, 63, 66, 71, 101, 104–106, 108, 115–116, 143, 148, 157, 159, 161, 181, 184, 194–195, 211, 240, 264–265
collective responsibility 122, 125, 128, 140
community resilience 9, 166–170, 175–176, 179–180, 259; *see also* resilience
community safety 39, 173, 177, 184, 235
compound 34, 50–52, 72–74, 193–194, 208–209, 211
CONTEST (UK national counter-terrorism strategy) 126, 151–153, 162, 169–174, 232, 264
control centre 236, 254; *see also* control room 193, 199, 203, 222, 254
Copenhagen (Denmark) 249, 251
cordon sanitaire 25, 34, 78–79, 94–95, 271
Counter Terrorism Preparedness Network (CTPN) 155, 179, 259, 280
Counter Terrorist Security Advisors (CTSAs) 103, 116
counter-terrorism 7, 9–17, 33, 38, 46–47, 52–53, 59–60, 62, 69, 74, 79,

81, 84–85, 87, 89, 91, 93–94, 96, 99–112, 115, 119–128, 132–137, 140–185, 189–193, 196, 198, 200–201, 204–210, 217–223, 229–232, 236–237, 239, 244, 246–247, 250–251, 254–268, 271
COVID-19 260–261
Coward, M. 13, 53, 142, 278, 280
crash-rated 119–120, 138, 196–197, 250, 262
Crime prevention through environmental design (CPTED) 40–42, 54, 125
criminologists (also criminology) 39–40
crisis 17, 129, 145, 152, 260–261, 263; see also crises 145, 151
critical security studies 12, 61, 161
critical terrorism studies 12, 18, 61–62, 122, 129
Croft, S. 129, 186, 280
crowded places 124, 126–128, 132, 155–156, 163, 190, 226, 230, 237, 245, 266, 269, 272

Dar es Salaam (Tanzania) 72, 173
Davies, S. 80, 200, 280
Davis, M. 36–37, 42–43, 50, 52–53, 62, 64–65, 72, 77, 94, 106, 113, 115, 280
de Certeau, M. 7–10, 12, 17, 66, 73, 165, 280
defence 5–6, 11, 17, 19–25, 27–37, 46, 52–53, 59–60, 64, 71, 76, 81, 90, 94, 99–110, 131, 138, 143, 148, 150–151, 159, 162–163, 193, 208, 210, 234, 236, 255
Defensible Space 38–44, 52, 64–65, 68, 72, 79, 101, 107–108, 125, 131, 142, 227
defensive design 6, 22, 38, 41, 54, 107
Deleuze, G. 80, 114, 183, 281
Department of Homeland Security (DNS) 111, 153–154, 220–222, 239, 271, 281
Derry (Northern Ireland) 54, 82
Design-out crime/terrorism 42, 59, 67, 78
Designing-in security 71, 120, 230, 231
Detroit (U.S.) 214, 221, 240
Domain Awareness System 205, 215–216
downing Street (London) 83, 86, 96
duty 5, 30, 168, 181–182; to prevent 168, 170, 182, 186; to protect 264, 272

effectiveness 120, 128, 138, 150, 201
Eiffel Tower (Paris) 251, 260

Eisenhower, D. 31, 216
Elden, S. 25, 38, 100, 191, 282
Ellin, N. 64, 79, 80, 282
embassy design 50–51, 71–72, 98, 102, 193–198, 210–212
emergency 8, 10–11, 15, 17, 32, 36, 66–67, 101, 146, 158, 166, 190, 208, 219, 228, 236, 244, 246, 258, 260
emergency planning 14, 29, 33, 90, 100, 123, 125, 144–145, 148–157
Emirates stadium (London) 135, 137
enclosure 14, 20–21, 33, 42, 78, 114, 191–192, 209, 218, 231
event security 218, 222, 232, 237, 239
everyday 4, 6, 8, 13–15, 18, 38, 61, 80, 106, 133, 202, 205, 209, 244, 265
everyday city 5, 7, 12, 36, 43, 52, 85, 94, 120, 122–123, 128, 131, 137, 164, 207–209, 230
everyday life 5, 7–10, 13, 15, 17, 24, 27–32, 38, 46–47, 52–53, 64, 66, 80–81, 93–94, 101, 104, 106, 119, 144, 147, 184, 208, 244–247, 256–259, 261–263, 265–266
everyday security 8, 18, 27, 65, 107–116, 140, 156–161, 164–184, 226, 238, 257, 265
exceptional 4, 9, 16–17, 107, 115, 146–147, 208, 217, 219, 222, 226–228, 237–238, 244–247, 253, 265; see also exceptionality 10, 112, 208, 210, 217–220, 230, 238, 244, 258, 265
eyes on the street 39, 42, 125, 173

facial recognition 200–203, 208–209, 213–215, 220, 239, 242, 262
facial recognition CCTV (FRCCTV) 110, 199, 200–203, 209, 214, 220, 230
Farish, M. 28–30, 32, 111, 282
FBI 55, 60, 66, 72, 74, 171, 228, 245, 282
Flusty, S. 64, 65, 281, 283
Flynn, S. 15, 154, 156, 283
Fussey, P. 95, 109, 161, 176–177, 191, 200–202, 217, 228–230, 233, 238–239, 241, 253, 257, 276, 279, 283–284
fortification 3, 5, 19–25, 27, 32–33
fortress 21, 23, 41–42, 63, 80, 108, 119, 124, 132, 190, 193–197, 207–208, 221, 223, 250, 252; fortress mentality, 42, 91
fortress city/fortress urbanism 63–64, 79, 102, 108, 112

Index

Foucault, M. 3, 5, 8, 78, 80, 95, 109, 130–131, 142, 147, 167, 181, 183, 190–192, 199, 208–209, 211, 218, 226, 265, 283
Fregonese, S. 13, 49, 77, 276, 283
Freidman, T. 36, 49, 52, 54, 283

gates 19, 43–44, 64, 68–69, 77, 79, 83, 86, 95, 101, 122, 194, 198, 201
Gaza Strip 46, 76
geography 8–10, 14, 28, 41, 43, 49, 61, 81, 102, 105, 122, 132, 264
geopolitics 3, 9, 11, 13, 15–16, 33, 38, 98, 101, 104–105, 178, 266
Glasgow airport (U.K.) 126, 176
Gold, J. 8, 22, 37, 81, 284
governance 4, 8, 13–16, 22, 100, 104–105, 111–112, 144–145, 147, 163, 165–168, 178–183, 191–192, 207–210, 218, 223, 227, 237, 239, 246, 253, 258–259, 264, 270
governmentality 17, 114, 140, 145, 159, 160, 165, 167, 182, 192, 208, 244, 258, 265
Graham, S. 13, 31, 33, 47, 78, 80, 94, 101, 104–107, 111, 113, 130, 199, 218, 285
Green Zone 194, 212, 252

Haggerty, K. 149, 238
Harvey, D. 8, 80, 286
Haussmann, B. 6, 25–27, 42, 46
Heath-Kelly, C. 179, 182, 286
Hezbollah 50–52, 55
Hinman, E. 68, 71, 286
Hobbes, T. 20, 37, 286
Hoffman, B. 59, 98, 286
homeland hecurity 9–10, 100, 106, 113, 115, 125, 154, 182, 201
Houses of Parliament (London) 102–103, 189, 267
human rights 15, 159, 169, 175, 200, 202, 203, 215, 236, 257–258, 270

insecurity 16, 20, 36, 39, 49, 106, 130, 138–139, 149, 209, 265
intelligence agencies 51, 60, 198, 209, 254
International Relations (see also IR) 3, 37, 100, 105, 122, 129–130, 142, 162
Iraq 74, 98, 123, 141, 172, 192, 194–197, 212
ISIS 246, 272
island security 220, 223–231, 237

Israel 38, 46–50, 53, 55, 65, 73, 76, 105, 213, 218, 245, 267
Israeli Defence Force (IDF) 46, 76
Italy 22–23, 49, 248–249, 267

Jackson, R. 12, 62, 115, 129, 146, 287
Jacobs, J. 39–40, 54, 173, 287
Jarman, N. 38, 43–44, 77, 81, 287
Jeffery, C.R. 40, 125, 288
Jerusalem (Israel-Palestine) 42, 47–49, 53, 55, 76

La Rambla (Barcelona) 6, 248, 268
Laqueur, W. 17, 76, 99, 289
Lebanon 38, 49–55, 193, 267
Local Resilience Forums (U.K.) 152, 224
lockdown security 14, 217–218, 220, 223, 227, 238, 243, 252, 261, 265, 269, 271–272
Loeffler, E. 289, 194–195, 211, 289
London 15, 24, 54–55, 60–61, 73–74, 77–97, 102–103, 109–110, 115–116, 123, 126, 133, 135–136, 141, 144, 150, 161–162, 169, 171, 173, 175–178, 184–186, 189, 195–200, 202–205, 211–215, 223, 229–237, 241–242, 246, 250, 259, 260, 267, 272
Los Angeles (LA) 63–65, 79
Los Angeles Police Department (LAPD) 64, 79
Lyon, D. 94–95, 109–110, 198, 200, 290

Madrid (Spain) 15, 110, 123, 141, 162, 170–171, 212, 223, 240
Manchester (U.K.) 15, 77, 91, 93, 151, 184, 213, 223–225, 240, 272
Manhattan (New York City) 7, 65, 68–69, 99, 111, 120, 204–205, 215, 268; Lower Manhattan Security Initiative 111, 204–205
Massumi, B. 11, 113, 114, 115, 147, 290
material turn 61, 80, 95
McDonald, M. 11, 155, 158, 290
Melbourne (Australia) 246, 250–251, 267–268
Metropolitan Police (London) 91, 110, 116, 162, 201–203, 213–214, 230, 234, 242–242, 252
Middle East 60, 69, 72, 194
Milan (Italy) 249, 267
military 5–6, 11, 14, 17, 19–20, 23–31, 38, 42, 50, 52–53, 59, 62, 72, 76, 100–101, 130, 144, 148, 191, 209, 218,

220, 228, 233–234, 236–237, 254, 256, 260–261, 265; technology 14, 23, 104, 110, 234
military architect 24, 42
military corridor/highway 25, 27, 46
military engineer 23–25, 32, 42, 70
military-industrial complex 66, 200, 209
military planner 20, 25, 32, 38, 46–47
military urbanism 23, 33, 98–116, 218
mobility 19, 23, 25, 37, 44, 47, 49, 52, 62, 68, 109, 114, 189, 190, 210, 223, 261
morals 30, 34, 164, 181, 183, 244, 259, 264, 266
Moscow (Russia) 15, 25, 235
Mumford, L. 3, 19–21, 24–27, 157–159, 292
Murakami Wood, D. 4, 13, 33, 100, 106, 132, 148, 157, 181, 198, 217, 219, 223, 232, 238, 243, 257, 292; *see also* Wood, D. 15, 17, 78, 101, 109–110, 112, 158, 199–200, 209
Mythen, G. 133, 180–181, 258, 292, 298

Nairobi (Kenya) 72, 193
National Capital Planning Commission (NCPC) 98, 109, 125, 292
National Counter Terrorism Security Office (NaCTSO) 116, 141, 153
national security 4, 11, 13–14, 29–31, 33, 53, 60, 76, 100, 110, 112, 115, 123–124, 126, 129, 131, 134, 141, 145, 147, 149, 154, 156–161, 164, 166, 171, 175, 177, 182, 193, 199, 201–202, 235, 254, 256, 258–259, 263, 272
National Security Agency (NSA, U.S.) 212, 270
national security strategy 143–144, 155, 160, 171, 232
New Orleans (U.S.) 156, 221
New York (U.S.) 7, 15, 36, 40, 60–61, 64–69, 74, 77, 107, 111, 120–121, 124, 134, 139–140, 142, 158, 204–205, 207, 215–216, 228, 246, 268
New York Police Department (NYPD) 205, 207, 215
New York Times 36, 54, 68, 108, 113, 197, 205, 212–215, 242, 269
Newham (London) 200, 203, 235
Newman, O. 6, 38, 40–43, 54, 65, 68, 108, 125, 142, 293
Nice (France) 6, 15, 17, 214, 246, 272

normalisation 49, 101, 113, 115, 140, 183, 192, 207, 209, 244, 247, 257, 265–266
Northern Ireland 36, 38, 43, 46, 53–54, 66, 76, 82, 84, 86

O'Hare, P. 65, 128, 133, 135, 159
obtrusive security 101, 109, 119, 123, 131, 133, 139, 142, 177
Oklahoma City (U.S.) 60–61, 64–65, 69–72, 77, 211, 239
Olympic Games security 200, 202, 218, 220, 226–243, 251, 254
Omand, D. 143, 148, 162, 293
Oslo (Norway) 15, 189, 264

Palestinian 46–50, 55, 65, 76, 105, 213, 267
pandemic 161, 260–262, 271–272
panopticon 80, 89, 95, 192, 207
Paris 5–6, 15, 25–27, 35, 144, 165, 190, 211, 214, 246, 250–251, 258, 268
Patriot Act (U.S.) 111, 153, 272
peace line 43, 231
policing 9, 22, 26, 33, 38, 39, 42, 46, 74, 79, 91, 94, 104, 154, 158, 168, 171–172, 174, 177–179, 183, 202, 207, 209, 219, 222, 224–232, 234, 240, 242, 254, 263
political violence 13, 36, 38, 47, 49, 105
pop-up security 217–239
preparedness 11, 16, 29–30, 33, 116, 144–145, 148–150, 155, 159–161, 182, 234, 257, 259–262, 264, 266
Prevent (counter-terrorism policy) 164–183; *see also* violent extremism
privacy 111, 154, 177, 200–203, 208–209, 213, 216, 220, 229, 256, 263, 265, 269, 272
private security 83, 89, 119, 132, 160, 205, 221, 224, 227, 234, 239, 256
Project Champion 176–178; *see also* Birmingham U.K.
proportionality (also proportionate) 122, 128, 140, 172, 198, 207, 217, 237, 247, 263; disproportionate 11, 42, 85, 111, 120, 200, 202, 205, 252
protective security 6, 67–68, 73, 98, 100, 111, 122, 124, 126–128, 131–132, 138, 141, 154, 189, 235, 245–248, 250, 252–253, 259, 262, 264, 271

306 *Index*

Provisional Irish Republican Army (Provisional IRA) 36, 43–44, 54, 78, 80, 82–97, 103, 201
public realm 8, 73, 80, 108, 121, 125, 127, 135, 140, 249, 250–251, 253, 262
public space 4, 6, 9, 13, 16, 27, 31–32, 34, 39–40, 64, 80, 108, 112–113, 119, 121, 124, 126–127, 132, 136, 158, 198, 200, 209, 214, 225–226, 231, 235, 250, 264, 268
Pullan, W. 47–48, 294

quality of life 39, 125, 158

radicalisation 161, 164–165 see also violent extremism
Ranciere, J. 14, 130, 294
Reeves, J. 30, 181, 294
resilience 9–10, 15–17, 23, 33, 90, 126, 143–163, 165–172, 175–186, 224–227, 230–233, 247, 257–262, 265, 271
responsibilisation 157, 167, 180–181, 183; deresponsibilisation 182
Revolution in Military Affairs (RMA) 104, 200
ring of steel 204, 223, 235, 237, 268; in Belfast 43–45, 74; in London; 83, 87–88, 91, 93, 96–97, 102, 104, 110, 116, 203–204, 215, 230, 250
Robustness 70, 119–120, 155
Rose, N. 32, 149, 158, 167, 181, 200–201

Saberi, P. 178, 295
Salt Lake City (U.S.) 228, 240
San Diego (U.S.) 253, 269
Saudi Arabia 72, 98, 102, 239
Schimmel, K. 218, 220, 222, 295–296
Secured by Design (SBD) 54, 232, 235
securitisation 8, 11–14, 62, 93, 113, 129, 137, 145–146, 158, 161, 164–167, 186, 238, 265
security cordon 14, 44, 78–79, 82, 85, 87, 89–96, 104, 203, 230–231, 237, 271
security governance I, 8, 14–15, 144, 159, 167, 210, 218, 223, 239, 246, 258–259, 264
security services 34, 53, 63, 82–83, 96, 112, 119, 123, 126, 131, 134, 138, 146, 152, 160, 173, 174, 184, 189, 224, 233, 244, 256, 259, 272
security zone 44, 46, 72, 77, 124, 135, 189–190, 215, 237, 269

security-driven urban resilience 15–16, 84, 145, 148–149, 156, 160–161, 178
Semtex 82, 84, 91–92, 96
separation wall/barrier 76, 245
set-back 70, 198, 247; *see also* stand-off
Sochi (Russia) 235–237, 242–243
soft targets 13, 119, 122–124, 126, 150, 162, 217, 221
Soja, E. 8, 61, 64, 80, 296
sovereign 10, 21, 23, 193, 208, 219
sovereignty 4, 10, 13, 32, 37, 49, 114, 179, 191, 216
spaces of exception 218–219, 227, 238
spaces of security 8, 130, 138, 191
spatial turn 8, 95
stand-off (see also set back) 68, 72, 89, 208, 230
state of emergency 8, 10, 32, 101, 158, 190, 236, 246, 258
state of exception 158, 162, 208, 237, 265
stealthy 133, 139, 196; *see also* unobtrusive
sterile space 6, 47, 124, 132, 236
Stockholm (Sweden) 246, 267
street furniture 93, 121, 133, 176, 268; street lamps 253
streetscape 108, 119–142, 247–248
suicide attacks 37, 46, 51–52, 76, 102–103, 109, 110, 115–116, 119, 123, 126, 141, 190, 209, 211–212, 235–236, 242, 254, 270
Super Bowl 200, 214, 220–223, 239–240
surveillance 1, 7, 10, 14–17, 23, 25, 29–31, 33–34, 39–41, 49, 65, 69, 74, 77–81, 86, 89, 91, 93–95, 103, 106–111, 116, 130, 132, 142, 153, 157, 159, 166, 168–171, 176–184, 189–192, 198–216, 218, 220, 222, 227–232, 235, 237, 239, 242, 245, 247, 253, 254–257, 260, 262–265, 267, 269–271
Syria 49–51, 172

Tampa (U.S.) 220–221
target hardening 19, 40–43, 52–53, 65, 72, 73, 93, 109, 158, 198, 227, 247
targeting 4, 6, 17, 20, 27–29, 31–32, 37, 52, 59, 68, 72–73, 77–78, 82–83, 95, 98, 105, 119, 123–124, 141, 169, 189, 249, 257
terrain 33, 38, 40, 106, 110, 189, 218, 220–221, 226, 228, 254–255, 257, 259
territorial security 63, 72, 81, 89, 91, 100, 189

Index

territoriality 6, 37–38, 40, 42–46, 52, 76, 78–79, 90, 102, 191
territory 5–7, 16, 25, 36–39, 49, 54, 60, 65, 80, 190, 194, 219, 254
tiger trap 135–139
Times Square (New York) 98, 121–122, 140, 205, 215
TNT 50, 54, 70, 82
Tokyo (Japan) 60–61, 162, 242–243
trust 109, 115, 166, 172, 175, 177–178, 183
Tulumello, S. 263, 297

unobtrusive 122, 128, 133, 177, 198, 231, 254, 257, 268; *see also* stealthy
urban design 6, 13, 25, 27, 32, 34, 38–40, 65, 81, 98, 102, 109, 120, 122, 140, 209, 237
urban planning 20, 23, 25, 27, 41–42, 48, 105–106, 124–125, 129
urbicide 47, 53, 55, 59
U.S. Embassies 51, 71, 98, 102, 192–193, 194–198, 210–212, 239

Vaughan-Williams, N. 9, 12, 18, 151, 158, 173, 298
vehicle bomb 43, 50, 54, 59–61, 119, 123, 189, 193, 196, 269; car bomb 36, 189
vehicle-as-weapon attack 245–250, 252, 266–267; vehicle ramming 245, 254, 267

violent extremism 156, 165, 168, 170–77, 182, 184–186, 258; *see also* Prevent
Virilio, P. 20, 66–67, 99, 112, 298
visibility of security features 41, 91, 122, 128, 131–134, 178, 232
Volgograd (Russia) 236, 242
vulnerability 4, 15–16, 33, 70–72, 96, 101, 104, 112, 127–128, 132, 150, 154, 156, 167, 208, 228, 266

Walklate, S. 133, 180, 181, 258, 298
walled city 21, 86, 96
walls 5, 19–23, 25, 29, 39, 43, 48, 51, 53, 64, 68, 76, 79, 183, 194, 196–197
War on Terror 4, 9–12, 14–15, 94, 96, 100–101, 104–106, 114–115, 131, 133–134, 136, 141, 143, 146–147, 153, 156, 158, 164–168, 171, 178, 193, 204, 207–210, 218, 223, 240, 244, 254, 269, 256, 260, 266
Washington D.C. 98, 101, 108, 112, 115, 144, 184, 215, 252
Weizman, E. 13, 25, 46–47, 76, 105, 299
World Trade Center (WTC, New York) 7, 9–10, 60, 68, 98, 99, 107, 108

Xinjiang province (China) 200, 254–255, 270

Zedner, L. 182, 300
Zulaika, J. 12, 61–62, 300

Lightning Source UK Ltd.
Milton Keynes UK
UKHW020106230722
406270UK00004B/212